INFORMATION SOURCES
FOR TEACHERS

Information Sources

for Teachers

Compiler
David Brown

Routledge
Taylor & Francis Group

LONDON AND NEW YORK

First published 1996 by Ashgate Publishing

Reissued 2018 by Routledge
2 Park Square, Milton Park, Abingdon, Oxon OX14 4RN
711 Third Avenue, New York, NY 10017, USA

Routledge is an imprint of the Taylor & Francis Group, an informa business

Publisher's Note
The publisher has gone to great lengths to ensure the quality of this reprint but points out that some imperfections in the original copies may be apparent.

Disclaimer
The publisher has made every effort to trace copyright holders and welcomes correspondence from those they have been unable to contact.

A Library of Congress record exists under LC control number : 96085392

ISBN 13: 978-1-138-31492-4 (hbk)
ISBN 13: 978-1-138-31493-1 (pbk)
ISBN 13: 978-0-429-45665-7 (ebk)

Contents

ADMINISTRATION

Administration

Educational standards and national administration

Awdurdod Cwricwlwm ac Asesu Cymru (ACAC)
Curriculum and Assessment Authority for Wales
Castle Buildings, Womanby Street
Cardiff
CF1 9SX
Telephone: 01222 344946
Facsimile: 01222 343612
Responsible in Wales for keeping under review all aspects of the curriculum for maintained schools and for schools examinations and assessment.

Belfast Education and Library Board
40 Academy Street
Belfast
BT1 2NQ
Telephone: 01232 329211
Facsimile: 01232 331714

Board of Education of the General Synod of the Church of England
Church House
Dean's Yard
London
SW1P 3NZ
Contact: David Lankshear, Schools Officer
Telephone: 0171-222 9011
The Board of Education represents the Church of England on all issues of policy to do with education. In particular it is concerned with legislation and its implementation.

Catholic Education Service
39 Eccleston Square
London
SW1V 1BX
Telephone: 0171-584 7491
Facsimile: 0171-823 7545
Supports all those working in and for Catholic education.

Council for Catholic Maintained Schools
160 High Street
Holywood
Co Down
BT18 9HT
Telephone: 01232 426972
Facsimile: 01232 424255
Seeks to promote effective management of Catholic schools, to promote and co-ordinate planning of the effective provision of Catholic schools, to advise other bodies in relation to Catholic schools and is the employing authority of all teachers in Catholic maintained schools.

Council of Churches and Associated Colleges
c/o Principal's Office
LSU College of Higher Education, The Avenue
Southampton
SO17 1BG
Telephone: 01703 212153
Facsimile: 01703 237324

OFSTED - Office for Standards in Education
Alexandra House
29-33 Kingsway
London
WC2B 6SE
Telephone: 0171-421 6800
An independent government department set up to administer the inspection of maintained schools in England and Wales.

Review Body on Schoolteachers' Pay and Conditions of Service
Office of Manpower Economics
76 Oxford Street
London
W1N 9FD
Contact: Miss M Hart, Secretariat
Telephone: 0171-636 1742
Facsimile: 0171-467 7248
Established in 1991 with a statutory duty to 'examine and report on such matters relating to the statutory conditions of employment of teachers in England and Wales'. It is independent of government who may decide to accept, reject or modify its recommendations.

Scottish Consultative Council on the Curriculum (Scottish CCC)
Gardyne Road
Broughty Ferry
Dundee
DD5 1NY
Contact: Mrs Tegwen R Wallace, Senior Administration Officer
Telephone: 01382 455053
Facsimile: 01382 455046
The principal advisory body to the Secretary of State for Scotland on all curriculum matters relating to 3-18-year-olds in Scottish schools.

Administration

Local Education Authorities

Avon
P.O. Box 57
Avon House North
St James Barton
Bristol
BS99 7EB
Telephone: 0117 987 4000

Barking and Dagenham
Town Hall
Barking
Essex
IG11 7LU
Telephone: 0181-592 4500
Facsimile: 0181-594 9837

Barnet
Educational Services
Friern Barnet Lane
London
N11 3DL
Telephone: 0181-368 1255
Facsimile: 0181-361 3794

Barnsley
Education Offices
Berneslai Close
Barnsley
S70 2HS
Telephone: 01226 773500

Bedfordshire
County Hall
Cauldwell Street
Bedford
MK42 9AP
Telephone: 01234 363222

Belfast Area
40 Academy Street
Belfast
BT1 2NQ
Telephone: 01232 329211

Berkshire
Shire Hall
Shinfield Park
Reading
Berkshire
RG2 9XE
Telephone: 01734 233625
Facsimile: 01734 750360

Bexley
Hill View
Hill View Drive
Welling
Kent
DA16 3RY
Telephone: 0181-303 7777
Facsimile: 0181-319 4302

Birmingham
Education Offices
Margaret Street
Birmingham
B3 3BU
Telephone: 0121-235 2590

Bolton
P.O. Box 53
Paderborn House
Civic Centre
Bolton
BL1 1JW
Telephone: 01204 22311
Facsimile: 01204 365492

Borders
Education Department
Regional Headquarters
Newtown St Boswells
Roxburghshire
TD6 0SA
Telephone: 01835 823301

Bradford
Flockton House
Flockton Road
Bradford
BD4 7RY
Telephone: 01274 752111

Brent
P.O. Box 1
Chesterfield House
9 Park Lane
Wembley
Middlesex
HA9 7RW
Telephone: 0181-904 1244

Administration

Local Education Authorities

Bromley
Civic Centre
Stockwell Close
Bromley
Kent
BR1 3UH
Telephone: 0181-464 3333
Facsimile: 0181-313 4049

Buckinghamshire
County Hall
Aylesbury
Buckinghamshire
HP20 1UZ
Telephone: 01296 395000

Bury
Athenaeum House
Market Street
Bury
BL9 0BN
Telephone: 0161-705 5000

Calderdale
Northgate House
Halifax
West Yorkshire
HX1 1UN
Telephone: 01422 357257
Facsimile: 01422 392515

Cambridgeshire
Castle Court
Castle Hill
Cambridge
CB3 0AP
Telephone: 01223 317111

Camden
Crowndale Centre
218-220 Eversholt Street
London
NW1 1BD
Telephone: 0171-911 1525
Facsimile: 0171-911 1536

Central
Central Regional Offices
Viewforth
Stirling
FK8 2ET
Telephone: 01786 442000

Cheshire
Education Services Group
County Hall
Chester
CH1 1SQ
Telephone: 01244 602424

Cleveland
Woodlands Road
Middlesbrough
Cleveland
TS1 3BN
Telephone: 01642 248155

Clwyd
Education Department
Shire Hall
Mold
Clwyd
CH7 6NB
Telephone: 01352 752121
Facsimile: 01352 754202

Cornwall
Education Department
County Hall
Truro
Cornwall
TR1 3AY
Telephone: 01872 320000

Coventry
New Council Offices
Earl Street
Coventry
CV1 5RS
Telephone: 01203 831511
Facsimile: 01203 831620

Croydon
Taberner House
Park Lane
Croydon
Surrey
CR9 1TP
Telephone: 0181-686 4433

Cumbria
5 Portland Square
Carlisle
Cumbria
CA1 1PU
Telephone: 01228 23456

Administration

Local Education Authorities

Derbyshire
County Offices
Matlock
Derbyshire
DE4 3AG
Telephone: 01629 580000

Devon
County Hall
Exeter
Devon
EX2 4QG
Telephone: 01392 382059

Doncaster
P.O. Box 266
The Council House
College Road
Doncaster
DN1 3AD
Telephone: 01302 737222
Facsimile: 01302 737223

Dorset
County Hall
Dorchester
Dorset
DT1 1XJ
Telephone: 01305 251000

Dudley
Westox House
1 Trinity Road
Dudley
DY1 1JB
Telephone: 01384 456000

Dumfries and Galloway
30 Edinburgh Road
Dumfries
DG1 1JQ
Telephone: 01387 61234
Facsimile: 01387 60453

Durham
County Hall
Durham
DH1 5UJ
Telephone: 0191-386 4411

Dyfed
Education Department
Pibwrlwyd
Carmarthen
Dyfed
SA31 2NH
Telephone: 01267 233333

Ealing
Perceval House
14-16 Uxbridge Road
London
W5 2HL
Telephone: 0181-579 2424

East Sussex
Education Department
P.O. Box 4
County Hall
Lewes
Sussex
BN7 1SG
Telephone: 01273 481000

Enfield
P.O. Box 56
Civic Centre
Enfield
Middlesex
EN1 3XQ
Telephone: 0181-366 6565
Facsimile: 0181-982 7375

Essex
P.O. Box 47
A Block, County Hall
Victoria Road South
Chelmsford
Essex
CM1 1LD
Telephone: 01245 492211

Fife
Regional Headquarters
Fife House
North Street
Glenrothes
KY7 5LT
Telephone: 01592 754411
Facsimile: 01592 610726

Administration

Local Education Authorities

Gateshead
Civic Centre
Regent Street
Gateshead
Tyne & Wear
NE8 1HH
Telephone: 0191-477 1011

Gloucestershire
Shire Hall
Gloucester
GL1 2TP
Telephone: 01452 425300

Grampian
Education Department
Woodhill House
Westburn Road
Aberdeen
AB9 2LU
Telephone: 01224 682222
Facsimile: 01224 664615

Greenwich
Riverside House
Beresford Street
London
SE18 6DF
Telephone: 0181-854 8888
Facsimile: 0181-855 2427

Guernsey
P.O. Box 32
Grange Road
St Peter Port
Guernsey
GY1 3AU
Telephone: 01481 710821
Facsimile: 01481 714475

Gwent
County Hall
Cwmbran
Gwent
NP44 2XG
Telephone: 01633 838838

Gwynedd
Education Offices
Castle Street
Caernarfon
Gwynedd
Telephone: LL55 1SH
Facsimile: 01286 672255

Hackney
Edith Cavell Building
Enfield Road
London
N1 5AZ
Telephone: 0171-214 8400
Facsimile: 0171-214 8531

Hammersmith and Fulham
Education Department
Cambridge House
Cambridge Grove
London
W6 0LE
Telephone: 0181-576 5366

Hampshire
The Castle
Winchester
Hampshire
SO23 8UJ
Telephone: 01962 841841
Facsimile: 01962 842355

Haringey
48 Station Road
Wood Green
London
N22 4TY
Telephone: 0181-975 9700
Facsimile: 0181-862 3864

Harrow
P.O. Box 22
Civic Centre
Harrow
Middlesex
HA1 2UW
Telephone: 0181-863 5611
Facsimile: 0181-427 0810

Administration
Local Education Authorities

Havering
Mercury House
Mercury Gardens
Romford
Essex
RM1 3RX
Telephone: 01708 772222
Facsimile: 01708 772672

Hereford and Worcester
County Hall
Worcester
WR5 2NT
Telephone: 01905 763763

Hertfordshire
County Hall
Hertford
SG13 8DF
Telephone: 01992 555827
Facsimile: 01992 555819

Highland
Regional Buildings
Glenurquhart Road
Inverness
IV3 5NX
Telephone: 01463 702000
Facsimile: 01463 702828

Hillingdon
Civic Centre
Uxbridge
Middlesex
UB8 1UW
Telephone: 01895 250111

Hounslow
Civic Centre
Lampton Road
Hounslow
Middlesex
TW3 4DN
Telephone: 0181-570 7728

Humberside
County Hall
Beverley
North Humberside
HU17 9BA
Telephone: 01482 867131
Facsimile: 01482 863684

Isle of Man
Murray House
Mount Havelock
Douglas
Isle of Man
Telephone: 01624 626262
Facsimile: 01624 685834

Isle of Wight
County Hall
Newport
Isle of Wight
PO30 1UD
Telephone: 01983 821000

Isles of Scilly
Town Hall
St Mary's
Isles of Scilly
T21 0LW
Telephone: 01720 22537

Islington
Education Offices
Laycock Street
London
N1 1TH
Telephone: 0171-457 5566
Facsimile: 0171-457 5555

Jersey
P.O. Box 142
St Saviour
Jersey
JE4 8QJ
Telephone: 01534 509500
Facsimile: 01534 509800

Kensington and Chelsea
Town Hall
Hornton Street
London
W8 7NX
Telephone: 0171-937 5464
Facsimile: 0171-937 0038

Kent
Education Offices
Springfield
Maidstone
Kent
ME14 2LJ
Telephone: 01622 671411
Facsimile: 01622 690892

Administration

Local Education Authorities

Kingston upon Thames
Guildhall 2
Kingston upon Thames
Surrey
KT1 1EU
Telephone: 0181-546 2121
Facsimile: 0181-547 5296

Kirklees
Oldgate House
2 Oldgate
Huddersfield
HD1 6QW
Telephone: 01484 422133
Facsimile: 01484 443336

Knowsley
Education Offices
Huyton Hey Road
Huyton
Merseyside
L36 5YX
Telephone: 0151-489 6000

Lambeth
234-244 Stockwell Road
London
SW9 9SP
Telephone: 0171-926 1000

Lancashire
P.O. Box 61
County Hall
Preston
Lancashire
PR1 8RJ
Telephone: 01772 254868

Leeds
Selectapost 17
Merrion House
Leeds
LS2 8DT
Telephone: 0113 234 8080
Facsimile: 0113 234 1394

Leicestershire
County Hall
Glenfield
Leicester
LE3 8RF
Telephone: 0116 232 3232

Lewisham
Education Directorate
Laurence House
1 Catford Road
Catford
London
SE6 4SW
Telephone: 0181-695 6000
Facsimile: 0181-690 4392

Lincolnshire
County Offices
Lincoln
LN1 1YL
Telephone: 01522 552222
Facsimile: 01522 553257

Liverpool
14 Sir Thomas Street
Liverpool
L1 6BJ
Telephone: 0151-227 3911

London, Corporation of
P.O. Box 270
Guildhall
London
EC2P 2EJ
Telephone: 0171-332 1750
Facsimile: 0171-332 1621

Lothian
40 Torpichen Street
Edinburgh
EH3 8JJ
Telephone: 0131-229 9166
Facsimile: 0131-229 0059

Manchester
Education Offices
Crown Square
Manchester
M60 3BB
Telephone: 0161-234 5000

Merton
Crown House
London Road
Morden
Surrey
SM4 5DX
Telephone: 0181-543 2222
Facsimile: 0181-545 3443

Administration
Local Education Authorities

Mid Glamorgan
County Hall
Cathays Park
Cardiff
Mid Glamorgan
CF1 3NF
Telephone: 01222 820820
Facsimile: 01222 780181

Newcastle upon Tyne
Civic Centre
Barras Bridge
Newcastle upon Tyne
NE1 8PU
Telephone: 0191-232 8520
Facsimile: 0191-211 4983

Newham
Broadway House
322 High Street
Stratford
London
E15 1PJ
Telephone: 0181-555 5552

Norfolk
County Hall
Norwich
NR1 2DL
Telephone: 01603 222146
Facsimile: 01603 222119

North Tyneside
Stevenson House
Stevenson Street
North Shields
NE30 1QA
Telephone: 0191-257 5544
Facsimile: 0191-296 2439

North Yorkshire
County Hall
Northallerton
North Yorkshire
DL7 8AE
Telephone: 01609 780780
Facsimile: 01609 778611

North-Eastern Area
County Hall
182 Galgorm Road
Ballymena
Co Antrim
BT42 1HN
Telephone: 01266 653333
Facsimile: 01266 46071

Northamptonshire
P.O. Box 149
County Hall
Guildhall Road
Northampton
NN1 1DN
Telephone: 01604 236236

Northumberland
County Hall
Morpeth
Northumberland
NE61 2EF
Telephone: 01670 533000
Facsimile: 01670 533750

Nottinghamshire
County Hall
West Bridgford
Nottingham
NG2 7QP
Telephone: 0115 982 3823
Facsimile: 0115 981 2824

Oldham
Old Town Hall
Middleton Road
Chadderton
Oldham
OL9 6PP
Telephone: 0161-678 4260
Facsimile: 0161-628 0443

Orkney
Council Offices
Kirkwall
Orkney
KW15 1NY
Telephone: 01856 873535

Administration

Local Education Authorities

Oxfordshire
Macclesfield House
New Road
Oxford
OX1 1NA
Telephone: 01865 792422

Powys
County Hall
Llandrindod Wells
Powys
LD1 5LG
Telephone: 01597 826000
Facsimile: 01597 826230

Redbridge
Lynton House
255-259 High Road
Ilford
Essex
IG1 1NN
Telephone: 0181-478 3020
Facsimile: 0181-553 0895

Richmond upon Thames
Regal House
London Road
Twickenham
Middlesex
TW1 3QB
Telephone: 0181-891 1411
Facsimile: 0181-891 1411

Rochdale
P.O. Box 70
Municipal Offices
Smith Street
Rochdale
OL16 1YD
Telephone: 01706 47474

Rotherham
Norfolk House
Walker Place
Rotherham
South Yorkshire
S60 1QT
Telephone: 01709 382121

Salford
Education Offices
Chapel Street
Salford
M3 5LT
Telephone: 0161-832 9751
Facsimile: 0161-835 1561

Sandwell
P.O. Box 41
Shaftesbury House
402 High Street
West Bromwich
B70 9LT
Telephone: 0121-525 7366
Facsimile: 0121-553 1582

Sefton
Town Hall
Bootle
L20 7AE
Telephone: 0151-933 6003

Sheffield
Leopold Street
Sheffield
S1 1RJ
Telephone: 0114 272 6444
Facsimile: 0114 273 6279

Shetland
21 Harbour Street
Lerwick
Shetland
ZE1 0JR
Telephone: 01595 3800
Facsimile: 01595 2810

Shropshire
Shirehall
Abbey Foregate
Shrewsbury
SY2 6ND
Telephone: 01743 251000

Solihull
P.O. Box 20
Council House
Solihull
B91 3QU
Telephone: 0121-704 6000

Administration

Local Education Authorities

Somerset
County Hall
Taunton
Somerset
TA1 4DY
Telephone: 01823 333451
Facsimile: 01823 338139

South Glamorgan
County Hall
Atlantic Wharf
Cardiff
South Glamorgan
CF1 5UW
Telephone: 01222 872000
Facsimile: 01222 872777

South Tyneside
Town Hall and Civic Offices
South Shields
NE33 2RL
Telephone: 0191-427 1717
Facsimile: 0191-427 0584

South-Eastern Area
18 Windsor Avenue
Belfast
BT9 6EF
Telephone: 01232 381188

Southern Area
3 Charlemont Place
The Mall
Armagh
BT61 9AX
Telephone: 01861 523811

Southwark
1 Bradenham Close
Walworth
London
SE17 2QA
Telephone: 0171-525 5001

St Helens
Rivington Road
St Helens
WA10 4ND
Telephone: 01744 24061
Facsimile: 01744 455350

Staffordshire
Education Offices
Tipping Street
Stafford
ST16 2DH
Telephone: 01785 223121
Facsimile: 01785 56727

Stockport
Stopford House
Stockport
SK1 3XE
Telephone: 0161-480 4949
Facsimile: 0161-953 0012

Strathclyde
Department of Education
Strathclyde House 12
20 India Street
Glasgow
G2 4PF
Telephone: 0141-204 2900

Suffolk
St Andrews House
County Hall
Ipswich
IP4 1LJ
Telephone: 01473 230000

Sunderland
Box 101
Civic Centre
Sunderland
SR2 7DN
Telephone: 0191-567 6161

Surrey
Education Department
County Hall
Kingston upon Thames
Surrey
KT1 2DJ
Telephone: 0181-541 9501

Sutton
The Grove
Carshalton
Surrey
SM5 3AL
Telephone: 0181-770 6568

Administration

Local Education Authorities

Tameside
Council Offices
Wellington Road
Ashton-under-Lyne
Lancashire
OL6 6DL
Telephone: 0161-342 8355
Facsimile: 0161-342 3260

Tayside
Tayside House
Dundee
DD1 3RJ
Telephone: 01382 23281

Tower Hamlets
Education Strategy Group
Mulberry Place
5 Clove Crescent
London
E14 2BG
Telephone: 0171-512 4200
Facsimile: 0171-512 4976

Trafford
P.O. Box 19
Tatton Road
Sale
Greater Manchester
M33 1YR
Telephone: 0161-872 2101

Wakefield
County Hall
Wakefield
WF1 2QW
Telephone: 01924 290900

Walsall
Civic Centre
Darwall Street
Walsall
WS1 1TP
Telephone: 01922 650000
Facsimile: 01922 722322

Waltham Forest
Municipal Offices
High Road
Leyton
London
E10 5QJ
Telephone: 0181-527 5544
Facsimile: 0181-556 8720

Wandsworth
Town Hall
Wandsworth High Street
London
SW18 2PU
Telephone: 0181-871 6000

Warwickshire
22 Northgate Street
Warwick
CV34 4SR
Telephone: 01926 410410
Facsimile: 01926 412746

West Glamorgan
County Hall
Swansea
West Glamorgan
SA1 3SN
Telephone: 01792 471111

West Sussex
County Hall
West Street
Chichester
Sussex
PO19 1RF
Telephone: 01243 777100
Facsimile: 01243 777229

Western Area
Headquarters Office
1 Hospital Road
Omagh
BT79 0AW
Telephone: 01662 240240
Facsimile: 01662 241443

Western Isles
Education Offices
Stornoway
Isle of Lewis
PA87 2BW
Telephone: 01851 703773

Westminster, City of
P.O. Box 240
Westminster City Hall
64 Victoria Street
London
SW1E 6QP
Telephone: 0171-828 8070

Administration

Local Education Authorities

Wigan
Gateway House
Standishgate
Wigan
WN1 1XL
Telephone: 01942 828891

Wiltshire
County Hall
Bythesea Road
Trowbridge
Wiltshire
BA14 8JG
Telephone: 01225 713000

Wirral
Hamilton Building
Conway Street
Birkenhead
Wirral
L41 4FD
Telephone: 0151-666 2121
Facsimile: 0151-666 4207

Wolverhampton
Civic Centre
St Peter's Square
Wolverhampton
WV1 1RR
Telephone: 01902 27811
Facsimile: 01902 314218

Administration

School support

Association of Head Teachers in Scotland
Northern College of Education
Gardyne Road
Dundee
DD5 1NY
Contact: James C Smith, General Secretary
Telephone: 01382 458802

Association of Heads of Independent Schools
Abbots Hill School
Bunkers Lane
Hemel Hempstead
Hertfordshire
HP3 8RP
Contact: Mrs J Kingsley, Hon Secretary
Telephone: 01442 403333
Facsimile: 01442 69981
The organisation exists to offer help to the Heads of small independent girls' schools.

Centre for Multicultural Education
Institute of Education
University of London
20 Bedford Way
London
WC1H 0AL
Contact: Dr Jagdish S Gundara
Telephone: 0171-612 6721
Facsimile: 0171-612 6733

Choir Schools' Association
The Minster School
Deangate
York
YO1
Contact: The Administrator
Telephone: 01904 625217
Facsimile: 01904 632418
Exists to promote the welfare of choir schools.

Conference for Independent Further Education
Buckhall Farm
Bull Lane
Bethersden, Ashford
Kent
TN26 3HB
Contact: Myles Glover, Secretary
Telephone: 01233 820797

Professional association for independent sixth form and tutorial colleges accredited, or aiming within 3 years to achieve accreditation, either by the British Accreditation Council for Independent Further and Higher Education or the Independent Schools Joint Council. The aim of the association is to safeguard and enhance academic standards, make provision for the welfare of students and standards of professional integrity among member colleges, and to promote good practice among them in all aspects of education.

Curriculum, Evaluation and Management Centre
Department of Education, University of Newcastle upon Tyne
St Thomas' Street
Newcastle upon Tyne
NE1 7RU
Contact: Prof Carol Taylor Fitz-Gib, Director
Telephone: 0191-222 6588
Facsimile: 0191-222 5021
Services offered include value added systems, full-scale monitoring (ALIS+, YELLIS, PIPS), full organisation of conferences and INSET.

European Council of International Schools
21 Lavant Street
Petersfield
Hampshire
GU32 3EL
Telephone: 01730 268244
Facsimile: 01730 267914
E-mail: 100412.242@compuserv.com
Supports international schools world-wide through the provision of recruitment services, professional development, accreditation, consultancies and publications.

Girls' Schools Association
130 Regent Road
Leicester
LE1 7PG
Contact: Mrs Sheila Cooper, General Secretary
Telephone: 0116 254 1619
Facsimile: 0116 255 3792

Administration

School support

Governing Bodies Association
Windleshaw Lodge
Withyham
Hartfield
Sussex
TN7 4DB
Contact: Mr D G Banwell, Secretary
Telephone: 01892 770879
Facsimile: 01892 770879
The advancement of education in co-
educational and boys' independent schools.

Governing Bodies of Girls' Schools
Association
Windleshaw Lodge
Withyham
Hartfield
Sussex
TN7 4DB
Contact: Mr D G Banwell, Secretary
Telephone: 01892 770879
Facsimile: 01892 770879
The advancement of education in member
independent schools for girls.

Grant-Maintained Schools Foundation
36 Great Smith Street
London
SW1P 3BU
Contact: Andrew Turner, Director
Telephone: 0171-233 4666
Facsimile: 0171-233 2795
Assists parents, teachers and governors to
consider grant-maintained (self-governing)
status for their schools. Nothing is charged
for the service.

Incorporated Association of Preparatory
Schools
11 Waterloo Place
Leamington Spa
Warwickshire
CV32 5LA
Contact: John Morris, General Secretary
Telephone: 01926 887883
Facsimile: 01926 888014
IAPS fosters the interchange of experience and
ideas on education between Heads of
preparatory schools, promoting their

collective ideas and providing a channel of
communication with senior independent
schools.

Independent Schools Bursars' Association
Woodlands
Closewood Road, Denmead
Waterlooville
Hampshire
PO7 6JD
Telephone: 01705 264506
Information service on school administration for
member schools (independent secondary).

Methodist Colleges and Schools
25 Marylebone Road
London
NW1 5JP
Contact: Derek Robson, Secretary
Telephone: 0171-935 3723
Facsimile: 0171-224 0702
Administrative office for Methodist independent
boarding and day schools.

National Association for Gifted Children
Park Campus
Boughton Green Road
Northampton
NN2 7AL
Telephone: 01604 792300
Facsimile: 01604 720636
Assists teachers to identify gifted children,
giving them strategies on coping with them.
Also gives advice on whole-school policies
towards the gifted. INSET is available from
an Education Consultants team.

National Association for the Support of
Small Schools
The Cottage
Little Barningham
Norwich
Norfolk
NR11 7LN
Contact: Mrs Molly Stiles, National Coordinator
Telephone: 01263 577553
Seeks to provide a voice and a link for those
who believe that small rural schools have
educational and social roles to perform and
are 'too precious to lose'.

Administration

School support

National Association of Governors and Managers
Suite 36-38
21 Bennetts Hill
Birmingham
B2 5QP
Telephone: 0121-643 5787
Facsimile: 0121-643 5787
National governors' helpline: 0800 241242.

National Consortium for Examination Results
Education Statistics Office, Cheshire Education Authority
County Hall
Chester
CH1 1SQ
Contact: Peter Richmond, Secretary
Telephone: 01244 602335/0860 377747
Facsimile: 01244 603821
Membership consists of 109 LEAs for whom NCER produces a full analysis of GCSE and A/AS results for its members each year. The data is produced at the various levels required (school, LEA and national).

National Grammar Schools Association
Grove House
19 Grove Road
Beaconsfield
Buckinghamshire
HP9 1UR
Contact: Mrs Margaret Dewar, Chairman
Telephone: 01494 673358
Facsimile: 01494 670121
Supports and conserves the remaining 161 grammar schools that remain in England.

Society of Headmasters and Headmistresses of Independent Schools
The Coach House
34a Heath Road
Upton-by-Chester
Cheshire
CH2 1HX
Contact: Mr I D Cleland, Secretary
Telephone: 01244 379649
Facsimile: 01244 379649
Represents the interests of independent schools and encourages high standards in all aspects of education.

Sports Turf Research Institute
St Ives Estate
Bingley
West Yorkshire
BD16 1AU
Contact: Dr Peter Hayes, Director
Telephone: 01274 565131
Facsimile: 01274 561891
Offers services to schools in both the independent and maintained sectors on the maintenance of pitches, and offers advice on the drainage of existing pitches and the construction of new playing fields.

The Sixth-Form Colleges' Association Ltd
10 Lombard Street
London
EC2V 9AT
Telephone: 0171-398 0077
Facsimile: 0171-283 9655
Seeks to provide a forum for the discussion of matters of common interest, and to provide a network of support for member colleges.

Administration

Parent-school liaison

Home and School Council
40 Sunningdale Mount
Sheffield
S11 9HA
Contact: Mrs B Bullivant, Hon Secretary
Telephone: 0114 236 4181
Facsimile: 0114 236 4181
The Council exists to publish reasonably priced booklets for parents, governors and teachers on aspects of home-school contact, and how parents can help their children. It also links the main parents' and teachers' associations.

National Confederation of Parent-Teacher Associations
2 Ebbsfleet Industrial Estate
Stonebridge Road
Gravesend
Kent
DA11 9DZ
Telephone: 01474 560618
Facsimile: 01474 564418
Committed to home-school partnership by encouraging and promoting the formation of home-school associations (PTAs).

Scottish Parent-Teacher Council
Cramond House, Kirk Cramond
Cramond Glebe Road
Edinburgh
EH4 6NS
Telephone: 0131-312 7226
Facsimile: 0131-312 7226
Encourages the fullest co-operation between home and school, education authorities, central government and all those concerned with education in Scotland. Membership includes PAs, PTAs, individuals and educational associations.

THE CURRICULUM

The Curriculum

Subject areas

GENERAL

Council for Education in World Citizenship
Seymour Mews House
Seymour Mews
London
W1H 9PE
Contact: Patricia Rogers, Director
Telephone: 0171-935 1752
Facsimile: 0171-935 5548
Helps to prepare young people for the rights and responsibilities of citizenship of our interdependent and multicultural world. Through the provision of materials, activities, information, services, workshops and conferences, it helps to bring international issues home to young people. Membership open to schools, colleges, organisations, LEAs and individuals.

Dartington Hall Trust
The Elmhirst Centre
Dartington Hall
Totnes
Devon
TQ9 6EL
Telephone: 01803 866688
Facsimile: 01803 865551
A charitable trust interested in education, the arts and research.

ARTS AND CRAFTS

Crafts Council
44a Pentonville Road
London
N1 9BY
Telephone: 0171-278 7700
Facsimile: 0171-837 6891
Promotes the contemporary crafts in Great Britain. It is an independent organisation funded by government and provides direct services to craftspeople and the public.

BUSINESS EDUCATION

Association of European Economics Education
Centre for Economics and Business Education
Staffordshire University Business School
Stoke-on-Trent
Staffordshire
ST4 2DF
Telephone: 01782 294085
Facsimile: 01782 747006
The advancement of economics and business education in Europe by supporting teachers with information, contacts and encouraging collaboration in research.

CLASSICS

Association for the Reform of Latin Teaching
15 Hardacre Close
Melbourne
Derbyshire
DE73 1GY
Contact: Dr A Henshaw, Secretary
Exists to promote by discussion, co-operation and experiment the teaching of Classics in all types of schools.

Classical Association
St John's College
Cambridge
CB2 1TP
Contact: Dr M Schofield, Joint Hon Secretary
Telephone: 01223 338644
Facsimile: 01223 337720
Seeks to increase public awareness of the contribution and importance of Classics to education and national life, by supporting classical learning in schools and creating opportunities for friendly exchange.

Joint Association of Classical Teachers
31-34 Gower Street
London
WC1H 0PY
Contact: The Executive Secretary
Telephone: 0171-387 0348
The promotion of the study of Classics in schools and universities.

The Curriculum

Subject areas

Society for the Promotion of Hellenic Studies
31-34 Gordon Square
London
WC1H 0PP
Contact: The Secretary
Telephone: 0171-387 7495
Facsimile: 0171-387 7495
Aims to advance the study of the Greek language, literature, history, art and archaeology in the Ancient, Byzantine and Modern periods.

Society for the Promotion of Roman Studies
31-34 Gordon Square
London
WC1H 0PP
Contact: The Secretary
Telephone: 0171-387 8157
Seeks to promote the study of the history, archaeology, literature and art of Italy and the Roman Empire, from the earliest times down to about AD700. Small grants are available to schools for textbooks and other teaching materials for the teaching of Latin/Roman studies.

DESIGN & TECHNOLOGY

Centre for Alternative Technology
Machynlleth
Powys
SY20 9AZ
Contact: Ann MacGarry, Education Officer
Telephone: 01654 703743
Facsimile: 01654 702782
Aims to educate about sustainable technologies, publishes materials for teachers and pupils and offers INSET.

Intermediate Technology
Myson House
Railway Terrace
Rugby CV21 3HT
Contact: Education Office
Telephone: 01788 560631
A number of moderately priced packs, books and slide sets describe a variety of cultures and contexts within which needs can be identified as the starting point for Design and Technology work.

Meat and Livestock Commission
P.O. Box 44
Winterhill House
Snowdon Drive
Milton Keynes
MK6 1AX
Contact: Education Manager
Telephone: 01908 677577
A wide range of free classroom resources which support Food Technology and Business Studies, software (Acorn), a video package and printed materials are available using fast food and product development themes.

National Association of Advisers and Inspectors in Design and Technology
124 Kidmore Road
Caversham
Reading
Berkshire
RG4 7NB
Contact: Mr R Welch, Hon Secretary
Telephone: 01734 470615
Facsimile: 01734 470615
Seeks to promote the teaching of good practice in Design and Technology in schools.

ENGLISH

Arthur Ransome Society
c/o Museum of Lakeland Life and Industry
Abbot Hall
Kirkland, Kendal
Cumbria
LA9 5AL
Contact: Dr Kirsty Cochrane, Hon Secretary
Telephone: 01539 722464
The Society celebrates the life, works and interests of the novelist Arthur Ransome. Members of all ages are welcome, with some regional groups having specific links with education. A junior newsletter is available and a junior sub-committee has been formed.

Books for Keeps & School Bookshop Association
6 Brightfield Road
London
SE12 8QF
Contact: Richard Hill, Managing Director

The Curriculum

Subject areas

Telephone: 0181-852 4953

Books for Keeps is a review magazine for teachers on children's books. The School Bookshop Association provides advice on setting up a school bookshop.

British Film Institute
21 Stephen Street
London
W1P 1PL
Contact: Cary Bazalgette, Principal Education Officer
Telephone: 0171-255 1444
Facsimile: 0171-436 7950

BFI Education supports the development of media education at all levels of schooling. The BFI is a government-funded body which includes the National Film Theatre, Museum of the Moving Image and the National Film Archive. A catalogue of educational publications is available.

Brontë Society
Brontë Parsonage Museum
Haworth
Keighley
West Yorkshire
BD22 8DR
Contact: Judith Warner, Education Consultant
Telephone: 01535 642323
Facsimile: 01535 647131

Seeks to establish closer contact with schools and colleges, assisting teachers in the communication of English, Drama, Art and History skills where they relate to the lives and works of the Brontës.

Burns Federation
Dick Institute
Elmbank Avenue
Kilmarnock
KA1 3BU
Telephone: 01536 572469
Facsimile: 01563 529661

Seeks to encourage Burns clubs and similar societies who honour the memory of Robert Burns and his works, arranges schools competitions and stimulates the teaching and study of Scottish literature, history, art and music.

Dalcroze Society
41A Woodmansterne Road
Coulsdon
Surrey
CR5 2DJ
Contact: Patricia Piqué, Secretary
Telephone: 0181-645 0714

Education through movement and music.

Dickens Fellowship
48 Doughty Street
London
WC1N 2LF
Contact: Edward G Preston, Hon General Secretary
Telephone: 0171-405 2127
Facsimile: 0171-831 5175

Seeks to bring together all who have any interest whatever in the life and works of Charles Dickens, and in his own concerns in social reform, particularly in education.

English Association
University of Leicester
128 Regent Road
Leicester
LE1 7PA
Contact: Helen Lucas, The Secretary
Telephone: 0116 252 5927
Facsimile: 0116 252 5928

Furthers the knowledge, understanding and enjoyment of the English language and its literature by means of conferences, lectures and publications.

John Buchan Society
16 Ranfurly Road
Bridge of Weir
Strathclyde
PA11 3EL
Contact: Russell Paterson, Secretary
Telephone: 01505 613116

The promotion of a wider understanding and appreciation of the life and works of John Buchan by holding regular meetings, producing a journal and supporting the John Buchan Centre.

ENGLISH

The Curriculum

Subject areas

National Association of Youth Theatres
Unit 1304, The Custard Factory
Gibb Street
Birmingham
B9 4AA
Telephone: 0121-608 2111
Facsimile: 0121-608 2333
Aims to increase the range and quality of youth theatre in the UK by generating public support at national and local levels, and is able to provide contacts for young people interested in joining a youth theatre.

National Youth Theatre of Great Britain
443/445 Holloway Road
London
N7 6LW
Contact: Marilyn Eardley, General Manager
Telephone: 0171-281 3863
Facsimile: 0171-281 8246
Aims to combine creative ensemble work together with social concern for young people and their right to opportunity and expression, regardless of background, through the medium of theatre.

Poetry Society
22 Betterton Street
London
WC2H 9BU
Contact: Education Officer
Telephone: 0171-240 4810
Facsimile: 0171-240 4818
Poetry Society Education aims to bring poetry alive in the classroom and to ensure that poetry is made accessible to all young people. To this end a practical guide is available from the Society, and they administer the WH Smith Poets in Schools scheme.

Reading and Language Information Centre
University of Reading
Bulmershe Court
Earley, Reading
RG6 1HY
Contact: Prof Viv Edwards, Director
Telephone: 01734 318820
Facsimile: 01734 318650
Provides professional development for teachers in the form of courses, conferences and INSET; makes accessible 12,000 resources (books, AV resources and software); and offers a package of services through a membership scheme.

Royal Society of Literature
1 Hyde Park Gardens
London
W2 2LT
Contact: Maggie Parham, Secretary
Telephone: 0171-723 5104
Facsimile: 0171-402 0144
Seeks to sustain and encourage all that is perceived as best, whether traditional or experimental, in English literature and to strive for a catholic appreciation of literature.

Shakespeare Centre
Henley Street
Stratford-upon-Avon
CV37 6QW
Contact: Bill Marriott, Education Assistant
Telephone: 01789 204016
Facsimile: 01789 296083
Offers educational work on Shakespeare's life, work and times, including practical workshops, illustrated slide lectures, stage histories, and use of videos. They are also happy to come out to schools and colleges.

Simplified Spelling Society
133 John Trundle Court
Barbican
London
EC2Y 8DJ
Telephone: 0171-628 5876
Facsimile: 0171-628 9147
Aims at producing a consistent and predictable spelling scheme with maximum benefit to future generations.

Society for Italic Handwriting
205 Dyas Avenue
Great Barr
Birmingham
B42 1HN
Contact: Nicholas Caulkin, Secretary & Editor of Newsletter
Telephone: 0121-358 0032
Encourages the use of italic handwriting and handwriting improvement generally.

The Curriculum

Subject areas

Tennyson Society
Tennyson Research Centre
Central Library, Free School Lane
Lincoln
LN2 1EZ
Contact: Hon Secretary
Telephone: 01522 552866
Facsimile: 01522 552858
Seeks to promote study and understanding of the life and work of Alfred, Lord Tennyson.

Young Book Trust
Book House
45 East Hill
London
SW18 2QZ
Telephone: 0181-870 9055
Facsimile: 0181-874 4790
Aims to promote children's books and reading. A subscription service for schools and libraries is available.

GEOGRAPHY

British Association for Canadian Studies
21 George Square
Edinburgh
EH8 9CD
Contact: Jodie Robson, Administrative Secretary
Telephone: 0131-662 1117
Facsimile: 0131-662 1118
Seeks to promote interest in Canada and Canadian culture in academic circles and in the general community in the UK, and to encourage and facilitate the study of Canada in schools. Publishes The British Journal of Canadian Studies and a termly newsletter.

Centre for Cartopedagogic Studies
Atlas House
46 Holtwood Road
Glenholt, Plymouth
Devon
PL6 7HU
Contact: Dr Herbert A Sandford, Director
Telephone: 01752 779621
Facsimile: 01752 761120

The Centre was set up to provide research and consultation in the design, use and production of maps of all kinds, with especial reference to school atlases.

Geographical Association
343 Fulwood Road
Sheffield
S10 3BP
Telephone: 0114 267 0666
Facsimile: 0114 267 0688
Reasonably priced books and packs on aspects of Geography, and teaching it, are available.

Met. Office, The
Education Service Room 124
London Road
Bracknell
Berkshire
RG12 2SZ
Telephone: 01344 854802
Facsimile: 01344 856151
Information, mostly free, about meteorology. A catalogue must be obtained first.

Northern Ireland Tourist Board
59 North Street
Belfast
BT1 1NB
Telephone: 01232 246609
Free tourism leaflets on Northern Ireland are available.

Places for People
Lewis Cohen Urban Studies Centre
68 Grand Parade
Brighton
Sussex
BN2 2JY
Contact: Mrs Selma Montford, Hon Treasurer
Telephone: 01273 673416
Facsimile: 01273 673416
Focuses on the urban environment in the country, promoting education and encouraging people of all ages to have a voice in the future of the places in which they live, work and play.

ENGLISH

The Curriculum

Subject areas

Relay Europe
Enterprise Centre
112 Malling Street
Lewes
Sussex
BN7 2RJ
Telephone: 01273 488666
Facsimile: 01273 488448
Free-loan videos on the EU, aimed at adults,
but many suitable for use in school. Also
manages a mobile exhibition vehicle for the
European Commission and has a range of
EU display materials for hire.

Royal Geographical Society, The (with the
Institute of British Geographers)
1 Kensington Gore
London
SW7 2AR
Contact: Mrs Shane Winser, Information Officer
Telephone: 0171-589 5466
Facsimile: 0171-584 4447
Supports the teaching of Geography in a variety
of ways, aimed at both teachers and
students, and provides student support for
choices of career and in the selection of
university degree courses.

Royal Meteorological Society
104 Oxford Road
Reading
Berkshire
RG1 7LJ
Telephone: 01734 568500
Facsimile: 01734 568571
A variety of reasonably priced aids to teaching
meteorology are available by mail order.

**Scottish Association of Geography
Teachers**
Geography Department, University of
Strathclyde
Jordanhill Campus
Glasgow
G13 1PP
Telephone: 0141-950 3399
Seeks to promote the teaching of Geography in
Scottish schools.

Scottish Tourist Board
23 Ravelston Terrace
Edinburgh
EH4 3EU
Telephone: 0131-332 2433
24-hour information line: 0891 666465. Calls
charged at 39p per min cheap rate and 49p
per min at all other times.
Facsimile: 0131-315 4545
Free information for tourists to Scotland.

Thames Water Customer Centre
P.O. Box 436
Swindon
SN38 1TL
Telephone: 01645 200800
Available are posters, booklets and a computer
game with water as the focus, relating to
Geography and Science, for schools in the
Thames Water area.

**United Kingdom Centre for European
Education**
The Central Bureau for Educational Visits and
Exchanges
Seymour Mews House, Seymour Mews
London
W1H 9PE
Telephone: 0171-486 5101
Facsimile: 0171-935 5741
Seeks to promote an awareness of Europe
throughout the curriculum through the
provision of information, conferences and in
the support of curriculum development.

HISTORY

**American Civil War Round Table (UK
Chapter)**
98 Kew Green
Kew
Richmond
Surrey
TW9 3AP
Contact: Michael F Barrett, Hon Secretary-
Treasurer
Telephone: 0181-940 9950
A serious and impartial study of the American
Civil War 1861-65. Membership for amateur
and professional historians.

The Curriculum

Subject areas

Archaeology in Education
Dept of Archaeology and Prehistory
University of Sheffield
Sheffield
S10 2TN
Contact: Prof Keith Branigan
Telephone: 0114 280 5030
Facsimile: 0114 272 2563
Provides a support service to teachers using archaeology at any level of the school curriculum. A range of teaching aids (slides, artefact kits, videos, replicas, packs, aerial photos, etc), a twice-yearly newsletter and a free advice and information service are available.

Avoncroft Museum of Buildings
Stoke Heath
Bromsgrove
Worcestershire
B60 4JR
Contact: Dr Simon Penn, Curator
Telephone: 01527 831886
A range of moderately priced materials based around this collection of historic buildings is available.

British Agricultural History Society
Department of History and Economic History
Taylor Building, University of Aberdeen
Old Aberdeen
AB9 2UB
Contact: Dr Richard Perren, Secretary
Telephone: 01224 272197
Facsimile: 01224 272203
Seeks to promote the study of agricultural history and the history of rural economy and society by publishing a journal, holding conferences, promoting the conservation of significant landscapes and promoting the teaching of the history of agriculture at all levels of education.

British Association for Local History
24 Lower Street
Harnham
Salisbury
Wiltshire
SP2 8EY
Telephone: 01722 320115
Facsimile: 01722 413242

Supports all those interested in local history, publishing two journals and a number of practical handbooks.

British Model Soldier Society
35 St Johns Road
Chelmsford
Essex
CM2 0TX
Telephone: 01245 262089
Seeks to promote research and scholarship in all aspects of military history, weaponry, uniforms, etc through the media of military models and the portrayal of historical events. Also provides support and instruction in museums and schools.

Corinium Museum
Park Street
Cirencester
Gloucestershire
GL7 2BX
Telephone: 01285 655611
Facsimile: 01285 643286
A number of reasonably priced replica Roman artefacts are available by mail order.

Council for British Archaeology
Bowes Morrell House
111 Walmgate
York
YO1 2UA
Contact: Don Henson, Education Officer
Telephone: 01904 671417
Facsimile: 01904 671384
Information service for teachers with some occasional publications.

Council for Scottish Archaeology
c/o National Museum of Scotland
York Building, Queen Street
Edinburgh
EH2 1JD
Contact: Patrick Begg, Director
Telephone: 0131-225 7534
Facsimile: 0131-557 9498
Promoting public education and appreciation of Scotland's archaeological heritage.

The Curriculum

Subject areas

Cromwell Association, The
Cosswell Cottage
Northedge
Tupton, Chesterfield
Derbyshire
S42 6AY
Contact: Miss P Barnes, Secretary
Exists to promote and encourage interest in Oliver Cromwell, the English Civil War and the Commonwealth and Protectorate period. Membership is open to anyone interested in the period.

Crown Imperial
37 Wolsey Close
Southall
Middlesex
UB2 4NQ
Telephone: 0181-574 4425
Formed to study the history, traditions and regalia of the forces of the crown (and their allies) and other insignia.

Dover Roman Painted House
New Street
Dover
Kent
CT17 9AJ
Contact: Mr B J Philp
Telephone: 01304 203279
A number of publications by the Kent Archaeological Rescue Unit are available dealing with excavations on sites of all periods.

Education at Beaulieu
Montagu Ventures Ltd
John Montagu Building
Beaulieu
Hampshire
SO42 7ZN
Telephone: 01590 612345
Facsimile: 01590 612624
Books and packs about the history of motoring and aspects of medieval life are available at moderate prices.

English Heritage
P.O. Box 229
Northampton
NN6 9RY
Telephone: 01604 781163
Facsimile: 01604 781714
A wide range of teachers' guides and site handbooks linking use of the historic environment to most curriculum subjects are available at reasonable prices. Videos are available on free loan. A magazine, Heritage Learning, is circulated to all schools each term.

Fishbourne Roman Palace
Salthill Road
Fishbourne
West Sussex
PO19 3QR
Telephone: 01243 785859
Facsimile: 01243 539266
A number of postcards, guides, slides, posters and booklets, and a teachers' resource pack (for KS2 & 3) related to Roman life in the Chichester area are available at reasonable prices.

Fountains Abbey
Ripon
North Yorkshire
HG4 3DY
Contact: Education Officer
Telephone: 01765 608888
A National Trust property providing educational literature for teachers and children.

Heritage Projects (Canterbury) Ltd
The Canterbury Tales
23 Hawks Lane
Canterbury
Kent
CT1 2NU
Contact: The Education Executive
Telephone: 01227 454888
Facsimile: 01227 765584
A moderately priced pack on medieval Canterbury is available.

HISTORY

The Curriculum

Subject areas

Historic Royal Palaces
Hampton Court Palace
East Molesey
Surrey
KT8 9AU
Contact: Education Service
Telephone: 0181-781 9750
Videos, posters, books and packs based on the history of Hampton Court, the Banqueting House, Kew Palace, The Tower of London and Kensington Palace are available at reasonable prices.

Historical Metallurgy Society Ltd
22 Easterfield Drive
Southgate
Swansea
SA3 2DB
Telephone: 01792 233223
Seeks to educate and instruct the public by the study, investigation, description and preservation of the historical and archaeological evidence of the extraction, working and use of metals.

Imperial War Museum
Duxford Airfield
Cambridgeshire CB2 4QR
Contact: Mail Order Section
Telephone numbers:
Resource orders: 01223 835000 ext 245
    (Facsimile: 01223 837267)
Visits:
    Duxford Airfield 01223 835000 ext 252
    Lambeth Road 0171-416 5313
    Cabinet War Rooms 0171-930 6961
    HMS Belfast 0171-407 6434
A comprehensive range of poster facsimile document packs, cassette tapes, videos and books are available on both World Wars, all reasonably priced.

Ironbridge Gorge Museum
Ironbridge
Telford
Shropshire
TF8 7AW
Contact: Education Department
Telephone: 01952 433522
A wide range of moderately priced packs, booklets and wallcharts are available from this 'birth-place of the Industrial Revolution'.

Kew Bridge Steam Museum
Green Dragon Lane
Brentford
Middlesex TW8 0EN
Telephone: 0181-568 4757
Beam engine sectional drawings, Cornish pump engine details and much more about Victorian steam-driven machinery is available at reasonable cost.

Museum of Antiquities
The University
Newcastle upon Tyne
NE1 7RU
Contact: Lindsay Allason-Jones
Telephone: 0191-222 7846
Facsimile: 0191-261 1182
Low-cost booklet about Mithraic temples on Hadrian's Wall.

National Maritime Museum
Greenwich
London
SE10 9NF
Contact: Education Services Section
Telephone: 0181-312 6608 (for bookings only)
0181-312 6700 (bookshop)
Teachers' resource packs, free fact files, wallcharts, all linked to the National Curriculum.

National Trust, Mercia Region
Attingham Park
Shrewsbury
SY4 4TP
Contact: Public Affairs Manager
Telephone: 01743 709343
Moderately priced teachers' guides to life in Elizabethan manor houses (Little Moreton Hall, Speke Hall and Moseley Old Hall), and a range of environmental education resources.

Oral History Society
c/o Dept of Sociology
University of Essex
Colchester
Essex
CO4 3SQ
Contact: Robert Perks, Secretary
Telephone: 01206 873333
Facsimile: 01206 873598

The Curriculum

Subject areas

Supports and encourages the recording and collection of personal memories and experiences, offering advice to individuals and groups through its regional network, journal and conferences. Educational work is supported through specialist advice and publications.

Rural History Centre
Box 229
Whiteknights
University of Reading
Reading
RG6 6AG
Contact: Education Office
Telephone: 01734 318669
A range of competitively priced teaching packs on the history of agriculture and rural life are available.

Siege Group
Flat 11, Marlborough Court
Marlborough Hill
Harrow
Middlesex
HA1 1UF
Contact: Dennis Wraight, Secretary
Telephone: 0181-861 0830
Seeks to promote interest in the mid-17th-century period of history by having displays and re-enactments. Also lectures in primary and middle schools, dressing in period costume and taking artefacts in to show the children.

Tutankhamun The Exhibition
25 High West Street
Dorchester
Dorset
DT1 1UW
Telephone: 01305 269571 (exhibition) and 01305 269741 (administration)
Facsimile: 01305 268885
A number of reasonably priced items are available from the museum shop.

IT

ORT
126 Albert Street
London
NW1 7NF
Contact: Dr Gideon Meyer, Director of Education
International organisation developing teaching materials in technology and IT applications for schools, colleges, teacher training institutes and resource centres.

MATHEMATICS

Association of Teachers of Mathematics
7 Shaftesbury Street
Derby
DE23 8YB
Contact: Marian V Keeling, Administrative Officer
Telephone: 01332 346599
Facsimile: 01332 204354
Encourages and enables an increased understanding of the teaching and learning of mathematics.

Centre for Studies in Science and Mathematics Education
University of Leeds
Leeds
LS2 9JT
Contact: Mr Colin Wood-Robinson, Director
Telephone: 0113 233 4611
Facsimile: 0113 233 4683
Provides continuing professional development, including higher degree teaching and supervision in Science, Maths and Technology education.

Mathematical Association
259 London Road
Leicester
LE2 3BE
Telephone: 0116 270 3877
Facsimile: 0116 244 8508
Works to improve mathematical education and publishes a range of journals, books and reports.

MATHEMATICS

The Curriculum

Subject areas

Shell Centre for Mathematical Education
University of Nottingham
University Park
Nottingham
NG7 2RD
Contact: Stephen Jeffery, Publications Officer
Telephone: 0115 951 4415
Facsimile: 0115 979 1813
Conducts research, develops materials and produces publications on Mathematical education particularly for students aged between 8 and 16. A particular interest is the use of IT and multimedia in the classroom.

MODERN LANGUAGES

An Commun Gaidhealach
91 Cromwell Street
Stornoway
Isle of Lewis
PA87 2DG
Contact: Donald John MacSween, Chief Executive
Telephone: 01851 703487
Facsimile: 01851 706967
Gaelic language promotion and development.

Association of Recognised English Language Services
2 Pontypool Place
Valentine Place
London
SE1 8QF
Contact: Oksana Higglesden, PR Officer
Telephone: 0171-242 3136
Facsimile: 0171-928 9378
Promotes the teaching of the English language to students both in this country and abroad.

Esperanto Teachers' Association
140 Holland Park Avenue
London
W11 4UF
Telephone: 0171-727 7821
Aims to have the international language Esperanto accepted into the National Curriculum as a first foreign language, in line with the recommendation of UNESCO.

Esperanto-Asocio de Britio
140 Holland Park Avenue
London
W11 4UF
Telephone: 0171-727 7821
An educational charity, existing to provide information to promote the international language Esperanto. Courses and examinations are available at all levels in the language.

MUSIC

Baylis Programme, The, at English National Opera
London Coliseum
St Martin's Lane
London
WC2N 4ES
Contact: Natalie Sinnadurai, Administrator
Telephone: 0171-836 0111
The Baylis Programme exists to introduce people of all ages to the enjoyment of opera and to deepen their understanding and appreciation of this artform. The aim is to stimulate creativity through participation.

British Association of Barbershop Singers
4 The Cottages
Maythorne
Southwell
Nottinghamshire
Contact: Glenn Cheyney, Manager, Youth Programme
Telephone: 01636 814377
Seeks to encourage the singing of the barbershop style in schools through presentations to pupils and teachers and by providing workshops, manuals, CD, tapes, etc.

British Federation of Young Choirs
37 Frederick Street
Loughborough
Leicestershire
LE11 3BH
Contact: Susan Lansdale, Director
Telephone: 01509 211664
Facsimile: 01509 233749
The aim of the Federation is to stimulate choral singing and to improve its quality through singing events and training courses.

MODERN LANGUAGES

The Curriculum

Subject areas

British Horn Society
Elmore
High Road
Chipstead, Coulsdon
Surrey
CR5 3SB
Contact: John Norman Wates
Telephone: 01737 557550
Facsimile: 01737 552918
Seeks to further interest in playing the French horn by running workshops and festivals in various music academies.

British Kodály Academy
11 Cotland Acres
Redhill
Surrey
RH1 6JZ
Contact: Mary Place, Secretary
Telephone: 01737 242974
Seeks to further and disseminate the principles and practice of music education found in the work of Zoltán Kodály and to relate these to our own cultural heritage and National Curriculum requirements. Organises demonstrations, courses and a summer school.

British Trombone Society
P.O. Box 817
London
SE21 7BY
Contact: Anthony Parsons, Editor
Promotes the trombone and its repertoire in all musical styles. Membership is aimed at anyone interested in the trombone regardless of age or whether they can play.

Clarinet & Saxophone Society of Great Britain
43 Keward Avenue
Wells
Somerset
BA5 1TS
Contact: Dr Kevin Murphy, Hon Secretary
Telephone: 01749 676378
The promotion of the clarinet and saxophone and their music. Membership is open to anyone regardless of age and whether they play or not.

Haydn Society of Great Britain
Music Dept, University of Lancaster
Bailrigg
Lancaster
LA1 4YW
Contact: Prof Denis McCaldin, Director
Telephone: 01524 593777
Seeks to promote a wider understanding of the music of Joseph Haydn and his circle.

Incorporated Association of Organists
11 Stonehill Drive
Bromyard
Herefordshire
HR7 4XB
Contact: Richard Popple MBE, Hon General Secretary
Telephone: 01885 483155
Facsimile: 01885 488609
Helps organists at all levels of proficiency to improve their playing. Affiliated associations in the UK arrange a programme of educational events, and there is an annual week-long IAO organ festival with master-classes, lectures, tutorials, etc. Bursaries are available for promising young students.

Ladies Association of British Barbershop Singers
59 Frensham Road
Lower Bourne
Farnham
Surrey
GU10 3HL
Contact: Penny Chisholm, National PR Officer
Telephone: 01251 794381
Facsimile: 01251 795344
Seeks to promote the art of ladies' four-part a cappella, known as barbershop singing, through clubs throughout the UK.

Music Advisers National Association
County Music Centre
Westfield Primary School, Bonsey Lane
Westfield, Woking
Surrey
GU22 9PR
Contact: Keith Willis, Secretary
Telephone: 01483 728711
Facsimile: 01483 725980
The advancement and improvement of Music education in schools, colleges and other educational establishments.

MUSIC

The Curriculum

Subject areas

National Association of Youth Orchestras
Ainslie House
11 St Colme Street
Edinburgh
EH3 6AG
Contact: Carol Main, Director
Telephone: 0131-225 4606
Facsimile: 0131-225 3568

National Music Council of Great Britain
Francis House
Francis Street
London
SW1P 1DE
Contact: Jennifer Goodwin, Administrator
Telephone: 0181-347 8618
Facsimile: 0181-347 8618
An organisation dedicated to promoting and representing the interests of music within Great Britain.

National School Band Association
52 Hall Orchard Lane
Frisby-on-the-Wreake
Melton Mowbray
Leicestershire
LE14 2NH
Contact: Peter Easton, Executive Officer
Telephone: 01664 434379
Facsimile: 01664 434137
Furthers the musical education of all young people by promoting the playing of brass and woodwind instruments in schools, colleges and the community.

National Youth Orchestra of Great Britain
Causeway House
Lodge Causeway
Bristol
Avon
BS16 3HD
Contact: Jill White, Director of Music
Telephone: 0117 965 0036
Facsimile: 0117 958 5311
Each year the NYO brings together over 150 of Britain's most talented young musicians, chosen at auditions held around the country. With tuition from leading professional musicians and teachers, and working with prestigious conductors, the NYO achieves standards which match or even surpass

those of the top professional orchestras. Auditions annually in September, October and November with the closing date for applications the end of July. Applicants must be under 18 on 1 September of year of application and a grade 8 distinction standard.

Rehearsal Orchestra
c/o London College of Music
Thames Valley University, St Mary's Road
London
W5 5RF
Contact: Miss Jean Shannon, Administrator
Telephone: 0181-231 2643
The Orchestra, founded in 1957, provides an opportunity to rehearse under professional conditions with professional leaders and conductors. Soloists may rehearse with the Orchestra. Courses are held at weekends in London and elsewhere, with a week-long residential course in Edinburgh during the Festival.

Royal Academy of Music
Marylebone Road
London
NW1 5HT
Telephone: 0171-873 7373
Facsimile: 0171-873 7374

Schools Music Association
71 Margaret Road
New Barnet
Hertfordshire
EN4 9NT
Contact: Maxwell Pryce, Hon Secretary
Telephone: 0181-440 6919
Facsimile: 0181-440 6919
Promotes music education by keeping its members informed, organising conferences and workshops, providing opportunities for children to perform at major venues (Royal Festival Hall, for example), and publishing a termly bulletin.

Sing for Pleasure
25 Fryerning Lane
Ingatestone
Essex
CM4 0DD

MUSIC

The Curriculum

Subject areas

Contact: Mrs L Parker, Administrator
Telephone: 01277 353691
Facsimile: 01277 353691
*Runs training courses for teachers and singing
days for children in schools. Residential
singing/activity weekends also offered.
Publishes songbooks with materials suited to
National Curriculum requirements.*

United Kingdom Harp Association
Pooks Hill
Woodland Way
Kingswood
Surrey
KT20 6NX
Telephone: 01737 832740
*An association for harpists, harp makers and
repairers and harp enthusiasts.*

United Kingdom Sibelius Society
5 Fitzwilliam Road
London
SW4 0DL
Contact: Edward Clark, President
Telephone: 0171-627 3056
Facsimile: 0171-430 1251
*The aims of the Society are to bring the
achievement of Sibelius's music to the largest
possible readership and audience. Benefits of
membership include a newsletter and
concerts hosted by the Society.*

Welsh Folk Song Society
9 High Street
Criccieth
Gwynedd
LL52 0BS
Contact: Mrs B Lloyd Roberts, Secretary
Telephone: 01766 522096
*Collects, preserves, interprets and performs
Welsh folk songs, publishes examples, and
fosters interest in folk literature and music in
general.*

Youth and Music
28 Charing Cross Road
London
WC2H 0DB
Telephone: 0171-379 6722
Facsimile: 0171-497 0345
*Aims to increase young people's access to the
arts. The main project is Stage Pass, a
membership scheme which provides
discounted tickets and an informative monthly
arts magazine. School and individual
subscriptions are available.*

PSE

Central Health Promotion Department
Northern Health and Social Services Board
2 George Street
Ballymena
BT43 5AP
Contact: Elaine O'Doherty
Telephone: 01266 46021
*Provides health education materials on behalf
of the Health Promotion Agency for Northern
Ireland.*

Family Planning Association
27-35 Mortimer Street
London
W1N 7RJ
Telephone: 0171-636 7866
Facsimile: 0171-436 5723
*Provides training, consultancy and resources
for teachers on sex and personal relations
education in schools.*

Health Promotion Department
Western Health and Social Services Board
Beech Villa, Clooney Road
Londonderry
BT47 1TF
Contact: Frances McReynolds
Telephone: 01504 860261
*Provides health education materials on behalf
of the Health Promotion Agency for Northern
Ireland.*

Health Promotion Unit
Eastern Health and Social Services Board
12-22 Linenhall Street
Belfast
BT2 8BS
Contact: David McCabe
Telephone: 01232 321313
*Provides health education materials on behalf
of the Health Promotion Agency for Northern
Ireland.*

PERSONAL & SOCIAL EDUCATION

The Curriculum

Subject areas

Kotex Product Advisory Service
Kimberly-Clark Ltd
Dept GM
Larkfield
Aylesford
Kent
ME20 7PS
Telephone: 01622 616282
A free pack is available to help teach girls and their parents about puberty and menstruation.

Life Education Centres
P.O. Box 137
London
N10 3JJ
Contact: Jill Pearman, National Director
Telephone: 0171-706 8966
Facsimile: 0171-706 8710
Provides preventative drug education which is specifically aimed at 3–15-year-olds by means of mobile classrooms visiting schools. LEC also provide HIV prevention programmes and publish a wide range of resources.

Polite Society
6 Norman Avenue
Henley-on-Thames
RG9 1SG
Telephone: 01491 572794
Facsimile: 01491 572794
A voluntary association of people committed to maintaining good manners and courtesy as the basis of everyday behaviour in British society.

Royal Society for the Prevention of Accidents
Cannon House
The Priory Queensway
Birmingham
B4 6BS
Telephone: 0121-200 2461
Facsimile: 0121-200 1254
RoSPA's purpose is to enhance the quality of life by exercising a powerful influence for accident prevention. One aspect of this is to produce a range of educational material aimed at young people.

PHYSICAL EDUCATION

Association for Archery in Schools
c/o Bloxham School
Bloxham
Banbury
Oxfordshire
OX15 4PE
Contact: C Fletcher-Campbell, Secretary
Telephone: 01295 720443
Facsimile: 01295 721714
Seeks to promote archery in UK schools by administering an achievement scheme, annual championships (outdoor and indoor), regional tournaments, postal leagues and a termly newsletter.

Benesh Institute
12 Lisson Grove
London
NW1 6TS
Contact: Tamsin McDowell, Administration Officer
Telephone: 0171-258 3041
Facsimile: 0171-724 6434
The centre for the study and analysis of movement through the Benesh Movement Notation.

British Association of Advisers and Lecturers in Physical Education
Nelson House
6 The Beacon
Exmouth
Devon
EX8 2AG
Contact: Geoff Edmondson, General Secretary
Telephone: 01395 263247
Facsimile: 01395 276348
Seeks to promote and maintain high standards of safe practice in all aspects and at all levels of physical education.

British Schools Gymnastics Association
Orchard House
15 North Common Road
Uxbridge
Middlesex
UB8 1PD

The Curriculum

Subject areas

Contact: Clive Hamilton, Secretary
Telephone: 01895 233377
Facsimile: 01895 814031
Promotes gymnastics in British schools.

British Schools Lawn Tennis Association
c/o The LTA Trust
The Queen's Club
West Kensington
London
W14 9EG
Contact: Mrs G Crump, Executive Director
Telephone: 0171-381 7000
Facsimile: 0171-381 6507
Seeks to encourage and promote the teaching of lawn tennis in schools through INSET, and provides a quality introduction to the sport with a competitive structure for all pupils.

Cymdeithas Ddawns Werin Cymru
(Welsh Folk Dance Society)
Ffynnonlwyd
Trelech, Caerfyrddin
Dyfed
SA33 6QZ
Telephone: 01994 484496
Assists Welsh schools in a practical way with teaching the Urdd Eisteddfod Dances and organises the Gwyl Plant Cymru, a bi-annual festival for primary and junior children throughout Wales.

Dance for Everyone
6 Milverton Road
London
NW6 7AS
Contact: N Benari, Artistic Director
Telephone: 0181-451 2000
Introduces children to dance and mime of all kinds through workshops, performances and videos, assisting teachers to deliver the National Curriculum.

England Rugby Football Schools' Union
National Centre for Schools and Youth
Castlecroft Stadium, Castlecroft Road
Wolverhampton
WV3 8NA
Telephone: 01902 380302

Promotes rugby union football in schools, arranges matches and trials, and safeguards correct coaching.

English Folk Dance and Song Society
Cecil Sharp House
2 Regent's Park Road
London
NW1 7AY
Contact: Carolyn Robson, Education Officer
Telephone: 0171-485 2206
Facsimile: 0171-284 0523
The Education Department promotes British traditional dance with young people (up to 25 years old).

English Schools Athletic Association
26 Newborough Green
New Malden
Surrey
KT3 5HS
Telephone: 0181-949 1506
Facsimile: 0181-949 1506
Organisation of schools' athletics (track & field, cross country and race walking) in England.

English Schools Badminton Association
National Badminton Centre
Bradwell Road
Loughton Lodge
Milton Keynes
MK8 9LA
Contact: Secretary
Telephone: 01908 568822
Facsimile: 01908 566922
Encourages, promotes and facilitates the playing of badminton at county, national and international levels by anyone up to age 16.

English Schools Cricket Association
38 Millhouse
Woods Lane
Cottingham
Hull
HU16 4QH
Contact: Lake Kenneth Stuart, General Secretary
Telephone: 01482 844446
Facsimile: 01482 844446

PHYSICAL EDUCATION

35

The Curriculum

Subject areas

English Schools Football Association
1-2 Eastgate Street
Stafford
ST16 2NQ
Contact: Mr M R Berry, Chief Executive
Telephone: 01785 51142
Facsimile: 01785 55485
*The mental, moral and physical development
and improvement of schoolchildren through
the medium of association football.*

English Schools Ski Association
17 Embleton Drive
Deneside View
Chester le Street
Co Durham
DH2 3JS
Contact: P D Neary, Secretary
Telephone: 0191-548 7174
*Seeks to encourage school skiing by promoting
competitive and social events.*

English Schools Swimming Association
Brackenridge
Guilsborough Hill
Hollowell
Northamptonshire
NN6 8RN
Contact: Mr N M Bramwell, Hon General
Secretary
Telephone: 01604 740919
Facsimile: 01604 820729
*Advances the physical education of
schoolchildren through the medium of life-
saving, diving, water polo and synchronised
swimming.*

Laban Centre for Movement and Dance
Laurie Grove
New Cross
London
SE14 6NH
Contact: Marion North, Director
Telephone: 0181-692 4070
Facsimile: 0181-694 8749
*The training of young dancers, choreographers,
teachers and writers in the field of
contemporary dance.*

Laban Guild for Movement and Dance
30 Ringsend Road
Limavady
Co Derry
BT49 0QL
Contact: Ann Ward, Membership Secretary
Telephone: 01504 762120
Facsimile: 01504 762120
*Seeks to promote and advance the study of
human movement, particularly recognising
the contribution made by the late Rudolph
Laban, a pioneer of modern educational
dance.*

**National Association of Teachers of Dancing
Ltd**
Suite 2, 56 The Broadway
Thatcham
Berkshire
RG19 4HP
Contact: Mrs Lyn Foster, Assistant General
Secretary
Telephone: 01635 868888
Facsimile: 01635 872301
*Fosters and improves the quality of all forms of
dance.*

National Coaching Foundation
114 Cardigan Road
Headingley
Leeds
LS6 3BJ
Contact: Information Centre
Telephone: 0113 274 4802
Facsimile: 0113 275 5019
*The NCF works closely with institutes of FE and
HE to provide a comprehensive range of
courses and resources for coaches, and
potential coaches, throughout the UK.
Teachers can access bibliographic database
searches on a wide range of topics through
the NCF's service, INFORM. Teachers are
encouraged to contact the NCF on behalf of
students regarding specific syllabus
enquiries.*

National Council for Schools' Sports
95 Boxley Drive
West Bridgford
Nottingham
NG2 7GN

The Curriculum

Subject areas

Contact: Mr Patrick Smith, Executive Officer
Telephone: 0115 923 1229
Facsimile: 0115 923 1229
*Co-ordinates the work of national schools'
sports associations and other national
associations responsible for the development
of their sport in schools.*

Physical Education Association Research Centre
University of Exeter
Heavitree Road
Exeter
EX1 2LU
Contact: Prof Neil Armstrong
Telephone: 01392 264812
Facsimile: 01392 264706
*Initiates research in health and physical
education and facilitates the continuing
education of PE teachers and students.*

Royal Life Saving Society UK
Mountbatten House
Studley
Warwickshire
B80 7NN
Telephone: for enquiries about training or
membership 01527 853943
For publications write to: RLSS UK Enterprises
Ltd at the address above
*A wide range of aids for teaching life-saving are
available by mail order.*

Royal Scottish Country Dance Society
12 Coates Crescent
Edinburgh
EH3 7AF
Telephone: 0131-225 3854
Facsimile: 0131-225 7783
*Seeks to preserve and further the practice of
traditional Scottish country dances by
assisting in the provision of instruction in
them, and publishing descriptions of them
with music and diagrams in a simple form.*

Rugby Fives Association
The Old Forge
Sutton Valence
Maidstone
Kent
ME17 3AW
Contact: Michael Beaman, General Secretary
Telephone: 01622 842278

*As the governing body of the game, they are
keen to support the game wherever it is
played and encourage its resurrection in
those schools where there are courts that are
no longer played on. A recently
commissioned coaching video is available.*

Schools Amateur Boxing Association
11 Beaconsfield Road
Ealing
London
W5 5JE
Contact: Dudley Savill, Hon General Secretary
Telephone: 0181-840 5519
*Seeks to advance amateur boxing among boys
as an important contribution to their overall
education and personal development, with an
eye on the welfare and safety aspects of the
sport.*

Schools' Association Football International Board
208 Stechford Road
Hodge Hill
Birmingham
B32 6BL
Contact: Mr C S Allatt
Telephone: 0121-783 7657
*Seeks to promote the welfare of schools'
football, and regulates and controls the
playing of international matches.*

Scottish Schools and Youth Hockey Association
c/o Scottish Hockey Union
48 Pleasance
Edinburgh
EH8 9JJ
Contact: The President
Telephone: 0131-650 8170

Scottish Schools' Football Association
50 Lochearn Crescent
Airdrie
ML6 6SQ
Contact: Mr John C Watson, General Secretary
Telephone: 01236 766929
*Seeks to foster the mental, moral and physical
development and improvement of pupils
through the medium of association football.*

PHYSICAL EDUCATION

The Curriculum

Subject areas

Scottish Schools Orienteering Association
Riversdale
Slitrig Crescent
Hawick
TD9 0EN
Telephone: 01450 377383
*Promotes the sport of orienteering within
Scotland by putting on local events and
providing instructors' courses for teachers
and others. In many regions there is a
schools orienteering association.*

Scottish Schools Rugby Union
59 Lochinver Crescent
Dundee
DD2 4TY
Telephone: 01382 667225 (business)
*Seeks to foster the game of rugby football in
Scottish schools.*

Scottish Schools Sailing Association
c/o 11 Stead's Place
Leith
Edinburgh
EH6 5DY
Contact: Mike Harrison, President
Telephone: 0131-554 7773
*Seeks to encourage the sport of sailing in
schools by promoting courses and
competitions and providing a structure for
school sailing.*

Scottish Women's Rugby Union
11 Bavelaw Crescent
Penicuik
Lothian
EH26
Contact: Maureen Sharp, Chairperson
Telephone: 01968 673355
*Administers a database of schools and clubs
playing girls' rugby (ages 12-16). Girls' rugby
is administered by Sue Brodie, 41 Royal Park
Terrace, Edinburgh EH8 8SA. Telephone:
0131-661 1179.*

Scottish Youth Hockey Board
'Marrald'
Brabloch Crescent
Paisley
PA3 4RG
Contact: Gerald C Ralph, Chairman
Telephone: 0141-887 9731 (home) and 0141-
882 6455 (business)
*Organises and co-ordinates inter-club and
district competitions (under 12 – under 18).
Promotes and encourages the development
of the sport from 8 to 18 using award
schemes.*

Student Rugby League
11 Inverness Road
Garforth
Leeds
LS23 2LS
Contact: Mr Simon Adamson
Telephone: 0113 286 9918
*Seeks to promote and develop rugby league in
schools (16-19 yrs).*

Swimming Teachers' Association
Anchor House
Birch Street
Walsall
WS2 8HZ
Contact: Mr A W Harvey, Administration
Director
Telephone: 01922 645097
Facsimile: 01922 720628
*Seeks to promote the study and teaching of the
administration, theory and practice of
swimming and aquatic activities of all types.*

Welsh Schools Basketball Association
Rhymney River Bridge Road
Cardiff
CF3 7YZ
Contact: Frank Daw, BAW Executive Secretary
Telephone: 01222 454395
Facsimile: 01222 454637
*Schools affiliated to the WSBA receive visits
from Basketball Association of Wales (BAW)
coaches to provide support for the staff.*

The Curriculum

Subject areas

RELIGIOUS EDUCATION

BFSS National Religious Education Centre
Brunel University, Osterley Campus
Borough Road
Isleworth
Middlesex
TW7 5DU
Contact: Maurice Lynch, Director
Telephone: 0181-568 8741
Facsimile: 0181-569 9198
Provides high-quality INSET in all aspects of religious education, the act of collective worship and the spiritual and moral dimensions of the curriculum. Also publishes books and provides loans to support this service.

Board of Deputies of British Jews
Woburn House
Tavistock Square
London
WC1H 0EZ
Contact: Yvonne Krasner, Education Officer
Telephone: 0171-387 3952
Facsimile: 0171-383 0629
The Education Department provides parents, teachers, young people and a variety of agencies both Jewish and non-Jewish with advice, information and action on issues surrounding Judaism.

British Buddhist Association
11 Biddulph Road
London
W9 1JA
Contact: A Haviland-Dye, Dhammacari, Director
Telephone: 0171-286 5575
Provides courses about Buddhism.

Buddhist Society
58 Eccleston Square
London
SW1V 1PH
Contact: Ronald C Maddox, General Secretary
Telephone: 0171-834 5858
Publishes and makes known the principles of Buddhism.

Jewish Education Bureau
8 Westcombe Avenue
Leeds
LS8 2BS
Contact: Rabbi Douglas Charing, Director
Telephone: 0113 266 3613
Facsimile: 0113 293 3533
Promotes the study of Judaism as part of an RE course in British schools by providing useful resources and INSET. Requests for information should be accompanied by an SAE.

National Society (C of E) for Promoting Religious Education
Church House
Great Smith Street
London
SW1P 3NZ
Telephone: 0171-222 1672
Facsimile: 0171-233 2592
The Society supports RE in all schools. It provides a range of services and publications as well as RE centres in London and York.

National Society's Religious Education Centre
36 Causton Street
London
SW1P 4AU
Telephone: 0171-932 1190
Facsimile: 0171-932 1199
Seeks to support everyone involved in RE by providing resources, information and advice for students, teachers, governors and parents with books (reference only), AV items and artefacts collections (loan).

RADIUS (The Religious Drama Society of Great Britain)
Christ Church and Upton Chapel
1a Kennington Road
London
SE1 7QP
Telephone: 0171-401 2422
Encourages all drama which throws light on the human condition, and helps the churches to use such drama for Christian understanding and communication.

The Curriculum

Subject areas

Religious Society of Friends
173-177 Euston Road
London
NW1 2BJ
Contact: H Gillman, Outreach Secretary
Telephone: 0171-387 3601
Facsimile: 0171-388 1977
Responds to pupils and teachers on issues
relating to Quakerism and the National
Curriculum.

World Congress of Faiths
2 Market Street
Oxford
OX1 3EF
Telephone: 01865 202751
Facsimile: 01865 202746
Arranges a variety of conferences, meetings,
retreats, visits and group travel with the aim
of providing opportunities to get to know
people of other faiths. Some meetings are of
particular interest to teachers or to health and
social workers.

SCIENCE

Area Health Promotion Department
Southern Health and Social Services Board
Tower Hill
Armagh
BT61 9DR
Contact: Lyn Donnelly
Telephone: 01861 522341
Provides health education materials on behalf
of the Health Promotion Agency for Northern
Ireland.

Association for Astronomy Education
c/o The Royal Astronomical Society
Burlington House, Piccadilly
London
W1V 0NL
Encourages and supports the teaching of
astronomy at all educational levels, and
provides training opportunities and resources
throughout the UK.

Association for Science Education
Contact: ASE Booksales
College Lane
Hatfield
Hertfordshire
AL10 9AA
Telephone: 01707 271216
Facsimile: 01707 266532
A wide range of moderately priced resources
supporting teaching of science at all levels
are available.

Biochemical Society
59 Portland Place
London
W1N 3AJ
Contact: The Education Officer
Telephone: 0171-580 5530
Facsimile: 0171-637 7626
The Society seeks to promote biochemistry
both as a career and a subject and produces
a series of booklets aimed at A level biology.

BNFL Education Unit
P.O. Box 10
Wetherby
West Yorkshire
LS23 7EL
Hotline: 01937 840209
Moderately priced packs, wallcharts and
computer software on electricity generation
and use, energy, technology, the world of
work and the environment are available.

British Association for the Advancement of Science
23 Savile Row
London
W1X 2NB
Contact: BAYS Office
Telephone: 0171-973 3500
Facsimile: 0171-973 3051
BAYS is the youth science club network
organised on a national level by the British
Association for the Advancement of Science.
Any science club for under-18s can join.
Information about Young Investigator Clubs
for under-13s and for 13-18s is available.

The Curriculum

Subject areas

British Astronomical Association
Burlington House
Piccadilly
London
W1V 9AG
Encourages all aspects of observational astronomy for all, whether beginners or advanced, and circulates information and observational material to its members. Membership is open to anyone.

British Interplanetary Society
27/29 South Lambeth Road
London
SW8 1SZ
Telephone: 0171-735 3160
Facsimile: 0171-820 1504
Videos available on international space programmes.

BT Education Service
P.O. Box 10
Wetherby
West Yorkshire
LS23 7EL
Telephone: 0800 622302
Booklets, wallcharts, packs, videos and computer software, some free, some low-cost, on the telecommunications industry, past, present and future are available.

Central Health Promotion Department
Northern Health and Social Services Board
2 George Street
Ballymena
BT43 5AP
Contact: Elaine O'Doherty
Telephone: 01266 46021
Provides health education materials on behalf of the Health Promotion Agency for Northern Ireland.

Centre for Research in Primary Science and Technology
University of Liverpool
126 Mount Pleasant
Liverpool
L69 3BX
Contact: Dr Terry Russell, Director
Telephone: 0151-794 3270
Facsimile: 0151-794 3271

Aims to support all aspects of research, assessment, evaluation and professional development in primary science and technology in both formal and informal environments.

Centre for Studies in Science and Mathematics Education
University of Leeds
Leeds
LS2 9JT
Contact: Mr Colin Wood-Robinson, Director
Telephone: 0113 233 4611
Facsimile: 0113 233 4683
Provides continuing professional development, including higher-degree teaching and supervision in Science, Maths and Technology education.

CLEAPSS School Science Service
Brunel University
Uxbridge
Middlesex
UB8 3PH
Telephone: 01895 251496
Facsimile: 01895 814372
Provides for subscribers information on safety and resources for teaching science and technology to A level. Subscribers are LEAs, GM schools, independent schools, incorporated colleges and education departments and individuals.

Ever-Ready Education Services
P.O. Box 480
London
SW9 9TH
A free pack for primary schools on electricity and battery power is available.

Health Education Authority
Hamilton House
Mabledon Place
London
WC1H 9TX
Contact: Mary Ryan, Resources Adviser
Telephone: 0171-383 3833
Facsimile: 0171-387 0550
Health education and health promotion issues.

The Curriculum

Subject areas

Health Promotion Department
Western Health and Social Services Board
Beech Villa, Clooney Road
Londonderry
BT47 1TF
Contact: Frances McReynolds
Telephone: 01504 860261
Provides health education materials on behalf of the Health Promotion Agency for Northern Ireland.

Health Promotion Unit
Eastern Health and Social Services Board
12-22 Linenhall Street
Belfast
BT2 8BS
Contact: David McCabe
Telephone: 01232 321313
Provides health education materials on behalf of the Health Promotion Agency for Northern Ireland.

Health Promotion Wales
Ffynnon-Las
Ilex Close, Ty-Glas
Llanishen, Cardiff
CF4 5DZ
Telephone: 01222 752222
Facsimile: 01222 756000
Provides general guidance on the place of health education in the National Curriculum in Wales, school policy development, and advice to governors on smoking, food policies and sex education. Resources are also available, especially for primary schools.

Institute of Physics
47 Belgrave Square
London
SW1X 8QX
Contact: Mr Chris Butlin, Educational Development Officer
Telephone: 0171-235 6111
Facsimile: 0171-259 6002
Promotes Physics and Science education through INSET, develops activities and events for students aged 7-18, develops links between industry and schools, and provides literature for teachers, comprehensive careers advice and lectures for teachers and students.

Inter-Action Trust
HMS President (1918)
Victoria Embankment
London
EC4Y 0HJ
Telephone: 0171-583 2652
Facsimile: 0171-583 2840
An educational charity dedicated to research, develop and implement creative methods of learning for young people and those who are disadvantaged. Stardome is a portable, inflatable planetarium which can be booked by schools, colleges and youth groups.

Jodrell Bank Science Centre, Planetarium and Arboretum
Macclesfield
Cheshire
SK11 9DL
Telephone: 01477 571339
Facsimile: 01477 571695
A wide range of mail order items about space, exploration and the Jodrell Bank Radio Telescopes are available.

Royal Society of Chemistry
The Royal Society of Chemistry
Burlington House
Piccadilly
London
W1V 0BN
Contact: Dr J A Johnston, Assistant Education Officer, Schools and Colleges
Telephone: 0171-437 8656, ext 289 (Dr N V Reed)
Facsimile: 0171-287 9825
A range of reasonably priced handbooks and reference books on aspects of chemistry in school is available.

SCSST Standing Conference on Schools' Science and Technology
1 Giltspur Street
London
EC1A 9DD
Contact: Ann Parkin, Chief Executive
Telephone: 0171-294 2431
Facsimile: 0171-294 2442
Seeks to enthuse young people about science and technology and motivate them to take up careers as scientists and engineers, and to

The Curriculum

Subject areas

promote joint activities between schools and industry. Activities include Young Engineers (clubs in schools for 11-18s), the CREST Award scheme (schools/industry partnership projects), and INSET. All these initiatives are delivered through the network of SATROs (listed on pages 199-204).

Society for Popular Astronomy
36 Fairway
Keyworth
Nottingham
NG12 5D
The Society is intended for beginners in astronomy, regardless of age. Through its publications, observing sections and advisory services members are encouraged to learn about and take part in astronomy. Any request for information must be accompanied by an SAE.

Welsh Scientific Society
Adran Ffiseg
Prifysgol Cymru Aberystwyth
Penglais, Aberystwyth
Dyfed
SY23 3BZ
Contact: Dr S E Pryse, Secretary
Telephone: 01970 622801
Promoting awareness of science through the medium of the Welsh language.

Wild Flower Society
68 Outwood Road
Loughborough
Leicestershire
LE11 3LY
Telephone: 01509 215598
Seeks to promote a greater knowledge of field botany among the general public and in particular among young people.

The Curriculum

Cultural links and exchanges

Africa Centre
38 King Street
London
WC2E 8JT
Contact: Education Officer
Telephone: 0171-836 1973
Facsimile: 0171-836 1975
Established to inform and educate the British and European public about Africa, its culture and affairs.

American Museum in Britain, The
The Education Centre
Claverton Manor
Bath
Avon
BA2 7BD
Contact: The Education Secretary
Telephone: 01225 463538
Publications and wallcharts on American history and culture.

Anglo-Albanian Association
38 Holland Park
London
W11 3RP
Contact: Mr Denys Salt, Hon Secretary
Telephone: 0171-727 0287
Acts as an unofficial clearing house and point of liaison for individuals and organisations channelling aid to Albania, and provides information on various aspects of Albanian life.

Anglo-Belgian Society
45 West Common
Haywards Heath
Sussex
RH16 2HA
Contact: Mrs A M Woodhead, Hon Secretary
Telephone: 01444 452183
Maintains and develops friendship between the British and Belgian people.

Anglo-Central American Society
30 Great Bounds Drive
Tunbridge Wells
Kent
TN4 0TR
Contact: Dr Janine Cooke, Secretary
Seeks to advance the education of the British about Central America, its people, history, language and literature, its institutions, folklore and culture and also its intellectual, artistic and economic life.

Anglo-Colombian Society
63A Union Street
London
SE1 1SG
Telephone: 0171-403 3088
Facsimile: 0171-403 7730

Anglo-Danish Society
25 New Street Square
London
EC4A 3LN
Contact: Mrs A-M Eastwood, Secretary
Telephone: 01753 884846
Exists to promote closer understanding and friendship between the UK and Denmark by arranging a variety of activities, such as visits to places of educational and cultural interest, informative talks and lectures as well as purely social gatherings.

Anglo-Israel Association
9 Bentinck Street
London
W1N 5RP
Telephone: 0171-486 2300
Facsimile: 0171-935 4690
Seeks to inform and educate the British public about Israel.

Anglo-Italian Society
Italian Consulate, Norfolk House
Smallbrook Queensway
Birmingham
B5 4LJ
Telephone: 0121-643 7794
Facsimile: 0121-643 7794
Seeks to foster relations between the UK and Italy.

Anglo-Ivorian Society
Embassy of the Republic of Côte d'Ivoire
2 Upper Belgrave Street
London
SW1X 8BJ
Contact: Secretary to His Excellency the Ambassador
Telephone: 0171-235 6991
Seeks to foster cultural and trade links between Britain and Côte d'Ivoire.

The Curriculum

Cultural links and exchanges

Anglo-Norse Society
25 Belgrave Square
London
SW1X 8QD
Telephone: 0171-235 7151
Seeks to promote friendship and cultural relations between the UK and Norway.

Anglo-Swedish Society
43 Kinburn Street
London
SE16 1DN
Contact: Margaretha Lewis, Hon Secretary
Telephone: 0171-231 3664
The promotion of good relations between the peoples of the UK and Sweden.

Arab British Centre
21 Collingham Road
London
SW5 0NU
Contact: The Director
Telephone: 0171-373 8414
Facsimile: 0171-835 2088
Advances Arab-British understanding and co-operation.

Britain-Australia Society
Swire House
59 Buckingham Gate
London
SW1E 6AJ
Telephone: 0171-630 1075
Facsimile: 0171-630 0353
Furthers links (cultural, educational, social and political) between Britain and Australia. A small educational trust provides grants.

British and American Schoolboy and Schoolgirl Scholarships Committee
English-Speaking Union
Dartmouth House
37 Charles Street
London
W1X 8AB
Contact: Natalie O'Neill, Scholarships Manager
Telephone: 0171-493 3328
Facsimile: 0171-495 6108
Aims to promote international understanding through the use of the English language.

British Italian Society
21-22 Grosvenor Street
London W1X 9FE
Contact: J F Cullis, Secretary
Telephone: 0171-495 5536
Seeks to increase the understanding in Great Britain of Italy and Italian civilisation and to encourage friendship between the two countries.

Commonwealth Linking Trust
Commonwealth House
7 Lion Yard
Tremadoc Road
London SW4 7NQ
Telephone: 0171-498 1101
An educational charity which makes links between schools within the Commonwealth so that they may exchange letters, or anything else. During the past 25 years 3000 schools have been linked by CLT in 40 Commonwealth countries.

Commonwealth Resource Centre
Commonwealth Institute
Kensington High Street
London W8 6NQ
Contact: Liz Craft, Schools Liaison Officer
Telephone: 0171-603 4535 ext 237
Facsimile: 0171-602 7374
Works to meet the needs of teachers and schools by the loan of packs, organising conferences, workshops and INSET, and providing educational programmes for pupils.

Commonwealth Youth Exchange Council
Commonwealth House
7 Lion Yard
Tremadoc Road
London SW4 7NQ
Contact: Maire Ni Threasaigh, Exchanges Officer
Telephone: 0171-498 6151
Facsimile: 0171-720 5403
Helps young Britons (16-25) to visit and host young people from other Commonwealth countries, and provides information and advice for planning and preparation of exchange visits. Also organises training courses and conferences.

The Curriculum

Cultural links and exchanges

Council for Education in World Citizenship, Cymru
Welsh Centre for International Affairs
Temple of Peace
Cathay's Park
Cardiff
CF1 3AP
Contact: Mr W R Davies, Secretary
Telephone: 01222 228549
The promotion and encouragement, within the educational system in Wales, of the study of world affairs.

Council of Europe
Documentation Centre for Education in Europe
F-67075 Strasbourg Cedex
France
Contact: Mr Wilson Barrett, Head of the Documentation Centre
Telephone: 88 41 25 93
Facsimile: 88 41 27 80
The Centre exists to provide a library and information service on education in a European context. Requests for information are welcomed from individuals and organisations. The Centre publishes a comparative review, Newsletter/Faits nouveaux, on educational developments throughout Europe.

Council on International Educational Exchange (CIEE)
33 Seymour Place
London
W1H 6AT
Contact: Louise Cook, Manager
Telephone: 0171-706 3008
Facsimile: 0171-724 8468
A non-profit organisation which exists to further international education. Study abroad opportunities for gap-year students, and international projects for teachers and educational administrators.

Embassy of Sweden
11 Montagu Place
London
W1H 2AL
Contact: Information Section
Promoting cultural and educational links between Britain and Sweden.

Experiment in International Living (UK)
Otesaga
Upper Wyche
Malvern
Worcestershire
WR14 4EN
Telephone: 01684 562577
Assists young people in their quest for international travel and inter-cultural understanding through the homestay concept.

Federal Trust
158 Buckingham Palace Road
London
SW1W 9TR
Telephone: 0171-259 9990
Facsimile: 0171-259 9505
Produces teaching materials and organises programmes related to its aim of providing students with an opportunity to test their own knowledge of the European Union and to engage in debate about the European dimension.

Franco-British Society
Room 623, Linen Hall
162-168 Regent Street
London
W1R 5TB
Contact: Mrs Marian Clarke, Executive Secretary
Telephone: 0171-734 0815
Facsimile: 0171-734 0815
Dedicated to encouraging closer relations with France, acting as a focus for those wishing to keep in touch with France, its language and people.

Friends of Israel Educational Trust
25 Lyndale Avenue
London
NW2 2QB
Contact: John D A Levy, Director
Telephone: 0171-435 6803
Facsimile: 0171-794 0291
Seeks to promote a critical awareness of the achievements, hopes and problems of Israel, its peoples and cultures, and to develop a range of voluntary programmes in Israel for British students.

The Curriculum

Cultural links and exchanges

Great Britain-China Centre
15 Belgrave Square
London
SW1X 8PS
Contact: Librarian
Telephone: 0171-235 4666
Facsimile: 0171-245 6885
Seeks to promote closer cultural, academic, economic and other relations between Britain and China. The Centre has an exchange programme with China and an information and advisory service.

Hispanic and Luso Brazilian Council
Canning House
2 Belgrave Square
London
SW1X 8PJ
Contact: The Education Department
Telephone: 0171-235 2303
Facsimile: 0171-235 3587
Seeks to promote understanding between Britain, Spain, Portugal and Latin America by offering courses and conferences for teachers and students, publications, a programme of cultural events, and an information service.

Institut Francais d'Ecosse
13 Randolph Crescent
Edinburgh
EH3 7TT
Telephone: 0131-225 5366
The IFE's aim, as part of the cultural network of the French Ministry of Foreign Affairs, is to promote French language and culture.

Iran Society
2 Belgrave Square
London
SW1X 8PJ
Contact: Alan D Ashmole, Hon Secretary
Telephone: 0171-235 5122
Promotes learning and advances education in the study of the languages, literature, art, history, religions, antiquities and customs of Iran, its people and culture.

Japan Information and Cultural Centre
101-104 Piccadilly
London
W1V 9FN
Telephone: 0171-465 6500
Facsimile: 0171-491 9347
Housed within the Embassy of Japan, the Centre aims to provide a comprehensive information service on Japan and to promote Japanese culture in Britain.

Malaysian High Commission
45 Belgrave Square
London
SW1X 8QT
Contact: Information Division
Telephone: 0171-235 8033
Facsimile: 0171-235 5161
Free leaflets and booklets on Malaysia are available, preferably when the request is accompanied by an SAE.

Royal Norwegian Embassy
25 Belgrave Square
London
SW1X 8QD
Contact: Press & Information Office
Telephone: 0171-235 7151
A free information pack is available.

Saudi-British Society
21 Collingham Road
London
SW5 0NU
Telephone: 0171-373 8414
Facsimile: 0171-835 2088
Advances Saudi-British understanding and co-operation.

Society for Anglo-Chinese Understanding Ltd
109 Promenade
Cheltenham
Gloucestershire
GL50 1NW
Contact: Jane Hadley, Education Correspondent
Telephone: 01242 226625
Seeks to improve cultural relations with the People's Republic of China, and provides information about current trends in education and other fields.

The Curriculum

Cultural links and exchanges

CULTURAL LINKS & EXCHANGES

Society for Co-operation in Russian and Soviet Studies
320 Brixton Road
London
SW9 6AB
Contact: Jane Rosen, Information Officer/Librarian
Telephone: 0171-274 2282
Facsimile: 0171-489 0391
Seeks to bring the peoples of the UK and the former USSR together through a range of cultural and educational contacts. An information service can provide packs for which a charge is made. Enquiries should be accompanied by an SAE.

Voluntary Service Overseas
317 Putney Bridge Road
London
SW15 2PN
Contact: Dr Ann Childs
Telephone: 0181-780 2266
Facsimile: 0181-780 1326
Enables men and women to work alongside people in poorer countries in order to share skills, build capabilities and promote international understanding and action, in the pursuit of a more equitable world.

Welsh Centre for International Affairs
Temple of Peace
Cathays Park
Cardiff
CF1 3AP
Contact: Mr W R Davies, Director
Telephone: 01222 228549
The fostering among the people of Wales, by every appropriate means, of the conception of a national obligation to world interest and a sense of loyalty to the international community.

The Curriculum

Issues of the day

ACTIONAID Education
Chataway House
Leach Road
Chard
Somerset
TA20 1FA
A charity working towards increasing knowledge and understanding of the nature and causes of poverty and the measures that can be taken to alleviate world inequality.

Advocates for Animals
10 Queensferry Street
Edinburgh
EH2 4PG
Telephone: 0131-225 6039
Facsimile: 0131-230 6377
Pamphlets are available relating to the work of this organisation which campaigns against all forms of animal abuse.

Age Concern England
1286 London Road
London
SW16 4ER
Contact: Sally Greengross, Director General
Telephone: 0181-679 8000
Facsimile: 0181-679 6069
Through a network of over 1500 organisations across the UK, Age Concern provides care and opportunity for older people.

Age Concern Scotland
113 Rose Street
Edinburgh
EH2 3DT
Contact: Maureen O'Neill, Director
Telephone: 0131-220 3345
Facsimile: 0131-220 2779
Aims to improve services for older people and campaign on their behalf. Brings together in membership national organisations and individuals, united in their commitment to improve the quality of life for older people in Scotland.

Aluminium Can Recycling Association Ltd
5 Gatsby Court
176 Holliday Street
Birmingham
B1 1TJ
Telephone: 0121-633 4656
Provides free teaching resources suitable for use in the National Curriculum, on aluminium can recycling, and a fundraising idea for school funds. A free-loan video for 8-16-year-olds is available to schools.

AMRIC
12 Whitehall
London
SW1A 2DA
Contact: Marjorie Johnson
Free literature explaining the role of animals in medicines research.

Animal Concern Ltd
62 Old Dumbarton Road
Glasgow
G3 8RE
Contact: Information Officer
Telephone: 0141-334 6014
Facsimile: 0141-445 6470
Seeks the total abolition of animal exploitation.

Animal Health Trust
Balaton Lodge
Snailwell Road
Newmarket
Suffolk
CB8 7DW
Telephone: 01638 661111
Facsimile: 01638 665789
Literature describing the work of the charity which aims to play a leading role in the diagnosis, treatment and cure of animal medical problems.

ASH - Action on Smoking and Health
109 Gloucester Place
London
W1H 4EJ
Telephone: 0171-935 3519
Facsimile: 0171-935 3463
Seeks to alert people to the dangers of smoking, and to campaign to prevent the death and disease caused by smoking.

The Curriculum

Issues of the day

Association for Nonsmokers' Rights
Melgund Centre
Melgund Terrace
Edinburgh
EH7 4BU
Contact: Margaret Whidden, Secretary
Telephone: 0131-557 3139
Facsimile: 0131-557 5055
Aims to protect people from the effects of other people's smoking. Although information is available, it will only be sent to teachers and librarians on receipt of an SAE.

Association for the Protection of Rural Scotland
483 Lawnmarket
Edinburgh
EH1 2NT
Contact: Mrs E J Garland, Manager
Telephone: 0131-225 7012
Facsimile: 0131-225 6592
Exists to stimulate and guide public opinion for the protection of rural scenery and the amenities of country districts in Scotland from unnecessary disfigurement or injury.

Biomedical Research Education Trust
Suite 501, International House
223 Regent Street
London
W1R 8QD
Telephone: 0171-287 2595
Facsimile: 0171-287 2595
A society established to provide information on the essential role of medical research.

Black Country Society, The
P.O. Box 71
Kingswinford
West Midlands
DY6 9YN
Telephone: 01922 24920
Fosters interest in the past, present and future of the Black Country, that area of the Midlands west of Birmingham wherein lay the 30-foot seam of coal.

British Butterfly Conservation Society Ltd
P.O. Box 222
Dedham
Colchester
CO7 6EY
Contact: Mrs Karen F Corley, Membership Secretary
Telephone: 01206 322342
Facsimile: 01206 322739
Dedicated to the saving of wild butterflies and their habitats by making people aware of their declining numbers, funding research and setting up reserves for the rarer species.

British Humanist Association
47 Theobalds Road
London
WC1X 8SP
Contact: Amanda Todd, Administrator
Telephone: 0171-430 0908
Facsimile: 0171-430 1271
A charity concerned with moral issues from a non-religious stance, seeking a more open, just and caring society. Publishes briefings on moral dilemmas and religion in schools, written specifically for schools.

British Temperance Society
Stanborough Park
Garston
Watford
WD2 6JP
Contact: Richard J B Willis, Director
Telephone: 01923 672251
Facsimile: 01923 893212
Promotes an alcohol- and drug-free lifestyle through lectures, literature distribution and the hire of films and videos.

Campaign for the Protection of Rural Wales
(Ymgyrch Diogelu Cymru Wledig)
Ty Gwyn, 31 High Street
Welshpool
Powys
SY21 7JP
Contact: Jenny Smith, Assistant Director
Telephone: 01938 552525/556212
Facsimile: 01938 552741
Exists to protect the local environment while encouraging sustainable rural development.

The Curriculum

Issues of the day

Cat Survival Trust
The Earth
The Mission Rainforest Foundation
The Centre
Codicote Road
Welwyn
Hertfordshire
AL6 9TU
Telephone: 01438 716873 or 716478 and ask
    for extension 29 (Rainforest Foundation and
    Cat Survival Trust), extension 30 (The Earth)
*The Cat Survival Trust aims to ensure that all
    species of wild cat are preserved, preferably
    in their own habitat.*
*The Earth is involved in the preservation of
    habitat for the benefit of all.*
*The Mission Rainforest Foundation saves
    rainforest and is attempting to purchase
    sufficient land in the Argentine to return
    jaguar to their old hunting ground.*

Centrepoint
Leaving Home Project
Bewlay House, 2 Swallow Place
London
W1R 7AA
Contact: Gillian Gholan, Schools Development
    Worker
Telephone: 0171-629 2229
Facsimile: 0171-409 2027
*Centrepoint aims to ensure that no young
    person is at risk because they do not have a
    place to stay. The Leaving Home Project
    aims to ensure that young people develop
    skills and access information on leaving
    home.*

Christian Aid
P.O. Box 100
London
SE1 7RT
Contact: Schools and Youth Team
Telephone: 0171-620 4444
*A charity working to help relieve poverty and
    suffering amongst the poorest people in over
    70 countries.*

Civil Liberties Trust
21 Tabard Street
London
SE1 4LA
Telephone: 0171-403 3888
Facsimile: 0171-407 5354
*Aims to protect and extend human rights and
    civil liberties, and to campaign for a Bill of
    Rights for the UK.*

Concord Video and Film Council Ltd
201 Felixstowe Road
Ipswich
Suffolk IP3 9BJ
Telephone: 01473 715754/ 726012
Facsimile: 01473 27453
*A charity which loans and sells films and videos
    on contemporary issues.*

Conservative Students
Conservative Central Office
32 Smith Square
London
SW1P 3HH
Telephone: 0171-222 9000
*Promotes the ideas and values of the
    Conservative Party in further and higher
    education through campaigns, debates and
    meetings.*

Council for Environmental Education
University of Reading
London Road
Reading
RG1 5AQ
*An information service and reference library
    provides support for policy development and
    good practice, with information held in a
    variety of formats. Various information
    sheets, newsletters and briefings are also
    available.*

Council for the Protection of Rural England
Warwick House
25 Buckingham Palace Road
London
SW1W 0PP
Telephone: 0171-976 6433
Facsimile: 0171-976 6373
*A registered charity working for a living and
    beautiful countryside.*

The Curriculum

Issues of the day

Dartmoor Preservation Association
Old Duchy Hotel
Princetown
Yelverton
Devon
PL20 6QF
Contact: Hon Secretary
Telephone: 01822 890646
*The conservation and preservation of
Dartmoor's landscape, flora and fauna,
archaeology, public access and freedom to
roam.*

Earthkind
Humane Education Centre
Avenue Lodge
Bounds Green Road
London
N22 4EU
Telephone: 0181-889 1595
*Promotes the concept that humankind can only
thrive if it shows respect for the living planet
and all the many forms of life which rely on
one another and on the earth. It is a dynamic
partnership of people working to improve the
well-being of all animals: pets, farm animals,
captive animals and wildlife.*

English Nature
Northminster House
Peterborough
PE1 1UA
Telephone: 01733 340345
Facsimile: 01733 68834
*Promotes the conservation of England's wildlife
and natural features, selects, establishes and
manages National Nature Reserves,
identifies Sites of Special Scientific Interest
and provides advice and information about
nature conservation.*

Friends of the Earth
26-28 Underwood Street
London
N1 7JQ
Contact: Information Department
Telephone: 0171-490 1555
Facsimile: 0171-566 1655
*Campaigns nationally, internationally and locally
helping individuals and communities to
become involved in protecting the
environment.*

Guide Dogs for the Blind Association
Hillfields
Burghfield
Reading
RG7 3YG
Telephone: 01734 835555
Facsimile: 01734 835211
The training organisation for guide dogs.

Hearing Dogs for the Deaf
Training Centre
London Road
Lewknor
Oxfordshire
OX9 5RY
Telephone: 01844 353898
Facsimile: 01844 353099
*A charity which trains hearing dogs, and a
member of Assistance Dogs (UK).*

Help the Aged
7 Kirkstall Park
Kirkstall Road
Leeds
LS4 2AZ
Contact: The Education Department
Telephone: 0113 279 6000
Facsimile: 0113 279 8989
*Works to improve the quality of life for elderly
people in the UK. By identifying needs,
raising public awareness and through
effective fundraising they develop aid
programmes of a high standard.*

Housing Corporation, The
149 Tottenham Court Road
London
W1P 0BN
Telephone: 0171-393 2000
*Assists housing associations in the provision of
good-quality, affordable homes to rent by
people on low incomes.*

Human Rights Society
Mariners Hard
Cley
Holt
Norfolk
NR25 7RX
Contact: Mrs Jennifer J Murray, Secretary
Telephone: 01263 740404

The Curriculum

Issues of the day

Facsimile: 01263 740404
Opposes the legalisation of voluntary euthanasia on the grounds that no law could provide the necessary safeguards.

International Children's Trust
50 Willesden Avenue
Peterborough
PE4 6EA
Telephone: 01733 576597
Facsimile: 01733 572136
Caring for children in parts of the world where there is poverty, hunger and lack of opportunity. Through education, training and personal development children are given the means of building their futures and benefiting the communities in which they live.

Irish Association for Cultural, Economic and Social Relations
35 Ailesbury Road
Dublin 4
Contact: Barbara Sweetman FitzGerald, Director
Telephone: 01 2695552
Facsimile: 01 2695518
Seeks to promote communication, understanding and co-operation between North and South, Unionist and Nationalist, Protestant and Catholic.

National Canine Defence League
17 Wakley Street
London
EC1V 7LT
Contact: Head of Public Relations
Telephone: 0171-837 0006
Facsimile: 0171-833 2830
The United Kingdom's largest dog welfare organisation with a nationwide network of rescue centres. The charity does not destroy any healthy animal coming into its care.

National Council of Women
36 Danbury Street
London
N1 8JU
Contact: The Office Manager
Telephone: 0171-354 2395
Facsimile: 0171-354 9214

Aims to secure the removal of all discrimination against women and to encourage the effective participation of women in the life of the nation.

National Society for Clean Air
136 North Street
Brighton
Sussex
BN1 1RG
Telephone: 01273 326313
Seeks to promote clean air through the reduction of air, water and land pollution, noise and other contaminants, while having due regard for other aspects of the environment.

Oxfam
274 Banbury Road
Oxford
OX2 7DZ
Telephone: 01865 311311
Seeks to relieve poverty, distress and avoidable suffering throughout the world; to educate people about the nature, causes and effects of them; and to campaign for a world without them.

Rare Breeds Survival Trust
National Agricultural Centre
Kenilworth
Warwickshire
CV8 2LG
Telephone: 01203 696551
Facsimile: 01203 696706
The promotion and conservation of rare breeds of British farm livestock and their re-introduction to livestock farming on a commercial and economic basis.

Royal Association for Disability and Rehabilitation, The
12 City Forum
250 City Road
London
EC1V 8AF
Telephone: 0171-250 3222
Facsimile: 0171-250 0212
Works with and for disabled people.

The Curriculum

Issues of the day

Scottish Natural Heritage
Battleby
Redgorton
Perth
PH1 3EW
Telephone: 01738 627921
Facsimile: 01738 630583
*Their aim is to help people enjoy Scotland's
natural heritage responsibly, understand it
more fully and use it wisely so that it can be
sustained for future generations.*

**Scottish Society for the Prevention of
Cruelty to Animals**
Education Department
19 Melville Street
Edinburgh
EH3 7PL
Contact: The Secretary
Telephone: 0131-225 6418
Facsimile: 0131-220 4675
Animal welfare in Scotland.

Socialist Educational Association
110 Humberstone Road
London
E13 9NJ
Telephone: 0181-470 3690
*Campaigns for comprehensive education and is
affiliated to the Labour Party.*

**Society for the Interpretation of Britain's
Heritage**
c/o 12 The Grove
Benton
Newcastle upon Tyne
NE12 9PE
Contact: Leslie Hehir, Secretary
Telephone: 0191-266 5804
Facsimile: 0191-384 4372
*Provides a forum for discussion and exchange
of ideas on the interpretation of Britain's
heritage, both rural and urban.*

Stroke Association, The
Whitecross Street
London
EC1Y 8JJ
Telephone: 0171-490 7999

Facsimile: 0171-490 2686
*Supports those who have suffered a stroke and
their families with activities, information and
other practical help.*

Tidy Britain Group
The Pier
Wigan
WN3 4EX
Contact: Anne Beazley, Education Manager
Telephone: 01942 824620 (enquiries only)
Facsimile: 01942 824778
*Grant-aided by the government, it is the
national agency for litter abatement, seeking
to make Britain a litter-free and beautiful
country.*

Voluntary Euthanasia Society
13 Prince of Wales Terrace
London
W8 5PG
Telephone: 0171-937 7770
Facsimile: 0171-376 2648
*Campaigns to change the law so that adults
who are suffering unbearably from an
incurable illness may receive medical help to
die at their own persistent and considered
request. Enquiries should be accompanied by
an SAE.*

Wildlife Watch
The Wildlife Trusts
The Green
Witham Park
Waterside South
Lincoln
LN5 7JR
*Wildlife Watch is the junior section of the
Wildlife Trusts.*

Wood Green Animal Shelters
Wood Green College
London Road
Godmanchester
Huntingdon
PE18 8LJ
Telephone (and facsimile): 01480 831177
*An animal charity caring for thousands of
unwanted, neglected and injured animals
every year. Once nursed back to health new
homes are found for them.*

The Curriculum

Issues of the day

WWF UK (World Wide Fund for Nature)
Weyside Park
Godalming
Surrey
GU7 1XR
Contact: Education Department
Telephone: 01483 426444
Facsimile: 01483 426409
An international environmental organisation with
offices in over 28 countries, committed to
environmental education by giving people the
skills and knowledge they need in order to
make informed personal judgements about
environmental issues.

The Curriculum

Assessment

Associated Board of the Royal Schools of Music
14 Bedford Square
London
WC1B 3JG
Contact: Richard Morris, Chief Executive
Telephone: 0171-636 5400
Facsimile: 0171-436 5420
Offers a graded system of music examinations (theory and practical) at all levels from preparatory test to professional diploma.

Associated Examining Board, The
Stag Hill House
Guildford
Surrey
GU2 5XJ
Telephone: 01483 506506
Facsimile: 01483 300152

English Speaking Board (International) Ltd
26a Princes Street
Southport
Merseyside
PR8 1EQ
Contact: Mrs Ros Brook, Chief Administrative Officer
Telephone: 01704 501730
Facsimile: 01704 539637
Aims to give learners, of whatever academic ability, the practice in and an assessment of their oral skills through a wide range of carefully graded oral assessments.

Independent Schools Examinations Board
Jordan House
Christchurch Road
New Milton
Hampshire
BH25 6QJ
Contact: Mrs J Williams, The Administrator
Telephone: 01425 621111
Facsimile: 01425 620044
Publishes the Common Entrance examinations which are used for assessing boys and girls who transfer to senior schools at the ages of 11+, 12+ and 13+. Candidates are normally entered for them if they have been offered a place at a senior school subject to their passing the examination.

Midland Examining Group
Head Office, Syndicate Buildings
1 Hills Road
Cambridge
CB1 2EU
Telephone: 01223 553311

Midland Examining Group (East Midland Office)
Robins Wood House
Robins Wood Road
Aspley, Nottingham
NG8 3NR
Telephone: 0115 929 6021
Facsimile: 0115 929 5261
The Midland Examining Group is a part of the University of Cambridge Local Examination Syndicate.

NFER-Nelson Publishing Co Ltd
Darville House
2 Oxford Road East
Windsor
Berkshire
SL4 1DF
Telephone: 01753 858961
Facsimile: 01753 858630
Publishes educational assessment material at all levels.

Northern Examinations and Assessment Board
Devas Street
Manchester
M15 6EX
Telephone: 0161-953 1180
Facsimile: 0161-273 7572

Northern Examinations and Assessment Board, Eastern District
31-33 Springfield Avenue
Harrogate
North Yorkshire
HG1 2HW
Telephone: 01423 840015
Facsimile: 01423 523678

The Curriculum

Assessment

Northern Examinations and Assessment Board, Eastern District
Scarsdale House
136 Derbyshire Lane
Sheffield
S8 8SE
Telephone: 0114 282 0014
Facsimile: 0114 255 3750

Northern Examinations and Assessment Board, Northern District
Wheatfield Road
Westerhope
Newcastle upon Tyne
NE5 5JZ
Telephone: 0191-286 2711
Facsimile: 0191-271 3314

Northern Examinations and Assessment Board, Western District
Orbit House
Albert Street
Manchester
M30 0WL
Telephone: 0161-953 1185
Facsimile: 0161-953 1203

Northern Ireland Council for the Curriculum, Examinations and Assessment
42 Beechill Road
Belfast
BT8 4RS
Contact: Margaret Quinn, Information Officer
Telephone: 01232 704666
Facsimile: 01232 799913

RSA Examinations Board
Progress House
Westwood Way
Coventry
CV4 8HS
Contact: Customer Information Bureau
Telephone: 01203 470033
Facsimile: 01203 468080
One of the leading providers of vocational qualifications in the UK.

School Curriculum and Assessment Authority
Newcombe House
45 Notting Hill Gate
London
W11 3JB
Telephone: 0171-229 1234
Facsimile: 0171-243 0542
The SCAA is responsible for advising the Secretary of State for Education on all matters relating to school examinations and assessment, and for developing the National Curriculum and its assessment arrangements at ages 7, 11, 14 and 16.

Scottish Examination Board
Ironmills Road
Dalkeith
Midlothian
EH22 1LE
Telephone: 0131-663 6601
Facsimile: 0131-654 2664

SEG
Stag Hill House
Guildford
Surrey
GU2 5XJ
Telephone: 01483 506506
Facsimile: 01483 300152

University of Cambridge Local Examinations Syndicate
Syndicate Buildings
1 Hills Road
Cambridge
CB1 2EU
Telephone: 01223 61111
Facsimile: 01223 460278

University of London Examinations and Assessment Council
Stewart House
32 Russell Square
London
WC1B 5DN
Telephone: 0171-331 4000
Facsimile: 0171-332 4044

ASSESSMENT

57

The Curriculum

Assessment

**University of Oxford Delegacy of Local
  Examinations**
Ewert House
Ewert Place, Banbury Road
Summertown
Oxford
OX2 7BZ
Telephone: 01865 54291
Facsimile: 01865 510085
*This is now a constituent part of the University
  of Cambridge Local Examinations Syndicate.
  Correspondence on the Delegacy's
  syllabuses should still be sent to the address
  above.*

The Curriculum

Book publishers and distributors

A & C Black (Publishers) Ltd
35 Bedford Row
London
WC1R 4JH
Contact: Charlotte Burrows, Publicity
Department
Telephone: 0171-242 0946
Facsimile: 0171-831 8478
Publishes books covering Maths, Science,
Poetry, History, Geography, Design &
Technology, Music and Social Education for
Key Stages 1 and 2.

Ann Arbor Publishers Ltd
P.O. Box 1
Belford
Northumberland
NE70 7JX
Contact: Peter Laverack
Telephone: 01668 214460
Facsimile: 01688 214484
A publisher and distributor of books for Special
Educational Needs teaching and learning for
ages 3-18.

B T Batsford Ltd
4 Fitzhardinge Street
London
W1H 0AH
Telephone: 0171-486 8484
Facsimile: 0171-487 4296
Publisher of books for ages 5-16.

BBC Educational Publishing
Room 5319
201 Wood Lane
London
W12 7TS
Telephone: 0181-752 5335
Facsimile: 0181-752 5340
A publisher of materials for primary (all
curriculum areas) and secondary (mainly
English, Geography and Modern Languages).

Better Books and Software
3 Paganel Drive
Dudley
DY1 4AZ
Contact: P J Wilkes, Proprietor
Telephone: 01384 253276
Facsimile: 01384 253285
A distributor of books and software for SEN
(dyslexia) for all ages from 3-18.

Bible Society
Stonehill Green
Westlea
Swindon
Wiltshire
SN5 7DG
Contact: Mrs Laura Jackson, Market
Development Executive
Telephone: 01793 513713
Publisher of Bibles and teacher/pupil resources
for teaching Christianity and the Bible as part
of the RE curriculum, for ages 5-16.

Blackwell Science
Osney Mead
Oxford
OX2 0EL
Contact: Julia Walker, Marketing Manager
Telephone: 01865 206206
Facsimile: 01865 791738
A publisher of books and software.

Books from India (UK) Ltd
45 Museum Street
London
WC1A 1LR
Contact: S Vidyarthi, Director
Telephone: 0171-405 7226
Facsimile: 0171-831 4517
Publishes and distributes books on or about
India and published in India, including some
in Indic languages, on various topics, and
suitable for ages 5-16.

British Museum Press
46 Bloomsbury Street
London
WC1B 3QQ
Contact: Marketing Dept
Telephone: 0171-323 1234
Facsimile: 0171-436 7315
Publisher of books and postcards, many aimed
at children of school age, related to displays
and exhibitions in the Museum.

PUBLISHERS

The Curriculum

Book publishers and distributors

Cambridge University Press
Edinburgh Building
Shaftesbury Road
Cambridge
CB2 2RU
Contact: Deborah Dunkley, Sales Controller
Telephone: 01223 312393
Facsimile: 01223 325573
Publisher of books covering English, Maths, Science, Technology, Modern Languages, History, Geography, Classics and Business Studies for ages 5-18.

Cassell Plc
Wellington House
125 Strand
London
WC2R 0BB
Contact: Huw Neill, Academic Promotion Executive
Telephone: 0171-420 5555
Facsimile: 0171-240 7261
Publisher of books covering Spelling, Modern Languages, Design & Technology, Education, Business Management, Counselling, Caring/Nursing, Hospitality and Tourism for ages 3-18.

Centaur Books
The Old Vicarage
Reades Lane
Dane-in-Shaw, Congleton
Cheshire
CW12 3LL
Contact: William Ball
Telephone: 01260 279276
Facsimile: 01260 298913
A publisher and distributor of books on History and the Classics (Greek and Latin) for ages 7-18.

Centre for Left-Handed Studies
P.O. Box 52
South DO
Manchester
M20 8PJ
Contact: Miss Diane Paul, Principal
Telephone: 0161-445 0159
Facsimile: 0161-445 0159

Assists those researching left-handedness, organises lectures and workshops and publishes books on the subject. Dextral Books (same address) can supply books on the subject and school equipment for left-handers.

Child's Play (International) Ltd
Ashworth Road
Bridgemead
Swindon
Wiltshire
SN5 7YD
Telephone: 01793 616299
Facsimile: 01793 512795
Publisher of books covering English, Maths, Science and Life Skills & Responsibilities suitable for ages 3-12.

Church House Publishing
Great Smith Street
London
SW1P 3NZ
Telephone: 0171-222 9011
Facsimile: 0171-340 0182
Publisher of books for RE (Christianity) for ages 3-12.

Collins Educational
HarperCollins Publishers
Westerhill Road
Bishopbriggs, Glasgow
G64 2QT
Contact: Customer Care Department
Telephone: 0141-306 3484
Facsimile: 0141-306 3750
A publisher of books for all ages from 3 to 18 in all subjects at primary level, and in most from age 12.

Datapower Publishing Ltd
Worthing House
Basingstoke
Hampshire
RG23 8PY
Telephone: 01256 842100
Facsimile: 01256 471079
Publisher of books for computer users (IBM compatibles) helping them to get more from some commonly used software.

PUBLISHERS

The Curriculum

Book publishers and distributors

David Fulton (Publishers) Ltd
2 Barbon Close
Great Ormond Street
London WC1N 3JX
Telephone: 0171-405 5606
Facsimile: 0171-831 4840
A publisher of books for professional teachers, teacher trainers and trainee teachers.

Dorling Kindersley Ltd
9 Henrietta Street
Covent Garden
London WC2E 8PS
Contact: Children's Publicity
Telephone: 0171-836 5411
Facsimile: 0171-836 7570
A publisher of books for ages 3-14.

Drake Educational Associates
St Fagans Road
Fairwater
Cardiff
CF5 3AE
Contact: Jonathan Drake, Sales and Marketing Manager
Telephone: 01222 560333
Facsimile: 01222 554909
Publisher and distributor of books for English, Science, Modern Languages, Geography and Special Needs for ages 5-14.

Educational Publishers Council
The Publishers Association
19 Bedford Square
London WC1B 3HJ
Telephone: 0171-580 6321
Facsimile: 0171-636 5375
A trade association producing publications on educational publishing and the provision of books and teaching materials.

Educational Television Company
P.O. Box 100
Warwick
CV34 6TZ
Telephone: 01926 433333
Facsimile: 01926 450178
Publisher of activity and resource books, teachers' guides, study guides and posters covering all curriculum areas for ages 3-18 and linked to Channel 4 Schools Programmes.

Elsevier Science Ltd
The Boulevard
Langford Lane
Kidlington
Oxfordshire
OX5 1GB
Contact: Myrica Stevens, Sales Development Manager
Telephone: 01865 843000
Facsimile: 01865 843010
Publishers of scientific, technical and medical journals, reference works and books. The publisher's aim is to facilitate communication among researchers across all major scientific, technical and medical disciplines.

Encyclopaedia Britannica International Ltd
Carew House
Station Approach
Wallington
Surrey
SM6 0DA
Contact: Tim Dare, National Sales Manager - Education
Telephone: 0181-669 4355
Facsimile: 0181-773 3631
A publisher and distributor of books for all curriculum areas for ages 5-18.

Environment Council, The
21 Elizabeth Street
London SW1W 9RP
Contact: Information Programme
Telephone: 0171-824 8411
Facsimile: 0171-730 9941
Publishes a series of directories listing non-commercial organisations in the country which are concerned with the environment.

European Schoolbooks Ltd
Ashville Trading Estate
The Runnings
Cheltenham
Gloucestershire
GL51 9PQ
Telephone: 01242 245252
Facsimile: 01242 224137
A publisher and distributor of books on Modern Languages (French, German, Spanish, Italian, Dutch and Portuguese) for all ages from 3 to 18.

PUBLISHERS

The Curriculum

Book publishers and distributors

Evans Brothers Ltd
2a Portman Mansions
Chiltern Street
London W1M 1LE
Telephone: 0171-935 7160
Facsimile: 0171-487 5034
Publisher of books for English, Maths, Science, History, Geography, Music, Art, Social Issues, RE, Design and Technology for ages 3-16.

Faber & Faber Ltd
3 Queen Square
London
WC1N 3AU
Telephone: 0171-465 0045
Facsimile: 0171-465 0034
Publisher of books for ages 15-18 on Poetry, Literature, Film and Theatre.

Falmer Press
4 John Street
London
WC1H 2ET
Contact: M W Clarkson, Managing Director
Telephone: 0171-400 3523
Publisher of books covering all curriculum areas and suitable for ages 3-18.

Folens Publishers
Albert House, Apex Business Centre
Boscombe Road
Dunstable
Bedfordshire
LU5 4RL
Contact: Justine Harrison
Telephone: 01582 662303
Facsimile: 01582 475524
A publisher of books for all Key Stages on all curriculum subjects.

Footprint Press Ltd
19 Moseley Street
Ripley
Derbyshire
DE5 3DA
Contact: John Merrill
Telephone: 01629 812143
Facsimile: 01629 812143
Publisher of local walk and cycle guidebooks to national parks and other scenic areas.

Franklin Watts Ltd
96 Leonard Street
London
EC2A 4RH
Telephone: 0171-739 2929
Publisher of books covering all curriculum areas, but specialising in Science, History, Geography and Social Studies for Key Stages 1-3.

Frederick Warne (Publishers) Ltd
27 Wrights Lane
London
W8 5TZ
Contact: Claire Baker, PR & Promotions Officer
Telephone: 0171-416 3000
Facsimile: 0171-416 3199
Publisher of books for Pre-school and Key Stage 1.

George Philip Ltd
Reed Books
Michelin House
81 Fulham Road
London
SW3 6RB
Telephone: 0171-581 9393
Facsimile: 0171-225 9477
Publisher of books covering Geography, Astronomy and Ecology for ages 5-18.

Gifted Children's Information Centre
Hampton Grange
21 Hampton Lane
Solihull
West Midlands
B91 2QJ
Telephone: 0121-705 4547
Supplies books, guides, teaching packs and equipment for gifted children, dyslexic children and left-handed children. Can arrange psychological assessments and offer legal advice and guidance for children with special educational needs.

Ginn & Co Ltd
Prebendal House
Parson's Fee
Aylesbury
Buckinghamshire
HP20 2QZ

The Curriculum

Book publishers and distributors

Telephone: 01296 88411
Facsimile: 01296 25487
A publisher of books for all areas of the curriculum for ages 5-14, including high-interest, low-ability reading books (for KS3).

Hawthorns Publications Ltd
Pond View House
6a High Street
Otford, Sevenoaks
Kent
TN14 5PQ
Telephone: 01959 522368 or 522325
Facsimile: 01959 522368
A publisher of books on Arithmetic and Spelling for Key Stages 1 & 2.

Heinemann Educational
Halley Court
Jordan Hill
Oxford
OX2 8EJ
Contact: Rod Smith, Marketing Manager
Telephone: 01865 311366
Facsimile: 01865 310043
Publishes books covering English, Maths, Science, History, Geography, RE, Technology, Modern Languages, Music, Business Studies, Economics, Drama, Health, PSE, School Management, Secretarial Studies and Special Needs for ages 5-18.

HLT Publications
200 Greyhound Road
London
W14 9RY
Telephone: 0171-385 3377
Facsimile: 0171-381 3377
Publisher of A level books covering Law, Applied Maths, Business Studies, Accounting, Maths, Statistics, Constitutional Law and GCSE Law.

HMSO Publications Centre
P.O. Box 276
London
SW8 5DT
Telephone: 0171-873 9090 (orders)
Facsimile: 0171-873 8200 (orders)
Publications for sale produced by the Department for Education & Employment and OFSTED. Other publications from various government departments and public bodies often relate to curriculum topics. Phone: 0171-873 0011 (enquiries).

Hodder & Stoughton Educational
Hodder Headline plc
338 Euston Road
London NW1 3BJ
Telephone: 0171-873 6000
Facsimile: 0171-873 6299
A publisher of books for ages 3-18 on English, Maths, Science, Modern Languages, Technology, History, Health & Social Care, RE, Business Studies, GNVQ, Psychology, Beauty Therapy, Teacher Education and Catering.

Home Health Education Service
Alma Park
Grantham
Lincolnshire
NG31 9SL
Contact: Mr E Johnson, Marketing Manager
Telephone: 01476 591800
Facsimile: 01476 77144
Publisher of books suitable for KS 2 & 3.

Hotel and Catering Training Company
International House
High Street
London
W5 5DB
Contact: Roy Hayter, Publications Manager
Telephone: 0181-579 2400
Facsimile: 0181-840 6217
Publisher and distributor of books on cookery, food, vocational training and careers in the hotel and catering industry for ages 16-18.

IT in Science Publishing and Consultancy
7 Sutton Place
London
E9 6EH
Contact: Roger Frost
Telephone: 0181-986 3526
Facsimile: 0181-986 3526
Publisher of books which review computer software and present ideas for using IT in science teaching with ages 7-18.

The Curriculum

Book publishers and distributors

James Nisbet & Co Ltd
78 Tilehouse Street
Hitchin
Hertfordshire
SG5 2DY
Telephone: 01462 438331
Facsimile: 01462 431528
A publisher of books on reading and English for all Key Stages.

John Murray (Publishers) Ltd
50 Albemarle Street
London
W1X 4BD
Contact: Judith Reinhold, Educational Marketing Director
Telephone: 0171-493 4361
Facsimile: 0171-499 1792
A publisher of books for ages 7-18 on Biology, Physics, Chemistry, History, French, Spanish, German, Maths, Geography, English, PSE & RE, Technology & IT, GNVQ, Business and Special Needs.

Jonathan Press/Claire Publications
Unit 8, Tey Brook Craft Centre
Great Tey
Colchester
Essex
CO6 1JE
Contact: Noel Graham
Telephone: 01206 211020
Facsimile: 01206 212755
A publisher and distributor of books for ages 3-16 on English, Maths and Science.

Julia MacRae Books
Random House
20 Vauxhall Bridge Road
London
SW1V 2SA
Telephone: 0171-973 9000
Facsimile: 0171-233 6058
Publisher of English Literature books some of which could also be used in teaching History and other Humanities areas with ages 3-18.

Kogan Page Ltd
120 Pentonville Road
London
N1 9JN
Telephone: 0171-278 0433
Facsimile: 0171-837 6348

A publisher of books on school management, professional skills for teachers, vocational education and GVNQs, careers, mentoring, and course materials design.

Ladybird Books Ltd
Beeches Road
Loughborough
Leicestershire
LE11 2NQ
Contact: Mary W Hagger, Publicity Manager
Telephone: 01509 268021
Facsimile: 01509 234672
A publisher of books for Key Stages 1 & 2 (English, Maths and Science) and Pre-school and Reception.

Learning Materials Ltd
Dixon Street
Wolverhampton
WV2 2BX
Contact: A Mellor, Director
Telephone: 01902 454026
Facsimile: 01902 457596
Publisher of books on English, Maths, Science and History for Special Needs only for Key Stages 1-4.

Letts Educational Ltd
Aldine House
Aldine Place
142/144 Uxbridge Road
London
W12 8AW
Telephone: 0181-743 7514
Facsimile: 0181-743 8451
Publisher of books for primary (English, Maths, Science) and secondary schools (all subjects), and also home study and revision books.

Lion Publishing plc
Peters Way
Sandy Lane West
Oxford
OX4 5HG
Contact: Pam Granger, Educational Sales Coordinator
Telephone: 01865 747550
Facsimile: 01865 747568
A publisher of books on RE and PSE for all ages from 3 to 18.

The Curriculum

Book publishers and distributors

Longman Education
Longman House
Burnt Mill
Harlow
Essex
CM20 2JE
Telephone: 01279 623921
Facsimile: 01279 414130
Publisher of books for all curriculum areas for all ages.

Lutterworth Press
c/o James Clark & Co
P.O. Box 60
Cambridge
CB1 2NT
Contact: Mary Hammond, PR/Publicity Manager
Telephone: 01223 350865
Facsimile: 01223 66951
A publisher of books on Science, History, RE, and children from other countries and cultures for ages 5-18.

Macmillan Children's Books
Cavaye Place
London
SW10 9PG
Telephone: 0171-373 6070
Facsimile: 0171-244 6379
A publisher of books for ages 3-18.

Macmillan Education Ltd
Houndmills
Basingstoke
Hampshire
RG1 6XS
Telephone: 01256 29242
Mainly publishes materials for the developing world. Many of their reading schemes and supplementary materials have proved useful in multi-ethnic schools in the UK.

Manchester University Press
Oxford Road
Manchester
M13 9PL
Contact: Debbie Smith, Inspection Copy Service
Telephone: 0161-273 5539

Facsimile: 0161-274 3346
Publisher of books for ages 16-18 on Politics, History, Literature, Cultural Studies, Art and Architecture.

Mary Glasgow Publications Ltd
Ellenborough House
Wellington Street
Cheltenham
Gloucestershire
GL50 1YD
Contact: Customer Services
Telephone: 01242 228888
Facsimile: 01242 221914
A publisher of books for ages 12-18 on Modern Languages.

McGraw-Hill Book Company Europe
Shoppenhangers Road
Maidenhead
Berkshire
SL6 2QL
Contact: Brenda Darbyshire, Sales & Marketing Manager
Telephone: 01628 23432
Facsimile: 01628 770224
Publisher of books suitable for ages 3-18.

National Christian Education Council
1020 Bristol Road
Selly Oak
Birmingham
B29 6LB
Contact: David Trenaman, Head of Publishing
Telephone: 0121-472 4242
Facsimile: 0121-472 7575
A Christian publisher with the objective of supplementing the work of churches and schools in their work of Christian education.

NFER-Nelson Publishing Co Ltd
Darville House
2 Oxford Road East
Windsor
Berkshire
SL4 1DF
Telephone: 01753 858961
Facsimile: 01753 858630
Publishes educational assessment material at all levels.

The Curriculum

Book publishers and distributors

Northcote House Publishers Ltd
Plymbridge House
Estover Road
Plymouth
Devon
PL6 7PZ
Contact: Brian Hulme, Managing Director
Telephone: 01752 705251
Facsimile: 01752 695699
A publisher of books for English Literature, Dance and Drama, Careers and Education Management for ages 16-18.

Northern Ireland Centre for Learning Resources
The Orchard Building
Stranmillis College
Belfast
BT9 5DY
Contact: Valerie Kinnen, Marketing Officer
Telephone: 01232 664525
Facsimile: 01232 681579
Produces educational videos and textbooks for use with the NI curriculum, and European Studies topics throughout the UK.

O M Publishing
P.O. Box 300
Carlisle
Cumbria
CA3 0QS
Contact: Pieter Kwant, Director of Publishing
Telephone: 01228 512512
Facsimile: 01228 514949
A publisher of RE books for Key Stages 1, 2 & 3.

Old Vicarage Publications
The Old Vicarage
Reades Lane
Dane-in-Shaw, Congleton
Cheshire
CW12 3LL
Contact: William Ball
Telephone: 01260 279276
Facsimile: 01260 298913
A publisher and distributor of books on History and the Classics (Greek and Latin) for ages 7-18.

Oliver & Boyd
Longman House
Burnt Mill
Harlow
Essex
CM20 2JE
Contact: Customer Service Department
Telephone: 01279 426721
A publisher of books for ages 3-18 on all National Curriculum and Exam Board subjects.

Open University Educational Enterprises
12 Cofferidge Close
Stony Stratford
Milton Keynes
MK11 1BY
Contact: Katherine Beele, Market Development Executive
Telephone: 01908 261662
Facsimile: 01908 261001
Distributor of books covering Maths, Science, Technology, Arts, Social Sciences and study skills for ages 16-18.

Ordnance Survey C454
Romsey Road
Southampton
SO16 4GU
Contact: Education Team
Telephone: 01703 792795
Facsimile: 01703 792039
A publisher of materials for Geography, History and IT for ages 5-16.

Oxford University Press
Walton Street
Oxford
OX2 6DP
Contact: Educational Marketing Department
Telephone: 01865 56767
Facsimile: 01865 56646
A publisher of books for all ages from 5 to 18. Publishers of the Oxford Reading Tree.

Paul Chapman Publishing Ltd
144 Liverpool Road
London
N1 1LA
Contact: Joyce Lynay, Marketing Coordinator

The Curriculum

Book publishers and distributors

Telephone: 0171-609 5315

A publisher of books for all areas of the curriculum for ages 3-18.

Penguin Group Distribution Ltd
Bath Road
Harmondsworth
Middlesex
UB7 0DA
Contact: Schools Line Coordinator
Telephone: 0500 807981
Facsimile: 0181-899 4020

A publisher of books for Reading (KS1, 2 & 3), History, Science and Geography (KS4).

Pictorial Charts Educational Trust
27 Kirchen Road
London W13 0UD
Telephone: 0181-567 9206

A supplier of photopacks, friezes and wallcharts on a wide range of curriculum subjects for all Key Stages, all very competitively priced.

Pitman Publishing
128 Long Acre
London
WC2E 9AN
Telephone: 0171-379 7383
Facsimile: 0171-240 5771

Publisher of books on educational management and professional development.

Religious and Moral Education Press
Chansitor Publications Ltd
St Mary's Works
St Mary's Plain, Norwich
Norfolk
NR3 3BH
Contact: Gordon Knights, Director
Telephone: 01603 615995
Facsimile: 01603 624483

Publishes books covering Religion and PSE for ages 5-18.

Routledge Customer Services
ITPS, Cheriton House
North Way
Andover
Hampshire
SP10 5BE
Telephone: 01264 332424
Facsimile: 01264 364418

Professional publications on all curriculum areas, general classroom skills, special educational needs, educational management, etc.

Sage Publications Ltd
6 Bonhill Street
London EC2A 4PU
Telephone: 0171-374 0645
Facsimile: 0171-374 8741

Publisher of books on the Social Sciences (sociology, psychology, management and organisation studies, media studies, research methods and evaluation, politics, education, social work and social policy, nursing, and public administration) for ages 16-18.

Sangam Books Ltd
57 London Fruit Exchange
Brushfield Street
London E1 6EP
Contact: Mr A de Souza, Executive in Charge
Telephone: 0171-377 6399
Facsimile: 0171-375 1230

Publisher and distributor of books for ages 3-14.

Schofield & Sims Ltd
Dogley Mill
Fenay Bridge
Huddersfield
HD8 0NQ
Telephone: 01484 607080
Facsimile: 01484 606815

Publisher of books for English, Maths, Science, Geography, History, French, German, Spanish, Technology, Music, Business Studies and reference books for ages 3-18.

Scholastic Publications Ltd
Villiers House
Clarendon Avenue
Leamington Spa
Warwickshire
CV32 5PR
Contact: Nikki Shaw, Marketing Executive
Telephone: 01926 887799
Facsimile: 01926 883331

A publisher and distributor of books for all curriculum areas for ages 3-12. It also distributes books to primary schools through its Book Fair and Book Club services.

PUBLISHERS

The Curriculum
Book publishers and distributors

Scripture Union
207-209 Queensway
Bletchley
Milton Keynes
MK2 2EB
Contact: Joanna Bicknell, Marketing Manager
Publisher of books covering RE for all ages.

Society for Promoting Christian Knowledge
Holy Trinity Church
Marylebone Road
London
NW1 4DU
Contact: Bridget Dewar, Head of Public
Relations
Telephone: 0171-387 5282
Facsimile: 0171-388 2352
*Publisher of books on RE and Christian
assemblies, health, and self-help books (eg.
helping children cope with bullying).*

Southgate Publishers
Glebe House
Church Street
Crediton
Devon
EX17 2AF
Telephone: 01363 777575
Facsimile: 01363 776007
*A publisher of books for English, Maths,
Science, Technology, Humanities, Music, PE,
PSE, collective worship and home-school
links for ages 5-12.*

Stanley Thornes (Publishers) Ltd
Ellenborough House
Wellington Street
Cheltenham
Gloucestershire
GL50 1YD
Telephone: 01242 228888
Facsimile: 01242 221914
*A publisher of books for all Key Stages and all
areas of the curriculum.*

**Sternberg Centre for Judaism, The, Centre
for Jewish Education**
80 East End Road
Finchley
London
N3 2SY

Contact: Pamela Hartog, Resource Centre
Consultant
Telephone: 0181-343 4303
Facsimile: 0181-349 0694
Provides resources for Jewish education.

TACADE
1 Hulme Place
The Crescent
Salford
M5 4QA
Contact: Mrs Mandy Broadbent, Head of
Marketing
Telephone: 0161-745 8925
Facsimile: 0161-745 8923
*The Advisory Council on Alcohol and Drug
Education (TACADE) works in the field of
personal, social and health education, and
has particular expertise and experience in
alcohol and drug education. TACADE works
in 3 key areas: resource materials, project
management, and consultancy, training and
conference administration.*

Thomas Nelson & Sons Ltd
Nelson House
Mayfield Road
Walton-on-Thames
Surrey
KT12 5PL
Telephone: 01932 252211
Facsimile: 01932 246109
*A publisher of books on all subject areas for
ages 5-18.*

Transworld Children's Books
61-63 Uxbridge Road
London
W5 5SA
Contact: Mary Archer, Sales Executive
Telephone: 0181-579 2652
Facsimile: 0181-231 6666
*Publisher of fiction for all ages under the
imprints of Corgi, Bantam and Doubleday.*

Trentham Books Ltd
Westview House
734 London Road
Oakhill, Stoke-on-Trent
Staffordshire
ST4 5NP

The Curriculum

Book publishers and distributors

Contact: Barbara Wiggins
Telephone: 01782 745567
Facsimile: 01782 745553
*Publisher of books for the staffroom on the
curriculum, assessment, special needs, equal
opportunities, management and staff training.
Also a range of professional magazines on
good practice.*

Trotman & Co Ltd
12-14 Hill Rise
Richmond
Surrey
TW10 6UA
Contact: Claire Dyball, Marketing Development
Officer
Telephone: 0181-940 5668
Facsimile: 0181-948 9267
*Publisher of books on careers and higher
education for ages 12-18.*

Usborne Publishing Co Ltd
Usborne House
83-85 Saffron Hill
London
EC1N 8RT
Contact: Anthony Keates, Promotions Executive
Telephone: 0171-430 2800
Facsimile: 0171-430 1562
*Publishers of books for English, History,
Science, Geography, Arts and Crafts, Music
and Languages for ages 3-18.*

Virago Press
20 Vauxhall Bridge Road
London
SW1V 2SA
Telephone: 0171-973 9750
Facsimile: 0171-233 6123
*A publisher of books on Literature, Sociology,
Politics and Women's Studies for ages 16-18.*

W Foulsham & Co Ltd
The Publishing House
Bennetts Close
Cippenham
Berkshire
SL1 5AP
Contact: Sue Peirce
Telephone: 01753 516769
Facsimile: 01753 535003
Publisher of educational books.

Ward Lock Educational Co Ltd
1 Christopher Road
East Grinstead
Sussex
RH19 3BT
Contact: Andrew Thraves
Telephone: 01342 318980
Facsimile: 01342 410980
*A publisher of books on English, Maths,
Science and Geography, with some other
curriculum areas also covered, for ages 3-16.*

Wayland (Publishers) Ltd
61 Western Road
Hove
Sussex
BN3 1JD
Telephone: 01273 722561
Facsimile: 01273 329314
*Publisher of books covering Maths, Science,
Geography, History, Environmental Studies,
Technology, Health and Nutrition and Social
Studies for ages 3-16.*

World of Education Ltd
2 The Courtyard
Denmark Street
Wokingham
Berkshire
RG11 2AZ
Contact: Gerald Mortimore, Education
Marketing Director
Telephone: 01734 773423
Facsimile: 01734 890550
*Distributor of books covering Science, English,
Maths, Geography, and cross-curricular
general reference books and encyclopaedias.*

PUBLISHERS

69

The Curriculum

Software and AV publishers and distributors

10 out of 10 Educational Systems
1 Percy Street
Sheffield
S3 8AU
Contact: Rick Sutcliff, General Manager
Telephone: 0114 278 0370
Facsimile: 0114 278 1091
Developer of software covering English, Maths, Science, History, Geography, IT, CDT, Music, RE, Languages (French, German, Italian, Spanish), Latin and PSE for ages 3-16 and suitable for Apple Mac, IBM and Archimedes. All the software incorporates assessment of the student's progress and an achievement record.

4Mation
14 Castle Park Road
Barnstaple
Devon
EX32 8PA
Contact: Neil Souch
Telephone: 01271 25353
Facsimile: 01271 22974
EMail: nsouch@cix.compulink.co.uk
Developer and distributor of software for all ages and abilities, suitable for Apple Mac, IBM, RM Nimbus, Archimedes, Master and BBC.

ABLAC Learning Works Ltd
South Devon House
Station Road
Newton Abbott
Devon
TQ12 2BP
Contact: Lesley M Ovens, Education Director
Telephone: 01626 332233
Facsimile: 01626 331464
Distributor of software covering language development, phonics, Maths, Science, Humanities, Geography, IT skills and creativity for ages 3-18, suitable for use on Apple Mac, IBM, RM Nimbus and Archimedes.

Advisory Unit: Computers in Education
126 Great North Road
Hatfield
Hertfordshire
AL9 5JZ
Contact: Diana Freeman, Director
Telephone: 01707 266714
Facsimile: 01707 273684
Developer and distributor of computer software covering Special Educational Needs, Geography and the Environment (on disk and CD-Rom), Logo and a weather data logging program, for ages 3-18 and suitable for use on IBM, RM Nimbus and Archimedes.

Amo Publishing
Mill House
Mill Lane
Carshalton
Surrey
SM5 2WZ
Contact: Julie Corbin, Sales
Telephone: 0181-401 1111
Facsimile: 0181-401 1112
Developer and distributor of software covering Science at secondary level, suitable for use on Apple Mac and IBM-compatible machines.

Andromeda Interactive Ltd
9-15 The Vineyard
Abingdon
Oxfordshire
OX14 3PX
Contact: Philippa Ravenscroft, Product Manager
Telephone: 01235 529595
Facsimile: 01235 559122
Publisher of general reference CD-Rom titles for ages 7-18, suitable for use on IBM-compatible machines.

Anglia Multimedia
Anglia Television Ltd
Anglia House
Norwich
NR1 3JG
Telephone: 01603 615151
Facsimile: 01603 622191
Developer and distributor of CD-Roms covering all curriculum subjects for ages 5-18 and suitable for use on Apple Mac, IBM, RM Nimbus, Archimedes, Master and BBC.

The Curriculum

Software and AV publishers and distributors

Appian Way Software
Old Cooperative Buildings
Langley Park
Durham
DH7 9XE
Contact: Peter Britton
Telephone: 0191-373 1389
Facsimile: 0191-373 1389
*Developer and distributor of software covering
cross-curricular subjects (primary) and
History (secondary), suitable for use on IBM,
RM Nimbus, Archimedes, Master and BBC.*

Apt Projects Ltd
P.O. Box 1066
Belton
South Yorkshire
DN8 1QX
Contact: Tony Rust, Sales Director
Telephone: 01427 875103
Facsimile: 01427 875104
*Developer and distributor of software covering
Modern Languages (English, Spanish,
French) and keyboard skills for ages 11-18,
suitable for use with IBM and RM Nimbus.*

Attica Cybernetics Ltd
Unit 2, Kings Meadow
Ferry Hinksey Road
Oxford
OX2 0DP
Contact: Tom Samuels, Sales Executive
Telephone: 01865 791346
Facsimile: 01865 794561
*Developer of software covering Science,
Language, History, Music, Art and reference
for ages 11-18, suitable for use on Apple
Mac, IBM and Archimedes.*

AVP
School Hill Centre
Chepstow
Gwent
NP6 5PH
Telephone: 01291 625439
Facsimile: 01291 629671
*Distributor and developer of software for ages
3-18 covering all curriculum subjects, suitable
for use with Apple Mac, IBM, RM Nimbus,
Archimedes, Master and BBC.*

BBC Education Information
Room G420, White City
201 Wood Lane
London
W12 7TS
Telephone: 0181-746 1111
*Developer and distributor of software for all Key
Stages, suitable for use on IBM, RM Nimbus,
Archimedes, Master and BBC.*

Beebug Ltd
117 Hatfield Road
St Albans
Hertfordshire
AL1 4JS
Contact: John Wallace, Software Manager
Telephone: 01727 840303
Facsimile: 01727 860263
*Developer and distributor of computer software
for word processing, communications,
languages and utilities, for ages 11-18 and
suitable for use on Archimedes machines.*

Bitfolio (Management Graphics) Ltd
67 Suttons Business Park
Reading
Berkshire
RG6 1AZ
Telephone: 01734 353100
Facsimile: 01734 263144
*General clipart collection with material suitable
for use at all levels on Apple Mac, IBM and
Archimedes.*

Blackburn College
Feilden Street
Blackburn
Lancashire
BB2 1LH
Telephone: 01254 681724
Facsimile: 01254 694291
*Software for timetable administration and ROA
preparation, suitable for use on IBM-
compatible machines.*

The Curriculum

Software and AV publishers and distributors

Book Data
Northumberland House
2 King Street
Twickenham
Middlesex
TW1 3RZ
Contact: Donna Wood
Telephone: 0181-892 2272
Facsimile: 0181-892 9109
*Developer and distributor of software on books
and other materials on all subjects and at all
levels. TES BookFind available termly on CD-
Rom for IBM (Windows).*

Boxford Ltd
Boy Lane
Wheatley
Halifax
West Yorkshire
HX3 5AF
Contact: Mr K Golding, Sales Office Manager
Telephone: 01422 358311
Facsimile: 01422 355924
*Manufactures CAD/CAM software and
machines for Key Stages 3 and 4.*

Brilliant Computing
P.O. Box 142
Bradford
BD9 5NF
Telephone: 01274 497617
Facsimile: 01274 497617
*Software developer specialising in special
needs early years programs of a cross-
curricular nature, with specific programs for
handwriting and keyboard skills, suitable for
use on IBM, RM Nimbus, Archimedes,
Master and BBC.*

**British Library National Bibliographic
Service**
Boston Spa
Wetherby
West Yorkshire
LS23 7BQ
Telephone: 01937 546585
Facsimile: 01937 546586
*Distributor of CD-Roms of machine-readable
catalogue records of interest to school
librarians.*

BTL Publishing
Business and Innovation Centre
Angel Way
Listerhills, Bradford
West Yorkshire
BD7 1BX
Contact: Matthew Hill, Marketing Executive
Telephone: 01274 841320
Facsimile: 01274 841322
*Developer of CD-Roms for secondary Science
and beginners programs for English, French
and German.*

Cambridgeshire Software House
The Computer Centre
8 Bramley Road
St Ives
Cambridgeshire
PE17 4WS
Telephone: 01480 467945
Facsimile: 01480 496442
*Software developer of cross-curricular
packages for Key Stages 1, 2, 3 & 4, suitable
for use on IBM, RM Nimbus, Archimedes,
Master and BBC.*

Capedia
Harford Centre
Hall Road
Norwich
Norfolk
NR4 6DG
Contact: Sue Armes
Telephone: 01603 259900
Facsimile: 01603 259444
*Distributor of software covering all curriculum
subjects for ages 5-18, suitable for Apple
Mac, IBM and RM Nimbus.*

Careersoft
31 Harrison Road
Halifax
West Yorkshire
HX1 2AU
Telephone: 01422 330450
Facsimile: 01422 248024
*Developer and distributor of software covering
careers education and guidance, mini-
enterprise and work experience for ages 12-
18 and suitable for use on IBM, RM Nimbus
and Archimedes.*

The Curriculum

Software and AV publishers and distributors

Caves Ltd
P.O. Box 204
St Albans
Hertfordshire
AL4 8JU
Contact: Hugh R Joiner, Director
Telephone: 01438 832695
Facsimile: 01582 762946
A 50-lesson audio-visual course 'Mathematics for A-level Physics' for use on IBM, RM Nimbus and Archimedes machines.

CD Sports Ltd
4 Wirral Business Centre
Dock Road
Birkenhead
Wirral
L41 1JW
Contact: Ms Sue Douglas, Managing Director
Telephone: 0151-691 0893
Facsimile: 0151-691 0893
Developer of CD-Rom and disk-based software covering sports health and safety for ages 5-18, suitable for use on IBM (Windows), RM Nimbus (Windows) and Archimedes (RISC OS 2/3).

CENMAC
Charlton Park School
Charlton Park Road
London
SE7 8HX
Contact: Myra Tingle, Director
Telephone: 0181-316 7589
Facsimile: 0181-317 3843
Develops and distributes a word processor for use with all those learning to write. It offers the ability to write word by word as well as letter by letter, and includes a choice of colours and 3 fonts, including large fonts for use with early learners and the visually impaired, and a read-back facility using a speech synthesiser. Suitable for use with ages 3-18 and compatible with IBM and RM Nimbus machines.

CFL Vision
P.O. Box 35
Wetherby
West Yorkshire
LS23 7EX
Telephone: 01937 541010
Facsimile: 01937 541083
Distributes videos for sale and on free loan covering Science, Health Education, Geography, Social Studies and Careers.

Chadwyck-Healey Ltd
The Quorum
Barnwell Road
Cambridge
CB5 8SW
Contact: Emma Robb, Sales Administrator
Telephone: 01223 215512
Facsimile: 01233 215514
Developer and distributor of computer software on CD-Rom of newspapers, English poetry and the 1991 census for ages 14-18 and suitable for use on Apple Mac and IBM-compatible machines.

Chartwell-Bratt Ltd
Old Orchard
Bickley Road
Bromley
Kent
BR1 2NE
Contact: Philip Yorke
Telephone: 0181-467 1956
Facsimile: 0181-467 1754
Distributor of software for Maths, specialising in geometry, for ages 11-18 and suitable for use on Apple Mac, IBM, RM Nimbus and Archimedes.

Children's Film and Television Foundation Ltd
Elstree Studios
Borehamwood
Hertfordshire
WD6 1JG
Contact: Mr S T Taylor, Chief Executive
Telephone: 0181-953 0844
Facsimile: 0181-207 0860
Promoting, by means of pump priming via script development and occasionally part-financing, feature films especially suitable for children between the ages of 5 to 12 and thereby, hopefully, the family.

SOFTWARE AND AV

The Curriculum

Software and AV publishers and distributors

CIA Training Ltd
North Sands Business Centre
Dame Dorothy Road
Sunderland
Tyne & Wear
SR6 0QA
Telephone: 0191-564 2450
Facsimile: 0191-565 2150
Distributor of open learning material for popular software applications for ages 14-18, suitable for use on IBM and RM Nimbus machines.

Clares Micro Supplies
98 Middlewich Road
Northwich
Cheshire
CW9 7DA
Contact: Gareth Owen, General Manager
Telephone: 01606 48511
Facsimile: 01606 48512
Developer of music and graphics software for all ages for use on Archimedes machines.

Claris International
1 Roundwood Avenue
Stockley Park
Uxbridge
Middlesex
UB11 1BG
Telephone: 0181-756 0101
Facsimile: 0181-573 4477
Software developer suitable for Apple Mac, IBM, RM Nimbus and Archimedes.

Colton Software
2 Signet Court
Swann's Road
Cambridge
CB5 8LA
Contact: Mrs A Sharman, Office Manager
Telephone: 01223 311881
Facsimile: 01223 312010
Developer of word processor, spreadsheet and database applications for use on IBM and Archimedes machines.

Comprix Ltd
P.O. Box 106
Altrincham
Cheshire
WA15 9RX

Contact: Peter Butzelaar, Managing Director
Telephone: 0161-926 9328
Facsimile: 0161-926 9419
Distributor of a computer-based keyboard training course for ages 7-18, suitable for use on Apple Mac and IBM machines.

Concord Video and Film Council Ltd
201 Felixstowe Road
Ipswich
Suffolk IP3 9BJ
Telephone: 01473 715754/ 726012
Facsimile: 01473 274531
Films and videos, some free-loan, some for hire and purchase.

Creative Curriculum Software
5 Clover Hill Road
Savile Park
Halifax
West Yorkshire
Telephone: 01422 340524
Facsimile: 01422 346388
Software distributor covering English, Maths, Science, Geography, History, Technology, Modern Languages, early learning, Special Needs, administration and leisure for ages 3-18, suitable for Apple Mac, IBM and Archimedes.

Crick Computing
123 The Drive
Northampton
NN1 4SW
Telephone: 01604 713686
Facsimile: 01604 458333
Producer of an on-screen overlay keyboard incorporating speech for special needs, a version of which has been developed for disabled users suitable for use on IBM, RM Nimbus (Windows) and Archimedes.

Datatechnology Datech Ltd
Sidcup Technology Centre
Maidstone Road
Sidcup
Kent
DA14 5HT
Contact: Sales Desk
Telephone: 0181-308 1800
Facsimile: 0181-308 0802

The Curriculum

Software and AV publishers and distributors

Supplier of CAD packages (hardware and software) suitable for IBM-compatible computers.

Dolphin Systems
P.O. Box 83
Worcester
WR3 8TU
Telephone: 01905 754577
Facsimile: 01905 754559
Developer and distributor of adaptive computer technology for the blind and partially sighted, for all ages and suitable for IBM-compatible machines.

Don Johnston Special Needs Ltd
18 Clarendon Court
Calver Road, Winwick Quay
Warrington
Lancashire
WA2 8QP
Telephone: 01925 241642
Facsimile: 01925 241745
Developer and distributor of software and hardware for special needs, including physical disabilities, visual impairments and learning disabilities, for all ages and for use on Apple Macs.

Dyslexia Educational Resources
Broadway Studios
28 Tooting High Street
London
SW17 0RG
Telephone: 0181-682 4522
Facsimile: 0181-767 3247
Provides a software distribution service for the dyslexia and special learning difficulties market suitable for use with Apple Mac, IBM, RM Nimbus, Archimedes, Master and BBC.

Education Distribution
Unit 2, Drywall Estate
Castle Road
Murston, Sittingbourne
Kent
ME10 3RL
Telephone: 01795 427614
Facsimile: 01795 474871
Distributor of films and videos covering a number of curriculum subjects and age ranges.

Educational Media Film and Video
235 Imperial Drive
Rayners Lane
Harrow
Middlesex
HA2 7HE
Contact: Lynda Morrell, Managing Director
Telephone: 0181-868 1908
Facsimile: 0181-868 1991
Distributes videos covering all curriculum subjects for a wide age range.

Educational Television Company
P.O. Box 100
Warwick
CV34 6TZ
Telephone: 01926 433333
Facsimile: 01926 450178
Developer and distributor of CD-Roms and disks, audio cassettes and videos covering all curriculum areas, linked to Channel 4 Schools Programmes for ages 3-18.

Electronic Font Foundry
Gibbs House
Kennel Ride
Ascot
Berkshire
SL5 7NT
Telephone: 01344 891355
Facsimile: 01344 891366
Developer of fonts suitable for reading, writing and special needs, join-writing fonts and foreign language fonts including Indic, for use on Apple Mac, IBM and Archimedes.

ERIC International
Pepabera
Findon Road
Findon
Sussex
BN14 0RD
Contact: Mrs Worley, Director
Telephone: 01903 872400
Facsimile: 01903 872400
Developer and distributor of software covering Maths, English, spreadsheets and databases, for ages 3-16 and suitable for IBM, RM Nimbus, Archimedes, Master and BBC.

The Curriculum

Software and AV publishers and distributors

Ernest Clarke Systems Ltd
103 Philbeach Gardens
London
SW5 9ET
Telephone: 0171-912 0600
Facsimile: 0171-370 3282
Developer and distributor of administration software covering planning, assessing and reporting in the classroom, and a management system for SEN co-ordinators, for all Key Stages and suitable for use on IBM, RM Nimbus and Archimedes.

ESM
Duke Street
Wisbech
Cambridgeshire
PE13 2AE
Telephone: 01945 63441
Facsimile: 01945 587361
Publisher of software covering all areas of the curriculum for Key Stages 1-4, including pupils with special educational needs, suitable for use with IBM, RM Nimbus, Archimedes, Master and BBC.

ExpLAN Computers Ltd
St Catherines House
20 Plymouth Road
Tavistock
Devon
PL19 8AY
Contact: Paul M Richardson, Director
Telephone: 01822 613868
Facsimile: 01822 610868
EMail: Paul@explan.demon.co.uk
Developer of software for use on the Acorn Pocket Book, diary software for school networks and multimedia Bible software for the Archimedes.

FACILITY Systems Ltd
Lenton Business Centre
Lenton Boulevard
Nottingham
NG7 2BY
Contact: Mr J Rootham, General Manager
Telephone: 0115 978 6556
Facsimile: 0115 978 7273
Developer and distributor of administration software covering timetabling and options, for all Key Stages and suitable for use on IBM (Windows) and RM Nimbus.

Famic
2 The Chase
Foxholes Business Park
Hertford
SG13 7NN
Telephone: 01992 505955
Facsimile: 01992 501091
Developer of software covering Technology at Key Stages 3 & 4 and NVQ.

Film Festival Video Club
Nacton
Ipswich
IP10 0JZ
Telephone: 01473 717088
Facsimile: 01473 274531
Rentals of videos of landmark films in the history of the cinema, and film versions of classics of literature. Priced catalogue of over 1200 titles.

Fisher-Marriott Educational Software
3 Grove Road
Ansty
Warwickshire
CV7 9JD
Contact: Richard Marriott
Telephone: 01203 616325
Facsimile: 01203 616325
A computer software developer covering English, Special Needs and cross-curricular topics for ages 5-18. Manufactures a spelling practice program, endorsed by the British Dyslexia Association and suitable for a wide age range. Programs are compatible with IBM, RM Nimbus, Archimedes, Master and BBC.

Flexible Software Ltd
P.O. Box 100
Abingdon
Oxfordshire OX13 6PQ
Telephone: 01865 391148
Facsimile: 01865 391030
Software developer of general purpose applications such as word processing, database and CAD, for ages 7-18 and suitable for use on IBM and RM Nimbus.

The Curriculum

Software and AV publishers and distributors

Force 2 International Ltd
Bridge House
Thame Station Industrial Park
Thame
Oxfordshire
OX9 3JA
Contact: Graham Kerry, Sales Director
Telephone: 01844 261872
Facsimile: 01844 216737
Distributor of software on CAD at Key Stages 2-4, suitable for IBM-compatible machines.

GST Software Publishing Ltd
Unit A
Meadow Lane Business Park
St Ives, Huntingdon
Cambridgeshire
PE17 4LG
Contact: Tracey Jarvis, Retail & Education
   Sales Executive
Telephone: 01480 496666
Facsimile: 01480 496189
Distributor and developer of desktop publishing and graphics software for producing fliers, posters, reports, letters, faxes, memos and promotional information, suitable for use on IBM-compatible machines.

Guildsoft Ltd
Software Centre
East Way, Lee Mill Industrial Estate
Ivybridge
Devon
PL21 9PE
Contact: Mr Mike Holman, Marketing Director
Telephone: 01752 895100
Facsimile: 01752 894833
Distributor of software on CD-Rom and disk covering English, Science, History, Modern Languages (French, German, Spanish) and general reference for all ages, suitable for use on Apple Mac and IBM-compatible machines.

Halloween
Amstel 204
1017 AH
Amsterdam
Netherlands
Telephone: 00 31 20 638 6383
Facsimile: 00 31 20 420 6160
Developer and distributor of CD-Rom- and disk-based language training programs (10 languages available), for ages 7-18 and suitable for use with IBM-compatible machines.

Hampshire Microtechnology Centre
Connaught Lane
Portsmouth
Hampshire
PO6 4SJ
Telephone: 01705 378266
Facsimile: 01705 379443
Developer and distributor of software covering English, Maths, Science, Geography, History, Modern Languages, Art & CAD and Technology, for ages 3-18 and suitable for use with Archimedes, Master and BBC.

Hazelnut (Specialist Educational Software)
197 Blackshots Lane
Grays
Essex
RM16 2LL
Contact: Hazel Thompson
Telephone: 01375 375514
Facsimile: 01375 375514
Developer and distributor of software covering Maths at Key Stages 1-4 with special needs versions available for KS 3 & 4, all suitable for use on Archimedes.

Hi Resolution
The Stables, Little Coldharbour Farm
Tong Lane
Lamberhurst
Kent
TN3 8AD
Telephone: 01892 891291
Facsimile: 01892 891291
Developer of software covering desktop and print control, password protection, access control and network management, for ages 7-18 and suitable for Apple Mac.

SOFTWARE AND AV

77

The Curriculum
Software and AV publishers and distributors

Hodder & Stoughton Educational
338 Euston Road
London
NW1 3BH
Contact: Tim Gregson-Williams, Editorial
    Director
Telephone: 0171-873 6250
Facsimile: 0171-873 6299
*Developer and distributor of software covering
vocational languages at Key Stages 3 & 4,
suitable for Apple Mac and IBM.*

iANSYST Ltd
United House
North Road
London
N7 9DP
Contact: Department DB
Telephone: 0171-607 5844
Facsimile: 0171-607 0187
*Develops and distributes general educational
software covering special needs and
dyslexia, for all ages and suitable for use on
Apple Mac, IBM, RM Nimbus, Archimedes,
Master and BBC.*

Iota Software
Iota House
Wellington Court
Cambridge
CB1 1HZ
Telephone: 01223 566789
Facsimile: 01223 566788
*Developer of software providing animation
creation for use in multimedia, training and
where full-motion video is not required to
illustrate a point, for ages 5-18 and suitable
for IBM, RM Nimbus and Archimedes.*

Key Solutions
Wharfe House
Ilkley Road
Otley
West Yorkshire
LS21 3JP
Contact: Peter Williams, Director of Marketing &
    Customer Services
Telephone: 01943 850970
Facsimile: 01943 464104
Software developer covering all aspects of

*school management and administration, also
a 'Personal Development Planner' for student
use in the preparation of CVs and ROAs.*

Kudlian Soft
8 Barrow Road
Kenilworth
Warwickshire
CV8 1EH
Contact: Gary Atkinson
Telephone: 01926 851147
Facsimile: 01926 851147
*Developer of software covering Maths, Art,
word processing and data handling
applications for ages 5-14, suitable for IBM,
RM Nimbus and Archimedes.*

Language Support
Unit 21, Lenton Business Centre
Lenton Boulevard
Nottingham
NG7 2BY
Contact: Barratt Hathaway-Taylor, Principal
Telephone: 0115 978 6969
Facsimile: 0115 978 7273
*Computer software developer and distributor
covering foreign language learning for ages
5-18, suitable for use on Apple Mac, IBM, RM
Nimbus and Archimedes.*

Libra Multimedia Ltd
5 Riverway
Barry Avenue
Windsor
Berkshire
Telephone: 01753 864547
Facsimile: 01753 864547
*Developer and distributor of CD-Roms covering
Modern Languages (French, German,
Spanish, Italian) for ages 14-18, suitable for
Apple Mac, IBM and RM Nimbus.*

Lindis International
Wood Farm
Linstead Magna
Halesworth
Suffolk
IP19 0DU
Telephone: 01986 785476
Facsimile: 01986 785460

The Curriculum

Software and AV publishers and distributors

Distributes Acorn hardware and supplies software on disk and CD-Rom for Acorn machines, covering graphics and reference at all Key Stages.

Literacy Development Company Ltd
8 Thorndales
Brentwood
Essex
CM14 5DE
Telephone: 01277 229093
Facsimile: 01277 260243
Developer and distributor of software covering reading, Maths and written English at a basic level for age 7 and up, suitable for Apple Mac and IBM machines.

Longman Logotron
124 Cambridge Science Park
Milton Road
Cambridge
CB4 4ZS
Contact: Customer Services Department
Telephone: 01223 425558
Facsimile: 01223 425349
Developer and distributor of software covering all areas of the curriculum for all Key Stages, and suitable for use on IBM, RM Nimbus, Archimedes, Master and BBC.

Lotus Development (UK) Ltd
Lotus Park
The Causeway
Staines
Middlesex
TW18 3AG
Telephone: 01784 455445
Facsimile: 01784 445618
Developer of spreadsheet, word processor and graphics software for ages 16-18, suitable for Apple Mac and IBM.

LTS Ltd
Hayden House
Alcester Road
Studley
Warwickshire
B80 7AN
Contact: Michael Trott, Managing Director
Telephone: 01386 792617

Facsimile: 01386 793147
Supplier of computer software covering Design Technology (DTP, graphics, modelling and animation) and suitable for ages 10-18.

MEU Cymru
WJEC, Unit A16/A17, Gwaelod y Garth Road
Treforest Industrial Estate
Treforest
Mid Glamorgan
CF37 5US
Contact: Mrs Maggie Buck, Information Officer
Telephone: 01443 841790
Facsimile: 01443 841792
Developer and distributor of software covering a range of curriculum subjects with an emphasis on Welsh/Celtic titles, for ages 5-18 and suitable for use on Apple Mac, IBM, RM Nimbus, Archimedes, Master and BBC.

Microsoft Ltd
Microsoft Place
Winnersh
Wokingham
Berkshire
RG11 5TP
Telephone: 01734 270001
Facsimile: 01734 270002
Develops a range of computer software covering administrative and curriculum needs for networking, communications, multimedia and general business needs and suitable for use on Apple Mac, IBM and RM Nimbus machines.

Mikrodaisy International Ltd
60 Hamble Lane
Hamble
Hampshire
SO31 4JS
Contact: Trevor Nice
Telephone: 01703 455004
Facsimile: 01703 457059
Developer and distributor of software for ages 3-12, suitable for use on Apple Mac, IBM and Archimedes.

The Curriculum

Software and AV publishers and distributors

Minerva Software
Minerva House
Baring Crescent
Exeter
Devon
EX1 1TL
Contact: Pat Cleaver, Software Sales Manager
Telephone: 01392 437756
Facsimile: 01392 421762
Developer of computer software covering Science, Geography, CDT, Art, IT, word processing and problem solving, for ages 5-18 and suitable for Archimedes machines.

MJP Geopacks
P.O. Box 23
St Just
Penzance
Cornwall
TR19 7JS
Contact: Michael Jay
Telephone: 01736 787808
Facsimile: 01736 787880
Suppliers of geography equipment and software for ages 5-18, suitable for use with IBM, RM Nimbus, Master and BBC.

Multimedia Solutions UK Ltd
11 Albion Park
Armley Road
Leeds
West Yorkshire
LS12 2SE
Telephone: 0113 234 2528
Facsimile: 0113 243 3142
Software distributor for ages 5-18, suitable for use on Apple Mac, IBM, RM Nimbus and Archimedes.

National Audio-Visual Library
Unit 16, Greenshield Industrial Estate
Bradfield Road
Silvertown
London
E16 2AU
Telephone: 0171-474 8707
Facsimile: 0171-511 1587

National Remote Sensing Centre Ltd
Arthur Street
Barwell
Leicestershire
LE9 8GZ
Contact: Lynette Rowbottom, Education Officer
Telephone: 01455 844513
Facsimile: 01455 841785
The Centre holds the world's largest commercial library of satellite and aerial images. This unique data source is made available to Geography teachers at all Key Stages, in the form of packs and CD-Rom products suitable for IBM and Archimedes machines and written by Geography teachers.

New Media
12 Oval Road
London NW1 7DH
Telephone: 0171-916 9999
Facsimile: 0171-482 4957
CD-Rom, 'The Chemistry Set', for use with secondary students and compatible with IBM machines.

News Multimedia
P.O. Box 481
Virginia Street
London E1 9BD
Contact: Tracey Walker
Telephone: 0171-782 3982
Facsimile: 0171-782 3987
Publisher of CD-Rom titles based on reports and articles which have appeared in The Times newspaper and which have relevance to a number of curriculum areas. Designed for use with ages 5-18 and suitable for Apple Mac, IBM, RM Nimbus and Archimedes.

Northern Micromedia/NORICC
University of Northumbria
Coach Lane Campus
Newcastle upon Tyne
NE7 7XA
Telephone: 0191-270 0424
Facsimile: 0191-227 4419
Software developer and teaching material in a variety of formats for a variety of subjects and age groups, but predominantly primary, suitable for use on Apple Mac, IBM, RM Nimbus, Archimedes, Master and BBC.

The Curriculum

Software and AV publishers and distributors

Northwest SEMERC
1 Broadbent Road
Watersheddings
Oldham
Lancashire
OL1 4LB
Telephone: 0161-627 4469
Facsimile: 0161-627 2381
*Framework-type programs for use across the
curriculum for ages 3-12, suitable for use with
IBM and Archimedes machines.*

Novell UK Ltd
Novell House
London Road
Bracknell
Berkshire
RG12 2UY
Contact: Customer Care Department
Telephone: 01344 724000
Facsimile: 01344 724419
*Developer of network-managing software for
use with Apple Mac and IBM-compatible
machines.*

Oak Solutions
Dial House
12 Chapel Street
Halton, Leeds
LS15 7RN
Telephone: 0113 232 6992
Facsimile: 0113 232 6993
*Developer of innovative multimedia software for
use across the curriculum, with CAD and
Design a speciality. Suitable for use with
ages 3-18 and compatible with IBM and
Archimedes machines.*

Oracle Educational Systems Ltd
Fiskerton Manor
Fiskerton
Southwell
Nottinghamshire
NG25 0UH
Contact: Russell Rogers and Ken Ald, Director
Telephone: 01636 830980
Facsimile: 01636 830305
*Developer and distributor of school
administration software suitable for use on
IBM-compatible machines.*

Pandora's Box Publishing
3 Central Drive
Castleford
West Yorkshire
WF10 1QG
Contact: David Baron
Telephone: 01977 511810
Facsimile: 01977 511810
*Developer of software including a library
management system and a ROA application
suitable for Apple Mac and IBM (Windows).*

Potential Software Ltd
26 Holmesdale Road
Reigate
Surrey
RH2 0BQ
Contact: Candace Robb, Sales Manager
Telephone: 01737 225570
Facsimile: 01737 249946
*Distributor of software covering all the
curriculum at Key Stages 1-4, suitable for
Apple Mac, IBM, RM Nimbus, Archimedes,
Master and BBC.*

Primary Source Media
P.O. Box 45
Reading
Berkshire
RG1 8HF
Contact: Helen Agutter, Customer Services
Manager
Telephone: 01734 583247
Facsimile: 01734 394334
*Developer of CD-Roms covering Humanities,
the Arts and Current Affairs, for ages 14-18
and suitable for use on IBM-compatible
machines.*

Projection Visual Communications
33/41 Dallington Street
London
EC1V 0BB
Telephone: 0171-250 1706
Facsimile: 0171-251 5957
*Sex education CD-Rom for ages 11-16, suitable
for use on IBM and RM Nimbus.*

SOFTWARE AND AV

The Curriculum

Software and AV publishers and distributors

Q-Multimedia (UK) Ltd
Orwell House
2 Orwell Road, Cowley Road
Cambridge
CB4 3WY
Contact: Paul Poulter, Managing Director
Telephone: 01223 576616
Facsimile: 01223 576617
*Developer and distributor of software for Key
    Stages 3 & 4.*

Question Mark Computing Ltd
5th Floor, Hill House
Highgate Hill
London
N19 5NA
Contact: Mr Murray Silver, Sales & Marketing
    Director
Telephone: 0171-263 7575
Facsimile: 0171-265 7555
*Develops and distributes a software package
    for computerising tests, exams and
    questionnaires, for Apple Mac and DOS +
    Windows. Suitable for ages 3-18.*

ReachOpen Ltd
8 Thorndales
Brentwood
Essex
CM14 5DE
Telephone: 01277 229093
Facsimile: 01277 260243
*Developer and distributor of form design
    software for use with OMRs and Chemistry
    simulations, suitable for use with IBM
    machines.*

REM (Rickitt Educational Media)
Great Western House
Langport
Somerset
TA10 9YU
Telephone: 01458 253636
Facsimile: 01458 253646
*Distributors of computer and audio-visual
    programs (over 2000) from all the major
    publishers for all ages, with the software
    suitable for use on Apple Mac, IBM, RM
    Nimbus, Archimedes, Master and BBC.*

Resource
The Resource Centre
51 High Street
Kegworth, Derby
DE74 2DA
Telephone: 01509 672222
Facsimile: 01509 672267
*Developer of software written and designed by
    teachers covering all curriculum areas, for
    ages 3-11 and suitable for use on Apple Mac,
    IBM, RM Nimbus, Archimedes, Master and
    BBC.*

Ridgeway CD-Rom Ltd
24 Bell Street
Princes Risborough
Buckinghamshire
HP27 0AD
Contact: Lydia Davis, Education Specialist
Telephone: 01844 342411
Facsimile: 01844 34281
*Distributor of CD-Roms covering all curriculum
    areas and all ages and suitable for use on
    Apple Mac and IBM-compatible machines.*

Robinson Marshall (Europe) plc
Nadella Building
Progress Close, Leofric Business Park
Coventry
CV3 2TF
Telephone: 01203 233216
Facsimile: 01203 233210
*Distributes computer software covering Maths
    and Science (electronics) for ages 12-18 and
    for use on Apple Mac, IBM and RM Nimbus
    machines.*

Rombo Ltd
2B Young Square
Brucefield Industrial Park
Livingston
EH54 9BX
Contact: S Wales, Marketing Manager
Telephone: 01506 414631
Facsimile: 01506 414634
*Developer of frame grabber and digitising
    software for use on IBM and Archimedes
    machines.*

The Curriculum

Software and AV publishers and distributors

Sally Systems Ltd
Upper Bumbles
Saxon Gardens
Taplow, Maidenhead
Berkshire
SL6 0DD
Contact: Max Lipman, Director
Telephone: 01628 24626
Facsimile: 01628 782224
*Distributes computer software called Dyspell.
Especially suitable for special needs
students, it teaches or revises spelling by
classifying words into 250 topics and uses
games and speech. Performance records are
kept. Suitable for 3-16-year-olds.*

Sanderson P S S Ltd
South Point
South Accommodation Road
Leeds LS10 1PP
Contact: Andrew Smith, National Sales
Manager
Telephone: 0113 254 2000
Facsimile: 0113 244 9420
*Developer of school administration software
covering staff/pupil records, finance,
subjects/options, exam entry and timetabling,
suitable for IBM compatible machines.*

Satellite Project, The
Dyfed LEA Satellite Centre
Aberard
Newcastle Emlyn
Dyfed SA38 9DB
Contact: Mrs Annette Temple
Telephone: 01239 710662
Facsimile: 01239 710985
*Developer and distributor of satellite images on
CD-Rom, for ages 7-18 and suitable for use
on Apple Mac, IBM and RM Nimbus.*

**SCET (Scottish Council for Educational
Technology)**
74 Victoria Crescent Road
Dowanhill
Glasgow
G12 9JN
Contact: Martin Jack
Telephone: 0141-337 5000
Facsimile: 0141-337 5050
*Software developer for all ages, suitable for
Apple Mac, IBM, Archimedes, Master and
BBC.*

School 2000
Philips Media
188 Tottenham Court Road
London
W1P 9LE
Contact: Beverley Scott
Telephone: 0171-911 3060
Facsimile: 0171-911 3053
*Distributor of computer software in CDi format
covering English, Maths and Science for
ages 3-18.*

Schools Direct CD-Rom
The Green
Ravensthorpe
Northampton
NN6 8EP
Contact: Len Hough
Telephone: 01604 770099
Facsimile: 01604 770702
*Distributor of CD-Roms (4000 titles) for all ages,
suitable for use on Apple Mac, IBM, RM
Nimbus and Archimedes.*

Selective Software
16 Park Road
Street
Somerset
BA16
Telephone: 01458 443079
Facsimile: 01458 443079
*Developer and distributor of software covering
English, Maths and general problem solving
for ages 3-16, suitable for use on
Archimedes, Master and BBC.*

Serious Statistical Software
Lynwood
Benty Heath Lane
Willaston
South Wirral
L64 1SD
Contact: Mr G R Edwards
Telephone: 0151-327 4268
*Developer of computer software covering
statistical analysis (applicable in Maths,
Science, Geography, Business Studies and
Psychology) for A level students and suitable
for use on Archimedes machines.*

The Curriculum

Software and AV publishers and distributors

Sherston Software Ltd
Angel House
Sherston
Malmesbury
Wiltshire
SN16 0LH
Telephone: 01666 840433
Facsimile: 01666 840048
*Developer of software covering English, Maths,
Science and History for ages 3-14, suitable
for use on Apple Mac, IBM, RM Nimbus,
Archimedes, Master and BBC.*

Sibelius Software
75 Burleigh Street
Cambridge
CB1 1DJ
Telephone: 01223 302765
Facsimile: 01223 351947
*Developer of music processing and publishing
software with midi facilities for ages 5-18.
Also retailers of Acorn hardware and music
technology equipment.*

SIMS Educational Services Ltd
Abbots Road
Priory Business Park
Cardington
Bedfordshire
MK44 3SG
Contact: Barbara Sturgess, Business
Development Coordinator (Schools)
Telephone: 01234 838080
Facsimile: 01234 838091
*Developer and distributor of administration
software for schools of all sizes, based on
IBM (Windows) and RM Nimbus.*

Soft Teach Educational
Sturgess Farmhouse
Longbridge Deverill
Warminster
Wiltshire
BA12 7EA
Telephone: 01985 840329
Facsimile: 01985 840331
*Developer and distributor of software covering
Maths, Science, Geography, History and
Design & Technology for ages 7-16, suitable
for use on IBM, RM Nimbus, Archimedes,
Master and BBC.*

Softease Ltd
The Old Courthouse
St Peters Church Yard
Derby
DE1 1NN
Telephone: 01684 73173
*Developer and distributor of a desktop publisher
suitable for Archimedes and IBM.*

SPA Ltd
P.O. Box 59
Tewkesbury
Gloucestershire
GL20 6AB
Contact: Spencer Instone
Telephone: 01684 833700
Facsimile: 01684 833718
*Software developer for ages 3-18, suitable for
use on Apple Mac, IBM, RM Nimbus,
Archimedes, Master and BBC.*

Speedwell Computing Services
The Courtyard
Orchard Hill
Little Billing, Northampton
NN3 9AG
Contact: June Patterson,
Administration/Marketing Manager
Telephone: 01604 410041
Facsimile: 01604 415551
*Developer of software to design, mark and
evaluate multiple-choice questions,
questionnaires and data entry forms.*

Storm Educational Software
Coachman's Quarters
Digby Road
Sherborne
Dorset
DT9 3NN
Telephone: 01935 817699
Facsimile: 01935 817699
*Developer of software covering English, Maths,
Science, Technology, Geography, History
and Special Needs for ages 4-13, suitable for
Apple Mac, IBM, RM Nimbus, Archimedes,
Master and BBC.*

The Curriculum

Software and AV publishers and distributors

Systems Integrated Research
4th Floor, East Mill
Bridgefoot
Belper
Derbyshire
DE56 1XQ
Contact: Graham Ford, Sales Manager
Telephone: 01773 820011
Facsimile: 01773 820206
Developer and distributor of software covering Maths (KS1-4), English, French, German, Spanish and Italian (KS2), suitable for IBM, RM Nimbus and Archimedes.

TAG Developments Ltd
25 Pelham Road
Gravesend
Kent
DA11 0HU
Contact: Rosemary Partridge, Marketing Manager
Telephone: 01474 357350
Facsimile: 01474 537887
Developer and distributor of software on CD-Rom and disk covering all curriculum subjects for ages 3-18, suitable for use on Apple Mac, IBM, RM Nimbus, Archimedes, Master and BBC.

Tandberg Educational Ltd
7 Hales Road
Leeds
LS12 4PL
Contact: Sales Department
Telephone: 0113 279 9116
Facsimile: 0113 279 8661
Developer and distributor of authoring software to provide a variety of learning outcomes for ages 12-18, suitable for IBM (Windows)-compatible machines.

TechSoft UK Ltd
The Grange
Eryrys
Mold
Clwyd
CH7 4DB
Contact: Mike Brown, Managing Director

Telephone: 01824 780318
Facsimile: 01824 780564
Software developer and distributor of CAD and CAD/CAM systems covering Design & Technology for ages 11-18, suitable for use on IBM, RM Nimbus, Archimedes, Master and BBC.

Timetabling Services UK
39 South Street
Emsworth
Hampshire
PO10 7EG
Contact: Neil Jepson
Telephone: 01243 379944
Facsimile: 01243 379944
Distributors of software for constructing school timetables and for preparing arrangements for daily staff cover, suitable for IBM, RM Nimbus and Archimedes.

Topologika Software
Islington Wharf
Church Hill
Penryn
Cornwall
TR10 8AT
Contact: B Kerslake
Telephone: 01326 377771
Facsimile: 01326 377771
Develops and distributes software for ages 3-18, suitable for use with Archimedes, IBM (Windows) and RM Nimbus.

TRO Learning (UK) Ltd
Brook House
Riverside Park, Poyle Road
Colnbrook
Berkshire
SL3 9JE
Contact: Geoff Fry, Business Development Manager (UK & Europe)
Telephone: 01753 799111
Facsimile: 01753 799199
Developer of CD-Rom software covering Reading, Writing, Maths, Science, and Life & Job Search skills for ages 7-18, suitable for use on IBM-compatible machines. All software has built-in assessment, testing and performance records.

The Curriculum

Software and AV publishers and distributors

Ultralab
Anglia Polytechnic University
Sawyers Hall Lane
Brentwood
Essex CM15 9BT
Contact: Professor Stephen Heppell, Director
Facsimile: 01277 211363
Developer and distributor of CD-Roms covering
IT in the classroom, for ages 3-18 and
suitable for Apple Mac.

University of Wales, Computers and RE
Project
Department of Theology and Religious Studies
University of Wales
Lampeter
Dyfed SA48 7ED
Contact: Revd Michael Morris
Telephone: 01570 424708
Facsimile: 01570 423641
Developer and distributor of software on CD-
Rom and disk covering RE at all Key Stages,
suitable for use on Apple Mac, IBM, RM
Nimbus, Archimedes, Master and BBC.

Vektor
The Oaks
Preston Road
Chorley
Lancashire PR7 1PL
Contact: Miss T Park, International Account
Manager
Telephone: 01257 232222
Facsimile: 01257 234039
Developer and distributor of software covering
Modern Languages (French, German,
Spanish, Italian, Japanese), for all ages and
suitable for use on IBM-compatible machines.

Viewtech Film & Video
161 Winchester Road
Brislington
Bristol
BS4 3NJ
Contact: Kate Bates
Telephone: 0117 977 3422
Facsimile: 0117 972 4292
Distributor of videocassettes covering English,
Maths, Science, Technology, Humanities, Art,
Music, PE and PSE for ages 5-18.

Wayland Multimedia
61 Western Road
Hove
Sussex BN3 1JD
Telephone: 01273 722561
Facsimile: 01273 723526
Developer and distributor of software covering
Science, History, Geography and
Technology, primarily at KS2 & 3, and
suitable for use on Apple Mac, IBM
(Windows) and RM Nimbus.

Widgit Software
102 Radford Road
Leamington Spa
Warwickshire
CV31 1LF
Telephone: 01926 885303
Facsimile: 01926 885293
Developer and distributor of software for special
needs and primary education, suitable for
IBM, RM Nimbus, Archimedes, Master and
BBC.

Wyddfa Software
3 Preswylfa
Llanberis
Gwynedd
LL55 4LF
Contact: Ms Anne Williams
Telephone: 01286 870101
Facsimile: 01286 871722
Developer of software that uses samples of
speech to stimulate the development of
spoken and written language. Covers English
at KS1 and available in Welsh, and suitable
for Archimedes machines.

YITM
TV Centre
Leeds
LS3 1JS
Contact: Louise Spicer, Customer Services
Executive
Telephone: 0113 246 1528
Facsimile: 0113 243 4884
Developer and distributor of software on CD-
Rom covering all curriculum areas, for ages
3-18 and suitable for IBM and Archimedes.
Also distributes videos for the same areas
and levels.

The Curriculum

Equipment suppliers and services

3M UK Plc
3M House
P.O. Box 1, Market Place
Bracknell
Berkshire
RG12 1JU
Contact: Customer Information Service
Telephone: 01344 858748
Facsimile: 01344 858278
A diversified manufacturing company which markets over 60,000 products for industrial, commercial, healthcare and consumer markets.

Abacus Teaching Systems Ltd
Bryn Eirw
Blaenau Ffestiniog
Gwynedd
LL41 3DL
Telephone: 01766 762579
Manufactures and supplies pneumatics training equipment.

Axis Visual Presentation
Unit 14, Windmill Industrial Estate
Birmingham Road
Coventry
CV5 9QE
Contact: Brian Johnson, Sales Director
Telephone: 01203 405040
Facsimile: 01203 407311
Manufactures and supplies visual presentation equipment including noticeboards, display systems, planning boards, literature displays and information cases.

Berol Limited
Oldmedow Road
Kings Lynn
Norfolk
PE30 4JR
Contact: Mr Will Hinks, Education Sales and Marketing Manager
Telephone: 01553 761221
Facsimile: 01533 766534
Manufactures and supplies educational writing, colouring, drawing and art and craft materials.

Blackfriars
Friars Lane
Barbican
Plymouth
Devon
PL1 2LH
Contact: David King
Telephone: 01752 665254
Facsimile: 01752 222402
Specialises in graphic design and print for schools and colleges. Also available is a full consultancy service for in-house reprographics.

Bromcom Computers plc
417-421 Bromley Road
Downham
Bromley
Kent
BR1 4PJ
Telephone: 0181-461 3737
Facsimile: 0181-461 3993
Manufactures electronic attendance registration systems for schools.

Casio Electronics Co Ltd
Unit 6
1000 North Circular Road
London
NW2 7JD
Contact: Mr S A Turner, Education Controller
Telephone: 0181-450 9131
Facsimile: 0181-452 6323
Manufacturer of calculators, musical instruments, watches and audio-visual products.

Centre for Left-Handed Studies
P.O. Box 52
South DO
Manchester
M20 8PJ
Contact: Miss Diane Paul, Principal
Telephone: 0161-445 0159
Facsimile: 0161-445 0159
Assists those researching left-handedness, organises lectures and workshops and publishes books on the subject. Dextral Books (same address) can supply books on the subject and school equipment for left-handers.

The Curriculum

Equipment suppliers and services

CfBT Education Service
Quality House
Gyosei Campus, London Road
Reading
Berkshire
RG1 5AQ
Telephone: 01734 756200
Facsimile: 01734 756365
Aims to be a leading independent provider of education services and training. It works with clients in the UK and worldwide to develop high-quality, innovative and cost-effective solutions to their needs. Services include the management of educational resources, providing all necessary leadership with professional and logistical support to educationalists in order to ensure that they can give of their best.

Commotion Ltd
Unit 11
Tannery Road
Tonbridge
Kent
TN9 1RF
Telephone: 01732 773399
Facsimile: 01732 773390
Supplies construction kits, tools, materials, science equipment and consumables, control and data logging equipment, covering Science, Maths, Technology and IT for ages 5-18.

Continental Sports Ltd
Paddock
Huddersfield
West Yorkshire
HD1 4SD
Contact: Mr A D Cockman, Sales, Planning and Marketing Manager
Telephone: 01484 542051
Facsimile: 01484 539148
Manufacturers of PE, sports and gymnastic equipment specifically designed to meet the needs of the National Curriculum at all Key Stages. Maintenance and repair services are also available.

Coomber Electronic Equipment Ltd
Croft Walk
Worcester
WR1 3NZ
Telephone: 01905 25168
Facsimile: 01905 612701
Manufactures and supplies cassette recorders for individual, group, classroom and hall use. Also portable public address and radio microphone systems.

Don Johnston Special Needs Ltd
18 Clarendon Court
Calver Road, Winwick Quay
Warrington
Lancashire
WA2 8QP
Telephone: 01925 241642
Facsimile: 01925 241745
Developer and distributor of software and hardware for special needs, including physical disabilities, visual impairments and learning disabilities, for all ages and for use on Apple Macs.

Eastlight Ltd
Ashton Road
Denton
Manchester
M34 3NA
Contact: Customer Services Department
Telephone: 0161-336 9431
Facsimile: 0161-320 8012
Manufactures stationery filing (lever arch box files and documents wallets).

Educational Co Ltd
1 Mallusk Park
Mallusk Road
Newtownabbey
Co Antrim
BT36 8GW
Contact: Bob Whitehead, Sales Director
Telephone: 01232 844023
Facsimile: 01232 840705
Edco is a general educational contractor with a range of over 8000 products for classroom use, covering all ages.

The Curriculum

Equipment suppliers and services

Elite Optics Ltd
Elite House
Llantrisant Business Park
Llantrisant
Mid Glamorgan
CF7 8LF
Contact: Ms Paula Howard, National Sales
 Manager
Telephone: 01443 238833
Facsimile: 01443 238008
*Manufactures overhead projectors,
 slide/filmstrip projectors and trolleys and also
 supplies computer projection products (LCD
 panels).*

Elliott-Medway Ltd
Glebe Court
Glebe Road
Peterborough
PE2 8EE
Contact: Ray Perkins, Sales Manager
Telephone: 01733 52151
Facsimile: 01733 313002
*Manufactures building systems, from
 relocatable classrooms to entire schools of
 four storeys.*

ERIC International
Pepabera
Findon Road
Findon
Sussex
BN14 0RD
Contact: Mrs Worley, Director
Telephone: 01903 872400
Facsimile: 01903 872400
Distributor for Acorn machines.

Esmond Hellerman Ltd
Hellerman House
Harris Way, Windmill Road
Sunbury-on-Thames
Middlesex
TW16 7EW
Contact: Mr Jonathan Fish, Managing Director
Telephone: 01932 781888
Facsimile: 01932 789573
*Manufacturers and suppliers of technical
 drawing equipment, graphic arts and
 educational equipment, specialising in the 11-
 18 age group.*

First Class Ltd
Sinclair House
Willoughby Lane
London
N17 0SP
Contact: Peter Berglas, Director of Educational
 Sales
Telephone: 0181-885 3311
Facsimile: 0181-808 4723
*Supplier of educational equipment covering
 Maths, Technology, Science and Art & Craft
 items for ages 3-12.*

Flight Electronics International Ltd
Flight House
Ascupart Street
Southampton
Hampshire
SO14 1LU
Contact: Andrew Padley
Telephone: 01703 227721
Facsimile: 01703 330039
*Manufactures and supplies Educational
 Electronics microprocessors and scientific
 test and measurement equipment, some
 suitable from age 11, but most for ages 16-18.*

Frank Berry Educational Products
Westhill Stationery Centre
North Wingfield Road
Grassmoor, Chesterfield
Derbyshire
S42 5EB
Telephone: 01246 852244
Facsimile: 01246 855317
*Supplier of general educational materials with a
 range of over 24,000 products.*

Franklin Electronic Publishers
7 Windmill Business Village
Brooklands Close
Sunbury-on-Thames
Middlesex
TW16 7DY
Contact: Customer Services
Telephone: 01932 770185
Facsimile: 01932 770176
*Distributor of hand-held electronic reference
 products, such as spelling machines,
 thesauruses and dictionaries, useful for SEN,
 English and IT.*

The Curriculum

Equipment suppliers and services

Gabbitas Educational Consultants
Broughton House
6-8 Sackville Street
Piccadilly
London
W1X 2BR
Telephone: 0171-734 0161
Facsimile: 0171-437 1764
*Offers parents and students individual,
independent guidance on education at all
levels, from age 5 upwards. For schools in
the UK and overseas a full range of staff
recruitment and consultancy services are
available.*

Galt Educational
Culvert Street
Oldham
Lancashire
OL4 2ST
Telephone: 0161-627 0795
Facsimile: 0161-627 1543
*Supplier of general educational equipment for
all ages.*

Group for Education in Museums
63 Navarino Road
London
E8 1AG
Contact: Susan Morris, Hon Secretary
Telephone: 0171-249 4296
*Promotes educational work in museums and
related institutions.*

Heckmondwike FB Ltd
P.O. Box 7
Wellington Mills
Liversedge
West Yorkshire
WF15 7XA
Telephone: 01924 406161
Facsimile: 01924 409972
*Manufactures a range of heavy-contract fibre-
bonded carpets and carpet tiles.*

Helix Ltd
P.O. Box 15
Lye
Stourbridge
West Midlands
DY9 7AJ

Contact: Ian Shipley, National Accounts
Manager
Telephone: 01384 424441
Facsimile: 01384 892617
*Manufacturers of mathematical and technical
drawing instruments (rules, compasses,
maths sets) and blackboard equipment.*

Heron Educational Ltd
Carrwood House
Carrwood Road
Chesterfield
Derbyshire
S41 9QB
Telephone: 01246 453354
Facsimile: 01246 260876
*Manufactures and supplies furniture and
resources for Science, Technology and
Geography for ages 5-13, and equipment and
storage for ages 3-6.*

HME Technology Ltd
Priory House
Saxon Park, Hanbury Road
Stoke Prior
Worcestershire
B60 4AD
Telephone: 01527 570900
Facsimile: 01527 570737
*Manufacturer of heat treatment equipment
(forges, brazing hearths, etc), fume extraction
systems, kilns, moulding/acid pickle benches,
woodworking equipment, wood dust
extraction systems, jewellery benches and
torches, PCB equipment, gas safety systems,
and equipment for school Design
Technology/Science/Art areas.*

Hope Education Ltd
Orb Mill
Huddersfield Road
Waterhead, Oldham
Lancashire
OL4 2ST
Telephone: 0161-633 6611
Facsimile: 0161-633 3431
*Supplier of over 10,000 items of general
educational equipment for all ages.*

The Curriculum

Equipment suppliers and services

Hunt & Broadhurst Ltd
Calderbank
River Street
Brighouse
West Yorkshire
HD6 1LU
Contact: Customer Service (Schools)
Telephone: 01484 400804
Facsimile: 01484 400839
Manufacturer and supplier of exercise books and papers.

John Farnell Ltd
24 Townhead Mill
Addingham
Ilkley
West Yorkshire
LS29 0PP
Contact: Mr John Farnell
Telephone: 01943 831504
Facsimile: 01943 831504
Suppliers of cassette tape recorders, headsets, televisions, video recorders and players to all schools.

Kuretake UK Ltd
10 Moons Park
Burnt Meadow Road
Redditch
Worcestershire
B98 9PA
Contact: Phill Jones, Key Accounts Manager Education
Telephone: 01527 62828
Facsimile: 01527 60765
Manufacturer of general writing instruments, and arts and crafts/graphics products for all age groups.

LEGO Dacta
LEGO UK Ltd
Ruthin Road
Wrexham
Clwyd
LL13 7TQ
Contact: Sue Williams, Sales Coordinator
Telephone: 01978 290900
Facsimile: 01978 296239
The educational division of the LEGO group which supplies materials covering Language, Maths, Science, Design Technology and IT.

LETA Telephone Training Ltd
15 Kingsway
Gerrards Cross
Buckinghamshire
SL9 8NS
Contact: Mrs Joyce Hill, Managing Director
Telephone: 01753 882130
Facsimile: 01753 887168
Manufactures telephone training equipment and foreign language material, of particular interest to teachers of business studies and of foreign languages.

Living and Learning (Cambridge) Ltd
Duke Street
Wisbech
Cambridgeshire
PE13 2AE
Telephone: 01945 63441
Facsimile: 01945 587361
Educational games from pre-school to 12 years.

London Emblem Plc
Emblem House
Blenheim Road, Longmead Industrial Estate
Epsom
Surrey
KT19 9AP
Contact: Shuana Baker, Sales Administrator
Telephone: 01372 745433
Facsimile: 01372 745462
Manufactures and supplies badgemaking kits, and distributor of a large-scale construction system ('Tactic') suitable for 4-18 years.

MJP Geopacks
P.O. Box 23
St Just
Penzance
Cornwall
TR19 7JS
Contact: Michael Jay
Telephone: 01736 787808
Facsimile: 01736 787880
Suppliers of geography equipment and software for ages 5-18, suitable for use with IBM, RM Nimbus, Master and BBC.

The Curriculum

Equipment suppliers and services

Peter Le Feuvre
3 Beacon Square
Emsworth
Hampshire
PO10 7HU
Telephone: 01243 373109
Facsimile: 01243 378498
Manufactures and supplies resources for SEN and dyslexic pupils, and language resources.

Playlink
The Co-op Centre
Unit 5, 11 Mowll Street
London
SW9 6BG
Contact: Sandra Melville, Director
Telephone: 0171-820 3800
Facsimile: 0171-793 0426
As part of its general aim to improve the quality and quantity of play opportunities for school-age children, PLAYLINK works with schools to develop their play policies and extend the range of play experience they offer their children during the school day.

Rahmqvist UK Ltd
Crabtree Road
Thorpe Industrial Estate
Egham
Surrey
TW20 8RN
Telephone: 01784 439888
Facsimile: 01784 471419
Manufactures and supplies markers, pens, paints, pencils, craft materials, adhesives and educational games.

ROMPA International
Goyt Side Road
Chesterfield
Derbyshire
S40 2PH
Contact: Bonny Britland, Marketing Manager
Telephone: 01246 211777
Facsimile: 01246 221802
Manufactures and supplies therapy, leisure, play and sport products for ages 3-18, primarily for those with profound learning disabilities or sensory impairments.

Saville Group Ltd
SchoolsVision, Millfield Lane
Nether Poppleton
York
YO2 6PQ
Contact: Maggie Read, Manager
Telephone: 01904 798979
Facsimile: 01904 781535
SchoolsVision (a division of the Saville Group) supplies audio-visual and video products to schools.

Scholaquip Limited
Weaver Point
Second Avenue
Crewe
Cheshire
CW1 1BZ
Telephone: 01270 251145
Facsimile: 01270 251042
Manufacturer of paints, crayons and chalks for classroom use.

Scottish Schools Equipment Research Centre
24 Bernard Terrace
Edinburgh
EH8 9NX
Telephone: 0131-668 4421
Facsimile: 0131-667 9344
Provides members with a variety of services: school equipment testing and advisory service; training in equipment usage, health and safety matters and IT usage; and a consultancy service for Science & Technology and Health & Safety.

Sibelius Software
75 Burleigh Street
Cambridge
CB1 1DJ
Telephone: 01223 302765
Facsimile: 01223 351947
Developer of music processing and publishing software with midi facilities for ages 5-18. Also retailers of Acorn hardware and music technology equipment.

The Curriculum

Equipment suppliers and services

SpaceKraft Ltd
Crowgill House
Rosse Street
Shipley
BD13 3SW
Telephone: 01274 581007
Facsimile: 01274 531966
Manufactures interactive multi-sensory
environments, including pools and sensory
gardens, for all ages.

Staedtler (UK) Ltd
Cowbridge Road
Pontyclun
Mid Glamorgan
CF7 8YJ
Contact: Caron Melin, Education Sales
Manager
Telephone: 01443 237421
Facsimile: 01443 238158
Manufacturer of writing, drafting, art and
colouring products suitable for all ages from 3
up.

Sundeala (Division of Celotex Ltd)
Warwick House
27 St Mary's Road
Ealing
London
W5 5PR
Telephone: 0181-579 0811
Facsimile: 0181-579 0106
Manufactures noticeboards and display boards.

Supertech International
4/5 Grosvenor Place
London
SW1X 7HH
Contact: Justin Barrett, Projects Manager
Telephone: 0171-235 2309
Facsimile: 0171-245 9046
Supplier of video imaging systems and security
solutions.

Teacherboards (1985) Ltd
Airedale Business Centre
Skipton
Yorkshire
BD23 2TZ

Contact: Belinda Chapman, Telesales
Telephone: 01756 700501
Facsimile: 01756 700502
Manufactures display boards, chalkboards,
rollerboards, noticeboards, projection screens
and display systems for all situations.

Technology Teaching Systems Ltd
Unit 4, Park Road
Holmewood
Chesterfield
Derbyshire
S42 5UY
Telephone: 01246 850085
Facsimile: 01246 855557
Manufactures and supplies resources for
Maths, Science, Technology, History and RE
suitable for ages 5-14.

Transaid Audio Visual Services
Francis Gregory & Son Ltd
Radley Road Industrial Estate
Abingdon
Oxfordshire
OX14 3RY
Contact: Mrs S I Gregory, Sales Desk
Telephone: 01235 555002
Facsimile: 01235 535940
Supplier of audio-visual equipment and
materials suitable for any age.

Treasure House of Make-up
197 Lee Lane
Horwich
Bolton
BL6 7JD
Telephone: 01204 668355
Facsimile: 01204 668355
Supplier of theatre make-up and water make-up
for face painting.

Two-Ten Communications Ltd
P.O. Box 5
Wetherby
West Yorkshire
LS23 7EH
Telephone: 01937 840210
Facsimile: 01937 845381
Distributor of free and subsidised educational
material.

EQUIPMENT - GENERAL

The Curriculum

Equipment suppliers and services

Valiant Technology Ltd
Myrtle House
69 Salcott Road
London
SW11 6DQ
Contact: Lee McGill, Sales Administrator
Telephone: 0171-924 2366
Facsimile: 0171-924 1892
Manufactures and supplies a range of products covering Maths, Science, Technology and IT at all Key Stages.

Visualex Ltd
3 Reading Road
Henley-on-Thames
Oxfordshire
RG9 1AB
Contact: Carolyn Ten-Holter, Marketing Department
Telephone: 01491 579789
Facsimile: 01491 578323
Supplies LCD panels and overhead projectors for classroom use and staff training.

RESOURCES RELATED TO SPECIFIC CURRICULUM AREAS

ABCeta Playthings Ltd
19 Torkington Road
Hazel Grove
Stockport
Cheshire
SK7 4RG
Contact: Terry J Denton, Managing Director
Telephone: 0161-483 4500
Facsimile: 0161-456 6896
Supplier specialising in mathematical equipment suitable for ages 3-10.

Acorn (Percussion) Ltd
Unit 34, Abbey Business Centre
Ingate Place
London SW8 3NS
Contact: Marguerite Vetter, Sales Director
Telephone: 0171-720 2243
Facsimile: 0171-627 8883

Manufactures and supplies a wide variety of mainstream, multicultural and special needs percussion instruments suitable for ages 3-18. Also available are electric and acoustic guitars and a book list for all areas of music.

Blundell Harling Ltd
Regulus Works
Lynch Lane
Weymouth
Dorset
DT4 9DW
Contact: Mr Colin Tucker, Sales Office Supervisor
Telephone: 01305 783275
Facsimile: 01305 760598
Manufacturer of drawing office equipment and accessories suitable for Key Stages 3-4 studying Design and Technical Drawing.

Conect Numerical Control Ltd
Trent Business Centre
Canal Street
Long Eaton, Nottingham
NG10 4HQ
Contact: Kevin Higgins, Sales Manager
Telephone: 0115 973 0315
Facsimile: 0115 946 3024
Manufactures a range of CNC lathes, mills and routers which can be used for training, suited to ages 12-18.

Data Harvest Group/Educational Electronics
Woburn Lodge
Waterloo Road
Linslade, Leighton Buzzard
Bedfordshire
LU7 7NR
Telephone: 01525 373666
Facsimile: 01525 851638
Designs and manufactures a range of data loggers and some 20 different calibrated sensors, for all Key Stages and suitable for use with IBM, Apple Mac and Acorn computers.

The Curriculum

Equipment suppliers and services

Dawsons Music Ltd
65 Sankey Street
Warrington
Cheshire
WA1 1SU
Contact: Keith Halligan, Education Department
  Manager
Telephone: 01925 632591
Facsimile: 01925 417812
*Supplies musical instruments to schools, and
  can provide INSET on music-related
  computer software.*

Denford Machine Tools Ltd
Birds Royd
Brighouse
West Yorkshire
HD6 1NB
Contact: Mr S E Conway, Marketing Manager
Telephone: 01484 712264
Facsimile: 01484 722160
*Manufactures computerised machines and
  systems (mills and lathes) for use across the
  curriculum from Key Stages 2 to 4, and
  GNVQ manufacturing and engineering.*

Donmar (Stage and Lighting) Ltd
Donmar House
54 Cavell Street
London
E1 2HP
Contact: Ms Miranda Hunt, Technical Sales
  Manager
Telephone: 0171-790 9937
Facsimile: 0171-790 6634
*Supplies, installs and services stage and studio
  lighting equipment in all schools.*

Educational and Scientific Products Ltd
A2 Dominion Way
Rustington
Sussex
BN16 3HQ
Telephone: 01903 773340
Facsimile: 01903 771108
*Manufactures and supplies plastic skeletons;
  animal and plant anatomical models;
  prepared zoology, botany and histology
  slides; and wallcharts for age 11 and above.*

ELE International Ltd
Eastman Way
Hemel Hempstead
Hertfordshire
HP2 7HB
Contact: Miss E Opperman, Marketing
  Coordinator
Telephone: 01442 218355
Facsimile: 01442 252474
*Manufactures an environmental monitoring
  station for education and research of
  weather, pollution and the environment,
  suitable for ages 11-18.*

Emco Maier Ltd
10 Woodshots Meadow
Croxley Business Park
Watford
Hertfordshire
WD1 8YZ
Telephone: 01923 250051
Facsimile: 01923 243908
*Manufactures PC-controlled lathes and milling
  machines for Design and Technology. Also
  supplies CAD/CAM software suitable for ages
  11-18.*

Emmerich (Berlon) Ltd
Wotton Road
Ashford
Kent
TN23 6JY
Telephone: 01233 622684
Facsimile: 01233 645801
*Craft and Technology workbenches, hand
  weaving looms and CAD/CAM systems, and
  storage cupboards with roller front.*

Griffin & George
Bishop Meadow Road
Loughborough
Leicestershire
LE11 0RG
Telephone: 01509 233344
Facsimile: 01509 231893
Supplier of science equipment and chemicals.

EQUIPMENT FOR SUBJECT AREAS

The Curriculum

Equipment suppliers and services

Irwin-Desman Ltd
Eurocrown House
23 Grafton Road
Croydon
CR9 3AZ
Telephone: 0181-680 2058
Facsimile: 0181-681 8429
Manufactures and supplies science equipment to the education market, for Key Stages 2 to 4.

LJ Technical Systems Ltd
Francis Way
Bowthorpe Industrial Estate
Norwich
NR5 9JA
Contact: Damian Breeze, Marketing Director
Telephone: 01603 748001
Facsimile: 01603 746340
Manufactures computer-based training systems for Technology at KS3 and above.

Locktronics Ltd
Unit 11, Chancellors Pound
Redhill
Avon
BS18 7TZ
Contact: Brian Chandler, General Manager
Telephone: 01934 863560
Facsimile: 01934 863561
Manufacturer of kits for teaching the principles of electricity and electronics.

Map Marketing Ltd
102/104 Carnwath Road
London
SW6 3HW
Contact: Mr Dominic West, Marketing Department
Telephone: 0171-736 0297
Facsimile: 0171-371 0473
Manufactures and supplies reversible political/physical wall maps, and satellite image maps suitable for all ages.

Mega Electronics Ltd
Grip Industrial Estate
Linton
Cambridgeshire
CB1 6NR
Contact: Tony Hawkins, Sales & Marketing Manager
Telephone: 01223 893900
Facsimile: 01223 893894
Manufactures and supplies printed circuit board production equipment for low-volume production and consumables, suited to Key Stages 3 and 4.

NCS Satellite Division
Belville House
Ponteland
Newcastle upon Tyne
NE20 9BD
Contact: Jon Malcolm, Division Manager
Telephone: 01661 825515
Facsimile: 01661 860069
Supplier of an Apple Mac- and Window-based weather satellite system, which receives, processes, analyses and displays live pictures of the earth from space allowing students to interpret weather formations as they happen.

P & B Weir Electrical
Unit 10, Leafield Way
Leafield Trading Estate
Corsham
Wiltshire
SN13 9SW
Contact: A E Hollins, Sales and Contracts Manager
Telephone: 01225 811449
Facsimile: 01225 810909
Manufactures electrical instruments and accessories for science teaching, suitable for ages 11-18.

Philip Harris Education
Lynn Lane
Shenstone
Lichfield
Staffordshire
WS14 0EE
Telephone: 01543 480077
Facsimile: 01543 480068
Manufactures and supplies measurement, control and science software for all ages. Also data logging hardware for science.

The Curriculum

Equipment suppliers and services

ProSonics Education
45 Douglas Road
Kingston-upon-Thames
Surrey
KT1 3PX
Contact: Mr Richard Todman
Telephone: 0181-974 9620
Music and multimedia technology training and support for music educators at Key Stages 2, 3 and 4 and A level.

R & D Electronics
12 Percy Avenue
Kingsgate
Broadstairs
Kent
CT10 3LB
Telephone: 01843 866662
Facsimile: 01843 866663
Manufactures weather monitoring instruments providing clear analogue and digital displays of weather parameters. All models can be connected via a computer interface and data logger to a PC to provide a picture of past weather either as a graph or in spreadsheet form.

Royal Sovereign Ltd
7 St Georges Industrial Estate
White Hart Lane
London
N22 5QL
Telephone: 0181-888 3232
Facsimile: 0181-888 9900
Supplies stationery and art materials, including hobby and craft colours, for all ages from 8 up.

Safemark Computer Security
Bentham House
30 Acomb Road
York
YO2 4EW
Contact: Neal K Williams, General Manager
Telephone: 01904 788494
Facsimile: 01904 788711
Manufacturers of security safes, cabinets, bolting-down plates and security cables to protect computers and peripherals. Also supplies anti-virus software and access control software to protect data.

T S Harrison and Sons
Union Street
Heckmondwike
West Yorkshire
WF16 0HN
Contact: Mr D H Smith, Sales Director
Telephone: 01924 403751
Facsimile: 01924 407285
Manufacturer of metal-cutting lathes, some with the facility of off-line programming with CAD/CAM.

Taskmaster Ltd
Morris Road
Leicester
LE2 6BR
Contact: Mrs D B Smith, Director
Telephone: 0116 270 4286
Facsimile: 0116 270 6992
Manufactures and supplies manipulatives, games, reproducible books and other learning aids for Maths, Speech and Language at KS1 & 2.

TecQuipment Ltd
Bonsall Street
Long Eaton
Nottingham
NG10 2AN
Contact: Customer Service Technical Representative
Telephone: 0115 972 2611
Facsimile: 0115 973 1520
Designs, manufactures, supplies and installs a range of proprietary products for engineering teaching and training suitable for trainees from age 16.

Unilab Ltd
The Science Park
Hutton Street
Blackburn
Lancashire
BB1 3BT
Contact: Ted Brewin, UK Sales Manager
Telephone: 01254 681222
Facsimile: 01254 681777
Manufactures a range of UK-designed resources for Science, Technology and practical Maths suitable for KS2 and up. Many products support the application of IT.

EQUIPMENT FOR SUBJECT AREAS

The Curriculum

Equipment suppliers and services

COMPUTER HARDWARE

Aleph One Ltd
The Old Courthouse
Bottisham
Cambridge
CB5 9BA
Telephone: 01223 811679
Facsimile: 01223 812713
Supplier of expansion cards for Acorn 300 and 400 series machines to provide compatibility with IBM software.

Apple Computer (UK) Ltd
6 Roundwood Avenue
Stockley Park
Uxbridge
Middlesex
UB11 1BB
Contact: Apple Assistance Centre
Telephone: 0181-569 1199
Facsimile: 0181-569 2957
Manufactures and supplies computers, monitors, printers and computer peripherals.

Ascot Systems
Woods Way
Goring-by-Sea
Sussex
BN12 4QY
Contact: Neil Kimmance, Marketing Manager
Telephone: 01903 503041
Facsimile: 01903 507250
Manufactures a computer hardware system in which instructor screen information is displayed onto student monitors for computer training. Suitable for ages 13-18.

Atomwide Ltd
7 The Metro Centre
Bridge Road
Orpington
Kent
BR5 2BE
Telephone: 01689 814500
Facsimile: 01689 814501
Supplier of Acorn computer hardware, upgrades, CD-Roms drives and RISC PC expansion kits, and creates and installs Ethernet networks.

AU Enterprises Ltd
126 Great North Road
Hatfield
Hertfordshire
AL9 5JZ
Contact: Diana Freeman, Director
Telephone: 01707 266714
Facsimile: 01707 273684
Provides an IT support service for all ages, which includes training, software and CD-Rom publications.

Boxford Ltd
Boy Lane
Wheatley
Halifax
West Yorkshire
HX3 5AF
Contact: Mr K Golding, Sales Office Manager
Telephone: 01422 358311
Facsimile: 01422 355924
Manufactures CAD/CAM software and machines for Key Stages 3 and 4.

Calligraph Ltd
53 Panton Street
Cambridge
CB2 1HL
Contact: Richard Piller, Director
Telephone: 01223 566642
Facsimile: 01223 566643
Manufactures and supplies laser printers suitable for classroom use.

Capital Electronic Developments Ltd
Balfour House
590 Uxbridge Road
Hayes
Middlesex
UB4 0RY
Contact: R C Wheeler, Director, Technical Sales
Telephone: 0181-573 3681
Facsimile: 0181-561 5356
Supplies a touchscreen suitable for all monitors compatible with IBM (incl. Windows), RM Nimbus and Archimedes machines, and suitable for all ages, particularly special needs.

The Curriculum

Equipment suppliers and services

Castle Technology
Ore Trading Estate
Woodbridge Road
Framlingham
Suffolk
IP13 9LL
Contact: Jack Lillington
Telephone: 01728 621222
Facsimile: 01728 621179
*Manufacturer and distributor of hardware
upgrades and peripherals for all Acorn 32-bit
computers.*

Computer Concepts Ltd
Gaddesden Place
Hemel Hempstead
Hertfordshire
HP2 6EX
Telephone: 01442 351000
Facsimile: 01442 351010
*Suppliers of publishing and multimedia products
on the Acorn platform, both software and
hardware.*

Concept Keyboard Company Ltd
Unit 6, Moorside Road
Winnall Industrial Estate
Winchester
Hampshire
SO23 7RX
Contact: Mr Mel Woodcock, Marketing
Department
Telephone: 01962 843322
Facsimile: 01962 841657
*Manufacturer of programmable keyboards
associated with all types of computer.*

Cumana Ltd
Pines Trading Estate
Broad Street
Guildford
Surrey
GU3 3BH
Telephone: 01483 503121
Facsimile: 01483 451371
*Manufactures and supplies CD-Rom and
multimedia products (both hardware and
software), and installs and services
Ethernet/Nexus networking hardware.*

Data Harvest Group/Educational Electronics
Woburn Lodge
Waterloo Road
Linslade, Leighton Buzzard
Bedfordshire
LU7 7NR
Telephone: 01525 373666
Facsimile: 01525 851638
*Designs and manufactures a range of data
loggers and some 20 different calibrated
sensors for all Key Stages and suitable for
use with IBM, Apple Mac and Acorn
computers.*

Datathorn Systems Ltd
The Seedbed Centre
Langston Road
Loughton
Essex
Telephone: 0181-502 4221
Facsimile: 0181-508 6660
*Designs, supplies and installs educational
computer networks supporting mixtures of
Acorn, IBM-compatible and Apple Mac
machines.*

Deltronics
Church Road Industrial Estate
Gorslas
Llanelli
Dyfed
SA14 7NF
Telephone: 01269 843728
Facsimile: 01269 845527
*Designs, manufactures and supplies computer
control interfaces, and data logging interfaces
and sensors for all ages.*

Economatics (Education) Ltd
Epic House
Darnall Road, Attercliffe
Sheffield
S9 5AA
Telephone: 0114 256 1122
Facsimile: 0114 243 9306
*Manufactures and supplies measurement and
control equipment for Apple Mac, IBM and
Archimedes machines.*

COMPUTER HARDWARE

99

The Curriculum

Equipment suppliers and services

Education Interactive Ltd
Hinton House
Hinton
Dorset
BH23 7EA
Telephone: 01425 272235
Facsimile: 01425 273784
Manufactures and distributes CD-Rom drives, towers, computer hardware and networking solutions to schools, colleges, universities and libraries.

Elonex plc
2 Apsley Way
London
NW2 7LF
Telephone: 0181-452 4444
Facsimile: 0181-452 6422
Manufacturer of IBM-compatible computers and associated hardware selling direct to the customer.

Eltec Computers
2 St Martins Avenue
Fieldhead Business Centre
Bradford
West Yorkshire
BD7 1LG
Telephone: 01274 309999
Facsimile: 01274 722680
Suppliers of computer systems, software and peripherals suitable for use with Apple Mac, Acorn and IBM-compatible machines.

Festo Ltd
Automation House
Harvest Crescent, Ancells Business Park
Fleet
Hampshire
GU13 8XP
Contact: Mr Stevan Stratfull, Didactic Product Manager
Telephone: 01252 775002
Facsimile: 01252 775012
Manufactures and supplies a learning system for automation technology, including pneumatics, hydraulics, electronics, robotics, sensors, PLCs, communications, software and books suitable for ages 12 to 18.

Highmead Technologies Ltd
Jupitor House
Travellers Lane
Welham Green, Hatfield
Hertfordshire
AL9 7DA
Contact: Jeff Baker, Education Director
Telephone: 01707 272627
Facsimile: 01707 267400
Supplies and installs IBM-compatible hardware for schools, including multimedia and network solutions.

Husqvarna
Viking House
Cheddar Business Park, Wedmore Road
Cheddar
Somerset
BS27 3EB
Telephone: 01934 744533
Facsimile: 01934 744811
Distributes a CAD/CAM sewing machine with unlimited free design potential via IBM-compatible software. Suitable for use with all Key Stages.

i-Cubed Ltd
Rustat House
62 Clifton Road
Cambridge
CB1 4GY
Contact: S Livingstone, Commercial Manager
Telephone: 01223 566113
Facsimile: 01223 566313
Suppliers of education Ethernet networking solutions, especially for the Acorn platform.

ICL Education Systems
CLASSICL Centre
FREEPOST (MR7541), Arndale House
Manchester
M4 3AR
Contact: Jenny Belfield, Telesales Manager
Telephone: 0800 252674
Facsimile: 0161-955 2711
EMail: J.Belfield@man1209.wins.icl.co.uk
Specialises in providing IT solutions to the education marketplace (from primary to university level). This includes hardware, software and services ranging from complex networks to PCs.

The Curriculum

Equipment suppliers and services

Insight International Corporation Ltd
P.O. Box 1293
Saltdean
Brighton
Sussex
BN2 8BD
Telephone: 01273 300338
Facsimile: 01273 309845
*Supplier of security equipment for computer
hardware.*

Instrutek (UK)
28 Stephenson Road Industrial Estate
St Ives
Cambridgeshire
PE17 4WJ
Contact: Doug Simpson, Managing Director
Telephone: 01480 460028
Facsimile: 01480 460340
*Manufactures and supplies IBM-compatible
hardware, and software and hardware for
electronics training, suitable for ages 9-18.*

Integrex Systems Ltd
Church Gresley
Swadlincote
Derbyshire
DE11 9PT
Contact: Jan Myshrall
Telephone: 01283 550880
Facsimile: 01283 552028
*Manufactures and supplies colour inkjet, dot
matrix and laser printers suitable for use with
IBM (including older variants) and
Archimedes A3000 machines.*

Irlam Instruments Ltd
Brunel Institute for Bioengineering
Brunel University
Uxbridge
Middlesex
UB8 3PH
Telephone: 01895 811401
Facsimile: 01895 811401
*Manufactures imaging instruments (scanners
and video digitisers) for Acorn RISC
machines.*

KCS Premier
73 Chapel Street
Leigh
Lancashire
WN7 2DA
Contact: Paul Leigh
Telephone: 01942 677777
Facsimile: 01942 672300
*Manufactures and supplies computer hardware,
specialising in school network installation.*

KCS Tools for the Computer-Enabled
P.O. Box 700
Southampton
Hampshire
SO17 1LQ
Telephone: 01703 584314
Facsimile: 01703 584320
*Supplies hardware and software access
systems to enable people with disabilities or
learning difficulties to get the best use of
computers regardless of age or ability.*

KRCS Group plc
Queens Court
Lenton Lane
Nottingham
NG7 2NR
Contact: Denise Hurt
Telephone: 0115 950 5352
Facsimile: 0115 986 0744
Supplier of computer hardware and software.

Lindis International
Wood Farm
Linstead Magna
Halesworth
Suffolk
IP19 0DU
Telephone: 01986 785476
Facsimile: 01986 785460
*Distributes Acorn hardware and supplies
software on disk and CD-Rom for Acorn
machines covering graphics and reference at
all Key Stages.*

COMPUTER HARDWARE

101

The Curriculum

Equipment suppliers and services

COMPUTER HARDWARE

Mayflower Business Systems Ltd
Unit 3, Heathgate Place
75-87 Agincourt Road
Hampstead
London
NW3 2NT
Contact: Mr Kim Menen, Managing Director
Telephone: 0171-267 0100
Facsimile: 0171-267 7800
Supplier of a colour-sensitive drawing board for use in conjunction with an IBM-compatible or Apple Mac computer.

Micro-Aid
Kildonan Courtyard
Barrhill
South Ayrshire
KA26 0PS
Contact: Mr Colin Chatfield
Telephone: 01465 821288
Facsimile: 01465 821288
Manufactures and supplies computer software for payroll, accounts and family history suitable for use with Acorn computers. Also supplies hardware and consumables.

Penny & Giles Computer Products Ltd
1 Airfield Way
Christchurch
Dorset BH23 3TE
Contact: Jack Randall, Operations Director
Telephone: 01202 481751
Facsimile: 01202 499279
Manufactures alternative computer input devices to the mouse, ranging from special needs tracker balls and joysticks to a ruggedised range of units intended for general classroom use. The SEN items are intended for those with a poor level of motor skills who have difficulty with standard mice.

Philip Harris Education
Lynn Lane
Shenstone
Lichfield
Staffordshire WS14 0EE
Telephone: 01543 480077
Facsimile: 01543 480068
Manufactures and supplies measurement, control and science software for all ages. Also data logging hardware for science.

Raised Dot Computing
408 S Baldwin Street
Madison
WI 53703
USA
Telephone: 00 1 608 257 9595
Facsimile: 00 1 608 257 4143
Braille production hardware and software, suitable for use by any age.

Research Machines Plc
New Mill House
183 Milton Park
Abingdon
Oxfordshire
OX14 4SE
Telephone: 01235 826000
Facsimile: 01235 826999
Designs, manufactures and supplies direct to schools a range of specialist IT resources. These include integrated software, hardware and services tailored to suit individual needs (primary, secondary, further and higher education).

Simnett Computers
Alperton House
Bridgewater Road
Wembley
Middlesex
HA0 1EH
Contact: Stewart Beeny, Sales Manager
Telephone: 0181-982 6383
Facsimile: 0181-982 6373
Supplies software and hardware for Apple Mac, IBM, RM Nimbus and Archimedes computers.

SRS Systems
Clock Chambers
78 Darlington Street
Wolverhampton
WV1 4LY
Contact: John Shermer, Managing Director
Telephone: 01902 711737
Facsimile: 01902 714558
Manufactures and supplies IBM-compatible hardware providing a new approach to the problem of giving people of any age with disabilities access to computers.

The Curriculum

Equipment suppliers and services

Swallow Systems
134 Cock Lane
High Wycombe
Buckinghamshire
HP13 7EA
Telephone: 01494 813471
Facsimile: 01494 813552
*Manufactures and supplies programmable
floor/table top robots (independent from the
computer), suitable for ages 3-12.*

System Insight
Units 1-3, East Burrowfield
Welwyn Garden City
Hertfordshire
AL7 4TB
Telephone: 01707 395500
Facsimile: 01707 395501
*Manufactures and supplies a range of refill kits
and other consumables for inkjet and
bubblejet printers, together with dustcovers
and specialist paper.*

Tandy Education Supplies & Services
Intertan UK Ltd, Tandy Centre
Leamore Lane
Bloxwich, Walsall
WS2 7PS
Telephone: 01922 434036
Facsimile: 01922 434042
*Supplier of notebook and laptop computers to
schools with particular emphasis on low-cost
notebooks. Other Tandy products offered at
educational discount.*

Unimatic Engineers Ltd
122 Granville Road
Cricklewood
London
NW2 2LN
Telephone: 0181-455 0012
Facsimile: 0181-209 1210
*Manufactures a complete CAM/CAD system for
Design Technology.*

Videk
Unit 10, Bowman Industrial Estate
Westmorland Road
Kingsbury
London
NW9 9RW

Telephone: 0181-204 6690
Facsimile: 0181-204 7624
*Manufactures and supplies computer cables
and accessories.*

Watford Electronics Ltd
Jessa House
1 Finway, Dallow Road
Luton
LU1 1TR
Contact: David Perry, Corporate Sales Manager
Telephone: 01582 745555
Facsimile: 01582 488588
*Manufactures and supplies a range of hardware
and software for both IBM-compatible and
Acorn machines.*

FURNITURE AND STAGING

Balmforth Engineering Ltd
Finway
Dallow Road
Luton
Bedfordshire
LU1 1TE
Telephone: 01582 31171
Facsimile: 01582 454103
*Manufactures library shelving and furniture
systems.*

Blyde-Barton Furniture Ltd
Reepham Road
Norwich
NR6 5LE
Contact: Mr David Cole, Office Sales Manager
Telephone: 01603 789000
Facsimile: 01603 405476
Manufactures educational furniture for all ages.

British Thornton ESF Ltd
Greenholme Mills
Iron Row
Burley in Wharfedale
West Yorkshire
LS29 7DB
Telephone: 01943 862504
Facsimile: 01943 862706
Manufacturer of furniture for all ages.

FURNITURE AND STAGING

The Curriculum

Equipment suppliers and services

FURNITURE AND STAGING

Budget Direct Plc
Global House
38/40 High Street
West Wickham
Kent
BR4 0NE
Telephone: 0181-777 0099
Facsimile: 0181-777 9355
Supplier of educational furniture, including storage, tables, chairs, AV furniture, computer furniture, lockers and staging systems.

Community Playthings
Darvell
Robertsbridge
Sussex
TN32 5DR
Contact: Ron Finlay, Sales Manager
Telephone: 01580 880626
Facsimile: 01580 882250
Manufacturer of furniture and play equipment for 3-8-year-olds and the disabled.

Crossbrook Furniture Ltd
Unit 8, Marshgate Trading Estate
Marshgate Drive
Hertford
SG13 7AJ
Contact: Mike Dobson, Designer
Telephone: 01992 584547
Facsimile: 01992 501666
Manufactures and supplies school furniture for all ages suitable for classrooms, laboratories, libraries and resource areas, and adjustable-height furniture for the disabled. Free design service.

Dexion Ltd
Maylands Avenue
Hemel Hempstead
Hertfordshire
HP2 7DF
Telephone: 01442 242261
Facsimile: 01442 248202
Manufactures plastic bins and containers, and steel shelving.

Diamik Ltd
Export House
Donisthorpe Street
Leeds
LS10 1PL
Telephone: 0113 244 3422
Facsimile: 0113 244 0201
Manufacturer of educational furniture for all ages.

EME Scotland
Blackaddie Road
Sanquhar
Dumfriesshire
DG4 6DE
Telephone: 01659 50404
Facsimile: 01659 50107
Manufactures and supplies educational furniture for all ages.

Felix Design
Unit 15, Tiverton Way
Tiverton Business Park
Tiverton
Devon
EX16 6SR
Telephone: 01884 255420
Facsimile: 01884 242613
Manufactures a modular staging system which can be packed flat for storage.

Gopak Ltd
Range Road
Hythe
Kent
CT21 6HG
Telephone: 01303 265751
Facsimile: 01303 268282
Manufactures lightweight folding tables and stacking benches for all ages.

Gratnells Ltd
258 Church Road
London
E10 7JQ
Telephone: 0181-556 9021
Facsimile: 0181-556 3502
Manufacturers of tray storage frames and trolleys.

The Curriculum

Equipment suppliers and services

Hostess Furniture Ltd
Vulcan Road
Bilston
West Midlands
WV14 7JR
Contact: Mr J T Cave, Sales Manager
Telephone: 01902 493681
Facsimile: 01902 353185
Manufactures and supplies school furniture for all levels and age groups, including furniture for classroom, creche, dormitory, lecture theatre, laboratory and assembly hall.

Interform Contract Furniture
8 West Hampstead Mews
London
NW6 3BB
Contact: Mr John Rodgers, Sales Director
Telephone: 0171-328 2340
Facsimile: 0171-624 1777
Manufactures and supplies school furniture, including residential accommodation furniture, seating and table ranges, storage and technology areas, libraries, laboratories and tailor-made furniture.

Klick Technology
Claverton Road
Wythenshawe
Manchester
M23 9FT
Telephone: 0161-998 9726
Facsimile: 0161-946 0419
Manufactures and supplies furniture for science, design technology and food technology for primary and secondary schools.

Magiboards Ltd
Stafford Park 12
Telford
Shropshire
TF3 3BJ
Contact: Mr L Bell, Sales Executive
Telephone: 01952 292111
Facsimile: 01952 292280
Manufactures and supplies a wide range of visual aids specifically for the education market.

Papworth Furniture Division
Papworth Everard
Cambridge
CB3 8RG
Contact: Peter Dix, Divisional Manager
Telephone: 01480 830345
Facsimile: 01480 830516
Manufactures and supplies classroom furniture, and assists with the design, supply and installation of laboratory furniture for all ages.

Safemark Computer Security
Bentham House
30 Acomb Road
York
YO2 4EW
Contact: Neal K Williams, General Manager
Telephone: 01904 788494
Facsimile: 01904 788711
Manufacturers of security safes, cabinets, bolting-down plates and security cables to protect computers and peripherals. Also supplies anti-virus software and access control software to protect data.

SICO Europe Ltd
Henwood Industrial Estate
Ashford
Kent
TN24 8DH
Contact: J Brian Scott, UK Sales Manager
Telephone: 01233 643311
Facsimile: 01233 645143
Manufactures and supplies folding, wheeling space-management furniture: combined table and seating systems (dining), classroom tables, and stage and tiering systems.

Stage Systems
P.O. Box 50, Stage House
Prince William Road
Loughborough
Leicestershire
LE11 0GN
Telephone: 01509 611021
Facsimile: 01509 233146
Manufactures and supplies portable staging/tiering systems suitable for ages 5-18.

FURNITURE AND STAGING

105

The Curriculum

Equipment suppliers and services

FURNITURE AND STAGING

Steltube Ltd
Leigh Industrial Estate
The Causeway
Maldon
Essex
CM9 7LW
Telephone: 01621 857273
Facsimile: 01621 851829
Manufacturer of classroom furniture.

Tubular Furniture Ltd
Units F2/F3
Coedcae Industrial Estate
Pontyclun
Mid Glamorgan
CF7 9HG
Telephone: 01443 229326
Facsimile: 01443 222657
*Manufactures a range of educational furniture
  suitable for all ages.*

Vari-Tech
Units 2, 3 & 7, Premier Mill
Begonia Street
Darwen
Lancashire
BB3 2DP
Contact: Sales Department
Telephone: 01254 773524
Facsimile: 01254 706617
*Manufactures and supplies educational furniture
  for all ages, with particular emphasis on
  height-adjustable furniture for special needs.*

W B Bawn & Co Ltd
Northern Way
Bury St Edmunds
Suffolk
IP32 6NH
Telephone: 01284 752812
Facsimile: 01284 752844
*Manufactures, supplies and supports lockers
  and associated cloakroom equipment
  (Helmsman brand).*

Wilson & Garden Ltd
17-21 Newtown Street
Kilsyth
Glasgow
G65 0JX
Contact: R A Cooper, Sales Manager
Telephone: 01236 823291
Facsimile: 01236 825683
*Manufactures and delivers visual
  communication equipment including
  whiteboards, pinboards, display stands,
  chalkboards, revolving surface writing
  boards, noticeboards and nursery furniture.
  Also supplies tables, chairs, chalkboards and
  various toys for age 3+.*

The Curriculum

Businesses and organisations providing low-cost resources

Abbeydale Industrial Hamlet
Abbeydale Road South
Sheffield
S7 2QW
Contact: The Secretary
Telephone: 0114 2367731
*A number of cards, slides and publications, and
a free Teachers' Pack illustrating working life
in this 19th-century agricultural tool-making
community.*

ACTIONAID Education
Chataway House
Leach Road
Chard
Somerset
TA20 1FA
*Moderately priced resources designed to
increase knowledge and understanding of the
nature and causes of poverty and the
measures that can be taken to alleviate world
inequality.*

Advocates for Animals
10 Queensferry Street
Edinburgh
EH2 4PG
Telephone: 0131-225 6039
Facsimile: 0131-230 6377
*Pamphlets relating to the work of the
organisation which campaigns against all
forms of animal abuse.*

Aluminium Can Recycling Association Ltd
5 Gatsby Court
176 Holliday Street
Birmingham
B1 1TJ
Telephone: 0121-633 4656
*Provides free teaching resources suitable for
use in the National Curriculum, on aluminium
can recycling, and a fundraising idea for
school funds. A free-loan video for 8-16-year-
olds is available to schools.*

American Museum in Britain
The Education Centre
Claverton Manor
Bath
Avon
BA2 7BD
Contact: The Education Secretary
Telephone: 01225 463538
*Publications and wallcharts on American history
and culture.*

AMRIC
12 Whitehall
London
SW1A 2DA
Contact: Marjorie Johnson
*Free literature explaining the role of animals in
medicines research.*

Animal Health Trust
Balaton Lodge
Snailwell Road
Newmarket
Suffolk
CB8 7DW
Telephone: 01638 661111
Facsimile: 01638 665789
*Literature describing the work of the charity
which aims to play a leading role in the
diagnosis, treatment and cure of animal
medical problems.*

Aquarian Advisory Service
P.O. Box 67
Elland
West Yorkshire
HX5 0SJ
Contact: Dr David Ford
Free literature on keeping fish.

Association for Science Education
College Lane
Hatfield
Hertfordshire
AL10 9AA
Contact: ASE Booksales
Telephone: 01707 271216
Facsimile: 01707 266532
*A wide range of moderately priced resources
supporting teaching of science at all levels.*

The Curriculum

Businesses and organisations providing low-cost resources

Association of the British Pharmaceutical Industry
12 Whitehall
London
SW1A 2DY
Contact: Education Coordinator
A range of moderately priced resources describing the way in which the work of the pharmaceutical industry helps in the fight against disease.

Avoncroft Museum of Buildings
Stoke Heath
Bromsgrove
Worcestershire
B60 4JR
Contact: Dr Simon Penn, Curator
Telephone: 01527 831886
A range of moderately priced materials based around this collection of historic buildings.

Biomedical Research Education Trust
Suite 501, International House
223 Regent Street
London
W1R 8QD
Telephone: 0171-287 2595
Facsimile: 0171-287 2595
Free leaflets, videos and other curriculum materials describing the care given to animals which help with medical research.

BNFL Education Unit
P.O. Box 10
Wetherby
West Yorkshire
LS23 7EL
Hotline: 01937 840209
Moderately priced packs, wallcharts and computer software on electricity generation and use, energy, technology, the world of work and the environment.

Botanical Society of the British Isles
The Natural History Museum
Cromwell Road
London
SW7 5BD
Contact: Department of Botany

Short pamphlets on growing wild flowers and the content of some selected books for the study of wild plants are available.

BP Educational Service
P.O. Box 934
Poole
Dorset
BH17 7BR
Telephone: 01202 669940
A large range of free and moderately priced packs, wallcharts, videos and booklets on the oil industry, the environment, technology and energy.

British Agrochemicals Association Ltd
4 Lincoln Court
Lincoln Road
Peterborough
PE1 2RP
Contact: Public Relations Officer
Telephone: 01733 349225
Classroom resource packs on crop production for primary, secondary and post-16 use.

British Architectural Library
Royal Institute of British Architects
66 Portland Place
London
W1N 4AD
Three free leaflets on environmental architecture, available on receipt of an SAE.

British Heart Foundation
14 Fitzhardinge Street
London
W1H 4DH
Contact: Education Department
Telephone: 0171-935 0185
Free publications and free-loan videos providing information about heart disease and helping people to understand the importance of heart research.

British Hedgehog Preservation Society
Knowbury House
Knowbury
Ludlow
Shropshire
SY8 3LQ

LOW-COST RESOURCES

The Curriculum

Businesses and organisations providing low-cost resources

Telephone: 01584 890287

A catalogue of items is available connected with hedgehog preservation, including an Education Pack, Project Packs, various leaflets and items related to the care of hedgehogs.

British Interplanetary Society
27-29 South Lambeth Road
London
SW8 1SZ
Telephone: 0171-735 3160
Videos on international space programmes.

British Museum Education Service
Great Russell Street
London
WC1B 3DG
Telephone: 0171-323 8511/8854
Free teachers' packs on subjects related to displays in the Museum.

British Museum Press
46 Bloomsbury Street
London
WC1B 3QQ
Contact: Marketing Dept
Telephone: 0171-323 1234
Facsimile: 0171-436 7315
Publisher of books and postcards, many aimed at children of school age, related to displays and exhibitions in the Museum.

British Red Cross
9 Grosvenor Crescent
London
SW1X 7EJ
Contact: Information Service
Telephone: 0171-235 5454
Facsimile: 0171-245 6315
Pamphlets on the work of the Red Cross.

British Steel Education Service
P.O. Box 10
Wetherby
Yorkshire
LS23 7EL
Telephone: 01937 840243
Moderately priced packs, games, booklets and videos on the steel industry and steel products.

BT Education Service
P.O. Box 10
Wetherby
West Yorkshire
LS23 7EL
Telephone: 0800 622302
Booklets, wallcharts, packs, videos and computer software, some free, some low-cost, on the telecommunications industry, past, present and future.

BTA Publications
Thames View Business Centre
Thames View
Abingdon
Oxfordshire
OX14 3LJ
Telephone: 01235 553233
Facsimile: 01235 553356
A variety of sponsored educational and learning resource materials, including wallcharts, booklets, leaflets, the BTA Studycard series for KS2,3 & 4, and BTA Directions for GCSE coursework, GNVQs and KS4.

Butter Council
Lime Tree House
15 Lime Tree Walk
Sevenoaks
Kent
TN13 1YH
Telephone: 01732 460060
Facsimile: 01732 459403
A selection of free teacher project packs are available on request covering KS1, 2 & 3.

Butterick/Vogue Patterns
New Lane
Havant
Hampshire
PO9 2ND
Telephone: 01705 486221
Special educational discounts on a wide range of patterns, books, magazines and OHP transparencies.

LOW-COST RESOURCES

109

The Curriculum
Businesses and organisations providing low-cost resources

Canned Food Information Centre
154 Great Charles Street
Birmingham
B3 3HU
Telephone: 0800 243364
Facsimile: 0121-236 7220
Free wallchart, leaflet and worksheets on cans
and canned food, including the production of
cans, the canning process and recycling.

Cat Survival Trust
The Earth
The Mission Rainforest Foundation
The Centre
Codicote Road
Welwyn
Hertfordshire
AL6 9TU
Telephone: 01438 716873 or 716478 and ask
for extension 29 (Rainforest Foundation and
Cat Survival Trust), extension 30 (The Earth).
The Cat Survival Trust aims to ensure that all
species of wild cat are preserved, preferably
in their own habitat.
The Earth is involved in the preservation of
habitat for the benefit of all.
The Mission Rainforest Foundation saves
rainforest and is attempting to purchase
sufficient land in the Argentine to return
jaguar to their old hunting ground.

Chemical Industry Education Centre
Department of Chemistry
University of York
Heslington
York
YO1 5DD
Contact: Ms Miranda Mapletoft
Telephone: 01904 432523
Reasonably priced activity packs, booklets and
worksheets developed specifically for schools
relating to the science curriculum and
targeted at age groups between 5 and 18.

Christian Aid
P.O. Box 100
London
SE1 7RT
Contact: Schools and Youth Team
Telephone: 0171-620 4444
Packs, videos, slides, posters, wallcharts,

magazines and booklets, some free, most
moderately priced, are available related to
the areas of the world and issues with which
the charity works.

Commonwealth Institute
Kensington High Street
London
W8 6NQ
Contact: Resource Centre
Telephone: 0171-603 4535
Ext 292 for general enquiries about loans
Ext 210 for enquiries about the reference
collection
Facsimile: 0171-602 7374
Wallcharts, packs, slides and books are
available for loan from their extensive
resource collection, on the Commonwealth.

Concord Video and Film Council Ltd
201 Felixstowe Road
Ipswich
Suffolk IP3 9BJ
Telephone: 01473 715754/726012
Facsimile: 01473 274531
Films and videos, some free-loan, some for hire
and purchase.

Confederation of Passenger Transport UK
Sardinia House
52 Lincoln's Inn Fields
London
WC2A 3LZ
Contact: Public Affairs Department
Telephone: 0171-831 7546
Facsimile: 0171-831 0487
A number of free leaflets on the passenger
transport industry.

Copper Development Association
Orchard House
Mutton Lane
Potters Bar
Hertfordshire
EN6 3AP
Contact: Information Department
Telephone: 01707 650711
Facsimile: 01707 642769
Free posters and a booklet on the copper and
brass industry and its products and uses.

The Curriculum

Businesses and organisations providing low-cost resources

Corinium Museum
Park Street
Cirencester
Gloucestershire
GL7 2BX
Telephone: 01285 655611
Facsimile: 01285 643286
A number of reasonably priced replica Roman artefacts are available by mail order.

Council for British Archaeology
Bowes Morrell House
111 Walmgate
York
YO1 2UA
Contact: Don Henson, Education Officer
Telephone: 01904 671417
Facsimile: 01904 671384
Information service for teachers, with some occasional publications.

Council for Environmental Education
University of Reading
London Road
Reading
RG1 5AQ
An information service and reference library provides support for policy development and good practice, with information held in a variety of formats. Various information sheets, newsletters and briefings are also available.

Dover Roman Painted House
New Street
Dover
Kent
CT17 9AJ
Contact: Mr B J Philp
Telephone: 01304 203279
A number of publications by the Kent Archaeological Rescue Unit are available dealing with excavations on sites of all periods.

Education at Beaulieu
Montagu Ventures Ltd
John Montagu Building
Beaulieu
Hampshire
SO42 7ZN
Telephone: 01590 612345
Facsimile: 01590 612624
Books and packs about the history of motoring and aspects of medieval life are available at moderate prices.

Education Training and Development Centre
St Mary's Passage
Warwick Street
Ryde
Isle of Wight
PO33 2RG
Telephone: 01983 811020
Facsimile: 01983 811006
A large number of teaching materials related to work on the island are available, all at reasonable prices.

Embassy of Sweden
11 Montagu Place
London
W1H 2AL
Contact: Information Section
Free leaflets on Sweden's life, culture, economy, geography, history and environment.

Engineering Council
10 Maltravers Street
London
WC2R 3ER
Contact: Dr J K Williams, Senior Executive - General Education
Telephone: 0171-240 7891
Facsimile: 0171-240 7517
A free booklet on problem solving in primary schools, low-cost photocopiable textbooks, resources and kits are available.

English Heritage
P.O. Box 229
Northampton
NN6 9RY
Telephone: 01604 781163
Facsimile: 01604 781714
A wide range of teachers' guides and site handbooks linking use of the historic environment to most curriculum subjects at reasonable prices. Videos are available on free loan. A magazine, 'Heritage Learning', is circulated to all schools each term.

The Curriculum

Businesses and organisations providing low-cost resources

LOW-COST RESOURCES

Esso UK Information Service
P.O. Box 46
Hounslow
Middlesex
TW4 6NF
Facsimile: 0181-759 4730
*Free wallcharts, booklets, leaflets and videos
are available on the oil industry, science and
technology, energy and the environment.*

Eurotunnel Exhibition Centre
St Martin's Plain
Folkestone
Kent
CT19 4QD
Telephone: 01303 270111
*Moderately priced booklets, packs, videos and
posters relating to the building and operation
of the tunnel and to its surrounding
countryside.*

Ever-Ready Education Services
P.O. Box 480
London
SW9 9TH
*A free pack for primary schools on electricity
and battery power is available.*

Federal Trust
158 Buckingham Palace Road
London
SW1W 9TR
Telephone: 0171-259 9990
Facsimile: 0171-259 9505
*Produces teaching materials and organises
programmes related to its aim of providing
students with an opportunity to test their own
knowledge of the European Union and to
engage in debate about the European
dimension.*

Firework Makers Guild
1 Waterloo Way
Leicester
LE1 6LP
Contact: Mr M R Schuster
Telephone: 0116 256 6000
Annual safety leaflet and poster available free.

Fishbourne Roman Palace
Salthill Road
Fishbourne
West Sussex
PO19 3QR
Telephone: 01243 785859
Facsimile: 01243 539266
*A number of postcards, guides, slides, posters
and booklets, and a teachers' resource pack
(for KS2 & 3) are available at reasonable
prices, related to Roman life in the Chichester
area.*

Food & Farming Information Service
The National Agricultural Centre
Stoneleigh Park
Warwickshire
CV8 2LZ
Contact: Information Officer
Telephone: 01203 535707
Facsimile: 01203 696388
*Produces free resource packs for teachers on
all aspects of food and farming, and advises
teachers wishing to visit a farm.*

Ford Education Service
Dept DSA
P.O. Box 1750
Billericay
Essex
CM12 9DF
Telephone: 01277 634176
*Free leaflets on aspects of car design,
manufacture and history, safety, environment
and recycling are available. Also videos
available on loan.*

Forestry Commission
231 Corstorphine Road
Edinburgh
EH12 7AT
Contact: Public Information (Schools)
Telephone: 0131-334 0303 ext 2322
*A number of free booklets and wallcharts on
aspects of forest life and forestry are
available.*

The Curriculum

Businesses and organisations providing low-cost resources

Forestry Trust
The Old Estate Office
Englefield Road
Theale
Reading
Berkshire
RG7 5DZ
Telephone: 01734 323523
Facsimile: 01734 304033
*An educational charity which aims to show
people what productive forestry is and how it
is compatible with conservation. A number of
reasonably priced educational packs and a
guide to the country's accessible woodlands
are available.*

Fountains Abbey
Ripon
North Yorkshire
HG4 3DY
Contact: Education Officer
Telephone: 01765 608888
*A National Trust property providing educational
literature for teachers and children.*

Friends of the Earth
26-28 Underwood Street
London
N1 7JQ
Contact: Information Department
Telephone: 0171-490 1555
Facsimile: 0171-566 1655
*A range of reasonably priced photocopiable
teaching resources, posters and leaflets
looking at key environmental issues are
available.*

Geographical Association
343 Fulwood Road
Sheffield
S10 3BP
Telephone: 0114 267 0666
Facsimile: 0114 267 0688
*Reasonably priced books and packs on aspects
of Geography, and teaching it, are available.*

Guide Dogs for the Blind Association
Hillfields
Burghfield
Reading
RG7 3YG
Telephone: 01734 835555
Facsimile: 01734 835211
*A range of free leaflets and educational posters
are available on the work of training guide
dogs, videos are available for loan and visits
by guide dog owners can be arranged.*

Hearing Dogs for the Deaf
Training Centre
London Road
Lewknor
Oxfordshire
OX9 5RY
Telephone: 01844 353898
Facsimile: 01844 353099
*A free information pack is available on the work
of the charity.*

**Hereford Cider Museum & King Offa
Distillery**
21 Ryelands Street
Hereford
HR4 0LW
Telephone: 01432 354207
*Postcards, Teachers' Guidelines, School Loan
Packs and slides are available at moderate
cost on the history of cider making.*

Heritage Projects (Canterbury) Ltd
The Canterbury Tales
23 Hawks Lane
Canterbury
Kent
CT1 2NU
Contact: The Education Executive
Telephone: 01227 454888
Facsimile: 01227 765584
*A moderately priced pack on medieval
Canterbury is available.*

Historic Royal Palaces
Hampton Court Palace
East Molesey
Surrey KT8 9AU
Contact: Education Service
Telephone: 0181-781 9750
*Videos, posters, books and packs based on the
history of Hampton Court, the Banqueting
House, Kew Palace, The Tower of London
and Kensington Palace are available at
reasonable prices.*

The Curriculum

Businesses and organisations providing low-cost resources

Home Office
Room 133
Queen Anne's Gate
London
SW1H 9AT
Contact: Fire Safety Publicity Material, Public
  Relations Branch
Telephone: 0171-273 4145
*Fire safety posters and leaflets are available
  free to publicly-funded organisations.*

Ilford Ltd
14-22 Tottenham Street
London
W1P 0AH
Telephone: 0171-636 7890
*A Manual of Classroom Photography and
  GCSE leaflets are available at reasonable
  prices.*

Imperial War Museum
Duxford Airfield
Cambridgeshire
CB2 4QR
Contact: Mail Order Section
Telephone numbers:
  Resource orders: 01223 835000 ext 245
  (Facsimile: 01223 837267)
  Visits: Duxford Airfield 01223 835000 ext 252
  Lambeth Road 0171-416 5313
  Cabinet War Rooms 0171-930 6961
  HMS Belfast 0171-407 6434
*A comprehensive range of poster facsimile
  document packs, cassette tapes, videos and
  books are available on both World Wars, all
  reasonably priced.*

Inland Waterways Association
114 Regents Park Road
London
NW1 8UQ
*Books, maps and guides are available by mail
  order on the history and construction of
  canals in Britain.*

Institute of Petroleum
61 New Cavendish Street
London
W1M 8AR
Contact: Information Services
*Case studies for GCSE Geography and
  Environmental Studies are available, together
  with information on other materials relevant to
  the oil and gas industry.*

Intermediate Technology
Myson House
Railway Terrace
Rugby
CV21 3HT
Contact: Education Office
Telephone: 01788 560631
*A number of moderately priced packs, books
  and slide sets describe a variety of cultures
  and contexts within which needs can be
  identified as the starting point for Design and
  Technology work.*

**International Centre for Conservation
  Education**
Greenfield House
Guiting Power
Cheltenham
Gloucestershire
GL54 5TZ
Contact: Dept GM
Telephone: 01451 850777
*Reasonably priced environmental education
  books, games, videos, packs, CD-Roms and
  slide sets are available.*

Ironbridge Gorge Museum
Ironbridge
Telford
Shropshire
TF8 7AW
Contact: Education Department
Telephone: 01952 433522
*A wide range of moderately priced packs,
  booklets and wallcharts are available from
  this 'birth-place of the Industrial Revolution'.*

**Jodrell Bank Science Centre, Planetarium
  and Arboretum**
Macclesfield
Cheshire
SK11 9DL
Telephone: 01477 571339
Facsimile: 01477 571695
*A wide range of mail order items about space,
  exploration and the Jodrell Bank Radio
  Telescopes are available.*

The Curriculum
Businesses and organisations providing low-cost resources

Kew Bridge Steam Museum
Green Dragon Lane
Brentford
Middlesex
TW8 0EN
Telephone: 0181-568 4757
Beam engine sectional drawings, Cornish pump engine details and information about Victorian steam-driven machinery are available at reasonable cost.

Kotex Product Advisory Service
Kimberly-Clark Ltd
Dept GM
Larkfield
Aylesford
Kent
ME20 7PS
Telephone: 01622 616282
A free pack is available to help teach girls and their parents about puberty and menstruation.

Landlife
The Old Police Station
Lark Lane
Liverpool
L17 8UU
Contact: Gillian Watson
Telephone: 0151-728 7011
A range of booklets, packs, plants and wildflower seeds are available.

Learning Through Landscapes Trust
Third Floor, Southside Offices
The Law Courts
Winchester
Hampshire
SO23 9DL
Contact: Jennie Day, Information and Publicity Officer
Telephone: 01962 846258
Facsimile: 01962 869099
A number of good-value booklets, videos and survey packs describing how to develop the school grounds are available. Also funding and technical advice can be provided.

London Transport Museum
Covent Garden
London
WC2E 7BB
Contact: School Visits Service
Telephone: 0171-379 6344

Facsimile: 0171-836 4118
A number of moderately priced packs and booklets describe the history of transport in London.

London Underground Ltd
55 Broadway
London
SW1H 0BD
Contact: Public Affairs Section
Telephone: 0171-918 3209
Facsimile: 0171-918 3447
Curriculum packs and a free-loan safety video and accompanying booklet are available providing activities based around travelling on London's Underground.

Malaysian High Commission
45 Belgrave Square
London
SW1X 8QT
Contact: Information Division
Telephone: 0171-235 8033
Facsimile: 0171-235 5161
Free leaflets and booklets on Malaysia are available, preferably when the request is accompanied by an SAE.

Marine Society
202 Lambeth Road
London
SE1 7JW
Contact: Head of Education
Telephone: 0171-261 9535
Facsimile: 0171-401 2537
A number of reasonably priced wallcharts and packs about the sea services, including both the Merchant and Royal Navy, are available. Sea Lines is a unique scheme offering schools an opportunity to forge a link with a serving seafarer.

Mark Hall Cycle Museum
Muskham Road
Harlow
Essex
CM20 2LF
Telephone and facsimile: 01279 439680
A free historical factsheet on bicycles is available.

The Curriculum
Businesses and organisations providing low-cost resources

MCS Sales Ltd
9 Gloucester Road
Ross-on-Wye
Herefordshire
HR9 5BU
Telephone: 01989 566017
A number of free and low-cost items about marine and seashore conservation are available, including study packs, factsheets and project information.

Meat and Livestock Commission
P.O. Box 44
Winterhill House
Snowdon Drive
Milton Keynes
MK6 1AX
Contact: Education Manager
Telephone: 01908 677577
A wide range of free classroom resources which support Food Technology and Business Studies, software (Acorn), a video package and printed materials are available using fast food and product development themes.

The Met. Office
London Road
Bracknell
Berkshire
RG12 2SZ
Contact: Education Service Room 124
Telephone: 01344 854802
Facsimile: 01344 856151
Information, mostly free, about meteorology. A catalogue must be obtained first.

Museum of Antiquities
The University
Newcastle upon Tyne
NE1 7RU
Contact: Lindsay Allason-Jones
Telephone: 0191-222 7846
Facsimile: 0191-261 1182
Low-cost booklet about Mithraic temples on Hadrian's Wall.

Museum of British Road Transport
St Agnes Lane
Hales Street
Coventry
CV1 1PN

Contact: Steven Bagley, Information Officer
Telephone: 01203 832425
A number of reasonably priced booklets and two resource packs about the history of road transport.

Museum of Mankind Education Service
Burlington Gardens
London
W1X 2EX
Telephone: 0171-323 8043
Free resource packs and leaflets on the subjects of the Museum's current (and some past) exhibitions.

Mushroom Bureau
27 King Edward Walk
London
SE1 7PR
Education Pack (70p stamp) on the use of cultivated mushrooms in cooking and a free-loan video describing their growing and culinary uses.

National Association for Environmental Education
University of Wolverhampton
Walsall Campus
Gorway
Walsall
West Midlands
WS1 3BD
Contact: The General Secretary
Telephone: 01922 31200
A number of reasonably priced practical guides to environmental activities at school. Also produces the termly journal 'Environmental Education'.

National Canine Defence League
17 Wakley Street
London
EC1V 7LT
Contact: Head of Public Relations
Telephone: 0171-837 0006
Facsimile: 0171-833 2830
Leaflets and posters related to the care of dogs and the work of the National Canine Defence League

LOW-COST RESOURCES

The Curriculum

Businesses and organisations providing low-cost resources

National Cavity Insulation Association Ltd
P.O. Box 12
Haslemere
Surrey
GU27 3AH
Telephone: 01428 654011
Facsimile: 01428 651401
Free leaflets about cavity insulation, loft insulation, draught proofing and external wall insulation.

National Dairy Council
5-7 John Princes Street
London
W1M 0AP
Contact: Education Department
Telephone: 0171-499 7822
Facsimile: 0171-408 1353
A wide range of free booklets and leaflets, and moderately priced wallcharts and teaching packs on all aspects of the dairy industry.

National Maritime Museum
Greenwich
London
SE10 9NF
Contact: Education Services Section
Telephone: 0181-312 6608 (for bookings only), 0181-312 6700 (bookshop)
Teachers' resource packs, free fact files, wallcharts, linked to the National Curriculum.

National Office of Animal Health Ltd
3 Crossfield Chambers
Gladbeck Way
Enfield
Middlesex
EN2 7HF
Contact: Mrs Alison Glennon, Communications & Marketing Executive
Telephone: 0181-367 3131
Free leaflets on aspects of pet and farm animal health are available, particularly relating to animal medicines.

National Society for Clean Air
136 North Street
Brighton
Sussex
BN1 1RG
Telephone: 01273 326313

A number of free and low-cost leaflets and packs on aspects of air pollution and noise.

National Trust
36 Queen Anne's Gate
London
SW1H 9AS
Contact: Education Office
Free education pack available containing a list of publications.

National Trust, Mercia Region
Attingham Park
Shrewsbury
SY4 4TP
Contact: Public Affairs Manager
Telephone: 01743 709343
Moderately priced teachers' guides to life in Elizabethan manor houses (Little Moreton Hall, Speke Hall and Moseley Old Hall), and a range of environmental education resources.

Nestlé UK Ltd
York
YO1 1XY
Contact: Consumer Services (B111)
Various information sheets describing Nestlé products are available free (for small quantities), including such subjects as coffee, chocolate, pickle and packaging.

Newspaper Society
Bloomsbury Square
74-77 Great Russell Street
London WC1B 3DA
Contact: Newspapers in Education Dept
Telephone: 0171-636 7014
Facsimile: 0171-631 5119
A number of reasonably priced packs providing activities which emphasise the multi-disciplinary value of newspapers in the classroom.

Northern Ireland Tourist Board
59 North Street
Belfast
BT1 1NB
Telephone: 01232 246609
Free tourism leaflets on Northern Ireland are available.

The Curriculum
Businesses and organisations providing low-cost resources

Northern Lighthouse Board
84 George Street
Edinburgh
EH2 3DA
Telephone: 0131-226 7051 extension 203/ 205
*A free pack (only available where a large SAE
is sent) on the work of the Board is available.*

Original Wallcharts
Wyke Lodge
London Road
Ryarsh
West Malling
Kent   ME19 5AS
Telephone: 01732 872626
*A number of reasonably priced wallcharts on a
range of subjects are available.*

Pedigree Petfoods Education Service
4 Bedford Square
London WC1B 3RA
*There is a wide range of packs, wallcharts and
other publications written specifically for
schools and related to pet care and working
animals. All are either free or very reasonably
priced.*

Pictorial Charts Educational Trust
27 Kirchen Road
London W13 0UD
Telephone: 0181-567 9206
*A supplier of photopacks, friezes and wallcharts
on a wide range of curriculum subjects for all
Key Stages, all very competitively priced.*

Port of London Authority
Devon House
58-60 St Katharine's Way
London E1 9LB
Contact: Public Relations Office
Telephone: 0171-265 2656
Facsimile: 0171-265 2699
*Free-loan video and an education pack for KS2
& 3 are available.*

Post Office Education Service
P.O. Box 145
Sittingbourne
Kent ME10 1NH
*A wide range of moderately priced packs are
available.*

Post Office Film and Video Library
P.O. Box 145
Sittingbourne
Kent
ME10 1NH
Telephone: 01795 426465
Facsimile: 01795 474871
*A supplier of free-loan films and videos on
stamp collecting, the story behind designs,
the work of the Post Office and the effect of
World War II on domestic life in Britain, many
supported by a range of educational
materials.*

Relay Europe
Enterprise Centre
112 Malling Street
Lewes
Sussex
BN7 2RJ
Telephone: 01273 488666
Facsimile: 01273 488448
*Free-loan videos on the EU, aimed at adults,
but many suitable for use in school. Also
manages a mobile exhibition vehicle for the
European Commission and has a range of
EU display materials for hire.*

Royal Anthropological Institute
50 Fitzroy Street
London
W1P 5HS
Telephone: 0171-387 0455
*A comprehensive Teachers' Resource Guide,
reasonably priced, is available.*

Royal Life Saving Society UK
Mountbatten House
Studley
Warwickshire
B80 7NN
Telephone: for enquiries about training or
membership 01527 853943.
For publications write to: RLSS UK Enterprises
Ltd at the address above
*A wide range of aids for teaching life saving are
available by mail order.*

The Curriculum

Businesses and organisations providing low-cost resources

Royal Meteorological Society
104 Oxford Road
Reading
Berkshire
RG1 7LJ
Telephone: 01734 568500
Facsimile: 01734 568571
A variety of reasonably priced aids to teaching meteorology are available by mail order.

Royal National Institute for the Blind (RNIB)
224 Great Portland Street
London
W1N 6AA
Telephone: 0171-388 1266
Facsimile: 0171-388 2034
A variety of teaching packs are available on the work of the RNIB, whose work provides over 60 different services to the blind and partially sighted.

Royal National Lifeboat Institution
West Quay Road
Poole
Dorset
BH15 1HZ
Contact: Youth Promotion Co-ordinator
Telephone: 01202 671133
Facsimile: 01202 660306
General Resource Pack and Primary Resource Packs (KS1 & KS2) on the work of the RNLI available at low cost. Films and videos available for loan or purchase.

Royal Norwegian Embassy
25 Belgrave Square
London
SW1X 8QD
Contact: Press & Information Office
Telephone: 0171-235 7151
A free information pack is available.

Royal Society for the Protection of Birds
The Lodge
Sandy
Bedfordshire
SG19 2DL
Contact: Head of Education
Telephone: 01767 680551
A comprehensive range of Project Guides, relevant to the National Curriculum and all very reasonably priced, are available.

Royal Society of Chemistry
The Royal Society of Chemistry
Burlington House
Piccadilly
London
W1V 0BN
Contact: Dr J A Johnston, Assistant Education Officer, Schools and Colleges
Telephone: 0171-437 8656
Facsimile: 0171-287 9825
A range of reasonably priced handbooks and reference books on aspects of chemistry in school is available.

RTZ Ltd
6 St James's Square
London
SW1Y 4LD
Contact: Miss S Marley
A range of teaching resources on the mining industry are available. Most are free with additional copies available at low cost.

Rural History Centre
Box 229
Whiteknights
University of Reading
Reading
RG6 6AG
Contact: Education Officer
Telephone: 01734 318669
A range of competitively priced teaching packs on the history of agriculture and rural life are available.

SCET (Scottish Council for Educational Technology)
74 Victoria Crescent Road
Glasgow
G12 9JN
Telephone: 0141-337 5000
Videos, publications, software and CD-Roms are available.

The Curriculum

Businesses and organisations providing low-cost resources

Scottish Society for the Prevention of Cruelty to Animals
Education Department
19 Melville Street
Edinburgh
EH3 7PL
Contact: The Secretary
Telephone: 0131-225 6418
Facsimile: 0131-220 4675
Free packs for Scottish schools on animal welfare if booking a visit from an SSPCA Education Officer, and a video loan service.

Scottish Tourist Board
23 Ravelston Terrace
Edinburgh
EH4 3EU
Telephone: 0131-332 2433
24-hour information line: 0891 666465. Calls charged at 39p per min cheap rate and 49p per min at all other times
Facsimile: 0131-315 4545
Free information for tourists to Scotland.

Sea Fish Industry Authority
18 Logie Mill
Logie Green Road
Edinburgh
EH7 4HG
A number of free packs and a video on the industry and the dietary value of fish.

Shell Education Service
P.O. Box 46
Newbury
Berkshire
RG14 2YX
Telephone: 01635 31721
Facsimile: 01635 529371
A free catalogue is available detailing resources on a wide variety of subjects which have been designed to support the National Curriculum. Many are free of charge.

Sopexa (UK) Ltd
Nuffield House
41-46 Piccadilly
London
W1V 9AJ

Contact: Promotions Department
Telephone: 0171-439 8371
Facsimile: 0171-434 9295
A range of charged promotional posters, leaflets and display aids for French wines, cheeses, and fruit and vegetables.

Tea Council
Sir John Lyon House
5 High Timber Street
London
EC4V 3NJ
Free information pack, Primary Schools Tea Resource Pack and KS3 Tea Resource Pack which covers Geography, History, Maths and Technology.

Thames Water Customer Centre
P.O. Box 436
Swindon
SN38 1TL
Telephone: 01645 200800
Available are posters, booklets and a computer game with water as the focus, relating to Geography and Science, for schools in the Thames Water area.

Tidy Britain Group
The Pier
Wigan
WN3 4EX
Contact: Anne Beazley, Education Manager
Telephone: 01942 824620 (enquiries only)
Facsimile: 01942 824778
A wide range of teaching materials, all reasonably priced, are available, and some free factsheets and posters on request.

Tree Council
51 Catherine Place
London
SW1E 6DY
Telephone: 0171-828 9928
Facsimile: 0171-828 9060
A number of resources are available related to trees and tree planting.

The Curriculum

Businesses and organisations providing low-cost resources

Trinity House Lighthouse Service
Trinity House
Tower Hill
London
EC3N 4DH
Contact: Records & Publications
A free information pack is available only on receipt of a large stamped (43p) addressed envelope.

Tutankhamun The Exhibition
25 High West Street
Dorchester
Dorset
DT1 1UW
Telephone: 01305 269571 (exhibition) and 01305 269741 (administration)
Facsimile: 01305 268885
A number of reasonably priced items are available from the museum shop.

Wildfowl and Wetlands Trust
Slimbridge
Gloucestershire
GL2 7BT
Contact: Director of Education & Public Affairs
Telephone: 01453 890333
A range of teaching resources are available, all very reasonably priced.

Wildlife Watch
The Wildlife Trusts
The Green
Witham Park
Waterside South
Lincoln
LN5 7JR
A variety of moderately priced project packs and other resources are available by mail order, together with a membership service for schools.

Wood Green Animal Shelters
Wood Green College
London Road
Godmanchester
Huntingdon
PE18 8LJ
Telephone (and facsimile): 01480 831177
A moderately priced book intended for GCSE on pet ownership is available. Project queries will be answered if an SAE (A4 envelope) is enclosed.

Worshipful Company of Goldsmiths
Goldsmiths Hall
Foster Lane
London
EC2V 6BN
Contact: The Librarian
Telephone: 0171-606 7010
Facsimile: 0171-606 1511
Publications and free-loan videos about precious metals and hallmarking are available.

WWF UK (World Wide Fund for Nature)
Weyside Park
Godalming
Surrey
GU7 1XR
Contact: Education Department
Telephone: 01483 426444
Facsimile: 01483 426409
A wide range of reasonably priced resources related to the National Curriculum and specifically written for schools.

LOW-COST RESOURCES

The Curriculum

School tour operators

Club Europe Holidays Ltd
Fairway House
53 Dartmouth Road
London
SE23 3HN
Contact: John Bristow
Telephone: 0181-699 7788
Facsimile: 0181-699 7770
*Offers tours throughout Europe for skiing,
Language, Music, Geography, Drama,
History, Technology and sports breaks. Also
operates in the USA, Canada and Israel. Age
range: 9 upwards.*

Edwin Doran Travel Ltd
9 York Street
Twickenham
Middlesex
TW1 3JZ
Telephone: 0181-744 1212
Facsimile: 0181-744 1169
*Provides school music and sports tours to every
continent of the world.*

Equity The Travel People
Dukes Lane House
47 Middle Street
Brighton
Sussex
BN1 1AL
Telephone: 01273 203202
Facsimile: 01273 203212
*Offers ski trips to Italy, Austria and France, and
educational courses on Technology, French
& Italian cookery, Music, Art, and the French
and German languages. All ages catered for.*

Euro Academy Ltd
77a George Street
Croydon
Surrey
CR0 1LD
Telephone: 0181-686 2363
Facsimile: 0181-681 8850
*Offers language study tours and courses in
France, Germany, Spain, Italy, Austria and
Portugal.*

European Study Tours
15 Pratt Mews
London
NW1 0AD
Telephone: 0171-388 9101
Facsimile: 0171-383 0029
*Offers educational tours for schools (students
aged 16-18), and specialist tours for Art,
Business and Language.*

Gower Tours Ltd
2 High Street
Studley
Warwickshire
B80 7HJ
Telephone: 01527 854822
Facsimile: 01527 857236
*Specialises in music performance tours to
Europe and the USA and ski tours to
Switzerland.*

Home & Overseas Educational Travel
4 Gypsy Hill
London
SE19 1NL
Telephone: 0181-761 4255
Facsimile: 0181-761 0646
*Educational tours of 3, 4 and 5 days to 25
centres in the UK. Also organises tours to
France, Belgium and Holland. Ages catered
for: 10-17.*

L H S School & Youth Travel
Sayto Studios
43 East Street
Bromley
Kent
BR1 1QQ
Contact: Tim Pretty
Telephone: 0181-313 3525
Facsimile: 0181-313 3622
*Educational tours for junior, middle and
secondary schools in the UK, to Europe and
beyond. Sports tours also offered (soccer,
rugby and hockey) with guaranteed fixtures.*

The Curriculum

School tour operators

N S T Ltd
Chiltern House
181 Bristol Avenue
Blackpool
Lancashire
FY2 0FA
Telephone: 01253 352525
Facsimile: 01253 356955
Offers a wide range of school tours within the UK and to the Continent backed up by a range of National Curriculum-linked study material.

Rank STS
Castle Mill
Lower Kings Road
Berkhamsted
Hertfordshire
HP4 2AP
Telephone: 01442 876641
Facsimile: 01442 877704
Offers tours in the UK (for ages 8-14), to Europe and worldwide (for ages 10-18) and ski trips (for ages 10-18).

Rayburn Tours Ltd
Rayburn House
Parcel Terrace
Derby
DE1 1LZ
Telephone: 01332 347828
Facsimile: 01332 371298
Offers educational, cultural, Language and History tours to Europe (particularly France, Spain and Germany) with support material. Specialises in music tours and concert arrangements to Europe, the USA, Canada and Russia.

School Journey Association
48 Cavendish Road
London
SW12 0DG
Telephone: 0181-673 4849/675 6636
Facsimile: 0181-673 4849
Tours in the UK and Europe for groups up to the age of 18 years.

Ski Partners
Friary House
Colston Street
Bristol
BS1 5AP
Telephone: 0117 925 3545
Facsimile: 0117 929 3697
Offers ski trips to Austria, France, Italy and Canada.

Top Class Travel
6 Laird Street
Coatbridge
Lanarkshire
ML5 3LJ
Telephone: 01236 433433
Facsimile: 01236 426442
Offers tours by coach to European and UK destinations for primary and secondary school groups.

Travelbound
Olivier House
18 Marine Parade
Brighton
Sussex
BN2 1TL
Telephone: 01273 677777
Facsimile: 01273 600999
Group travel for students from age 11/12 years to Europe, the USA, China, Israel and Russia.

Wyvern Schooltours Ltd
28 Westbourne Gardens
Trowbridge
Wiltshire
BA14 9AW
Telephone: 01225 766346
Facsimile: 01225 777936
Educational visits by coach to western Europe, tailor-made to suit each leader.

SCHOOL TOUR OPERATORS

The Curriculum

Outdoor provision

UK-WIDE & ABROAD

Alpback Mountaineering
61 Mossmill Park
Mosstodloch
Fochabers
Moray
IV32 7JX
Contact: Ray Treadwell
Telephone: 01343 820829
Facsimile: 01343 820829
Provides mountaineering instruction throughout the UK.

CCI/UK Venue-Finding
P.O. Box 169
Coventry
CV1 4PW
Contact: Mr L Belcham
Telephone: 01203 559099
Facsimile: 01203 559099
Offers a free service to find a venue for whatever purpose for a group of any size. Apply by phone, fax or post providing numbers, age, catering requirements, programme, general location and dates. Within 48 hours of receiving the information you will be phoned with a list of available venues. The booking is then up to you.

Chris Chrystal
Farr Cottage
Corpach
Fort William
Inverness-shire PH33 7LR
Telephone: 01397 772315
Available for instruction in mountaineering, rock climbing, abseiling and skiing (Nordic).

Dave Monteith
Gordonstoun School
Elgin
Morayshire IV30 2RF
Telephone: 01343 835470
Available for instruction in mountaineering in the British Isles for groups of up to 10 in number aged over 14, and for rock climbing in small groups for students aged over 16. Only available in the school holidays.

Discover Ltd
Timbers
Oxted Road
Godstone
Surrey
RH9 8AD
Telephone: 01883 744392
Facsimile: 01883 744913
A specialist company which arranges customised fieldwork trips in Geography/Geology and Biology, and expeditions in France and Morocco.

Endeavour (Scotland)
Ancaster Business Centre
Cross Street
Callander
FK17 8EA
Telephone: 01877 5293
Facsimile: 01877 331666
Personal development programmes using experiential learning methods.

Footprint Press Ltd
19 Moseley Street
Ripley
Derbyshire
DE5 3DA
Contact: John Merrill
Telephone: 01629 812143
Facsimile: 01629 812143
Publisher of local walk and cycle guidebooks to national parks and other scenic areas.

International Adventure
9 Teasdale Close
Royston
Hertfordshire
SG8 5TD
Telephone: 01763 242867
Facsimile: 01736 242586
Organises self-drive activity holidays in Sweden (canoe camping and timber rafting) and France (canoe camping) for students aged over 11 years.

The Curriculum

Outdoor provision

Pennine Outdoor Pursuits
Wharfedale House
Springfield Close
Midway
Derbyshire
DE11 0DB
Telephone: 01283 216507
Facsimile: 01283 214436
*Provides instructors for activities in any region
from half-day tasters to full-day skills learning
courses. They may be used by both school
students of any age or adults wishing to
improve their skill level or training for a
qualification. Activities include caving and
potholing, rock climbing, abseiling, rafting,
scrambling, map and compass, mountain
navigation, mountain expeditions, mountain
biking, night abseiling, orienteering, guided
walks, sailing, canoeing, paragliding, pony
trekking and residential programmes.*

PGL Adventure
Alton Court
Penyard Lane
Ross-on-Wye
Herefordshire
HR9 5NR
Telephone: 01989 764211
Facsimile: 01989 765451
*Runs 13 activity centres in the UK and 12
abroad. The courses provided in the UK are
mainly multi-activity tasters, with watersports
in Spain and France.*

Scottish Centres
Loaningdale House
Carwood Road
Biggar
Lanarkshire
ML12 6LX
Telephone: 01899 21115
Facsimile: 01889 20644
*Five residential outdoor education centres are
operated in Scotland catering for groups of
10-250 people and with a minimum age of 8
years. A range of environmental and activities
programmes are offered.*

Scottish Youth Hostels Association
7 Glebe Crescent
Stirling
Central
FK8 2JA
Telephone: 01786 451181
Facsimile: 01786 450198
*Over 80 youth hostels throughout Scotland
providing good-value, comfortable, friendly
accommodation. Information pack available.*

Young Explorers' Trust
at The Royal Geographical Society
1 Kensington Gore
London
SW7 2AR
Telephone: 01623 861027
Facsimile: 01623 861027
*Seeks to encourage young people (aged 14-20)
to take part in expeditions. YET offers an
advice service and operates an
approval/grant aid scheme for youth
expeditions. It does not organise expeditions
itself.*

**Youth Hostels Association (England and
Wales)**
8 St Stephen's Hill
St Albans
Hertfordshire
AL1 2DY
Contact: Natalie Husak, Marketing Assistant
Telephone: 01727 845047
Facsimile: 01727 844126
*Provides budget accommodation for those of
limited means.*

AVON

Charter Centre
Charter House
Blagdon
Bristol
BS18 6XR
Telephone: 01761 462267
Facsimile: 01761 462267
*Activities including environmental education,
caving, climbing, orienteering and problem
solving.*

The Curriculum

Outdoor provision

Mendip Outdoor Pursuits
Laurel Farm House
Summer Lane
Banwell, Weston-Super-Mare
Avon
BS24 6LP
Telephone: 01934 820518
Facsimile: 01934 820518
A residential centre offering caving, climbing, abseiling, canoeing, surf skiing, sailing, windsurfing, archery, orienteering, hill walking, surfing and group initiative exercises.

Mendip Riding Centre/Avon Ski Centre
Lyncombe Lodge
Churchill
Avon
BS19 5PQ
Telephone: 01934 852335
Facsimile: 01934 853314
Residential accommodation or day/half-day visit. Courses offered include horse riding, skiing (dry), archery, pistol shooting, swimming and quad biking.

BERKSHIRE

Adventure Dolphin
Dolphin House
Whitchurch Road
Pangbourne, Reading
Berkshire
RG8 7DA
Telephone: 01734 843162
Facsimile: 01734 841055
Non-residential activity courses for schools and colleges in canoeing, orienteering and climbing, and specific PE courses designed to meet the needs of the National Curriculum, outdoor and adventurous activities.

Challenge of Excellence
Tudor Cottage
Buckle Lane
Moss End, Warfield
Berkshire
RG12 5SB
Telephone: 01344 483740
Facsimile: 01344 483906
An education project integrating adventure and team building with the curriculum, run in conjunction with Project America Inc.

Eton Dorney Centre, The
Lake End Road
Dorney
Windsor
Berkshire
SL4 6QS
Telephone: 01628 662823
Facsimile: 01628 662583
Residential youth centre accommodating groups of up to 34 full-board, with one acre of land for outdoor activities. Suitable for those wishing to organise their own activities.

Leckhampstead Countryside Centre
Education Department
60 North Brook St
Newbury
Berkshire
RG13 1AH
Telephone: 01635 43115 Education Dept
A self-catering residential centre for up to 20 people, situated in the Berkshire Ridgeway Country.

Ufton Court Residential Centre
Green Lane
Ufton Nervet
Reading
Berkshire
RG7 4HD
Telephone: 01734 832099
Residential accommodation for up to 48 and 4 staff. Activities provided include orienteering, adventurous journeys, archery and environmental studies.

The Curriculum

Outdoor provision

BUCKINGHAMSHIRE

Caldecotte Project
George Amey Centre
366 Simpson
Milton Keynes
Buckinghamshire
MK6 3AG
Telephone: 01908 232042
Facsimile: 01908 232042
Courses provided in sailing, windsurfing, canoeing, rock climbing, orienteering, problem-solving activities and team building.

Woodrow High House
Cherry Lane
Woodrow
Amersham
Buckinghamshire
HP7 0QG
Telephone: 01494 433531
Facsimile: 01494 431391
Residential accommodation for up to 55 people. Suitable as a centre for environmental studies in the 24 acres of grounds.

CAMBRIDGESHIRE

Burwell House Residential Centre
North Street
Burwell
Cambridgeshire
CB5 0BA
Telephone: 01638 741256
Facsimile: 01638 741256
Residential accommodation for up to 55. Courses offered include environmental studies, geography, history and biology. Facilities include a TV studio for technical and communication skills training. Situated close to the Fens.

CAC Watersports
Grafham Water
Perry
Huntingdon
Cambridgeshire
PE18 0BU
Telephone: 01480 812288
Instruction in watersports.

CENTRAL SCOTLAND

Abernethy Trust
Ardeonaig Outdoor Centre
By Killin
Perthshire
FK21 8SY
Telephone: 01567 820523
Facsimile: 01567 820523
Residential accommodation and courses in outdoor education provided.

Scottish Youth Hostels Association
7 Glebe Crescent
Stirling
Central
FK8 2JA
Contact: Alan Mitchell, Groups Manager
Telephone: 01786 451181
Facsimile: 01786 450198
Provides good-quality budget accommodation for both groups and individuals at locations throughout Scotland.

CHESHIRE

Beeston Outdoor Education Centre
Tarporley
Cheshire
CW6 9TR
Telephone: 01829 260535
Residential accommodation for 44 students and 4 staff, specialising in short residential courses for primary age.

Grisdale Cottages
c/o 36 Wilton Crescent
Alderley Edge
Cheshire
SK9 7RG
Telephone: 01625 586552
Self-catering accommodation for 10 people, situated at 1200 feet.

Middlewich Narrowboats
Canal Terrace
Middlewich
Cheshire CW10 9BD
Telephone: 01606 832460
Narrowboat hire.

The Curriculum

Outdoor provision

CLEVELAND

Cleveland Youth Association
Richard Crosthwaite Centre
Sotherby Road
Middlesborough
Cleveland
TS3 8BT
Telephone: 01642 230973
Portland Lodge, near Stanhope in the north Pennines, is a self-catering residential centre sleeping 34.

CLWYD

Clwyd Outdoor Adventure
Dee Kayak School
65 Harwoods Lane
Rossett, Wrexham
Clwyd
LL12 0EU
Telephone: 01244 570157
Facsimile: 01244 571244
A canoe centre offering all levels of kayak instruction, also Canadian canoeing, dragon boat racing, mountain biking and whitewater rafting.

CORNWALL

Adventure Sports
Carnkie Farm House
Carnkie
Redruth
Cornwall
TR16 6RZ
Telephone: 01209 218962
Provides students aged 16-18+ with paragliding, water skiing, surfing, windsurfing, sailing, wave-ski and rock climbing.

CAC Watersports
Mylor Yacht Harbour
Falmouth
Cornwall
TR11 5UF
Telephone: 01326 376191
Facsimile: 01326 376192
Residential centre offering a wide range of watersport activities.

Churchtown Outdoor Education Centre
Lanlivery
Bodmin
Cornwall
P30 5BT
Telephone: 01208 872148
Outdoor activities to enable students with physical disabilities to discover what they can do for themselves. Activities include sailing, rock climbing, canoeing, sea fishing, orienteering and environmental studies.

Chyvarloe Basecamp
Chyvarloe
Gunwalloe
Helston
Cornwall
TR12 7PY
Residential self-catering accommodation for up to 14 students and 2 leaders, managed by The National Trust. Enquiries to Mr A Sandham, Cornwall Regional Office, Lanhydrock, Bodmin, Cornwall PL30 4DE, telephone 01208 74281.

Cornwall County Council Outdoor Education Centres
Dalvanie House
County Hall
Truro
Cornwall
TR1 3AY
Telephone: 01872 322448
Facsimile: 01872 323806
The Authority run four multi-activity centres in Cornwall providing a wide range of outdoor activities and field study programmes in fully equipped accommodation.

Delaware Outdoor Education Centre
Gunnislake
Cornwall
PL18 9EH
Telephone: 01822 833885
Facsimile: 01822 833885
Residential accommodation for up to 64 people, catered or self-catering. Activities available include canoeing, rock climbing, abseiling, walking, camping, archery, orienteering, problem solving, and pond and mine studies.

The Curriculum

Outdoor provision

Endeavour Club Centre
John Keay House
St Austell
Cornwall
PL25 4DJ
Telephone: 01726 623469
Duke of Edinburgh's Award Operating Authority.

Freetime Holidays
Runnelstone Cottages
St Levan
Penzance
Cornwall
TR19 6LU
Telephone: 01736 871302
Activities are offered to singles and families and include surfing, windsurfing, climbing, abseiling, coastal walking and mountain biking.

Mike Raine
19 Rosevean Road
Penzance
Cornwall
TR18 2DY
Telephone: 01736 67889
Instructor providing rock climbing from basic to instructor level.

National Trust Beach Head Basecamp
Pentire Farm
St Eval
Wadebridge
Cornwall
PL27 7UU
Residential self-catering accommodation for up to 12 students and 2 leaders, situated on the north Cornwall coast, and administered by The National Trust. Enquiries to Mr R Calvert, Wayside Cottage, Churchtown, St Agnes, Cornwall TR5 0QP, telephone 01872 552412.

Porthpean Outdoor Education Centre
Castle Gotha
St Austell
Cornwall
PL26 6AZ
Telephone: 01726 72901
Facsimile: 01726 72901
Residential outdoor activities provided.

St Ives Wesley Youth Hostel
Street An Garrow
St Ives
Cornwall
TR26 1SG
Telephone: 01736 796829
Residential self-catering accommodation for 52 students and staff. Situated in the centre of St Ives. Booking via Mrs Kemp, Runnelstone, Ayr, St Ives, Cornwall TR26 1EQ.

TM International School of Horsemanship
Sunrising Riding Centre
Henwood
Liskeard
Cornwall
PL14 5BP
Telephone: 01579 362895
Facsimile: 01579 362895
Residential accommodation for up to 20 for instruction in horse riding, care and stable management. Situated close to Bodmin Moor.

CUMBRIA

Ashness Hut and Campsite
Greta Bank Farm
Keswick
Cumbria
CA12 4NS
Contact: Mrs J Gilbert
Telephone: 017687 72590
Wooden bunkhouse with 12 bunks and mattresses. Calor cooking and lighting, chemical toilet, no running water, adjacent area for tents. Situated on fellside 3 miles out of Keswick.

Bendrigg Trust
Bendrigg Lodge
Old Hutton
Kendal
Cumbria
LA8 0NR
Telephone: 01539 723766
Facsimile: 01539 722446
Residential activity centre specialising for disabled and disadvantaged young people.

The Curriculum

Outdoor provision

Blaithwaite Christian Centre
Blaithwaite House
Wigton
Cumbria
CA7 0AZ
Contact: The Centre Manager
Telephone: 016973 42319
Facsimile: 016973 42319
Self-catering accommodation for up to 100, and catered accommodation for smaller groups.

Brathay Hall Trust
Ambleside
Cumbria
LA22 0HP
Telephone: 015394 33041
Facsimile: 015394 34424
Personal and social development training for young people over 14.

Calvert Trust Centre for Disabled People
Little Crossthwaite
Keswick
Cumbria
CA12 4QD
Telephone: 01768 772254
Facsimile: 01768 73941
Residential centre providing a variety of outdoor activities for those with special needs.

Carlisle Diocesan Youth Centre
St John's in the Vale Vicarage
Naddle
Keswick
Cumbria
CA12 4TF
Telephone: 01768 772542
Self-catering residential accommodation for 28 students and 8 staff. Situated in the northern Lake District.

Castle Head Field Centre
Grange-over-Sands
Cumbria
LA11 6QT
Contact: F C Dawson
Telephone: 015395 34300
Day programmes for ages 9-18 in wildlife watching and A level fieldwork. Also activities including climbing, abseiling, canoeing, rafting, caving and orienteering.

Castlerigg Manor
Manor Brow
Keswick
Cumbria
CA12 4AR
Telephone: 017687 72711
Facsimile: 017687 75302
Residential accommodation, mainly in use with school leaver groups, but also available for field and geography trips planned independently.

Catholes Bunkhouse Barn
Catholes Farm
Dent Road
Sedburgh
Cumbria
LA10 5SS
Telephone: 01539 620334
Self-catering barn sleeping 15 people in 4 rooms. Facilities include washing and toilets, a shower, drying room, cookers, fridge and cutlery and crockery. Sleeping bags required.

Country Venture Activity Centre
The Old School
Tebay
Penrith
Cumbria
CA10 3TP
Telephone: 015396 24286
Facsimile: 015396 24286
Residential accommodation for up to 46. Activities offered include navigation, scrambling, rock climbing, hill walking and winter skills.

Cumbria Outdoors
Portinscale
Keswick
Cumbria
Contact: Barbara Hunter, Business Development Officer
Telephone: 017687 72816
Facsimile: 017687 75108
Three residential centres, a watersport centre and a campsite in the Lake District. Self-programming or full instruction in a wide variety of outdoor activities and environmental courses.

The Curriculum

Outdoor provision

Derwent Hill Outdoor Education Centre
Portinscale
Keswick
Cumbria
CA12 5RD
Telephone: 017687 72005
Facsimile: 017687 75422
*Residential centre offering outdoor education
courses for students aged 9-18. GCSE
Geography and PE courses, and social
development courses using a mixture of
outdoor activities, including hill walking, rock
climbing, canoeing, orienteering and sailing.*

Eden Valley Centre
Ainstable
Carlisle
Cumbria
CA4 9QA
Telephone: 01768 896202
Facsimile: 01768 896202
*Residential centre providing tailor-made
courses in outdoor education for schools and
colleges.*

Eskdale Youth Hostel
Boot
Holmrook
Cumbria
CA19 1T
Telephone: 019467 23219
Facsimile: 019467 23219
*Accommodation for 54, either self-catering or
catered, with a wide range of outdoor
activities available. Classroom suitable for 30
people.*

Freetime Activities
Sun Lea
Joss Lane
Sedburgh
Cumbria
LA10 5AS
Contact: Paul Ramsden
Telephone: 01539 620828
Courses in caving (all levels) and abseiling.

Ghyll Head Outdoor Education Centre
Windermere
Cumbria LA23 3LN
Telephone: 015394 43751

Facsimile: 015394 43751
*Residential accommodation for up to 36
students aged 10 years upwards. Activities
on the site (17 acres wooded) and at venues
throughout the southern Lake District.*

Grizedale Forest Hostel
Hawkshead
Ambleside
Cumbria
LA22 0QJ
Telephone: 01229 860373
Facsimile: 01229 860273
Residential self-catering accommodation for 16.

High Borrans Centre
High Borrans
Windermere
Cumbria
LA23 1JS
Telephone: 01539 442816
*Residential centre offering courses for groups of
up to 36 people from age 8 to adult. Activities
include mountain walking, climbing, caving,
canoeing, raft building, gorge scrambling,
archery and mountain biking. GCSE and A
level subjects are also available. Special
rates are offered to all North Tyneside
establishments.*

High Loaning Head Adventure
Garrigill
Alston
Cumbria
CA9 3EY
Contact: Lindsay Williams
Telephone: 01434 381929
*Residential centre catering for up to 17 people.
Instruction in outdoor activities can be
arranged or groups can be self-tutored.*

Howtown Outdoor Education Centre
Pooley Bridge
Penrith
Cumbria CA10 2ND
Telephone: 01768 486508
Facsimile: 01768 486875
*Outdoor education courses for students aged
10-17 years.*

The Curriculum
Outdoor provision

Longrigg Residential Centre
Frostrow Lane
Sedburgh
Cumbria
LA10 5JU
Contact: Rob Gregory
Telephone: 015396 21161
*Self-catering accommodation for 24 students
and 4 staff, run by Buckinghamshire County
Council.*

**Low Bank Ground Outdoor Education
Centre**
Coniston
Cumbria
LA21 8AA
Telephone: 015394 41314
Facsimile: 015394 41525
*Residential accommodation primarily for Wigan
schools, but with some vacancies for outside
groups. Self-catering available. Courses
include canoeing, sailing, mountain walking,
climbing, orienteering, environmental studies,
geography and biology fieldwork.*

Low Gillerthwaite Field Centre
Ennerdale
Cleator
Cumbria
CA23 3AX
Telephone: 01946 861229
*Self-catering farmhouse sleeping 40. Activities
available include canoeing, orienteering,
climbing, abseiling and environmental
studies.*

Mere Mountains
Pleasure-in-Leisure
Keldwyth Park
Windermere
Cumbria
LA23 1HG
Contact: John & Elspeth Mason
Telephone: 015394 88002
Facsimile: 015394 88288
*Activity sessions, adventure days and outdoor
education courses in climbing, canoeing,
abseiling, orienteering, windsurfing, raft
building, gorge walking and initiative
challenges. Accommodation can be arranged
in Youth Hostels.*

Mike Margeson
8 Long Row
Marshside
Kirkby-in-Furness
Cumbria
LA17 7UP
Telephone: 01229 889721
*Instruction in all mountain activities, climbing,
abseiling, orienteering, caving and
watersports.*

Nexus Training and Development
Blencathra House
High Carleton
Penrith
Cumbria
CA11 8SW
Telephone: 01768 890939
Facsimile: 01768 890933
*Specialists in the design and provision of
development programmes for sixth-formers.*

**Northern Council for Outdoor Education,
Training and Recreation**
Adventure Education
12 St Andrew's Churchyard
Penrith
Cumbria
CA11 7YE
Telephone: 01768 891065
Facsimile: 01768 891914
*The representative organisation for outdoor
providers in the north.*

Outward Bound Eskdale
Eskdale Green
Holmrook
Cumbria
CA19 1TE
Telephone: 01946 723281
Facsimile: 01946 723393
*Residential courses for 14-18-year-olds
providing personal development through
challenging, exciting and enjoyable outdoor
activities.*

The Curriculum

Outdoor provision

Outward Bound Ullswater
Watermillock
Penrith
Cumbria
CA11 0JL
Telephone: 01768 486347
Facsimile: 01768 486405
*Provider of personal development courses for
young people using adventurous activities as
a medium.*

Pardshaw Methodist Holiday Centre
c/o 7 Fern Bank
Cockermouth
Cumbria
CA13 0DF
Telephone: 01900 823273
*A residential self-catering centre in the Lake
District catering for up to 18.*

R & L Adventures
The Byre, Knotts Farm
Patterdale Road
Windermere
Cumbria
LA23 1NL
Contact: Linda Rutland
Telephone: 015394 45104
*Courses provided in canoeing, abseiling, rock
climbing, ghyll scrambling, mountain walking,
caving and orienteering.*

Sticklebarn
Dungeon Ghyll
Great Langdale
Ambleside
Cumbria
LA22 9JY
Telephone: 015394 37356
*Bunkbarn accommodation for 20 people. Meals
are available in the adjacent pub.*

Tower Wood Outdoor Education Centre
Windermere
Cumbria
LA23 3PL
Telephone: 015395 31519
Facsimile: 015395 30071
*Residential and day courses primarily for
Lancashire schools.*

DERBYSHIRE

Cliff Conference Centre Complex
Cliff College
Calver
Derbyshire
S30 1XG
Telephone: 01246 582321
Facsimile: 01246 583739
*Activities available include badminton, netball,
table tennis and outdoor tennis.*

Cromford Wharf Shed
c/o Lea Green
Lea
Matlock
Derbyshire
DE4 5GJ
Telephone: 01629 534561
Facsimile: 01629 534071
*Self-catering accommodation designed for use
by groups, situated adjacent to the High Peak
trail close to Cromford. It may be possible to
arrange low-key adventurous activities
through Lea Green.*

Crowden Outdoor Centre
Hadfield
Hyde
Greater Manchester
SK14 7HZ
Telephone: 01457 862821
Facsimile: 01457 869569
*Residential centre situated in the Peak District
on the Pennine Way, offering caving,
canoeing, moorland walking and climbing.*

Dovedale House
Lichfield Diocesan Centre for Young People
Ilam
Ashbourne
Derbyshire
DE6 2AZ
Telephone: 01335 350365
Facsimile: 01335 350441
*Residential accommodation for up to 45 people.
A wide variety of activities are available or
can be organised locally.*

The Curriculum

Outdoor provision

Dukes Barn
School Lane
Beeley
Derbyshire
DE4 2NU
Telephone: 01629 733039
*Accommodation for up to 45 with adventurous
    activities provided.*

Edale YHA Activity Centre
Rowland Cote
Nether Booth
Edale, Sheffield
Derbyshire
S30 2ZH
Telephone: 01433 670302
*Residential accommodation (Youth Hostel) with
    141 beds. Activities provided for 8 years up
    include climbing, caving, canoeing, walking,
    navigation, abseiling and problem solving.
    Situated in the Peak National Park.*

Gateway Residential Youth Centre
2 George Street
Ashbourne
Derbyshire
DE6 1DW
Telephone: 01335 346136
*Self-catering residential centre for up to 27
    people.*

Glenorchy Rural Activity Centre
Wirksworth United Reformed Church
Coldwell Street
Wirksworth
Derbyshire
DE4 4YB
Contact: Mrs E M Butlin, Secretary
Telephone: 01629 824323
*Self-catering accommodation for 30 people.
    Situated on the edge of the Peak National
    Park.*

Grin Low Cottage
c/o White Hall Centre
Long Hill
Buxton
Derbyshire
SK17 6SX
Telephone: 01298 23260
Facsimile: 01298 25945

*Self-catering accommodation for group use.
    Outdoor adventurous activities can be
    arranged through White Hall Centre. Grin
    Low Cottage is situated on the southern
    outskirts of Buxton.*

Hopton Cottage
c/o Lea Green
Lea
Matlock
Derbyshire
DE4 5GJ
Telephone: 01629 534561
Facsimile: 01629 534071
*Self-catering centre designed for use by groups,
    situated on the High Peak trail between
    Middleton Top and Tissington. It may be
    possible to arrange low-key outdoor
    adventurous activities through Lea Green.*

Lea Green
Lea
Matlock
Derbyshire
DE4 5GJ
Telephone: 01629 534561
Facsimile: 01629 534071
*Educational residential centre providing
    opportunities in arts education, environmental
    education, PE and outdoor education.*

Lockerbrook Outdoor Activities Centre
Snake Road
Bamford
Derbyshire
S20 2BJ
Telephone: 01433 651412
*Residential accommodation for groups of up to
    28. Suitable as a base for walking, climbing
    and environmental activities.*

Overton Park Camp
c/o White Hall Centre
Long Hill
Buxton
Derbyshire SK17 6SX
Telephone: 01298 23260
Facsimile: 01298 25945
*Semi-permanent campsite accommodating up
    to 50 people. Situated between Matlock and
    Chesterfield.*

The Curriculum

Outdoor provision

Peak National Park Environmental Education Service
Losehill Hall
Castleton
Derbyshire
S30 2WB
Telephone: 01433 620373
Facsimile: 01433 620346
Offers a range of activities and programmes for junior and secondary groups at various locations in the National Park.

Peak Training Services
6 Millcliff
Buxton
Derbyshire
SK17 6QP
Telephone: 01298 25031
Facsimile: 01298 72343
Instruction provided in canoeing (Canadian), climbing, abseiling, caving, orienteering, hill walking, scrambling and field study courses.

Rock Lea Activity Centre
Station Road
Hathersage
Derbyshire S30 1DD
Telephone: 01433 650345
Residential (groups of up to 20 in number) and non-residential (can be more than 20) courses offered in rock climbing, abseiling, orienteering, mountain biking, caving, potholing, gorge walking, problem-solving activities and geography and ecology field-work. Activities are suitable for ages 9-18.

Talbrager Training
High Street
Tideswell
Buxton
Derbyshire SK17 8LD
Contact: Mr Nigel Smee
Telephone: 012988 71245/71827
Courses offered include self-development, leadership and teamwork skills for upper secondary age.

Thornbridge Education Centre
Great Longstone
Bakewell
Derbyshire DE45 1NY

Telephone: 01629 640491
Facsimile: 01629 640494
Self-catering accommodation and camping facilities for organised groups.

Turnlee Centre
c/o White Hall Centre
Long Hill
Buxton
Derbyshire
SK17 6SX
Telephone: 01298 23260
Facsimile: 01298 25945
Self-catering accommodation for use by groups, situated on the southern outskirts of Glossop. Outdoor adventurous activities can be arranged through White Hall Centre.

Unitarian Holiday and Conference Centre
Great Hucklow
Buxton
Derbyshire
SK17 8RH
Contact: Elizabeth McCutcheon, General Manager
Telephone: 01298 871218
Accommodation for accompanied groups.

Unstone Grange
Crow Lane
Unstone
Sheffield
S18 5AL
Telephone: 01246 412344
Residential accommodation for 31 people. Situated close to the Peak District.

White Hall Centre
Long Hill
Buxton
Derbyshire
SK17 6SX
Telephone: 01298 23260
Facsimile: 01298 25945
Residential centre providing outdoor activities including rock climbing, abseiling, caving, canoeing, mountain biking, sailing, orienteering, hill walking, problem solving and a ropes course.

The Curriculum

Outdoor provision

DEVON

Beaford Centre, The
Beaford
Winkleigh
Devon
EX19 8LU
Telephone: 01805 603201
*Residential centre for up to 36 people
specialising in Arts-based activities.
Specialist artist/teachers providing art,
drama, dance, storytelling, music and
ceramics.*

Buckland Monachorum Residential Hostel
c/o 14 Parker Close
Plymton
Plymouth
Devon
PL7 3FD
Telephone: 01752 342101
Self-catering accommodation for 26.

Dartmoor Expedition Centre
Rowden
Widecombe-in-the-Moor
Newton Abbot
Devon
TQ13 7TX
Telephone: 01364 621249
*Residential centre offering courses for groups of
over 6 in climbing, canoeing, caving,
moorland walking, mountain rescue, sailing,
pony trekking and problem-solving tasks.*

Dartmoor Training Centre
The Old Duchy Hotel
Princetown
Yelverton
Devon
PL20 6QF
Contact: Tim Dawson, Head of Centre
Telephone: 01822 890672
*Residential self-catering accommodation
providing opportunities for activities and
fieldwork in and around Dartmoor. Jointly
managed by Dartmoor National Park and
Devon County Council.*

Fort Bovisand Underwater Centre
Fort Bovisand
Plymouth
Devon
PL9 0AB
Telephone: 01752 408021
Facsimile: 01752 481952
*Residential accommodation for those
undertaking courses in scuba diving (for over-
15s) and sailing.*

Grenville House
Berry Head Road
Brixham
Devon
TQ5 9AF
Contact: Mike Bennett, Centre Manager
Telephone: 01803 852797
*Self-catering accommodation for groups of up
to 42 students and 10 staff, providing courses
in sailing. Managed by a charity, The British
Seamens' Boys Home, and supported by
Devon County Council.*

Haven Banks Outdoor Education Centre
61 Haven Road
Exeter
Devon
EX2 8BP
Contact: Janet Bradford, Centre Manager
Telephone: 01392 434668
*Activity centre (non-resident) providing courses
for individuals and groups in canoeing,
sailing, windsurfing, climbing (wall or rock),
orienteering, caving, abseiling, moorland
walking, environmental studies and problem
solving. Supported by Devon County Council.*

ISCA Children's Holidays
Bonnaford
Brentor
Tavistock
Devon
PL19 0LX
Telephone: 01822 810514
Facsimile: 01822 810514
*Residential accommodation for up to 42
students. Activities provided include archery,
riflery and pony trekking, with other activities
available at nearby sites.*

The Curriculum

Outdoor provision

National Trust Exmoor Basecamp
1 Town Farm Cottages
Contisbury
Lynton
Devon
EX35 6NE
Telephone: 01598 741297
Self-catering bunkhouse accommodation for up
to 27 people. Suitable for activities in the
Exmoor area.

Pixies Holt Residential Centre
Dartmeet
Yelverton
Devon
PL20 6SG
Contact: Ann Tribe, Centre Manager
Telephone: 01364 631248
Fully catered residential accommodation for
groups of up to 35 students, useful as a base
for work in the area. Outdoor clothing and
equipment for camping, climbing and
moorland walking. Supported by Devon
County Council.

River Dart Residential Centre
Holne Park
Ashburton
Devon
TQ13 7NP
Telephone: 01364 652511
Facsimile: 01364 652020
A multi-activity centre set in 92 acres of
parkland on the south-east edge of Dartmoor
catering for groups of up to 90.

Sheldon Centre, The
Dunsford
Exeter
Devon
EX6 7LE
Telephone: 01647 252203
Self-catering residential accommodation for up
to 52 people. Situated close to Dartmoor and
the coast. Resident warden and staff on hand
if required.

Skern Lodge Outdoor Centre
Appledore
Bideford
Devon
EX39 1NG
Telephone: 01237 475992
Facsimile: 01237 421203
Residential accommodation with instruction in
surfing, sailing, water skiing, canoeing,
rafting, abseiling, climbing, archery and
coastal exploration.

Slade Centre, The
Sidmouth
Devon
EX10 0NU
Contact: Dr E Svendsen MBE, Hon
Administrator
Telephone: 01395 578222
Facsimile: 01395 579266
Provides riding activities for children with
special needs and disabilities, using donkeys.

St Georges House
Georgham
Devon
EX33 1JN
Telephone: 01271 890755
Facsimile: 01271 890060
Provides geography field trips and a wide range
of outdoor activities.

Start Bay Centre, The
Slapton
Kingsbridge
Devon
TQ7 2RA
Contact: Angela Wiggett, Centre Manager
Telephone: 01548 580321
Self-catering accommodation for groups of up
to 39. Supported by Devon County Council.

Stonelands School of Ballet and Theatre
Arts
Ashcombe Road
Dawlish
Devon EX7 9BL
Telephone: 01626 866708
Tuition in all branches of dance.

The Curriculum
Outdoor provision

University of Exeter
Devonshire House
Stocker Road
Exeter
Devon
EX4 4PZ
Telephone: 01392 215566
Facsimile: 01392 263512
Accommodation in university halls with flexible catering arrangements. An activity and leisure holiday programme is available.

Wembworthy Centre, The
Wembworthy
Chumleigh
Devon
EX18 7QR
Contact: Fran Sendell, Centre Manager
Telephone: 01769 580667
A self-catering residential centre for groups of up to 34 students suitable as a base for work in the area. Supported by Devon County Council.

West Devon Outdoor Education Centre
Martinsgate
Bretonside
Plymouth
Devon
PL4 0AT
Contact: Martin Northcott, Centre Director
Telephone: 01752 253264
Non-residential activity centre providing courses in sailing, canoeing, caving, rock climbing, orienteering and problem solving. Supported by Devon County Council.

DORSET

Allnatt Centres
35 Ulwell Road
Swanage
Dorset
BH19 1LG
Telephone: 01929 422122
Facsimile: 01929 421075
The Centres provide a range of 5 outdoor education programmes for schools and youth groups. Activities include climbing, canoeing and a range of low-risk activities, all designed to provide a taster experience, rather than proficiency in the activity.

Hamworthy Outdoor Education Centre
Hamworthy Park
Hamworthy
Poole
Dorset
BH15 4LZ
Telephone: 01202 677272
Facsimile: 01202 677272
Activities provided include sailing, canoeing, rock climbing, abseiling and orienteering.

Springhead Trust
Springhead
Fontmell Magna
Shaftsbury
Dorset
SP7 0NU
Telephone: 01747 811853
Facsimile: 01747 811853
Provides activities related to the exploration of the countryside and man's impact on it.

Weymouth Outdoor Education Centre
Knightsdale Road
Weymouth
Dorset
DT4 0HS
Telephone: 01305 784927
Facsimile: 01305 766362
The Centre provides the following activities: sailing, canoeing, climbing, caving, archery, and multi-activity courses.

CO DURHAM

Faverdale Training & Adventure Ltd
Faverdale Hall
Darlington
Co Durham
DL3 0UU
Telephone: 01325 3844640
Facsimile: 01325 467352
Activities provided for ages 15-18: climbing, abseiling, caving, canoeing and fell walking.

The Curriculum

Outdoor provision

Four Seasons
44 The Bank
Barnard Castle
Co Durham
DL12 8PN
Telephone: 01833 637829/01642 678000
*Canoeing and whitewater rafting for students
aged 12-14 years.*

Hamsterley Forest
Forest Enterprise
Redford Hamsterley
Bishop Auckland
Co Durham
DL13 3NL
Telephone: 01388 488312
*Courses in habitat studies, minibeast hunts,
forest management and earth education.*

High Force Training Centre
The Old Vicarage
Forest-in-Teesdale
Co Durham
DL12 0HA
Telephone: 01833 622302
Facsimile: 01833 622337
*Activities provided include climbing, abseiling
and gorge walking.*

Kingsway Adventure Centre
Alston Road
Middleton-in-Teesdale
Co Durham
DL12 0UU
Telephone: 01833 640881
Facsimile: 01833 640881
*Family-run Christian residential outdoor centre
for all ages. Instruction provided in a wide
range of outdoor activities.*

Northumbria Horse Holidays
East Castle
Annfield Plain
Stanley
Co Durham
DH9 8PH
Telephone: 01207 235354
Courses in horse riding.

Base Camp Field Study/Activity Centre
Llawhaden
Narberth
Pembrokeshire
SA67 8DS
Contact: Sharon & Chris Bannis
Telephone: 01437 541318
*Accommodation providing a range of outdoor
activities.*

Maesnant Centre
Maesnant
Ponterwyd
Dyfed
Telephone: 0181-421 4648
*Self-catering accommodation for up to 16 in
number situated on the slopes of Plynlimon in
mid-Wales. Facilities include gas lighting and
heating, showers, WCs and fully equipped
kitchen. Additional space for camping. For
booking contact: Booking Secretary, 18 High
View, Pinner, Middlesex HA5 3PA.*

Orielton Field Centre
Pembroke
Dyfed
SA71 5EZ
Telephone: 01646 661225
Facsimile: 01646 661737
*Week-long courses in Ecology, Environmental
Science and Geography for all ages, but
especially KS4 and A level.*

The Stackpole Centre
Home Farm
Stackpole
Pembroke
Dyfed
SA71 5DG
Telephone: 01646 661425
Facsimile: 01646 661456
*Residential accommodation for up to 34
students. Activities offered include canoeing,
archery and abseiling.*

VISITS - DYFED

The Curriculum
Outdoor provision

ESSEX

Bradwell Outdoor Education Centre
Bradwell Waterside
Bradwell-on-Sea
Southminster
Essex
CM0 7QY
Telephone: 01621 776256
Facsimile: 01621 776378
Residential centre offering one-day courses in dinghy sailing, canoeing and offshore sailing. Groups can be resident for up to 5 days.

Clarance House Residential Study Centre
Thaxted
Dunmow
Essex
CM6 2PJ
Telephone: 01371 830245
Facsimile: 01371 830245
Day trips for KS2 & 3 in History and Geography locally.

Diocese of Chelmsford Youth Service
Asheldham Youth Church
6 Bakery Close
Tillingham
Essex
CM0 7TT
Telephone: 01621 778017
Converted 14th-century church providing self-catering accommodation for groups of up to 28 and 8 leaders. Kitchen, workroom and chapel.

Epping Forest Field Centre
High Beach
Loughton
Essex
IG10 4AF
Telephone: 0181-508 7714
Facsimile: 0181-508 8429
Provides curricular and non-curricular activity-based learning programmes for all ages.

Fellowship Afloat
The Sail Lofts
Woodrolfe Road
Tollesbury
Essex
CM9 8SE
Telephone: 01621 868113
Facsimile: 01621 868533
Residential accommodation on a converted Trinity House lightvessel for 36. Activities provided include windsurfing, sailing, fishing, bird watching, art and craft, music and photography.

Field Studies Council Flatford Mill Field Centre
East Bergholt
Colchester
Essex
CO7 6UL
Telephone: 01206 298283
Facsimile: 01206 298892
Residential and day courses for primary and secondary schools linked with the National Curriculum, GCSE and A level syllabuses.

Lee Valley Park Youth & Schools Service
Lee Valley Park Countryside Centre
Abbey Gardens
Waltham Abbey
Essex
EN9 1QX
Telephone: 01992 713838
Facsimile: 01992 893118
Provides half- and full-day programmes in Science, Geography, Environmental Studies and History for KS1 & 2. Also individually-tailored programmes for KS3 & 4, GNVQ, B.Tech and A level.

Mansfield Outdoor Centre
Manor Road
Lambourne End
Essex
RM4 1NB
Telephone: 0181-500 3047
Facsimile: 0181-559 8481
Self-catering accommodation mainly for Newham and inner-city groups, providing a wide range of outdoor activities for personal and group development.

The Curriculum

Outdoor provision

GLAMORGAN

Atlantic College Extramural Centre
Llantwit Major
South Glamorgan
CF6 9WF
Telephone: 01446 792711
Facsimile: 01446 794163
Multi-activity courses offered at all levels.

Clyne Farm Activity Centre
Westport Avenue
Mayals
Swansea
West Glamorgan
SA3 5AR
Telephone: 01792 403333
Facsimile: 01792 403339
Residential and non-residential centre offering abseiling, climbing, canoeing, caving, gorge walking, rock hopping, archery, horse riding, camping, assault course and field study programmes for Geography, Geology, Biology and Ecology.

Dolygaer Outdoor Education Centre
Pontsticill
Merthyr Tydfil
Mid Glamorgan
CF48 2UR
Telephone: 01685 389677
Facsimile: 01685 388059
The Centre caters for students aged 10 and above in outdoor adventurous activities.

Kilvrough Manor Outdoor Education Centre
Parkmill Gower
Swansea
West Glamorgan
SA3 2EE
Telephone: 01792 232743
Facsimile: 01792 233637
Courses provided in rock climbing, canoeing, surfing, orienteering, walking and mountaineering. Minimum age 9.

GLOUCESTERSHIRE

Admiral Collier Centre, The
Diocesan Education Office
St Mary's Gate, St Mary's Street
Gloucester
GL1 2QR
Contact: Heather Hodges, Administrator
Telephone: 01452 410022
Situated in Blockley in the Cotswolds, the Centre is self-catering with accommodation for up to 40 people.

Clearwell Caves
Coleford
Gloucestershire
GL16 8JR
Telephone: 01594 832535
Guided tours round ancient iron ore mines and caving deeper underground for students aged 9-10 years old.

Gloucestershire DART
St Mary's Gate
St Mary's Street
Gloucester
GL1 2QR
Contact: Heather Hodges, Administrator
Telephone: 01452 410022
Gloucestershire Disabled Afloat Riverboats Trust (DART) is a riverboat available for hire at reasonable rent to groups of disabled people, for cruising the Rivers Severn and Avon and the Gloucester–Sharpness Canal.

GYPCE
St Mary's Gate
St Mary's Street
Gloucester
GL1 2QR
Contact: Heather Hodges, Administrator
Telephone: 01452 410022
A narrowboat available for hire to groups of up to 10 young people, primarily for use by those who are considered to be in some way 'at risk'.

The Curriculum

Outdoor provision

Lord's Hill Centre, The
St Mary's Gate
St Mary's Street
Gloucester
GL1 2QR
Contact: Heather Hodges, Administrator
Telephone: 01452 410022
Situated in Coleford, the Centre is self-catering and accommodates up to 24 people.

Severn Valley Sports
9 Orchard Street
Wotton-under-Edge
Gloucestershire
GL12 7EZ
Telephone: 01453 842892
Facsimile: 01453 843572
Residential and day camps in the Easter and summer holidays involving soccer coaching and multi-sports.

South Cerney Outdoor Education Centre
Spine Road
South Cerney
Cirencester
Gloucestershire
GL7 5TY
Telephone: 01285 860388
Facsimile: 01285 862107
Residential centre (or day or half-day) offering courses in rafting, orienteering, windsurfing, canoeing, snorkelling and problem solving.

Viney Hill Christian Adventure Centre
St Mary's Gate
St Mary's Street
Gloucester
GL1 2QR
Contact: Heather Hodges, Administrator
Telephone: 01452 410022
Situated near Lydney, 20 miles outside Gloucester near the Forest of Dean, the Centre is a self-catering camping venue with cooking facilities catering for about 50.

Wyedean Canoe and Adventure Centre
Holly Barn
Symonds Yat Rock
Coleford
Gloucestershire
GL16 7NZ

Telephone: 01594 833238
Facsimile: 01594 833238
Residential accommodation and a programme of activities are available. Situated in the Wye Valley.

GRAMPIAN

Braemar Outdoor Centre
Mar Road
Braemar
Grampian
AB3 5YL
Telephone: 013397 41517
Facsimile: 013397 41496
Bunkhouse/independent hostel accommodation offering winter skills and cross-country skiing courses.

GWENT

Brittons Outdoor Education Centre
School House
Cwmavon Road
Blaenafon
Gwent
NP4 9LD
Contact: Ian Kyle
Telephone: 01495 792067
Facsimile: 01873 890517
A wide range of outdoor pursuits in the Brecon Beacons.

GWYNEDD & ANGLESEY

Aberglaslyn Hall Outdoor Education Centre
Beddgelert
Caernarfon
Gwynedd
LL55 4YF
Contact: D Shearman, Secretary
Telephone: 01766 866233
Facsimile: 01766 890255
Situated within the Snowdonia National Park, the Centre offers a full range of outdoor education activities and can accommodate up to 36 people.

The Curriculum

Outdoor provision

Andy Newton Mountain Activity Services
16 Goodman Street
Llanberis
Gwynedd
LL55 4HL
Telephone: 01286 872317
Instructor for all mountain-related activities for groups and individuals.

Anglesey Sea & Surf Centre
Porthadfarch
Treaddur Bay
Anglesey
LL65 2LP
Telephone: 01407 2525
Facsimile: 01407 2525
Residential accommodation for 45 students providing multi-activity courses. Specialises in sea canoeing, sailing and windsurfing.

Bala Adventure & Watersports Centre
Bala Lake Foreshore
Bala
Gwynedd
LL23 7SR
Contact: Centre Office
Telephone: 01678 521059
Facsimile: 01678 521059
Courses offered in canoeing, windsurfing, sailing, rock climbing, abseiling, raft building and mountain biking.

Barry Skinner
Turnpike Cottage
Traeth
Beddgellert
Gwynedd LL55 4YF
Telephone: 01766 890283
Instruction in all levels of mountain walking, scrambling, rock climbing, canoeing, nordic skiing (dry and real), downhill skiing (dry) and orienteering.

Beics Betws
Tan Lan
Betws y Coed
Gwynedd LL24 0AB
Telephone: 01690 710766
Facsimile: 01690 710766
Hire of mountain bikes.

C R Ashe-Cregan
Namaste
Morfa Crescent
Tywyn
Gwynedd
LL36 9AU
Telephone: 01654 711389
Provides activities including slate mine tours, overnight expeditions and navigation courses.

Caban Cader Idris
Tal-Sarn
Llanllechid
Bangor
Gwynedd
LL57 3AJ
Telephone: 01248 600478
Residential accommodation, either self-catering or fully serviced. Caban Cader Idris is an old school situated in Islawdref, near Dolgellau. Sleeps 16 and has kitchen, two dormitories, toilets, showers and a drying room. Local activities include climbing, hill walking, pony trekking, biking, canoeing and rafting.

Canolfan Tryweryn National White Water Centre
Frongoch
Bala
Gwynedd
LL23 7NU
Telephone: 01678 521083
Facsimile: 01678 521158
Whitewater rafting for over-12s.

Chris Smith
Ty Cappel Dinas
Roman Bridge
Dolwyddelan
Gwynedd
LL25 0JQ
Telephone: 01690 6337
Provides instruction in mountain walking, rock climbing, abseiling, scrambling, canoeing and navigation, and leads gorge walks and mine and cave trips.

The Curriculum

Outdoor provision

Conway Centre, The
Llanfairpwll
Anglesey
LL61 6DJ
Telephone: 01248 714501
Facsimile: 01248 714504
Residential accommodation for up to 350, and day use. Courses offered include outdoor activities, development training, field studies and cross-curricular courses.

Cwm Pennant Centre of Outdoor Education
Garndolbenmaen
Porthmadog
Gwynedd
LL51 9AQ
Telephone: 01766 5300682
Facsimile: 01766 530682
Outdoor education centre offering self-catering or catered courses for groups of up to 60. In the Snowdonia National Park close to the sea, mountains, rivers, beaches and Tremadog cliffs.

Fairbourne Adventure
64 Belgrave Road
Fairbourne
Gwynedd
LL38 2BQ
Telephone: 01341 250613
Facsimile: 01341 250800
Activity centre for students aged over 9 offering canoeing, climbing, abseiling, slate mine exploration, orienteering, gorge walking, mountain biking, whitewater rafting and raft building. Accommodation is in hotels or guest houses, if required.

Jesse James
The Bunkhouse
Penisarwaen
Carnarfon
Gwynedd
LL55 3DA
Telephone: 01286 870521
Residential accommodation for groups of up to 24 plus staff, with meals provided as required. Courses offered include hill walking and mountain skills, navigation, climbing, abseiling and canoeing (lake only), or do your own thing.

Kent Mountain Centre
Glyn Padarn
Llanberis
Gwynedd
LL55 4EL
Telephone: 01286 870216
Facsimile: 01286 872353
Residential centre providing full board for all age ranges. Activities offered include climbing, walking, canoeing and scrambling. Geography field trips can also be provided.

Llanrug Outdoor Education Centre
Llanrug
Caernarfon
Gwynedd
LL55 4EL
Telephone: 01286 672136
Facsimile: 01286 675697
Provides adventurous activity courses and A level field study courses. Run by Hereford & Worcester County Council.

Marle Hall Outdoor Centre
Marl Lane
Llandudno Junction
Gwynedd LL31 9JA
Telephone: 01492 581218
Residential accommodation for up to 70 people. Courses either taught by centre staff, or self-tutored.

Marty Kelly
Gwenallt Waunfawr
Caernarfon
Gwynedd LL55 4YU
Telephone: 01286 650238
Facsimile: 01286 870200
General outdoor instruction and supervision provided for individuals or groups in mountain guiding, canoeing and rock climbing.

Michael Brown
1 Dolafon
Dolwyddellan
Gwynedd LL25 0DX
Telephone: 01690 6322
Instruction in canoeing, climbing, abseiling, raft building, mountain walking, scrambling, gorge walking and mine trips. Bunkhouse accommodation available locally.

The Curriculum

Outdoor provision

Mountain Ventures Ltd
Bryn Du
Ty Du Road
Llanberis
Gwynedd
LL55 4TY
Telephone: 01286 870454
Facsimile: 01286 870454
*Self-catering or full catering hostel
accommodation for groups and individuals
aged 3-18, with drying room and games
room.*

**Nant Bwlch yr Haearn Outdoor Education
Centre**
Llanrwst
Gwynedd
LL27 0JB
Telephone: 01492 640735
Facsimile: 01492 640967
*Provides courses in outdoor activities and
environmental studies.*

Outdoor Alternative
Rhoscolyn
Holyhead
Anglesey
LL65 2NQ
Contact: Ian and Margaret Wrig
Telephone: 01407 860469
Facsimile: 01407 860469
*Self-catering or fully catered accommodation for
up to 36. Caters for those with their own
programme as well as those who require
support for their outdoor activities.*

Pen y Pass Mountain Centre
Nant Gwynant
Caernarfon
Gwynedd LL55 4NY
Telephone: 01286 870428
Facsimile: 01286 872434
*Residential accommodation and courses in rock
climbing, photography, mountain navigation
and mountain walking.*

Plas Dôl y Moch
City of Coventry Outdoor Education Centre
Maentwrog
Blaenau Ffestiniog
Gwynedd LL41 3YT

Telephone: 01766 762623
Facsimile: 01766 762438
*Residential centre for groups of up to 50
students and 7 staff providing a range of
adventure and environmental activities.*

Plas Menai National Watersports Centre
Llanfairsgaer
Caernarfon
Gwynedd
LL55 1UE
Telephone: 01248 670964
Facsimile: 01248 670964
*Catering for ages 8-18, the Centre offers
sailing, windsurfing, canoeing and multi-
activity.*

Plas y Brenin
The National Mountain Centre
Capel Curig
Gwynedd
LL24 0ET
Telephone: 01690 720214
Facsimile: 01690 720394
*Residential centre providing courses in
mountain sports. As a national sports centre,
it is responsible for training and assessing
leaders, instructors and coaches.*

Ranch, The
Pensarn Harbour
Llanbedr
Gwynedd
LL45 2HS
Telephone: 01341 23358
Facsimile: 01341 241530
*Residential accommodation providing a range
of supervised activities. Situated on the
Snowdonia coastline.*

Rhos-y-Gwaliau Outdoor Education Centre
Bala
Gwynedd
LL23 7ET
Telephone: 01678 520395
*Caters for 40 students (10-adult) plus staff.
Courses provided in field studies, hill walking,
rock climbing, mine exploration, canoeing,
sailing, camping, mountaineering and
problem solving.*

The Curriculum
Outdoor provision

Rhydau Duon Farmhouse
Brynrefail
Caernarfon
Gwynedd
LL55 3NR
Contact: Hugh and Judy Walton
Telephone: 01286 870744
Self-catering accommodation for up to 30 people. A variety of activities can be provided on request.

Rob Hastings Adventure Ltd
25 Southcourt Avenue
Leighton Buzzard
Bedfordshire
LU7 7QD
Telephone: 01525 379881
Facsimile: 01525 379881
Provides two types of holiday: adventure holidays in North Wales for schools, special needs groups and deprived children's charities; and adventure courses in the Spanish Pyrenees in July and August.

Snowdonia National Park Education Service
Penrhyndeudraeth
Gwynedd
LL48 6LS
Telephone: 01766 770701
Facsimile: 01766 771211
Provides advice on safety and access in the Snowdonia National Park, and information and advice on environmental education for students and teachers.

Tyddyn Philip Activity Centre
Brynteg
Anglesey
LL78 8JF
Telephone: 01248 853439
Activities offered on a daily basis include canoeing, mountain biking, raft building, climbing, abseiling, gorge walking, target shooting, archery and orienteering. Accommodation can be arranged.

HAMPSHIRE

Avon Tyrell, Youth Clubs UK
Bransgore
Hampshire
BH23 8EE
Telephone: 01425 672347
Facsimile: 01425 673883
Residential catered or self-catering accommodation. Staff available to provide activities, if required. Situated in the New Forest.

Bramley Frith Study Centre
Bramley
Basingstoke
Hampshire
RG26 5BJ
Contact: Andrew Cleave, Warden
Telephone: 01256 882094
Facsimile: 01256 880174
A study centre run by Hampshire County Council.

British Automobile Racing Club
Thruxton Racing Circuit
Thruxton
Andover
Hampshire
SP11 8PN
Telephone: 01264 772607
Facsimile: 01264 773794
Local schools are helped whenever possible. Some early driving courses have been organised at the circuit.

Calshot Activities Centre
Calshot Spit
Fawley
Southampton
SO4 1BR
Telephone: 01703 892077
Facsimile: 01703 891267
A residential centre with full catering offering courses in dinghy sailing, windsurfing, powerboating, skiing, canoeing and special courses for young people.

The Curriculum

Outdoor provision

Fairthorne Manor
YMCA National Centre
Curdridge
Southampton
SO30 2GH
Contact: Cheryl Jayne, Assistant to Director of
  Operations
Telephone: 01489 785228
Facsimile: 01489 798936
Outdoor Education centre offering activities on
a residential and daily basis. Programmes
can be designed to suit the needs of the
group and the Centre is ideally suited for field
studies.

Hampshire Outdoor Centre - Portsmouth
Eastern Road
Portsmouth
PO3 5LY
Telephone: 01705 663873
Facsimile: 01705 666531
A non-residential centre offering dinghy sailing,
windsurfing, canoeing and multi-activity
watersports for children.

Hampshire Outdoor Centre - Southampton
Floating Bridge Road
Chapel
Southampton
SO14 3FL
Telephone: 01703 225525
Facsimile: 01703 233063
A non-residential centre offering courses in
sailing and windsurfing.

Hampshire Outdoor Centre - Tile Barn
Church Hill
Brockenhurst
Hampshire
SO42 7UB
Contact: Mike Davies, Warden
Telephone: 01590 623160
Facsimile: 01590 623160
A camping site exclusively for the use of groups
of young people, situated in the New Forest.

Minstead Rural Study Centre
Minstead
Lyndhurst
Hampshire
SO43 7GJ

Contact: Jane Pownall, Warden
Telephone: 01703 813437
A study centre run by Hampshire County
Council.

QE2 Silver Jubilee Activity Centre
Manor Farm Country Park
Pylands Lane
Burlesdon
Hampshire
SO31 1BH
Contact: Phil Oates, Centre Manager
Telephone: 01703 404844
Activity centre providing canoeing, climbing,
rowing, orienteering and an obstacle course,
primarily for people with special needs, but
any groups from schools or day centres are
welcome.

Stubbington Centre
182-184 Stubbington Lane
Stubbington
Fareham
Hampshire
PO14 2ND
Telephone: 01829 662244
A study centre run by Hampshire County
Council.

Wellington Riding Ltd
Heckfield
Basingstoke
Hampshire
RG27 0LG
Telephone: 01734 326308
Tuition in horse riding at all levels.

Woodmill
Woodmill Lane
Swaythling
Southampton
SO18 2JR
Telephone: 01703 555993
Facsimile: 01703 556641
A non-residential centre offering courses in
canoeing, rock climbing, orienteering, dragon
boating, mountain biking and a variety of
special courses for children.

The Curriculum

Outdoor provision

HEREFORD & WORCESTER

Barnes Close Centre
Chadwich Manor Estate
Money Lane
Worcester
B61 0RA
Telephone: 01562 710231
Residential accommodation for up to 40 people.

Bishop Wood Environmental Education Centre
Crossways Green
Stourport-on-Severn
Worcestershire
DY13 9SE
Telephone: 01299 250513
Facsimile: 01299 250131
Provision of environmental education programmes for students of all school ages.

Bredwardine Lodge Centre
Bredwardine
Herefordshire
HR3 6BT
Telephone: 01981 500510
Residential centre offering canoeing, orienteering, caving and environmental work.

Dunfield House Residential Centre
Stanner Road
Kington
Hereford
HR5 3NN
Telephone: 01544 230563
Facsimile: 01544 231189
Residential accommodation for up to 100 people.

Frank Chapman Centre
Park End
Bewdley
Hereford & Worcester
DY12 2TY
Telephone: 01299 403292
Facsimile: 01299 402724
Purpose-built accommodation for groups of up to 70. Courses relate directly to the National Curriculum and cater for all school ages.

Glasbury House Outdoor Education Centre
Glasbury-on-Wye
Hereford
HR3 5NW
Contact: Head of Centre
Telephone: 01497 847231
Facsimile: 01497 847807
Residential accommodation (limited) run by the London Borough of Redbridge. Self-catering bunkhouse available.

Hanbury Hall Basecamp
Droitwich
Worcestershire
WR9 7EA
Contact: Mr J P Blades, Property Manager
Telephone: 01527 821214
Bunk accommodation for 20, with cooking facilities. Located at a National Trust property (Hanbury Hall), 4 miles east of Droitwich in Worcestershire.

Highball Children's Holiday Centre, The
Handley Swan
Malvern
Worcestershire
Contact: Mr Dave Benton, Bookings Officer
Telephone: 0121-354 2799
Self-catering residential accommodation for up to 57 people. Available between Easter and Christmas. Situated close to the Malvern Hills.

Kerne Bridge Adventure Centre
c/o Young Gloucestershire
Peter Scott House, 78 London Road
Gloucester
GL1 3PG
Telephone: 01452 520048
Facsimile: 01452 380248
Self-catering accommodation for 10 students and 2 staff. Situated on the River Wye in the Forest of Dean.

Longtown Outdoor Education Centre
The Court House
Longtown
Hereford & Worcester
HR2 0LD
Contact: The Bursar
Telephone: 01873 860225

The Curriculum

Outdoor provision

Facsimile: 01873 860333

Residential activity centre situated on the eastern edge of the Brecon Beacons National Park and supported by Northamptonshire County Council.

Pioneer Centre

Cleobury Place
Kidderminster
DY14 8JG
Telephone: 01299 271217
Facsimile: 01299 270948

Residential accommodation providing a range of activities which include abseiling, climbing, orienteering and initiative exercises.

Toc H Weirside

The Hedges
10 Cropthorne Drive
Hollywood
Worcestershire
B47 5PZ
Contact: Mr D Ridgway
Telephone: 0121-474 4685

Residential accommodation for 16 in bunks, with cooking facilities and showers. Room for camping beside building.

Upton Warren County Youth Sailing Centre

Upton Warren
Bromsgrove
Worcestershire
B61 7ER
Contact: Brian George, Warden
Telephone: 01527 861426
Facsimile: 01527 861799

Developmental courses based on week-long residential water activity programmes or termly/sessional attendances. Sailing, canoeing, windsurfing and problem-solving team games.

Ursa Major Adventure

Little Dewchurch
Hereford
HR2 6PW
Telephone: 01432 840542

Residential accommodation providing activities: canoeing, climbing, rafting, mountain walking and orienteering.

West Malvern Outdoor Education Centre

Old Hollow
Malvern
Hereford & Worcester
WR14 4NR
Telephone: 01684 574546
Facsimile: 01684 893931

Residential accommodation for groups of between 30 and 80, run by Hereford & Worcester County Council. Wide range of outdoor activities available.

Western Adventure

2 Wye Terrace
Bridge Terrace
Hereford
HR4 9DW
Contact: Nick Eve
Telephone: 01432 279030

Provides instruction in climbing, abseiling, caving, canoeing and gorge walking. This is not a residential centre.

HERTFORDSHIRE

Crusader Holidays

2 Romeland Hill
St Albans
Hertfordshire
AL3 4ET
Contact: Nigel Hall
Telephone: 01727 862731
Facsimile: 01727 848518

Organises activity holidays for students in the age range 9-18.

Cuffley Outdoor Education Centre

Carbone Hill
Cuffley
Potters Bar
Hertfordshire
EN6 4PR
Telephone: 01707 872632
Facsimile: 01707 875705

Residential accommodation maintained by the local authority. Activities provided include mountain biking, parachute games, assault course, problem solving and trampolining.

The Curriculum
Outdoor provision

Reach Out Projects
Education Centre
Hall Grove
Welwyn Garden City
Hertfordshire
AL7 4PJ
Telephone: 01707 335968
Facsimile: 01707 373089
Traditional narrowboats for day hire on Grand Union Canal. Self-catering residential centre in north Bedfordshire. Reach Out Projects is a charity.

West Hyde Residential Centre
Old Uxbridge Road
West Hyde
Rickmansworth
Hertfordshire
WD3 2XL
Telephone: 01923 720747
Facsimile: 01923 720747
Self-catering accommodation for up to 34 in modern heated building with all catering equipment provided.

HIGHLAND

Alan Kimber
Calluna
Heathercroft
Fort William
Inverness-shire
PH33 6RE
Telephone: 01397 700451
Facsimile: 01397 700489
Self-catering accommodation providing mountain activities in winter and summer.

Craigower Lodge Outdoor Centre
Golf Course Road
Newtonmore
Inverness-shire
PH20 1AT
Telephone: 01540 673319
Facsimile: 01540 673319
Residential centre providing skiing, canoeing and environmental studies for pupils aged 8-18.

John Patchett
Mandalay
Old Distillery Road
Kingussie
Inverness-shire
PH21 1EZ
Telephone: 01540 661800
Advises, lectures, leads and instructs in mountaineering in the Cairngorms in summer and winter.

Lagganlia Outdoor Education Centre
Kincraig
Kingussie
Inverness-shire
PH21 1NG
Telephone: 01540 651265
Facsimile: 01560 651240
Residential centre providing a wide variety of courses in outdoor education for all ages.

Loch Insh Watersports and Skiing Centre
Insh Hall
Kincraig
Kingussie
Inverness-shire PH21 1NU
Telephone: 01540 651272
Facsimile: 01540 651208
Residential centre offering canoeing, sailing, windsurfing, fishing, skiing (dry and real), mountain biking, hill walking and river trips.

Mountain Craft
Glenfinnan
Fort William
PH37 4LT
Telephone: 01397 722213
Facsimile: 01397 722300
Courses provided for students aged 16 upwards.

Outward Bound Scotland
Loch Eil Centre
Achdalieu
Fort William
Inverness-shire
PH33 7NN
Telephone: 01397 772866
Facsimile: 01397 772869
Provides outdoor development training courses for up to 75 11-18-year-olds.

The Curriculum

Outdoor provision

Peter Cliff
Ardenberg
Grant Road
Grantown-on-Spey
Perthshire
PH26 3LD
Telephone: 01479 2824
*Self-catering accommodation for 26 people.
Instruction is available from mountain
instructors and guides.*

HUMBERSIDE

Humberside Youth Association Ltd
36 Market Place
Beverley
North Humberside
HU17 9AG
Telephone: 01482 868630
Facsimile: 01482 882592
*Self-catering residential accommodation for 54
at Muston Grange Centre. Close to the beach
and the North Yorkshire Moors.*

ISLE OF MAN

Ardwhallin Outdoor Pursuits Centre
West Baldwin
Douglas
Isle of Man
Contact: Lesley Sleight
Telephone: 01624 852208
Facsimile: 01624 852208
*Accommodation for up to 22 with equipment for
archery, pistol shooting, canoeing,
orienteering, climbing and abseiling.*

Eary Cushlin Youth Adventure Centre
c/o Ardwhallin Outdoor Pursuits Centre
West Baldwin
Douglas
Isle of Man
Contact: Lesley Sleight
Telephone: 01624 852208
Facsimile: 01624 852208
*Situated near Dalby, the Centre has
accommodation for groups of up to 18*
*students with equipment for orienteering,
walking and field studies. Canoeing, climbing
and abseiling equipment can be borrowed
from Ardwhallin.*

Venture Centre
Lewaigue Farm
Maughold
Isle of Man
IM7 1AW
Telephone: 01624 814240
Facsimile: 01624 815615
*Centre providing activities for students aged 9
and up. Courses include abseiling, canoeing,
air rifle shooting, archery, assault course, raft
building, map and compass, go-karting, horse
management, campcraft, hill walking and
sailing.*

ISLE OF WIGHT

Wight Water Adventure Sports
19 Orchardleigh Road
Shanklin
Isle of Wight
PO37 7NP
Telephone: 01983 866269
Facsimile: 01983 866269
*Non-residential activity centre open April to
September. Provides catamaran sailing,
windsurfing, canoeing, wave-skiing, surfing,
bodyboarding and mountain biking.*

KENT

Arethusa Venture Centre
Lower Upnor
Rochester
Kent
ME2 4XB
Telephone: 01634 719933/711566
Facsimile: 01634 295905
*Residential accommodation for up to 90 people.
Courses are provided in outdoor and
environmental education.*

The Curriculum

Outdoor provision

Bewl Water Outdoor Education Centre
Bewl Water
Lamberhurst
Kent
TN3 8JH
Telephone: 01892 890716
Centre run by Kent County Council providing courses in outdoor pursuits.

Bowles Outdoor Centre
Eridge Green
Tunbridge Wells
Kent
TN3 9LW
Telephone: 01892 665665
Facsimile: 01892 669556
Residential accommodation for up to 70 students plus staff. On-site facilities include rock climbing (sandstone), skiing (dry) and swimming. Also available are canoeing, orienteering and initiative/team-building activities. Suitable for age 9 upwards.

LANCASHIRE

Adventure Centre Ltd
Evans House
Off Orford Lane
Warrington
Lancashire
WA2 7HW
Telephone: 01925 411385
Outdoor pursuits superstore for walking, climbing and camping equipment.

Arnside Youth Hostel
Oakfield Lodge
Redhills Road
Carnforth
Lancashire
LA5 0AT
Telephone: 01524 761781
Facsimile: 01524 762589
Comfortable hostel accommodation popular with ages 8-13. Most outdoor activities can be provided via a specialised independent team of instructors.

Borwick Hall Residential Centre
Borwick
Carnforth
Lancashire
LA6 1JU
Telephone: 01524 732508
Facsimile: 01524 732590
Residential centre providing accommodation for up to 90, including 20 self-catering. Camping facilities. Equipment available. Situated near the Lake District, the Yorkshire Dales and Morecambe Bay.

Cattleshaw Centre
Waterworks Road
Delph
Oldham
Lancashire
OL3 5LZ
Contact: Mike Green
Telephone: 01457 874276
Facsimile: 01457 820551
Residential accommodation (catered or self-catering) for 32 students and 4 staff. Courses available in outdoor or environmental activities.

Ingleborough Hall
Clapham
Lancaster
LA2 8EF
Telephone: 01524 251265
Facsimile: 01524 251020
Residential accommodation for up to 100 students, with outdoor activities provided by the centre staff. Run by Bradford Metropolitan District Council.

Moor Crag Water Activity Centre
c/o Waddecar Scout Camp
Beacon Fell
Wigton
Lancashire
PR3 2ER
Telephone: 01995 61336
Facsimile: 01995 61178
Indoor accommodation for 26 in modern premises. Available for 7-18-year-olds for canoeing, sailing, climbing, shooting, abseiling and archery.

The Curriculum

Outdoor provision

Venture Forth Base
W Lancs County Scout Office
Wood Top, Beacon Fell
Goosnargh
Lancashire
PR3 2ER
Telephone: 01995 61336
Facsimile: 01995 61178
Accommodation in Scandinavian-style chalets to a maximum of 76. Available to ages 7-18 for canoeing, sailing, climbing, shooting, abseiling and archery.

LEICESTERSHIRE

Adventure Afloat
c/o Leicester Outdoor Pursuits Centre
Loughborough Road
Leicester
LE4 5PN
Telephone: 0116 266 2010
Narrowboats, each with 12 bunks, catering and residential facilities and wheelchair access.

Arnesby Christian Conference Centre
St Peter's Road
Arnesby
Leicestershire
LE8 5WJ
Telephone: 0116 247 8392
Area suitable for camping and outdoor games.

Hothorpe Hall
Theddingworth
Lutterworth
Leicestershire
LE17 6QX
Telephone: 01858 880257
Facsimile: 01858 880979
Residential accommodation for 57 people.

LINCOLNSHIRE

Hot Rocks
97 Swineshead Road
Wyberton Fen
Boston
Lincolnshire
PE21 7JG
Telephone: 01205 311700/359909
Facsimile: 01205 311777
Instruction provided in climbing, abseiling, caving, canoeing, raft building, river running and initiative-based exercises.

LONDON

Beauchamp Lodge Settlement
2 Warwick Crescent
Harrow Road
London
W2 6NE
Telephone: 0171-289 3388
Narrowboat trips.

International Students Housing Society
International House
109 Brookhill Road
London
SE18 6RZ
Telephone: 0181-854 1418
Facsimile: 0181-855 9257
Residential accommodation.

Laburnum Boat Club
Laburnum Street
Hackney
London E2 8BA
Telephone: 0171-729 2915
Provides canoeing, narrowboat trips and a school canal study programme.

The Curriculum

Outdoor provision

Wildside Trust
5-11 Worship Street
London EC2A 2BH
Telephone: 0171-628 7261
The Wildside Trust offers unique experiences to young people aged 8-25 of differing abilities and needs. The creative workshop programme is based around countryside arts and adventure, and explores our relationship to nature, conservation and integration.

LOTHIAN

Port Edgar Watersports Centre
Port Edgar Shore Road
South Queensferry
West Lothian
EH30 9SQ
Telephone: 0131-331 3330
Facsimile: 0131-331 4878
Courses provided in sailing, canoeing and powerboating at all levels. Minimum age 8 years.

MANCHESTER

The Station House
c/o Burnage High School
Burnage Lane
Burnage
Manchester
M19 1BU
Telephone: 0161-432 1527
Facsimile: 0161-442 2366
Self-catering centrally heated accommodation for up to 24 people, located at Buxworth in the Peak District.

MERSEYSIDE

Dave Hardy
Outdoor Education Unit, School of Education
John Moores University
Barkhill Road
Liverpool
L17 6BD
Telephone: 0151-231 5249
Facsimile: 0151-729 0136

Provides consultation for schools and other educational establishments on outdoor education curriculum development and associated administrative details.

Merlin Holidays (MV) Ltd
Brecon House
120 Allerton Road
Liverpool
L18 2DG
Telephone: 0151-734 2477
Facsimile: 0151-734 2997
Residential centre providing courses in outdoor activities suitable for ages 3-18.

Merseysport
110 Mariners Wharf
Queens Dock
Liverpool
L3 4DG
Telephone: 0151-708 9322
Facsimile: 0151-709 5141
Courses in canoeing, sailing and windsurfing for all levels.

Wirral Outdoor Pursuits
Barnston Dale Centre
Storeton Lane
Barnston
Wirral L61 1BX
Telephone: 0151-648 4148
Facsimile: 0151-648 4148
Courses provided in canoeing, climbing, orienteering, hill walking and problem solving.

MIDDLESEX

Hillington Outdoor Activities Centre
Dews Lane
Harvil Road
Harefield
Middlesex UB9 6JN
Telephone: 01895 824171
Facsimile: 01895 824171
Campsite available for students aged 8-18, with barbecue and washing-up areas plus separate shower and toilet block. Suitable for raft building, sailing, windsurfing and canoeing, instructors provided or bring your own.

The Curriculum

Outdoor provision

Youth Hostels Association
133-135 High Street
Staines
Middlesex
TW18 4PD
Telephone: 01784 452989
*Sells a range of outdoor clothing, tents,
sleeping bags, rucksacks and boots.
Discount for YHA members and Duke of
Edinburgh Award participants.*

NORFOLK

Break
20 Hooks Hill Road
Sheringham
Norfolk
NR26 8NL
Telephone: 01263 823170
Facsimile: 01263 825560
*Provides holidays and respite care for children
and adults with learning difficulties at centres
in Norfolk.*

Hilltop Outdoor Centre
Old Wood
Beeston Regis
Sheringham
Norfolk
NR26 8TS
Telephone: 01263 824514
Facsimile: 01263 824514
*Residential accommodation for groups of up to
65. Outdoor pursuits and field studies for
ages 6-13 and development training for 16
upwards. Activities include mountain biking,
archery, air rifle shooting, climbing,
orienteering, sailing, canoeing, horse riding,
geography, history, ecology and science.*

Horsted Centre
Rectory Road
Horsted
Norwich
NR12 7EP
Telephone: 01603 737215
Facsimile: 01603 737494

*Accommodation for between 12 and 36 people
close to the Norfolk Broads. Activities include
canoeing, sailing, archery and abseiling.*

How Hill Trust
How Hill
Ludham
Great Yarmouth
Norfolk
NR29 5PG
Telephone: 01692 678555
*Structured field study courses in biology and
geography for school groups in the 360-acre
nature reserve.*

Pleasaunce, The
Overstrand
Cromer
Norfolk
NR27 0PN
Telephone: 01263 579212
Residential accommodation for up to 30 people.

The Old Bakery
Hindolveston
Dereham
Norfolk
NR20 5DF
Telephone: 01263 861325
*Residential accommodation with all meals for
up to 12 people.*

Winterton Adventure Centre
c/o Martham Youth & Community Centre
Coronation Recreation Ground, Off Rollesby Rd
Martham, Great Yarmouth
Norfolk
NR29 4SN
Telephone: 01493 748838
*Accommodation with showers for approximately
24 young people. One main hall with
partition. Kitchen. Supply own camp beds,
etc. Organise own activities. Close to beach.*

The Curriculum
Outdoor provision

NORTHAMPTONSHIRE

Frontier Centres
Welford Avenue
Irthlingborough
Wellingborough
Northamptonshire
NN9 5XA
Telephone: 01933 651718
Facsimile: 01933 651893
Residential accommodation providing courses in canoeing, abseiling, climbing, archery, orienteering, overnight bivvies and expeditions.

NORTHERN IRELAND

Bushmills Education Centre
7 Priestland Road
Bushmills
Co Antrim
BP57 8QP
Telephone: 012657 31599
Facsimile: 012657 31591
Accommodation for 72 people. Activities offered include canoeing, deep-sea fishing, sailing, surfing, archery, snorkelling, camping, hill walking, orienteering, climbing and scrambling. A laboratory is also available for environmental work.

Gortatole Outdoor Education Centre
Florencecourt
Co Fermanagh
BT92 1ED
Activities provided include climbing (wall) and a ropes course. Classrooms and a laboratory are available.

Southern Education and Library Board
3 Charlemont Place
The Mall
Armagh BT61 9AX
Telephone: 01861 512234
Outdoor education facilities for schools and recognised youth organisations at two Outdoor Education Centres and some self-catering bases. Priority is given to youth groups at weekends and in the school holidays.

Tollymore Mountain Centre
Bryansford
Newcastle
Co Down
BT33 0PT
Telephone: 013967 22623
Facsimile: 013967 26155
Courses provided in mountaineering, rock climbing and canoeing. Multi-activity sessions also available.

Youth Hostel Association of Northern Ireland Ltd
22-26 Donegall Road
Belfast
BT12 5JN
Contact: Ken Canavan, General Secretary
Telephone: 01232 324733
Facsimile: 01232 439699
Seeks to encourage an appreciation of the countryside among young people through the provision of hostel accommodation. It takes any action possible to preserve the beauties of the countryside and to obtain or maintain access across rights of way.

NORTHUMBERLAND

Bearsports Group
Windy Gyle
Belford
Northumberland
NE70 7QE
Telephone: 01668 213289
Residential outdoor education courses in Northumberland for groups of up to 43. Activities include canoeing, climbing, windsurfing, orienteering, bivouacs and surfing. School leader packs available.

Calvert Trust Kielder
Kielder Water
Hexham
Northumberland
NE48 1BS
Telephone: 01434 250232
Accommodation for 50 offering tailor-made courses.

The Curriculum

Outdoor provision

City of Newcastle Outdoor Education Service
121 Trewhitt Road
Heaton
Newcastle upon Tyne
NE5 6DY
Telephone: 0191-265 1311
Facsimile: 0191-276 5686
Self-catering accommodation for groups of up to 32 people at Kielder Water in Northumberland.

Featherstone Castle
Haltwhistle
Northumberland
NE49 0BP
Telephone: 01434 320363/320202
Self-catering accommodation for groups of up to 100 students and staff situated close to the Roman Wall and the Pennine Way.

Outdoor Education Centre
Clock Tower Annexe
Ford Castle
Ford, Berwick-on-Tweed
Northumberland
Contact: Roger Homyer, Centre Director
Telephone: 01890 820257
Facsimile: 01890 820413
Residential centre offering courses. Run by Northumberland County Council.

OXFORDSHIRE

Middle Aston House
Middle Aston
Oxford
OX6 3PT
Telephone: 01869 340361
Team-building and leadership outdoor exercises designed for over-16s.

POWYS

Argoed Lwyd
Libanus
Brecon
Powys
Telephone: 01874 611947
Facsimile: 01874 623485
A residential centre catering for 50 situated in the Brecon Beacons National Park and administered by Hampshire County Council.

Birch Grove
Heol Senni
Brecon
Powys
Telephone: 01874 636464
A residential centre catering for 18 situated in the Brecon Beacons National Park and administered by Hampshire County Council.

Cadarn Trail Riding Farm
Velindre
Three Cocks
Brecon
Powys
LD3 0SP
Telephone: 01497 847351
Facsimile: 01497 847680
Residential centre with full board providing mountain riding courses in the Brecon Beacons National Park.

Dinefwr Treks
Caban Cwmffynnon
Cefn Gorwydd
Llangammarch Wells
Powys
LD4 4DW
Telephone: 01591 610638
Bunkhouse accommodation for 24 people. Activities offered include birdwatching and map and compass work.

Joe's Lodge Mountain Centre
Hay Road
Talgarth
Brecon
Powys
LD3 0AL
Telephone: 01874 711845
Self-catering bunkhouse groups of up to 26. Facilities include heating, showers, drying room, TV. Meals can be provided. Well located for activities in the Brecon Beacons National Park.

The Curriculum

Outdoor provision

Kevin Walker Mountain Activities
74 Beacons Park
Brecon
Powys
LD3 9BQ
Telephone: 01874 625111
Facsimile: 01874 625111
Instruction in rock climbing, abseiling, caving, hill walking and associated activities.

Lewisham Education Authority Outdoor Education Centre
Tyn y Berth Mountain Centre
Corris Uchaf
Machynlleth
Powys
SY20 9RH
Telephone: 01654 761678
Two centres, each catering for up to 28 students and staff and offering courses in mountain walking, camping, rock climbing, abseiling, orienteering, pony trekking, and gorge walking and ropes courses.

Maes y Lade Outdoor Education & Environmental Centre
Tregoyd
Brecon
Powys
LD3 0SS
Telephone: 01497 847287
Facsimile: 01497 847287
Residential centre offering activities including canoeing, caving, climbing, abseiling, camping & expeditions, pony trekking and mountain walking.

Mount Severn Centre
Llanidloes
Powys
SY18 6PP
Telephone: 01686 412344
Facsimile: 01686 412344
Residential multi-activity courses in climbing, abseiling, hill walking, archery, canoeing, whitewater rafting, orienteering, caving, pony trekking and a ropes course.

Pendarren House Outdoor Education Centre
Llangenny
Crickhowell
Powys
NP8 1HE
Telephone: 01873 810694
Facsimile: 01873 811986
Outdoor and environmental courses for Key Stages 2, 3 & 4.

SHROPSHIRE

Bishop Mascall Centre
Lower Galdeford
Ludlow
Shropshire
SY8 1RZ
Telephone: 01584 873882
Facsimile: 01584 877945
Self-catering or full catering residential accommodation for groups of up to 47. Useful as a base to explore the locality.

Edgmond Hall Residential Centre
Edgmond
Newport
Shropshire
TF10 8JY
Telephone: 01952 810799
Residential accommodation for 38 students and 4 staff, run by Sandwell Metropolitan Borough Council and open to outside groups. Subjects offered include environmental education, geography, history, art, science, drama, English, PSE and team-building courses.

Quinta Christian Centre
Weston Rhyn
Oswestry
Shropshire
SY10 7LR
Contact: Peter Bevington, Centre Manager
Telephone: 01691 773696
Facsimile: 01691 774687
Self-catering accommodation or full-board equivalent for groups of 10-140. Sports facilities.

The Curriculum

Outdoor provision

Telford Ski Slope
Madley Court Centre
Court Street
Telford
Shropshire
TF7 5DZ
Contact: Ms Frances Jackson, Booking
    Secretary
Telephone: 01952 586862
Facsimile: 01952 586862
*Instruction provided in skiing, snowboarding
    and Alpine tobogganing.*

Ysgol Natur Maengwynedd
Llanrhaedr-yr-Mochnant
Oswestry
Shropshire
SY10 0DE
Contact: Head of Centre
Telephone: 01691 780581
Facsimile: 01691 780581
*Residential centre offering a wide range of
    adventurous and environmental activities.*

SOMERSET

Black Rock Outdoor Education
16 St Andrews Road
Cheddar
Somerset
BS27 3NE
Telephone: 01934 744389
Facsimile: 01934 744389
*Residential accommodation providing courses
    in caving, climbing, mountain biking,
    canoeing and archery.*

Burnworthy Activity Centre
Churchstanton
Taunton
Somerset
TA3 7DR
Contact: Dave Regan & Mike Hicks
Telephone: 019184 656691
*Activities provided: archery, climbing, abseiling,
    expeditions, mountain biking, raft building,
    canoeing, caving and windsurfing. Self-
    catering accommodation for up to 45 is in
    tents.*

Mill on the Brue Activity Centre
Trendle Farm
Bruton
Somerset
BA10 0BA
Telephone: 01749 812307
Facsimile: 01749 812706
*Residential and day visits. Activities on site
    include 1-2 hour activity and team-building
    tasks. Outdoor activities include canoeing,
    climbing, high ropes, archery, orienteering,
    rafting and problem solving.*

Millfield Village of Education
Millfield School
Street
Somerset
BA16 0YD
Telephone: 01458 445823
Facsimile: 01458 840584
*Summer holiday residential accommodation
    and a wide range of courses for all ages.*

Pinkery Outdoor Education Centre
Simonsbath
Minehead
Somerset
TA24 7LL
Telephone: 01643 831437
Facsimile: 01598 753435
*Provides accommodation, advice, resources
    and tuition for self-planned, self-catering
    groups of up to 36 students and staff.*

STAFFORDSHIRE

Kingswood Centre Ltd
Barn Lane
Albrighton
Wolverhampton
Staffordshire
WV7 3AW
Telephone: 01902 847000
Facsimile: 01902 845424
*Fully residential courses for school groups,
    linking outdoor pursuits, environmental
    studies, educational visits and IT with the
    National Curriculum.*

The Curriculum

Outdoor provision

Orchard Farm
38 Cross Street
Ware
Hertfordshire
SG12 7AM
Contact: Mrs I R Mansfield, Registrar
Telephone: 01920 462863
*Self-catering residential accommodation for up
to 50 people in a farmhouse situated in
Cauldon, between Ashbourne and Leek, in
the Southern Peak District. Facilities include
electricity, water, toilets, washing facilities,
dining room and kitchen.*

Shepherds Buildings
c/o Diocesan Youth Office
St Mary's House, The Close
Lichfield
Staffordshire
WS13 7LD
Telephone: 01543 414551
Facsimile: 01543 250935
*Self-catering accommodation for 22 students.
Situated in the village of Burnhill Green on
the Staffordshire/Shropshire border.*

STRATHCLYDE

Achnamara Outdoor Education Centre
Achnamara
Lochgilphead
Argyll
PA31 8PX
Telephone: 01546 850247
Facsimile: 01546 850247
*Activities centre offering sailing, canoeing,
windsurfing and hill walking with half-day
taster courses or week-long skills courses.*

Ardroy Outdoor Centre
Lochgoilhead
Argyle
Strathclyde
PA24 8AE
Telephone: 01301 703391
Facsimile: 01301 703479
*A residential centre accommodating groups of
up to 44 of either primary or secondary age.
Outdoor activities include canoeing,
abseiling, orienteering and hill walking.*

Arnhall Centre
Whiting Bay
Brodick
Isle of Arran KA27 8PX
Telephone: 01770 700533
Facsimile: 01770 700533
*Self-catering or fully catered residential
accommodation providing courses to suit all
needs. Adapted and experienced in special
needs.*

Arran Outdoor Centre
Shiskine
Isle of Arran
KA27 8EW
Telephone: 01770 860333
Facsimile: 01770 860333
*Outdoor activity weeks and weekends for
students aged 5-14 in canoeing, gorge
walking, fishing, cycling, hill walking and
cruising.*

Arrochar Outdoor Education Centre
Arrochar
Argyll
G83 7AA
Telephone: 01301 702355
Facsimile: 01301 702664
*Courses offered in curricular, social/personal
development or skills training.*

Blairvadach Outdoor Pursuits Centre
Hellensburgh
Dunbartonshire
G84 8NN
Telephone: 01436 820491
Facsimile: 01436 820668
*Residential accommodation for groups of up to
60 during school holidays. Activities offered
include sailing, canoeing, hill walking,
orienteering and environmental studies, or
you can organise your own programme.*

Cartsdyke Resource Centre
1-3 Riverside Road
Greenock
Renfrewshire PA15 3AQ
Telephone: 01475 892335
Facsimile: 01475 892335
*Hire of equipment: tents, sleeping bags, boots,
waterproofs, etc.*

The Curriculum

Outdoor provision

Primary Adventure
12 St Modans Way
Rosneath
Helensburgh
Dunbartonshire
G84 0SQ
Telephone: 01436 831288
Facsimile: 01436 831288
Residential centre providing a range of outdoor activities. Situated in the western Highlands, one hour from Glasgow.

Tom Redfern
2 Riverside Cottages
Benmore
Dunoon
Argyll
PA23 8QU
Telephone: 01369 706474
Instruction in rock climbing and mountaineering.

SUFFOLK

Jarman Centre
Cambridgeshire East Guides
119 Duchess Drive
Newmarket
Suffolk
CB8 9HB
Telephone: 01223 356615
Facsimile: 01223 356615
Self-catering accommodation for 36 students and 6 adults. Campsites also available.

SURREY

Action Packs
The Booking Hall
Boxhill Station
Westhumble
Surrey
RH5 6BT
Telephone: 01306 886944
Facsimile: 01306 880332
Mountain biking centre.

Grafham Centre, The
The Education Centre
The Cathedral
Guildford
Surrey
GU2 5UP
Telephone: 01483 450423
Facsimile: 01483 450424
Residential accommodation for 24 students and staff.

Surrey Association of Youth Clubs
Felbury House
Holmbury St Mary
Dorking
Surrey
RH5 6NL
Telephone: 01306 730929
Facsimile: 01306 730610
Residential centre catering for up to 46 people (and fully equipped for disabled guests), offering archery, orienteering, mountain biking and a challenge course.

SUSSEX

Adur Outdoor Activities Centre
Brighton Road
Shoreham-by-Sea
Sussex
BN4 5LT
Telephone: 01273 462968
Residential accommodation for 16. Activities include canoeing (kayak and Canadian), orienteering, climbing, walking, raft building, mountain biking, environmental studies and problem solving.

Ashburnham Christian Trust
Ashburnham Place
Battle
Sussex
TN33 9NF
Telephone: 01424 892244
Facsimile: 01424 892243
Residential accommodation suitable for school groups.

The Curriculum

Outdoor provision

Cobnor Activities Centre
Cobnor Point
Chidham
Chichester
Sussex
PO18 8TE
Telephone: 01243 572791
Self-catering accommodation for 30 including facilities for the disabled. Activities include canoeing, sailing and windsurfing. Situated in Chichester harbour.

TAYSIDE

Compass Christian Centre
Glenshee Lodge
By Blairgowrie
Perthsire
PH10 7QD
Telephone: 01250 885209
Facsimile: 01250 885209
Centre providing the following activities: canoeing, orienteering, climbing, abseiling, skiing and environmental studies.

Croft na Caber Ltd
Kenmore
Loch Tay
Perthshire
PH15 2HW
Telephone: 01887 830588
Facsimile: 01887 830649
Courses in watersports and outdoor activities.

Highland Adventure
Knockshannoch
Glenisla
By Alyth
Perthshire
PH11 8PE
Telephone: 01575 582238
Facsimile: 01575 582207
Accommodation for up to 60 people for downhill and cross-country skiing in winter, and in summer, orienteering, rifle shooting, climbing (wall), abseiling and problem solving.

Mains of Taymouth
The Barn Bunkhouse
Kenmore

Perthshire
PH15 2HN
Telephone: 01887 830226
Facsimile: 01887 830211
Self-catering accommodation for up to 35 people. Situated close to centres offering watersports, pony trekking, mountain biking, walking and fishing.

PGL Dalguise
Dunkeld
Tayside
PH8 0JX
Telephone: 01350 727339
Facsimile: 01350 728933
Multi-activity taster sessions for ages 6-18.

TYNE & WEAR

Rising Sun Countryside Centre
Whitley Road
Newcastle upon Tyne
NE12 9SS
Telephone: 0191-266 7733
Facsimile: 0191-266 8455
Non-residential study centre in the heart of North Tyneside providing a full environmental studies service related to the National Curriculum.

WARWICKSHIRE

Coventry Young People's Centre
c/o Mr & Mrs Heighton
21 Dalkeith Avenue
Bilton, Rugby
Warwickshire
CV22 7NN
Telephone: 01788 815514
Self-catering residential accommodation for groups of up to 32 at Southam.

Purley Chase New Church Centre
Purley Chase Lane
Mancetter
Atherstone
Warwickshire CV9 2RQ
Contact: The Manager
Telephone: 01827 712370

The Curriculum

Outdoor provision

A residential centre offering meals and accommodation for groups wishing to organise their own activities.

Wroxhall Abbey Enterprises Ltd
Wroxhall Abbey School
Warwick
CV35 7NB
Telephone: 01926 484541
Facsimile: 01926 484531
Summer holiday activities for students aged 4-12, including archery, fencing, pottery, swimming, laser shooting and canoeing.

WEST MIDLANDS

Ackers, The
Golden Hillock Road
Small Heath
Birmingham
B11 2PY
Telephone: 0121-772 3739
Facsimile: 0121-766 7870
Activities centre offering discounted rates to schools on skiing, climbing, canoeing, rope courses, tobogganing and snowboarding.

Acorn Venture Ltd
Worcester Road
Hagley
Stourbridge
West Midlands
DY9 0NW
Telephone: 01562 882151
Facsimile: 01562 887091
Multi-activity courses in Wales, France and Spain. All centres BCU/RYA-approved with NGB-qualified instructors.

Associated Cruises
c/o Mr L R Still
29a The Grove
Great Barr, Birmingham
Telephone: 0121-357 9418
Two 12-berth narrowboats available (with skipper) for navigation of inland canals. Both operate from Wolverhampton and are available for weekends or 7-day journeys.

Bell's Farm
Bell's Close
157 Bell's Lane
Druids Heath, Birmingham
B14 5QH
Telephone: 0121-784 6408
Tudor building for hire as overnight centre for up to 12 children with leaders. Special needs teacher available for craft and historical projects. Sundry outdoor pursuits and specialist craft workshops in textiles, woodwork, metalwork, etc. Contact Roz Sheard, Bell's Farm Schools Liaison, 43 Croft Road, Yardley, Birmingham B26 1SQ. Telephone: 0121-784 6408.

Bentley Leisure Pavilion
Bentley Road North
Walsall
WS2 0EA
Contact: Ms Carole Harris, Centre Manager
Telephone: 01922 616165
Facsimile: 01922 30757
Facilities provided: outdoor climbing tower and tennis court.

Birmingham Wheels
1 Adderley Road South
Saltley
Birmingham
B8 1AD
Contact: Mr M Boy, Manager
Telephone: 0121-771 0725
Facsimile: 0121-771 2167
Urban farm, nature trail, rollerskating, skateboarding and a variety of motorised and wheel-based activities.

Coven Outdoor Centre
Laches Lane
Slade Heath
Wolverhampton
West Midlands
WV10 7PA
Telephone: 01902 790388
Facsimile: 01902 790376
Residential accommodation for 46 students, providing courses in environmental studies, canoeing, archery, climbing and air rifle shooting.

The Curriculum

Outdoor provision

VISITS - WEST MIDLANDS

Coventry Waterways Scheme
Canal House
Drapers Fields
Coventry
CV1 4LG
Telephone: 01203 831698
Facsimile: 01203 831698
Two 65ft residential narrowboats each with 12
berths, a gas cooker, cabin heater, toilets,
fridge and electric lights. Part of Coventry
City Council Education Department's
educational provision.

Elisabeth Svendsen Trust for Children and
Donkeys, The
Sutton Park
Birmingham
B74 2YT
Contact: Dr E Svendsen MBE, Hon
Administrator
Telephone: 01395 578222
Facsimile: 01395 579266
Provides riding activities for children with
special needs and disabilities, using donkeys.

Kingsbury Water Park
Bodymoor Heath Lane
Sutton Coldfield
West Midlands
B76 0DY
Telephone: 01827 872660
Facsimile: 01827 875161
Lakes available for environmental work and
watersports.

Queensway Trust
6 South Street
Harborne
Birmingham
B17 0DB
Telephone: 0121-428 4590
Facsimile: 0121-428 3817
The Trust hires out to groups 2 cottages
sleeping 14 people, and a fully equipped
camp sleeping 25 people. The cottages are
located at Burwarton and Button Oak, and
the camp is on Burcot.

Sneyd Community School Water Activities
Centre
Vernon Way
Bloxwich
Walsall
West Midlands
WS3 2PA
Contact: David Hart, Head of Centre
Telephone: 01922 710020
Courses provided in windsurfing, sailing and
canoeing. Also equipment for hire for self-
tuition.

St Peters College
College Road
Saltley
Birmingham
B8 3TE
Telephone: 0121-327 3734
Facsimile: 0121-327 3734
Self-catering group hostel with camping
facilities.

Urban Outdoor Education Centre
Chillingholme Road
Birmingham
B36 8QJ
Telephone: 0121-748 6868
Facsimile: 0121-776 6473
A centre run by Birmingham for Birmingham
schools, offering canoeing, sailing, rock
climbing, skiing, orienteering, mountaineering
and expeditions.

Youth Afloat Sailing Centre
Fordbridge Road
Kingshurst
Solihull
West Midlands
B37 6LY
Contact: R F Williams, Principal
Telephone: 0121-788 8943
Teaching establishment providing water-based
activities for young people.

The Curriculum

Outdoor provision

WESTERN ISLES

Uist Outdoor Centre
1 Cearn Dusgaidh
Lochmaddy
Isle of North Uist
Outer Hebrides
HS6 5AE
Telephone: 01876 500480
*Provider of outdoor activities for all ages on hill,
sea and beach.*

WILTSHIRE

Legge House
Church Hill
Wroughton
Swindon
Wiltshire
SN4 9JS
Telephone: 01793 813273
Facsimile: 01793 814582
*Self-catering dormitory accommodation for up
to 32 people.*

YORKSHIRE

Barrowby House
Barrowby
Kirkby Overblow
Harrogate
North Yorkshire
HG3 1HY
Telephone: 0113 288 6240
Facsimile: 0113 288 6428
*A country house providing full-board
accommodation for groups of up to 38.*

Bewerley Park Centre for Outdoor Education
Pateley Bridge
Harrogate
North Yorkshire
HG3 5JB
Contact: Mrs A Barrand, Bursar
Telephone: 01423 711287
Facsimile: 01423 712648
*LEA Centre available to out-county groups at
weekends and school holidays. Suitable for
groups of between 20 and 130.*

Birchcliffe Centre, The
Birchcliffe Road
Hebden Bridge
West Yorkshire
HX7 8DG
Contact: Simon Booth
Telephone: 01422 843626
Facsimile: 01422 842424
Catered accommodation for up to 64.

Buckden House
Buckden
Skipton
North Yorkshire
BD23 5JA
Contact: Rick Halsall
Telephone: 01756 760254
Facsimile: 01756 760423
*Run by Bradford Metropolitan District Council,
activities provided include caving, climbing,
canoeing and fieldwork.*

Castleton Rotary Centre
c/o Robert Jackson
14 The Grove, Totley
Sheffield
S17 4AS
Telephone: 0114 236 5218
Self-catering accommodation for 70-75 people.

Champion House
Edale
Sheffield
South Yorkshire
S30 2ZA
Telephone: 01433 670254
Facsimile: 01433 670254
*Accommodation for 44 with staff providing
climbing, abseiling, orienteering, hill walking
and team-building exercises.*

Dales Centre Ltd, The
Grassington
North Yorkshire
BD23 5AU
Telephone: 01756 752757
Facsimile: 01756 752522
*Activities provided for ages 10-18 include
climbing, caving, navigation, mountain biking,
pony trekking, raft building and gorge
scrambling.*

The Curriculum
Outdoor provision

David Shepherd
36 Mount Street
Harrogate
HG2 8DQ
Telephone: 01423 873301
Trains and assesses teachers wishing to take young people rock climbing.

David Smith
30 Garsdale Road
Newsome
Huddersfield
South Yorkshire
HD4 6QZ
Telephone: 01484 541301
Instruction for individuals or groups provided in any land-based outdoor activity.

Draco Enterprises
10 Ford Close
Dronfield
Sheffield
South Yorkshire
S18 6TG
Telephone: 01246 414260
Guided walks and field trips within the White and Dark Peak District, also navigation, canoeing and orienteering.

Emmaus Centre, The
York Diocesan Centre
Brompton by Sawden
Scarborough
North Yorkshire
YO13 9DG
Telephone: 01723 859777
Facsimile: 01723 859702
Self-catering accommodation situated on the southern edge of the North Yorkshire Moors.

Glenmoor Centre, The
Wells Road
Ilkley
West Yorkshire
LS29 9JF
Telephone: 01943 816359
Facsimile: 01943 816359
Residential accommodation situated on the edge of Ilkley Moor.

Great Hucklow Activity Centre
c/o 16 Chapel Street
Woodhouse
Sheffield
S13 7JN
Telephone: 0114 269 2755
The Centre is owned by Sheffield City Scout Council. It is self-catering, sleeps 54 people, is suitable for mixed parties and is fully centrally heated. It is in the middle of the Peak District.

Highfield House Residential Centre
Hangingstone Road
Ilkley
West Yorkshire
LS29 8BT
Contact: Mr and Mrs Mann
Telephone: 01943 607454
Residential centre catering for groups of between 20 and 56. Outdoor pursuits and field trips can be arranged.

Low Mill Residential Centre
Askrigg
Leyburn
North Yorkshire
DL8 3HZ
Telephone: 01969 650432
Residential accommodation catering for up to 40 people of all ages and abilities, including those with special needs. Activities provided include abseiling, caving, watersports, orienteering, mountain biking, snowsports, archery and initiative games.

Marrick Priory Outdoor Education Centre
Richmond
North Yorkshire
DL11 7LD
Telephone: 01748 884434
Facsimile: 01748 884434
Catered accommodation providing courses in climbing, caving, canoeing, orienteering, ropes, and team and initiative exercises.

The Curriculum

Outdoor provision

Middle Head Outdoor Pursuits Centre
Stape
Pickering
North Yorkshire
YO18 8QL
Contact: Ian Williams
Telephone: 01751 473120
Facsimile: 01751 477370
Provides outdoor education programmes.

Nell Bank Centre, The
Denton Road
Ilkley
West Yorkshire
LS29 0AA
Contact: Bruce Fowler
Telephone: 01943 602032
Facsimile: 01943 601690
Residential accommodation with staff-led sessions in activities related to the National Curriculum, including environmental education and orienteering. Run by Bradford Metropolitan District Council.

North York Moors Adventure Centre
Park House
Ingleby Cross
Northallerton
North Yorkshire
DL6 3PE
Telephone: 01609 882571
Residential accommodation for 24 people. Activities provided include climbing, canoeing, caving, mountain biking, orienteering, problem solving, raft building, pony trekking and bivouacs.

Parson Cross Centre, Sheffield College
Remington Road
Sheffield
South Yorkshire
S5 9PB
Telephone: 0114 260 2500
Facsimile: 0114 260 2501
Courses for students of 16 upwards, in NVQ Outdoor Education, GNVQ Outdoor Pursuits, GCSE and A level subjects.

Parson House Farm Outdoor Pursuits Centre
Longshaw
Sheffield
South Yorkshire
S11 7TZ
Telephone: 01433 631017
Facsimile: 01433 630794
Accommodation for up to 30. Activities provided include canoeing, climbing, abseiling, caving, orienteering, pony trekking and hill walking. Camping facilities.

Stones Environmental Training Centre
Upper Oakes
Dyson Lane
Ripponden, Sowerby Bridge
West Yorkshire
HX6 4JX
Telephone: 01422 824030
Self-catering accommodation for 42 students. Pennine location.

Toc H Centre
Colsterdale
Masham
Ripon
North Yorkshire
HG4 4NN
Telephone: 01765 689382
Residential self-catering accommodation for up to 28 people. Situated in the Yorkshire Dales.

Trig Point 49
Staithes
Whitby
North Yorkshire
TS13 5AH
Telephone: 01947 840757
Residential accommodation for groups of up to 250 people with full board. Activities offered include dinghy sailing, canoeing, rock climbing, abseiling, bivouac, expeditions, river walking, pony trekking and mountain biking. Alternatively leaders can organise their own activities, using the Centre as a base. Special needs groups are particularly catered for.

VISITS - YORKSHIRE

The Curriculum

Outdoor provision

Widdop Gate Hostel
c/o 5 Brow Top Road
Haworth
West Yorkshire
BD22 9PH
Telephone: 01535 643773
*Self-catering accommodation for up to 25.
Situated close to the Pennine Way.*

York Youth Hostel
Bishophill House
11-13 Bishophill Senior
York
YO1 1EF
Telephone: 01904 625904
Facsimile: 01904 612494
*Residential accommodation in the centre of the
city.*

Yorkshire Dales Field Centre
Square House
Church Street
Giggleswick, Settle
North Yorkshire
BD24 0BE
Telephone: 01729 824180
Facsimile: 01729 824180
*Residential accommodation providing
programmes on geography, geology, biology,
environmental science and outdoor pursuits.*

Youth Clubs North Yorkshire
Carlton Lodge Activity Centre
Carlton Miniott
Thirsk
North Yorkshire
YO7 4NJ
Telephone: 01845 522145
Facsimile: 01845 522145
*Residential self-catering or fully catering
accommodation for those aged 8 and above.
Activities can be provided. Camping is also
available.*

The Curriculum

Careers

ADMINISTRATION, BUSINESS, CLERICAL AND MANAGEMENT
General
Civil service
Health service administration
Public service administration
Business management
Personnel management and industrial relations
Clerical and secretarial work
Computer work
Politics
Management services
Operational research
Trading standards and consumer protection
Occupational safety and hygiene

ART AND DESIGN
General
Graphic art, design and illustration
Industrial and craft design
Fashion and clothing design
Surface and two-dimensional design
Interior design and display
Photography

TEACHING AND CULTURAL ACTIVITIES
Teaching and teacher support
Journalism and writing
Publishing
Museum and art gallery work
Library and information work
Historical and related work
Archaeology
Religion and church work

ENTERTAINMENT AND LEISURE
Theatre and drama
Music
Dance
Sport and recreation management and support staff
Radio, television, films and video work
Theatre
Travel and tourism

CATERING AND OTHER SERVICES
Hotel, catering and institution management
Catering and domestic work
Rig catering
Home economics
Beauty culture

Hairdressing
Burial and cremation
Graphology

HEALTH AND MEDICAL SERVICES
Medicine and surgery
Nursing
Dentistry and dental ancillary occupations
Pharmacy
Optics and orthoptics
Physiotherapy
Radiography and radiotherapy
Occupational therapy
Chiropody and podiatry
Medical research and laboratory sciences
Neurophysiology technicians
Physiological measurement and medical physics
Ambulance work
Complementary medicine and therapies

SOCIAL AND RELATED SERVICES
General
Social, probation and care work
Careers advisory and employment agency work
Youth and community work
Psychology
Charities and voluntary work

LAW AND RELATED WORK
Barrister and advocate
Solicitor
Legal executive
Court services
Patents and trademarks
Crown Prosecution Service
Conveyancing
Barristers' clerk

SECURITY AND PROTECTIVE SERVICES
General
Police and related work
Fire service

FINANCE AND RELATED WORK
General
Accountancy
High street banking
Merchant banking
Building societies
Insurance
Insurance broking

CAREERS

The Curriculum

Careers

Actuarial work
Financial services
Stock Exchange work
Pensions management

BUYING, SELLING AND RELATED SERVICES

Marketing and market research
Advertising
Specialist shops/sales
Public relations
Wholesale distribution
Modelling (London area)

SCIENCES, MATHEMATICS AND RELATED WORK

Chemistry
Biology
Microbiology and biotechnology
Mathematics
Statistics
Earth and environmental sciences
Oceanography, marine sciences, subsea engineering
Food science and technology
Materials science
Scientific laboratory work

ENGINEERING

General
Automobile engineering
Chemical engineering
Electrical engineering
Lighting
Electronic engineering
Energy engineering
Maritime engineering
Marine engineering
Marine technology, science & engineering
Mechanical engineering
Mining, quarrying and drilling
Shipbuilding, chandlery and naval architecture
Engineering testing

MANUFACTURING INDUSTRIES

Food, drink and tobacco
Glass, clay and ceramics

Textiles and carpets
Clothing and fashion
Iron, steel and other metals
Paper and paper products
Printing
Oil refining and oil products
Chemicals, paints and dyestuffs
Traditional crafts

CONSTRUCTION AND LAND SERVICES

Architecture
Building technology and management
Construction crafts and other construction work
Housing management
Building services engineering
Landscape architecture
Surveying and related work
Civil, structural and related engineering work
Town and country planning
Mapping and charting, cartography

ANIMALS, PLANTS AND NATURE

Agriculture
Horticulture
Fish farming
Sea fishing
Veterinary science and animal health welfare
Other work with animals
Environmental and nature conservation

TRANSPORT

General
Air transport
Flying training
Pilots
Bus and coach transport
Road transport
Rail transport
Ports and inland waterways
Sea transport
Chartering, broking and freight forwarding
Materials handling, delivery and storage

ENTERTAINMENT AND LEISURE

Music
Music publishing

The Curriculum

Careers

Skill: National Bureau for Students with Disabilities
336 Brixton Road
London
SW9 7AA
Contact: Emma Delap, Information Officer
Telephone: 0171-274 0565
Facsimile: 0171-274 7840

Skill aims to improve opportunities for young people and adults in post-16 education, training and employment. It does this by providing an information service which can deal with individual queries, by producing a range of information sheets and publications and by working at a national level to influence policy.

ADMINISTRATION, BUSINESS, CLERICAL AND MANAGEMENT

GENERAL

Institute of Chartered Secretaries and Administrators
16 Park Crescent
London
W1N 4AH
Telephone: 0171-580 4741

CIVIL SERVICE

Fast Stream and European Staffing Division
Room 127/2
Horse Guards Road
London
SW1P 3AL
Telephone: 0171-270 5696
Facsimile: 0171-270 5764

Foreign and Commonwealth Office, Recruitment Section
Personnel Management Dept, 3-4 Central Buildings
Matthew Parker Street
London
SW1H 9NL
Telephone: 0171-210 0417
Facsimile: 0171-210 0427

HEALTH SERVICE ADMINISTRATION

Institute of Health Services Management
39 Chalton Street
London
NW1 1JD
Telephone: 0171-388 2626
Facsimile: 0171-388 2386

PUBLIC SERVICE ADMINISTRATION

Post Office Management Recruitment Centre
FREEPOST
Coton House
Rugby
CV23 0BR
Contact: Norma Beck, Graduate Recruitment

BUSINESS MANAGEMENT

Institute of Chartered Secretaries and Administrators
16 Park Crescent
London
W1N 4AH
Contact: Education Help Desk
Telephone: 0171-580 4741

PERSONNEL MANAGEMENT AND INDUSTRIAL RELATIONS

Trades Union Congress
Congress House
Great Russell Street
London
WC1B 3LS
Telephone: 0171-636 4030
Facsimile: 0171-666 0632

CLERICAL AND SECRETARIAL WORK

Association of Medical Secretaries, Practice Administrators and Receptionists
Tavistock House North
Tavistock Square
London
WC1H 9LN
Telephone: 0171-387 6005

The Curriculum

Careers

Institute of Agricultural Secretaries & Administrators
National Agricultural Centre
Stoneleigh
Kenilworth
Warwickshire
CV8 2LZ
Telephone: 01203 696592
Facsimile: 01203 417937

Institute of Qualified Private Secretaries
68 Longmoor Road
Long Eaton
Nottingham
NG10 4FP
Contact: Mrs Nancy Harris, General Manager
Telephone: 0115 973 3235

COMPUTER WORK

British Computer Society
1 Sandford Street
Swindon
Wiltshire
SN1 1HJ
Contact: Miss T L Tueton
Telephone: 01793 417411
Facsimile: 01793 480270

POLITICS

Liberal Democrats
4 Cowley Street
London
SW1P 3NB

MANAGEMENT SERVICES

Institute of Management Services
1 Cecil Court
London Road
Enfield
Middlesex
EN2 6DD
Telephone: 0181-363 7452
Facsimile: 0181-367 8149

OPERATIONAL RESEARCH

Operational Research Society
Seymour House
12 Edward Street
Birmingham
B1 2RX

Contact: Dr J F Miles, Secretary & General Manager
Telephone: 0121-233 9300
Facsimile: 0121-233 0321

TRADING STANDARDS AND CONSUMER PROTECTION

Chartered Institute of Environmental Health
Chadwick Court
15 Hatfields
London
SE1 8DJ
Telephone: 0171-928 6006
Facsimile: 0171-928 1951

OCCUPATIONAL SAFETY AND HYGIENE

Health and Safety Executive
St Hughes House
Stanley Precinct, Trinity Road
Bootle
L20 3QY
Contact: Mrs S Horrocks, Education Officer
Telephone: 0151-951 4000
Facsimile: 0151-951 3934

ART AND DESIGN

GENERAL

Art & Design Admissions Registry
Penn House
9 Broad Street
Hereford
HR4 9AP
Contact: Tony Charlton, Information Officer
Telephone: 01432 266653
Facsimile: 01432 343367

GRAPHIC ART, DESIGN AND ILLUSTRATION

Institute of Medical Illustrators
Bank Chambers
8 Onslow Gardens
London
SW7 3AH

CAREERS

172

The Curriculum

Careers

INDUSTRIAL AND CRAFT DESIGN

Chartered Society of Designers
29 Bedford Square
London
WC1B 3EG
Contact: Information Department
Telephone: 0171-631 1510
Facsimile: 0171-580 2338

Institution of Engineering Designers
Courtleigh
Westbury Leigh
Westbury
Wiltshire
BA13 3TA
Telephone: 01373 822801
Facsimile: 01373 858085

FASHION AND CLOTHING DESIGN

CAPITB Trust
80 Richardshaw Lane
Pudsey
Leeds
LS28 6BN
Contact: Mrs Sheila Relton, Secretarial
   Assistant
Telephone: 0113 239 3355
Facsimile: 0113 239 3155

SURFACE AND TWO-DIMENSIONAL DESIGN

British Society of Master Glass Painters
The Honorary Secretary
6 Queen Square
London
WC1
Send SAE for information.

INTERIOR DESIGN AND DISPLAY

Interior Decorators and Designers
   Association
1-4 Chelsea Harbour Design Centre
Chelsea Harbour, Lots Road
London
SW10 0XE
Telephone: 0171-349 0800
Facsimile: 0171-349 0500

PHOTOGRAPHY

Association of Photographers
9-10 Domingo Street
London
EC1Y 0TA
Telephone: 0171-608 1441
Facsimile: 0171-253 3007

British Institute of Professional Photography
2 Amwell End
Ware
Hertfordshire
SG12 9HN
Telephone: 01920 464011

Newspaper Society
74-77 Great Russell Street
London
WC1B 3DA
Contact: Training Department
Telephone: 0171-636 7014
Facsimile: 0171-631 5119

TEACHING AND CULTURAL ACTIVITIES

TEACHING AND TEACHER SUPPORT

General Teaching Council for Scotland
5 Royal Terrace
Edinburgh
EH7 5AF
Telephone: 0131-556 0072
Facsimile: 0131-557 6773

Scottish Office Education Department
Room 3/06, New St Andrews House
St James Centre
Edinburgh
EH1 3TG
Contact: Mr Iain Prior
Telephone: 0131-556 8400
Facsimile: 0131-244 4466

Teacher Education Admissions Clearing
   House
P.O. Box 165
Edinburgh
EH8 8AT

The Curriculum

Careers

Teacher Training Agency
Portland House
Stag Place
London
SW1E 5TT
Contact: Information Section
Telephone: 0171-925 5880/5882

JOURNALISM AND WRITING

National Union of Journalists
Acorn House
314-320 Grays Inn Road
London
WC1 8DP
Contact: Bob Norris, Assistant Secretary
Telephone: 0171-278 7916
Facsimile: 0171-837 8143

Newspaper Society
Bloomsbury House
74-77 Great Russell Street
London
WC1B 3DA
Training Department
Telephone: 0171-636 7014
Facsimile: 0171-631 5119

Scottish Newspaper Publishers' Association
48 Palmerston Place
Edinburgh
EH12 5DE
Telephone: 0131-220 4353
Facsimile: 0131-220 4344

PUBLISHING

Publishers' Association
19 Bedford Square
London
WC1B 3JH
Telephone: 0171-580 6321

MUSEUM AND ART GALLERY WORK

Museums Association
42 Clerkenwell Close
London
EC1R 0PA
Telephone: 0171-608 2933
Facsimile: 0171-250 1929

LIBRARY AND INFORMATION WORK

The Library Association
7 Ridgmount Street
London
WC1E 7AE
Contact: Information Service
Telephone: 0171-636 7543

HISTORICAL AND RELATED WORK

Historical Association
59a Kennington Park Road
London
SE11 4JH
Telephone: 0171-735 3901
Facsimile: 0171-582 4989

Society of Archivists
Information House
Old Street
London
EC1V 9AP
Contact: Executive Secretary
Telephone: 0171-253 5087
Facsimile: 0171-253 3942

Society of Genealogists
14 Charterhouse Buildings
Goswell Road
London
EC1M 7BA
Telephone: 0171-251 8799

ARCHAEOLOGY

Council for British Archaeology
Bowes Morrell House
111 Walmgate
York
YO1 2EP
Contact: Don Henson, Education Officer
Telephone: 01904 671417

The Curriculum

Careers

RELIGION AND CHURCH WORK

Advisory Board of Ministry
Church House
Great Smith Street
London
SW1P 3NZ
Contact: Vocations Officer
Telephone: 0171-222 9011
Facsimile: 0171-976 7625

Christians Abroad
1 Stockwell Green
London
SW9 9HP
Contact: Claire Pedrick, Guidance Manager
Telephone: 0171-737 7811
Facsimile: 0171-737 7237
Send SAE for information.

Church of Scotland
Education Department
121 George Street
Edinburgh
EH2 4YN
Contact: Rev Mrs Evelyn M Young, Deputy
   Secretary
Telephone: 0131-225 5722
Facsimile: 0131-220 3113

Diocesan Vocations Service for England and
   Wales
c/o 39 Eccleston Square
London
SW1V 1BX
Telephone: 01772 726166
Facsimile: 01772 769614

Methodist Church
25 Marylebone Road
London
NW1 5JR
Telephone: 0171-636 5422

National Religious Vocation Centre
82 Margaret Street
London
W1N 8LH
Telephone: 0171-631 5173

United Reformed Church
86 Tavistock Place
London
WC1H 9RT
Contact: Kathryn Brown
Telephone: 0171-916 2020
Facsimile: 0171-916 2021

ENTERTAINMENT AND LEISURE

THEATRE AND DRAMA

British Actors Equity Association
Guild House
Upper St Martins Lane
London
WC2H 9EG
Telephone: 0171-379 6000

National Council for Drama Training
5 Tavistock Place
London
WC1H 9SS
Contact: Adele Bailey, Secretary
Telephone: 0171-387 3650
Facsimile: 0171-387 3650

Stage Management Association
South Bank House
Black Prince Road
London
SE1 7SJ
Contact: Joy Cruikshank, Assistant Secretary
Telephone: 0171-587 1514

MUSIC

Incorporated Society of Musicians
10 Stratford Place
London
W1N 9AE
Contact: Neil Hoyle, Chief Executive
Telephone: 0171-629 4413
Facsimile: 0171-408 1538

The Curriculum

Careers

DANCE

Council for Dance Education and Training
Riverside Studios
Crisp Road
London
W6 9RL
Telephone: 0181-741 5084
Facsimile: 0181-748 4604
Send SAE for information.

SPORT AND RECREATION MANAGEMENT AND SUPPORT STAFF

Institute of Leisure and Amenity Management
ILAM House
Lower Basildon
Reading
Berkshire
RG8 9NE
Telephone: 01491 874222

Scottish Sports Council
Caledonia House
South Gyle
Edinburgh
EH12 9DQ
Contact: Publications Section
Telephone: 0131-317 7200
Facsimile: 0131-317 7202

RADIO, TELEVISION, FILMS AND VIDEO WORK

ITV Network Centre
200 Gray's Inn Road
London
WC1X 8XZ
Telephone: 0171-843 8000
Facsimile: 0171-843 8158

Skillset
124 Horseferry Road
London
SW1P 2TX
Telephone: 0171-306 8585
Facsimile: 0171-306 8372

THEATRE

Association of British Theatre Technicians
47 Bermondsey Street
London
SE1 3XT
Telephone: 0171-403 3778
Send SAE for information.

TRAVEL AND TOURISM

English Tourist Board
Thames Tower
Blacks Road
London
W6 9EL
Contact: Business Support Department
Telephone: 0181-846 9000

The Travel Training Company
The Cornerstone
The Broadway
Woking
Surrey
GU21 5AR
Telephone: 01483 727321
Facsimile: 01483 756698

CATERING AND OTHER SERVICES

HOTEL, CATERING AND INSTITUTION MANAGEMENT

HCIMA (Hotel & Catering International Management Association)
191 Trinity Road
London
SW17 7HN
Telephone: 0181-672 4251
Facsimile: 0181-682 1707

CATERING AND DOMESTIC WORK

City and Guilds of London Institute
1 Giltspur Street
London
EC1A 9DD
Telephone: 0171-294 2468
Facsimile: 0171-294 2400

The Curriculum

Careers

RIG CATERING

Institute of Petroleum
61 New Cavendish Street
London W1M 8AR
Contact: Information Service
Telephone: 0171-467 7100
Facsimile: 0171-255 1472

HOME ECONOMICS

Institute of Home Economics
Hobart House
40 Grosvenor Place
London
SW1X 7AE
Telephone: 0171-823 1109
Facsimile: 0171-823 1109

National Association of Teachers of Home Economics
Hamilton House
Mabledon Place
London
WC1H 9JB
Contact: Geoffrey Thompson, Association Secretary
Telephone: 0171-387 1441
Facsimile: 0171-383 7230

BEAUTY CULTURE

Institute of Electrolysis
251 Seymour Grove
Manchester
M16 0DS
Contact: Examination Secretary

International Health and Beauty Council
46 Aldwick Road
Bognor Regis
Sussex
PO21 2PN
Telephone: 01243 860320

HAIRDRESSING

Hairdressing Training Board
3 Chequer Road
Doncaster
DN1 2AA
Telephone: 01302 342837

Institute of Trichologists (Incorporated)
228 Stockwell Road
Brixton
London
SW9 9SU
Telephone: 0171-733 2056
Facsimile: 0171-733 2056

BURIAL AND CREMATION

British Institute of Embalmers
21c Station Road
Knowle
Solihull
West Midlands
B93 0HL
Contact: L M Stephens, Administrative Secretary
Telephone: 01564 778991

British Institute of Funeral Directors
63A Union Street
London
SW1 1SG
Telephone: 0171-403 3088
Facsimile: 0171-403 7730

GRAPHOLOGY

British Institute of Graphologists
24-26 High Street
Hampton Hill
Middlesex
TW12 1PD
Contact: Hon Secretary

HEALTH AND MEDICAL SERVICES

MEDICINE AND SURGERY

British Medical Association
BMA House
Tavistock Square
London
WC1H 9JP
Contact: Public Information Officer
Telephone: 0171-387 4499
Facsimile: 0171-383 6403

The Curriculum

Careers

British Medical Association - Scottish Office
3 Hill Place
Edinburgh
EH8 9EQ
Contact: Mrs E A Sharp, Regional Officer
Telephone: 0131-662 4820
Facsimile: 0131-667 6933

NURSING

English National Board for Nursing, Midwifery and Health Visiting
P.O. Box 2EN
London
W1A 2EN
Contact: ENB Careers Service
Telephone: 0171-391 6200/6205
Facsimile: 0171-391 6207

NMCCH (Nurses and Midwives Central Clearing House)
P.O. Box 9017
London
W1A 0XA
Telephone: 0171-388 3131
Facsimile: 0171-391 6252

Welsh National Board for Nursing, Midwifery and Health Visiting
Floor 13, Pearl Assurance House
Greyfriars Road
Cardiff
South Glamorgan
CF1 3AG
Telephone: 01222 395535
Facsimile: 01222 229366

DENTISTRY AND DENTAL ANCILLARY OCCUPATIONS

British Association of Dental Nurses
110 London Street
Fleetwood
Lancashire
FY7 6EU
Telephone: 01253 778631
Send SAE for information.

Dental Laboratories Association Ltd
Chapel House
Noel Street
Nottingham
NG7 6AS
Telephone: 0115 970 4321

PHARMACY

National Pharmaceutical Association
Mallinson House
38-42 St Peters Street
St Albans
Hertfordshire
AL1 3NP
Contact: Mrs M A Benson, Head of Training
Telephone: 01727 832161

Royal Pharmaceutical Society of Great Britain
1 Lambeth High Street
London
SE1 7JN
Contact: Education Division
Telephone: 0171-735 9141
Facsimile: 0171-735 7629

OPTICS AND ORTHOPTICS

Association of British Dispensing Opticians
6 Hurlingham Business Park
Sullivan Road
London
SW6 3DU
Contact: Derek Baker, Registrar
Telephone: 0171-736 0088
Facsimile: 0171-731 5531

British College of Optometrists
10 Knaresborough Place
London SW5 0TG
Coontact: Academic Assistant
Telephone: 0171-373 7765
Facsimile: 0171-373 1143

British Orthoptic Society
Tavistock House North
Tavistock Square
London WC1H 9HX
Contact: The Secretary
Telephone: 0171-387 7992
Facsimile: 0171-383 2584

The Curriculum

Careers

General Optical Council
41 Harley Street
London
W1N 2DJ
Contact: Richard Wilshin, Registrar
Telephone: 0171-580 3898
Facsimile: 0171-436 3525

PHYSIOTHERAPY

Chartered Society of Physiotherapy
14 Bedford Row
London
WC1R 4ED
Contact: Diane Kinsella, Careers Adviser
Telephone: 0171-306 6600
Facsimile: 0171-306 6611

RADIOGRAPHY AND RADIOTHERAPY

College of Radiographers
14 Upper Wimpole Street
London
W1M 8BN
Telephone: 0171-935 5726
Facsimile: 0171-224 2186

OCCUPATIONAL THERAPY

College of Occupational Therapists
6-8 Marshalsea Road
London
SE1 1HL
Contact: Education Department
Telephone: 0171-357 6480

CHIROPODY AND PODIATRY

Society of Chiropodists and Podiatrists
53 Welbeck Street
London W1M 7HE
Contact: Mr J Trouncer, General Secretary
Telephone: 0171-486 3381
Facsimile: 0171-935 6359

MEDICAL RESEARCH AND LABORATORY SCIENCES

Biochemical Society
59 Portland Place
London W1N 3AJ
Contact: Education Officer
Telephone: 0171-580 5530

Institute of Biomedical Science
12 Coldbath Square
London
EC1R 5HL
Telephone: 0171-636 8192

Medical Research Council
20 Park Crescent
London
W1N 4AL
Contact: Careers Information

NEUROPHYSIOLOGY TECHNICIANS

Electrophysiological Technologists Association
EEG Department
St Bartholomews Hospital
London
EC1A 7BE
Contact: Mrs P E Carter, Hon Secretary

PHYSIOLOGICAL MEASUREMENT AND MEDICAL PHYSICS

British Society of Audiology
80 Brighton Road
Reading
Berkshire
RG6 1PS
Telephone: 01734 660622
Facsimile: 01734 351915

AMBULANCE WORK

The Scottish Ambulance Service NHS Trust
National HQ
Tipperlinn Road
Edinburgh
EH10 5UU
Contact: Personnel Department

The Curriculum

Careers

COMPLEMENTARY MEDICINE AND THERAPIES

British Acupuncture Association & Register
34 Alderney Street
London
SW1V 4EU
Contact: Dr A C Cecil, Hon President
Telephone: 0171-834 1012

British Association of Art Therapists
11a Richmond Road
Brighton
Sussex
BN2 3RL
Contact: Mrs E M Waller, Secretary
Provides information on training to become an art therapist.

British Chiropractic Association
29 Whitley Street
Reading
Berkshire
RG2 0EG
Contact: S A Wakefield, Executive Director
Telephone: 01734 757557
Facsimile: 01734 757257

British College of Naturopathy and Osteopathy
Frazer House
6 Netherall Gardens
London
NW3 5RR
Contact: Judith Marshall, Registrar
Telephone: 0171-435 6464
Facsimile: 0171-431 3630

British Homeopathic Association
27a Devonshire Street
London
W1N 1RJ
Contact: Mrs Enid Segall, General Secretary
Telephone: 0171-935 2163

British Hypnotherapy Association
1 Wythburn Place
London
W1H 5WL
Telephone: 0171-935 2163

British School of Osteopathy
1-4 Suffolk Street
London
SW1Y 4HG
Contact: Sophia Kovank, Admissions Officer
Telephone: 0171-930 9254
Facsimile: 0171-839 1098

British Society for Music Therapy
25 Rosslyn Avenue
East Barnet
Hertfordshire
EN4 8DH
Contact: Mrs Denise Christophers, Administrator
Telephone: 0181-368 8879
Facsimile: 0181-368 8879

Council for Complementary and Alternative Medicine
179 Gloucester Place
London
NW1 6DX
Telephone: 0171-724 9103

Institute for Complementary Medicine
P.O. Box 194
London
SE16 1QZ
Telephone: 0171-237 5165
Facsimile: 0171-237 5175

International Institute of Sports Therapy
46 Aldwick Road
Bognor Regis
Sussex
PO21 2PN
Telephone: 01243 860320

National Institute of Medical Herbalists
56 Longbrook Street
Exeter
Devon
EX4 6AH
Telephone: 01392 426022
Facsimile: 01392 498963

The Curriculum

Careers

SOCIAL AND RELATED SERVICES

GENERAL

Community Service Volunteers
237 Pentonville Road
London
N1 9NJ
Telephone: 0171-278 6601

Royal Anthropological Institute
50 Fitzroy Street
London
W1P 5HS
Telephone: 0171-387 0455
Facsimile: 0171-383 4235

SOCIAL, PROBATION AND CARE WORK

Central Council for Education and Training in Social Work
Derbyshire House
St Chad's Street
London
WC1H 8AD
Coontact: Information Service
Telephone: 0171-278 2455

CAREERS ADVISORY AND EMPLOYMENT AGENCY WORK

Institute of Careers Guidance
27a Lower High Street
Stourbridge
West Midlands
DY8 1TA
Telephone: 01384 376464
Facsimile: 01384 440830

YOUTH AND COMMUNITY WORK

Central Council for Education and Training in Social Work
Derbyshire House
St Chad's Street
London
WC1H 8AD
Contact: Information Service
Telephone: 0171-278 2455

Scottish Community Education Council
Roseberry House
9 Haymarket Terrace
Edinburgh
EH12 5EZ
Contact: Gordon Mactie, Senior Development Officer
Telephone: 0131-313 2488
Facsimile: 0131-313 6800

PSYCHOLOGY

Association of Child Psychotherapists
Burgh House
New End Square
London
NW3 1LT
Contact: Angela Lee-Lazone, Secretary
Telephone: 0171-794 8881
Facsimile: 0171-433 1874

British Association of Psychotherapists
37 Mapesbury Road
London
NW2 4HJ
Telephone: 0181-452 9823
Facsimile: 0181-452 5182

British Psychological Society
St Andrew's House
48 Princess Road East
Leicester
LE1 7DR
Telephone: 0116 254 9568
Facsimile: 0116 247 0787

CHARITIES AND VOLUNTARY WORK

Community Service Volunteers
237 Pentonville Road
London
N1 9NJ
Contact: Volunteer Programme
Telephone: 0171-278 6601
Facsimile: 0171-833 0149

The Curriculum

Careers

LAW AND RELATED WORK

BARRISTER AND ADVOCATE

Faculty of Advocates, Scotland
Advocates' Library
Parliament House
Edinburgh
EH1 1RF
Contact: Clerk of Faculty
Telephone: 0131-226 5071
Facsimile: 0131-225 3642

General Council of the Bar
3 Bedford Row
London
WC1R 4DB
Telephone: 0171-242 0082

SOLICITOR

Law Society of Scotland
26 Drumsheugh Gardens
Edinburgh
EH3 7YR
Contact: Liz Campbell, Deputy Secretary Legal
  Education
Telephone: 0131-226 7411
Facsimile: 0131-225 2935

LEGAL EXECUTIVE

Institute of Legal Executives
Kempston Manor
Kempston
Bedford
MK42 7AB
Telephone: 01234 841000
Facsimile: 01234 840373

COURT SERVICES

British Institute of Verbatim Reporters
61 Carey Street
London
WC2A 2JG

Institute of Legal Cashiers & Administration (ILCA)
2nd Floor, 146-148 Eltham Hill
Eltham
London
SE9 5DX
Telephone: 0181-294 2887
Facsimile: 0181-859 1662

PATENTS AND TRADEMARKS

Chartered Institute of Patent Agents
Staple Inn Buildings
High Holborn
London
WC1V 7PZ
Contact: M C Ralph, Secretary
Telephone: 0171-405 9450
Facsimile: 0171-430 0471

CROWN PROSECUTION SERVICE

Crown Prosecution Service
50 Ludgate Hill
London
EC4M 7EX
Contact: Personnel Branch 2
Telephone: 0171-273 3000

CONVEYANCING

Council for Licensed Conveyancers
16 Glebe Road
Chelmsford
Essex
CM1 1QG
Contact: Mrs Enid Watson, Assistant Director
Telephone: 01245 349599
Facsimile: 01245 348380

BARRISTERS' CLERK

Institute of Barristers' Clerks
4A Essex Court
Temple
London
EC4Y 9AJ
Telephone: 0171-353 2699

The Curriculum

Careers

SECURITY AND PROTECTIVE SERVICES

GENERAL

Association of British Investigators
10 Bonner Hill Road
Kingston-upon-Thames
Surrey
KT1 3EP
Contact: Elizabeth Wrixton, General Secretary
Telephone: 0181-546 3368
Facsimile: 0181-546 7701

International Professional Security Association
IPSA House
3 Dendy Road
Paignton
Devon
TQ4 5BZ
Contact: P W Rabbitts, International Secretary
Telephone: 01803 554849
Facsimile: 01803 529203

POLICE AND RELATED WORK

British Transport Police
P.O. Box 260
15 Tavistock Place
London
WC1H 9SJ
Contact: Inspector Michael Foster

Home Office (Police Recruiting Department)
Division F5
Queen Anne's Gate
London
SW1H 9AT
Telephone: 0171-273 3797

Metropolitan Police Careers
Central Recruitment and Selection
26 Aybrook Street
London
W1M 3JL
Contact: Terry Mason, Marketing and Careers Adviser
Telephone: 0171-321 9516

Scottish Home and Health Department (Police Division)
Room 364A
St Andrew's House
Edinburgh
EH1 3DE
Contact: Ann Tocher
Telephone: 0131-244 2156
Facsimile: 0131-244 2666

FIRE SERVICE

London Fire and Civil Defence Authority
Albert Embankment
London
SE1 7SD
Contact: Firefighter Selection
Telephone: 0171-586 6176

FINANCE AND RELATED WORK

GENERAL

Insolvency Practitioners' Association
Moor House
119 London Wall
London
EC2Y 5ET
Contact: S N Milner, Secretary
Telephone: 0171-374 4200
Facsimile: 0171-588 7216

ACCOUNTANCY

Association of Accounting Technicians
154 Clerkenwell Road
London
EC1R 5AD
Telephone: 0171-837 8600

Chartered Association of Certified Accountants (ACCA)
29 Lincoln's Inn Fields
London
WC2A 3EE
Contact: Student Recruitment Section
Telephone: 0171-396 5701
Facsimile: 0171-396 5858

The Curriculum

Careers

Chartered Association of Certified Accountants Scottish Branch
2 Woodside Place
Glasgow
G3 7QF
Telephone: 0141-309 4099
Facsimile: 0141-309 4141

Chartered Institute of Management Accountants
63 Portland Place
London
W1N 4AB
Contact: The Registry
Telephone: 0171-637 2311
Facsimile: 0171-637 2311

Chartered Institute of Public Finance and Accountancy
3 Robert Street
London
WC2N 6BH
Contact: Natalie Lofts, Student Marketing Officer
Telephone: 0171-895 8823
Facsimile: 0171-895 8825

Institute of Chartered Accountants in Scotland
27 Queen Street
Edinburgh
EH2 1LA
Contact: Jennifer Deas, Careers Development Manager
Telephone: 0131-225 5673
Facsimile: 0131-479 4872

Institute of Company Accountants
80 Portland Place, London W1N 4DP and at
40 Tyndalls Park Road
Bristol
BS8 1PL
Telephone: 0117 923 8261
Facsimile: 0117 923 8292

Institute of Cost and Executive Accountants
141-149 Fonthill Road
London
N4 3HF
Telephone: 0171-272 3925
Facsimile: 0171-281 5723

Institute of Financial Accountants
Burford House
44 London Road
Sevenoaks
Kent
TN13 1AS
Contact: Mrs Carolyn Anderson, Education Officer
Telephone: 01732 458080
Facsimile: 01732 455848

HIGH STREET BANKING

Banking Information Service
10 Lombard Street
London
EC3V 9AT
Telephone: 0171-398 0066
Facsimile: 0171-283 9655

MERCHANT BANKING

London Investment Banking Association
6 Frederick's Place
London
EC2R 8BT

BUILDING SOCIETIES

Building Societies Association
3 Savile Row
London
W1X 1AF
Contact: Louise Coffey, Under Secretary, Personnel
Telephone: 0171-437 0655
Facsimile: 0171-734 6416

INSURANCE

Chartered Insurance Institute
20 Aldermanbury
London
EC2V 7HY
Telephone: 0171-417 0495
Facsimile: 0171-417 0563

The Curriculum

Careers

INSURANCE BROKING

British Insurance and Investment Brokers' Association
BIIBA House
14 Bevis Marks
London
EC3A 7NT
Contact: The Education Department
Telephone: 0171-623 9043
Facsimile: 0171-626 9676

ACTUARIAL WORK

Faculty of Actuaries, Scotland
40 Thistle Street
Edinburgh
EH2 1EN
Telephone: 0131-557 1575/220 4555
Facsimile: 0131-220 2280

Institute of Actuaries
Napier House
4 Worcester Street
Oxford
OX1 2AW
Contact: Pauline Simpson, Academic Registrar
Telephone: 01865 794144
Facsimile: 01865 794094

FINANCIAL SERVICES

Association of Taxation Technicians
12 Upper Belgrave Street
London
SW1X 8BB
Telephone: 0171-235 2544
Facsimile: 0171-235 2562

Institute of Credit Management
The Water Mill
Station Road
South Luffenham, Oakham
Leicestershire
LE15 8NB
Contact: Education and Membership Department
Telephone: 01780 721888
Facsimile: 01780 721333

The Chartered Institute of Taxation
12 Upper Belgrave Street
London
SW1X 8BB
Telephone: 0171-235 9381
Facsimile: 0171-253 2562

STOCK EXCHANGE WORK

London Stock Exchange, Human Resources (T/15)
Stock Exchange Tower
Old Broad Street
London
EC2N 1HP
Contact: Resourcing Centre
Telephone: 0171-797 1000

PENSIONS MANAGEMENT

Pensions Management Institute
PMI House
4-10 Artillery Lane
London
E1 7LS
Telephone: 0171-247 1452
Facsimile: 0171-247 0603

BUYING, SELLING AND RELATED SERVICES

MARKETING AND MARKET RESEARCH

Communication Advertising and Marketing Education Foundation Ltd
Abford House
15 Wilton Road
London
SW1V 1NJ
Contact: J A Knight, General Secretary
Telephone: 0171-828 7506
Facsimile: 0171-976 5140
Provides examinations and qualifications for those working in Advertising, Public Relations, Sales Promotion and Direct Marketing.

The Curriculum

Careers

CAREERS

Market Research Society
15 Northburgh Street
London
EC1V 0AH
Telephone: 0171-490 4911
Facsimile: 0171-490 0608

The Chartered Institute of Marketing
Moor Hall
Cookham
Maidenhead
Berkshire
SL6 9QH
Contact: Student Registration Department
Telephone: 01628 524922
Facsimile: 01628 531382

ADVERTISING

Advertising Association
Abford House
15 Wilton Road
London
SW1V 1NJ
Contact: Philip Spink, Head of Information
Telephone: 0171-828 4831
Facsimile: 0171-931 0376

SPECIALIST SHOPS/SALES

British Antique Dealers' Association
20 Rutland Gate
London
SW7 1BD
Contact: Mrs E D Eza
Telephone: 0171-589 4128
Facsimile: 0171-581 9083

Floristry Training Council
Roebuck House
Newbury Road
Hermitage, Newbury
Berkshire
RG16 9RZ
Telephone: 01635 200465

Institute of the Motor Industry
Fanshaws
Brickenden
Hertford SG13 8PQ
Telephone: 01992 511521
Facsimile: 01992 511548

National Association of Goldsmiths
78a Luke Street
London
EC2A 4PY
Contact: Clare Wetherall, Education Manager
Telephone: 0171-613 4445
Facsimile: 0171-613 4450

Retail Motor Industry Training
201 Great Portland Street
London
W1N 6AB
Telephone: 0171-580 9122

PUBLIC RELATIONS

Institute of Public Relations
The Old Trading House
15 Northburgh Street
London
EC1V 0PR
Telephone: 0171-253 5151
Facsimile: 0171-490 0588

WHOLESALE DISTRIBUTION

Institute of Grocery Distribution
Grange Lane
Letchmore Heath
Watford
Hertfordshire
WD2 8DQ
Contact: T Radford, Personnel Officer
Telephone: 01923 857141
Facsimile: 01923 852531

MODELLING (LONDON AREA)

Association of Model Agents
6 St Catherine's Mews
Milner Street
London
SW3 2PX
Telephone: 0891 517644

The Curriculum

Careers

SCIENCES, MATHEMATICS AND RELATED WORK

CHEMISTRY

Biochemical Society
59 Portland Place
London
W1N 3AJ
Contact: Education Officer
Telephone: 0171-580 5530

Royal Society of Chemistry
Burlington House
Piccadilly
London
W1V 0BN
Contact: Dr John A Johnston, Assistant
    Education Officer
Telephone: 0171-437 8656
Facsimile: 0171-287 9825

BIOLOGY

Biochemical Society
59 Portland Place
London W1N 3AJ
Contact: Education Officer
Telephone: 0171-580 5530

Institute of Biology
20-22 Queensbury Place
London
SW7 2DZ
Contact: Anne Jordan, Head of Education
Telephone: 0171-581 8333
Facsimile: 0171-823 9409

MICROBIOLOGY AND BIOTECHNOLOGY

Society for General Microbiology
Marlborough House
Basingstoke Road, Spencers Wood
Reading
Berkshire RG7 1AE
Contact: Mrs J Hurst, External Relations
    Administrator
Telephone: 01734 885577
Facsimile: 01734 885656

MATHEMATICS

Institute of Mathematics and its Applications
16 Nelson Street
Southend-on-Sea
Essex
SS1 1EF
Telephone: 01702 354020
Facsimile: 01702 354111

STATISTICS

Royal Statistical Society
12 Errol Street
London
EC1Y 8LX
Telephone: 0171-638 8998
Facsimile: 0171-256 7598

EARTH AND ENVIRONMENTAL SCIENCES

Geographical Association
343 Fulwood Road
Sheffield
S10 3BP
Telephone: 0114 267 0666
Facsimile: 0114 267 0688

Geological Society
Burlington House
Piccadilly
London
W1V 0JV
Contact: Education Officer
Telephone: 0171-434 9944
Facsimile: 0171-439 8975

Institution of Environmental Sciences
14 Princes Gate
Hyde Park
London
SW7 1PU

Natural Environment Research Council
Polaris House
North Star Avenue
Swindon
Wiltshire
SN2 1EU
Telephone: 01793 411500

Royal Meteorological Society
104 Oxford Road
Reading
Berkshire
RG1 7LJ
Telephone: 01734 568500
Facsimile: 01734 568571

OCEANOGRAPHY, MARINE SCIENCES, SUBSEA ENGINEERING

James Rennel Centre for Ocean Circulation
Gamma House, Chilworth Research Centre
Chilworth
Southampton
SO1 7NS
Contact: Stephen Hall, School Links Officer
Telephone: 01703 766184
Facsimile: 01703 767507

FOOD SCIENCE AND TECHNOLOGY

Institute of Food Science and Technology
5 Cambridge Court
210 Shepherd's Bush Road
London
W6 7NJ
Telephone: 0171-603 6316

MATERIALS SCIENCE

Institute of Materials
1 Carlton House Terrace
London
SW1Y 5DB
Contact: Education Department
Telephone: 0171-839 4071

SCIENTIFIC LABORATORY WORK

Institute of Animal Technology
5 South Parade
Summertown
Oxford
OX2 7JL
Contact: Mrs S C Mackrell, Principal Animal
Technician
Telephone: 01920 882688

ENGINEERING

GENERAL

Engineering Training Authority (ECIS)
41 Clarendon Road
Watford
Hertfordshire
WD1 1HS
Telephone: 0800 282167

Initiative Training & Enterprise Ltd
ITE Autotech and Marine Training Centre
Dominion Road
Wallisdown
Bournemouth
BH11 8LH
Contact: Ms S Duddington, Sales and
Marketing Coordinator
Telephone: 01202 570341
*Offers career opportunities and national
vocational qualifications in Automotive and
Marine Engineering, Mechanical and
Electrical Engineering, Business and Office
Skills and Information Technology.*

Institution of Engineering Designers
Courtleigh
Westbury Leigh
Westbury
Wiltshire
BA13 3TA
Telephone: 01373 822801
Facsimile: 01373 858085

The Smallpeice Trust
Smallpeice House
27 Newbold Terrace East
Leamington Spa
Warwickshire
CV32 4ES
Contact: Jayne Clark, Industry/Education
Liaison Assistant
Telephone: 01926 336423
Facsimile: 01926 450679
*An educational charity specialising in running
courses for students between 13 and 20
years of age. A development programme is
available to Year 9 students who are
interested in learning through first-hand
experience more about Industry/Engineering
and related career options.*

The Curriculum

Careers

Women's Engineering Society
Imperial College
Imperial College Road
London
SW7 2BV
Contact: The Secretary
Telephone: 0171-584 6025

AUTOMOBILE ENGINEERING

Institute of Road Transport Engineers
22 Greencoat Place
London
SW1P 1PR
Telephone: 0171-630 1111
Facsimile: 0171-630 6677

Institute of the Motor Industry
Fanshaws
Brickenden
Hertford
SG13 8PQ
Telephone: 01992 511521
Facsimile: 01992 511548

Institution of Plant Engineers
77 Great Peter Street
London
SW1P 2EZ
Contact: Peter F Tye, Secretary
Telephone: 0171-233 2855
Facsimile: 0171-233 2604

Society of Motor Manufacturers and Traders Ltd
Forbes House
Halkin Street
London
SW1X 7DS
Contact: Michael Stedman, Public Affairs Manager
Telephone: 0171-235 7000
Facsimile: 0171-235 7112

Vehicle Builders' and Repairers' Association Ltd
Belmont House
Finkle Lane
Leeds
LS27 7TW
Telephone: 0113 253 8333
Facsimile: 0113 238 0496

CHEMICAL ENGINEERING

Institution of Chemical Engineers
Davis Building
165-189 Railway Terrace
Rugby
Warwickshire
CV21 3HQ
Contact: Education Liaison Unit
Telephone: 01788 578214
Facsimile: 01788 560833

ELECTRICAL ENGINEERING

Institution of Electrical Engineers
Michael Faraday House
Six Hills Way
Stevenage
Hertfordshire
SG1 2AY
Contact: Mrs Dorie Giles, Schools Education and Liaison
Telephone: 01438 313311
Facsimile: 01438 742856

LIGHTING

Institution of Lighting Engineers
Lennox House
9 Lawford Road
Rugby
Warwickshire
CV21 2DZ
Telephone: 01788 576492
Facsimile: 01788 540145

ELECTRONIC ENGINEERING

Institution of Electrical Engineers
Michael Faraday House
Six Hills Way
Stevenage
Hertfordshire
SG1 2AY
Contact: Mrs Dorie Giles, Schools Education and Liaison
Telephone: 01438 313311
Facsimile: 01438 742856

The Curriculum

Careers

Institution of Electronics and Electrical Incorporated Engineers
Savoy Hill House
Savoy Hill
London
WC2R 0BS
Contact: Graham Guest, Manager, Qualifications
Telephone: 0171-836 3357
Facsimile: 0171-497 9006

ENERGY ENGINEERING

Institution of Gas Engineers
21 Portland Place
London
W1N 3AF
Telephone: 0171-636 6603
Facsimile: 0171-636 6602

MARITIME ENGINEERING

Institute of Marine Engineers
Memorial Building
76 Mark Lane
London
EC3R 7JN
Contact: Miss N Waggon, Membership Clerk
Telephone: 0171-481 8493
Facsimile: 0171-488 1854

MARINE ENGINEERING

Royal Institution of Naval Architects
10 Upper Belgrave Street
London
SW1X 8BQ
Contact: David C Bragger, Manager of Professional Affairs
Telephone: 0171-235 4622
Facsimile: 0171-245 6959

MARINE TECHNOLOGY, SCIENCE & ENGINEERING

Society for Underwater Technology Ltd
76 Mark Lane
London
EC3R 7JN
Telephone: 0171-481 0750
Facsimile: 0171-481 4001

MECHANICAL ENGINEERING

Institution of Mechanical Engineers
Northgate Avenue
Bury St Edmunds
Suffolk
IP32 6BN
Contact: Schools Liaison Service
Telephone: 01284 763277
Facsimile: 01284 704006

MINING, QUARRYING AND DRILLING

Institute of Petroleum
61 New Cavendish Street
London
W1M 8AR
Contact: Information Service
Telephone: 0171-467 7100
Facsimile: 0171-255 1472

SHIPBUILDING, CHANDLERY AND NAVAL ARCHITECTURE

British Marine Industries Federation
Meadlake Place
Thorpe Lea Road
Egham
Surrey
TW20 8HE
Telephone: 01784 473377

ENGINEERING TESTING

British Institute of Non-Destructive Testing
1 Spencer Parade
Northampton
NN1 5AA
Contact: Mr P A Kolbe, Technical Secretary
Telephone: 01604 230124
Facsimile: 01604 231489

MANUFACTURING INDUSTRIES

FOOD, DRINK AND TOBACCO

Institute of Food Science and Technology
5 Cambridge Court
210 Shepherd's Bush Road
London
W6 7NJ
Telephone: 0171-603 6316

Institute of Grocery Distribution
Grange Lane
Letchmore Heath
Watford
Hertfordshire
WD2 8DQ
Contact: T Radford, Personnel Officer
Telephone: 01923 857141
Facsimile: 01923 852531

National Association of Master Bakers
21 Baldock Street
Ware
Hertfordshire
SG12 9DH
Telephone: 01920 468061
Facsimile: 01920 461632

National Dairy Council
5-7 John Princes Street
London
W1M 0AP
Telephone: 0171-499 7822

GLASS, CLAY AND CERAMICS

British Ceramic Confederation
Federation House
Station Road
Stoke-on-Trent
Staffordshire
ST4 2SA
Contact: Mr Francis Morrall, Human Resources
Executive
Telephone: 01782 744631
Facsimile: 01782 744102

Glass Training Ltd
BGMC Building
Northumberland Road
Sheffield
South Yorkshire
S10 2UA
Contact: Julia Warne, National Development
Manager
Telephone: 0114 266 1494
Facsimile: 0114 266 0738

Institute of Materials
1 Carlton House Terrace
London
SW1Y 5DB
Contact: Education Department
Telephone: 0171-839 4071

TEXTILES AND CARPETS

Confederation of British Wool Textiles Ltd
Merrydale House
Roydsdale Way
Bradford
BD4 6SB
Telephone: 01274 652207

CLOTHING AND FASHION

CAPITB Trust
80 Richardshaw Lane
Pudsey
Leeds
LS28 6BN
Contact: Mrs Sheila Relton, Secretarial
Assistant
Telephone: 0113 239 3355
Facsimile: 0113 239 3155

IRON, STEEL AND OTHER METALS

Engineering Training Authority (ECIS)
41 Clarendon Road
Watford
Hertfordshire
WD1 1HS
Telephone: 0800 282167

CAREERS

The Curriculum

Careers

Institute of Materials
1 Carlton House Terrace
London
SW1Y 5DB
Contact: Education Department
Telephone: 0171-839 4071

PAPER AND PAPER PRODUCTS

Institute of Packaging
Syonby Lodge
Nottingham Road
Melton Mowbray
Leicestershire LE13 0NU
Contact: Mr J McDermott, Head of Training
Telephone: 01664 500055
Facsimile: 01664 64164

National Association of Paper Merchants
Hamilton Court
Gogmore Lane
Chertsey
Surrey
KT16 9AP
Contact: Mrs V Bowen, Information Officer
Telephone: 01932 569797
Facsimile: 01932 569749

The Paper Federation of Great Britain
Papermakers' House
Rivenhall Road
Westlea, Swindon
Wiltshire
SN5 7BE
Contact: Information Office
Telephone: 01793 886086
Facsimile: 01793 886182

PRINTING

British Printing Industries Federation
11 Bedford Row
London WC1R 4DX
Contact: Education and Training
Telephone: 0171-242 6904
Facsimile: 0171-405 7784

Scottish Print Employers' Federation
48 Palmerston Place
Edinburgh EH12 5DE
Telephone: 0131-220 4353
Facsimile: 0131-220 4344

OIL REFINING AND OIL PRODUCTS

Institute of Petroleum
61 New Cavendish Street
London
W1M 8AR
Contact: Information Service
Telephone: 0171-467 7100
Facsimile: 0171-255 1472

CHEMICALS, PAINTS AND DYESTUFFS

Association of the British Pharmaceutical Industry
12 Whitehall
London
SW1A 2DY
Contact: Publications Department
Telephone: 0171-930 3477 Ext1446

British Coatings Federation Ltd
James House
Bridge Street
Leatherhead
Surrey
KT22 7EP
Telephone: 01372 360660
Facsimile: 01372 376069

Chemical Industries Association
King's Building
Smith Square
London
SW1P 3JJ
Contact: Mrs S A Tooth, Publications Department
Telephone: 0171-834 3399

National Pharmaceutical Association
Mallinson House
38-42 St Peter's Street
St Albans
Hertfordshire
AL1 3NP
Contact: Mrs M A Benson, Head of Training
Telephone: 01727 832161

The Curriculum

Careers

Royal Pharmaceutical Society of Great Britain
1 Lambeth High Street
London
SE1 7JN
Contact: Education Division
Telephone: 0171-735 9141
Facsimile: 0171-735 7629

Society of Dyers and Colourists
P.O. Box 244
Perkin House, Grattan Road
Bradford
West Yorkshire
BD1 2JB
Contact: Mr Mike Roberts, Education and
Qualifications Officer
Telephone: 01274 725138
Facsimile: 01274 392888

TRADITIONAL CRAFTS

Farriery Training Service
P.O. Box 49
East of England Showground
Peterborough
Cambridgeshire
PE2 6GU
Contact: Miss J R Bailey, Senior Administrator
Telephone: 01733 394848
Facsimile: 01733 371103

CONSTRUCTION AND LAND SERVICES

ARCHITECTURE

Architects' and Surveyors' Institute
15 St Mary Street
Chippenham
Wiltshire SN15 3WD
Telephone: 01249 444505
Facsimile: 01249 443602

British Institute of Architectural Technologists
397 City Road
London
EC1V 1NE
Contact: Education Officer

Telephone: 0171-278 2206
Facsimile: 0171-857 3194

Royal Institute of British Architects
66 Portland Place
London W1N 4AD
Contact: Frances Mills, Education Department
Telephone: 0171-580 5533
Facsimile: 0171-255 1541

BUILDING TECHNOLOGY AND MANAGEMENT

Association of Building Engineers
Jubilee House
Billing Brook Road
Northampton
NN3 8NW
Contact: Mr Leslie Lewis, Educational
Admissions Officer
Telephone: 01604 404121
Facsimile: 01604 784220

Chartered Institute of Building
Englemere
Kings Ride
Ascot
Berkshire
SL5 8BJ
Telephone: 01344 23355
Facsimile: 01344 23467

CONSTRUCTION CRAFTS AND OTHER CONSTRUCTION WORK

Institute of Carpenters
35 Hayworth Road
Sandiacre
Nottingham
NG10 5LL
Telephone: 0115 949 0641
Facsimile: 0115 949 1664

Institute of Roofing
24 Weymouth Street
London
W1N 3FA
Contact: Mrs J Wells, Secretary
Telephone: 0171-436 0103
Facsimile: 0171-637 3215

CAREERS

The Curriculum

Careers

HOUSING MANAGEMENT

Chartered Institute of Housing
Octavia House
Westwood Business Park, Westwood Way
Coventry
CV4 8JP
Contact: Membership Section
Telephone: 01203 694433
Facsimile: 01203 695110

BUILDING SERVICES ENGINEERING

Institute of Refrigeration
Kelvin House
76 Mill Lane
Carshalton
Surrey
SM5 2JR
Telephone: 0181-647 7033
Facsimile: 0181-773 0165

LANDSCAPE ARCHITECTURE

Landscape Institute
6-7 Barnard Mews
London
SW11 1QU
Contact: Mr G S Royston, Director General
Telephone: 0171-738 9166
Facsimile: 0171-738 9134

SURVEYING AND RELATED WORK

ISVA (Incorporated Society of Valuers and Auctioneers)
3 Cadogan Gate
London
SW1X 0AS
Telephone: 0171-235 2282
Facsimile: 0171-235 4390

National Association of Estate Agents
Arbon House
21 Jury Street
Warwick
CV34 4EH
Telephone: 01926 496800
Facsimile: 01926 400953

Royal Institution of Chartered Surveyors
Surveyor Court
Westwood Way
Coventry
CV4 8JE
Telephone: 0171-222 7000
Facsimile: 0171-334 3800

Royal Institution of Chartered Surveyors, Scotland
9 Manor Place
Edinburgh
EH3 7DN
Contact: Careers Coordinator
Telephone: 0131-225 7078
Facsimile: 0131-226 3599

CIVIL, STRUCTURAL AND RELATED ENGINEERING WORK

Civil Engineering Careers Service
1-7 Great George Street
London
SW1P 3AA
Contact: Mrs Razvana Kurkic, Careers Officer
Telephone: 0171-222 7722
Facsimile: 0171-222 7500

Institution of Structural Engineers
11 Upper Belgrave Street
London
SW1X 8BH
Telephone: 0171-235 4535
Facsimile: 0171-235 4294

TOWN AND COUNTRY PLANNING

Royal Town Planning Institute
26 Portland Place
London
W1N 4BE
Telephone: 0171-636 9107
Facsimile: 0171-323 1582

Society of Town Planning Technicians
c/o 26 Portland Place
London
W1N 4BE
Contact: M I Grigsby, Hon Secretary
Telephone: 0171-636 9107
Facsimile: 0171-323 1582

The Curriculum

Careers

MAPPING AND CHARTING, CARTOGRAPHY

School of Construction and Earth Sciences
Oxford Brookes University
Headington
Oxford
OX3 0BP
Contact: Mr R W Anson, Principal Lecturer,
Cartography
Telephone: 01865 483346

ANIMALS, PLANTS AND NATURE

AGRICULTURE

ADAS (Agricultural Development Advisory Service)
Oxford Spires Business Park
The Boulevard
Kidlington, Oxford
OX5 1NZ
Contact: Ms Susan Evanson, Personnel Officer
Telephone: 01865 842742

British Crop Protection Council
Bear Farm
Binfield
Bracknell
Berkshire
RG12 3QE
Telephone: 01734 342727
Facsimile: 01734 341998

HORTICULTURE

Horticultural Trades Association
19 High Street
Theale
Reading
Berkshire
RG7 5AH
Telephone: 01734 303132

Institute of Horticulture
14-15 Belgrave Square
London SW1X 8PS
Contact: General Secretary
Telephone: 0171-245 6943
Facsimile: 0171-245 6943

FISH FARMING

Institute of Fisheries Management
22 Rushworth Avenue
West Bridgford
Nottingham
NG2 7LF
Telephone: 0115 982 2317

SEA FISHING

Seafish Industry Authority
Seafish House
St Andrews Dock
Hull
HU3 4QE
Contact: Librarian
Telephone: 01482 327837
Facsimile: 01482 223310

VETERINARY SCIENCE AND ANIMAL HEALTH WELFARE

British Veterinary Nursing Association
The Seedbed Centre
Coldharbour Road
Harlow
Essex
CM19 5AF
Telephone: 01279 450567

Royal College of Veterinary Surgeons
Belgravia House
62-64 Horseferry Road
London
SW1P 2AF
Telephone: 0171-222 2001
Facsimile: 0171-222 2004

OTHER WORK WITH ANIMALS

Association of British Wild Animal Keepers
12 Tackley Road
Eastville
Bristol
BS5 6UQ
Send SAE for information.

British Horse Society
Training Office
Stoneleigh
Kenilworth
Warwickshire CV8 2LR
Telephone: 01203 696697

The Curriculum

Careers

British Trust for Ornithology
The Nunnery
Nunnery Place
Thetford
Norfolk
IP24 2AU
Telephone: 01842 750050

National Pony Society
Willingdon House
102 High Street
Alton
Hampshire
GU34 1EN
Telephone: 01420 88333
Facsimile: 01420 80599

Royal Society for the Prevention of Cruelty
  to Animals
Causeway
Horsham
Sussex
RH12 1HG
Telephone: 01403 264181

ENVIRONMENTAL AND NATURE CONSERVATION

Countryside Commission
P.O. Box 124
Walgrave
Northampton
NN6 9TL
Telephone: 01604 781848
Facsimile: 01604 781752

Scottish Natural Heritage
Recruitment Section
12 Hope Terrace
Edinburgh
EH9 2AS
Telephone: 0131-447 4784

TRANSPORT

GENERAL

Institute of Transport Administration
32 Palmerston Road
Southampton
Hampshire
SO1 1LL
Contact: P F Green, Director
Telephone: 01703 631380
Facsimile: 01703 635164

AIR TRANSPORT

British Airways plc
Meadowbank
P.O. Box 59
Hounslow
Middlesex
TW5 9QX
Contact: Recruitment and Selection
Telephone: 0181-564 1450

FLYING TRAINING

British Aerospace Flying College Ltd
Prestwick International Airport
Prestwick
Ayrshire
KA9 2RW
Telephone: 01292 671022
Facsimile: 01292 476151

PILOTS

Civil Aviation Authority
Aviation House
Gatwick
RH6 0YR
Telephone: 01293 573725
Facsimile: 01293 573999

BUS AND COACH TRANSPORT

Bus and Coach Training Ltd
Regency House
43 High Street
Rickmansworth
Hertfordshire
WD3 1ET
Telephone: 01923 896607
Facsimile: 01923 896881

The Curriculum

Careers

ROAD TRANSPORT

Road Haulage Association
35 Monument Hill
Weybridge
Surrey
KT13 8RN
Contact: Controller: Employment & Distribution
Telephone: 01932 841515

RAIL TRANSPORT

Institute of Transport Administration
32 Palmerston Road
Southampton
Hampshire
SO1 1LL
Contact: P F Green, Director
Telephone: 01703 631380
Facsimile: 01703 635164

PORTS AND INLAND WATERWAYS

Chartered Institution of Water and Environmental Management
15 John Street
London
WC1N 2EB
Telephone: 0171-831 3110
Facsimile: 0171-405 4967

National Rivers Authority
Rivers House, Waterside Drive
Aztec West
Almondsbury, Bristol
BS12 4UD
Telephone: 01454 624400
Facsimile: 01454 624479

SEA TRANSPORT: DECK AND ENGINEERING OFFICER

Merchant Navy
Carthusian Court
12 Carthusian Street
London
EC1M 6EB
Contact: Officer Careers
Telephone: 0171-417 8400

SEA TRANSPORT: OFFICER CADETSHIPS, ENGINEER & DECK

Royal Fleet Auxiliary
COMRFA, North Office Block
Room F9, Portsmouth Naval Base PP29
Portsmouth
Hampshire
Contact: RFA Recruitment Officer
Telephone: 01705 725244
Facsimile: 01705 726021

SEA TRANSPORT

Institute of Transport Administration
32 Palmerston Road
Southampton
Hampshire
SO1 1LL
Contact: P F Green, Director
Telephone: 01703 631380
Facsimile: 01703 635164

CHARTERING, BROKING AND FREIGHT FORWARDING

British International Freight Association
Redfern House
Browells Lane
Feltham
Middlesex
TW13 7EP
Contact: Training and Education Department
Telephone: 0181-844 2266
Facsimile: 0181-890 5546

Institute of Chartered Shipbrokers
3 Gracechurch Street
London
EC3V 0AT
Contact: The Secretary
Telephone: 0171-626 3058
Facsimile: 0171-626 2139

MATERIALS HANDLING, DELIVERY AND STORAGE

British Association of Removers
3 Churchill Court
58 Station Road
North Harrow
Middlesex
HA2 7SA
Contact: Mrs Paulina Aston
Telephone: 0181-861 3331
Facsimile: 0181-861 3332

ENTERTAINMENT AND LEISURE

MUSIC

Association of Professional Recording Services Ltd
2 Windsor Square
Reading
Berkshire
RG1 2TH
Telephone: 01628 663725

Institute of Musical Instrument Technology
134 Crouch Hill
London
N8 9DX
Telephone: 0181-340 2271

Music Retailers Association
P.O. Box 249
Chiswick
London
W4 5EX
Telephone: 0181-994 7592

Phonographic Industry Ltd
25 Savile Row
London
W1X 1AA
Telephone: 0171-287 4422

Professional Lighting & Sound Association
7 Highlight House
St Leonards Road
Eastbourne
Sussex
BN21 3UH
Telephone: 01323 410335

Scottish Musical Instrument Retailers Association
33 Bath Street
Glasgow
G2 1HT
Telephone: 0141-332 6644

MUSIC PUBLISHING

Music Publishers Association
3rd Floor, Strandgate
18-20 York Buildings
London
WC2N 6JU
Telephone: 0171-839 7779

The Curriculum

Science & Technology Regional Organisations

Avon & Somerset SATRO
School of Education
University of Bath
Claverton Down
Bath
BA2 7AY
Director: Mr John Poole & Mr John Trickett
Telephone: 01225 826930
Facsimile: 01225 826113

Bedfordshire SATRO
Bedfordshire County Council
Teaching Media Resource Service
Science Unit, Russell House
14 Dunstable Street
Ampthill, Bedford
MK45 2JT
Director: Ms Joan O'Sullivan, Bedfordshire
    Science Adviser
Telephone: 01525 405220
Facsimile: 01525 405128

Berkshire SATRO
Education Department
Shire Hall
Shinfield Park
Reading
Berkshire
RG2 9XE
Director: Mr Bob Welch
TIC Coordinator: Mr Alan Wills. Phone: 01734
    790229, fax: 01734 790265
Telephone: 01734 233682
Facsimile: 01734 750360

Birmingham SATRO
The University of Birmingham
School of Electronic and Electrical Engineering
Edgbaston
Birmingham
B15 2TT
Director: Mr Colin Baldyga
Projects Consultant: Carole Gallant
Telephone: 0121-414 4318
Facsimile: 0121-414 4291

Bradford & Leeds SATRO
c/o Greenhead Grammar School
Greenhead Road
Utley
Keighley
BD20 6EB
Director: Mr David Ross
Telephone: 01535 690836
Facsimile: 01535 690836

Cheshire SATRO
Science, Design & Technology Centre
Middle Lane
Kingsley
Frodsham
Cheshire
WA6 6TZ
Director: Mr Roy Palin
Young Engineers: Mr Don Daunt, Ford
    Industrialist in Residence
Engineering Education Scheme: Mr Norman
    Davies
SATRO National Coordinator: Mr David Merrell
Telephone: 01928 788854
Facsimile: 01928 787112
Mailbox No YNX014

Cleveland SATRO
School of Science and Technology
University of Teesside
Middlesbrough
Cleveland
TS1 3BA
Director: Mr Miles Garnett
Telephone: 01642 218121 ext 3432
Facsimile: 01642 342478 and marked for the
    attention of Cleveland SATRO

County Durham SATRO
Durham Business & Education Support Team
Broom Cottages Primary School
Ferryhill
County Durham
DL17 8AN
Director: Miss Jane Ritchie
TIC Coordinator: Mr Robin Nodding
Telephone: 01740 652681
Facsimile: 01740 657005

SATROs

Devon & Cornwall SATRO
Devon Education Business Partnership
c/o Parkins Ltd
20 Trusham Road
Marsh Barton, Exeter
Devon
EX2 8DF
Director: Mrs Ann Forsyth
Telephone: 01392 494488
Facsimile: 01392 433404

Dudley & Sandwell SATRO
Saltwells Education Development Centre
Bowling Green Road
Dudley
DY2 9LY
Director: Mr Gareth Large
Telephone: 01384 634155
Facsimile: 01384 410436

Dumfries & Galloway SATRO
Penninghame Centre
Auchenden Road
Newton Stewart
DG8 6HD
Director: Mr Keith Best
Telephone: 01671 403455
Facsimile: 01671 402915

Gloucestershire SATRO
Hucclecote Centre
Churchdown Lane
Hucclecote
Gloucester
GL3 3QN
Director: Mrs Jan Greenhalgh (Acting)
CREST: Mr John Perriman
Telephone: 01452 427233
Facsimile: 01452 372347

Greater Manchester SATRO
CISTEL
The Manchester Metropolitan University
Didsbury
Manchester
M20 2RR
Director: Dr Jim Dewey
Telephone: 0161-434 3273
Facsimile: 0161-446 2325 and marked for the
attention of Pauline Adshead, CISTEL

Heart of England SATRO
c/o Technology Associates
Gable End
Hatford
Faringdon
Oxfordshire SN7 8JF
Director: Richard Speed
Telephone: 01367 710593
Facsimile: 01367 710593

Hereford & Worcester SATRO
Education-Industry Liaison Office
County Careers Centre, County Buildings
St Mary's Street
Worcester WR1 1TW
Director: Mr Andrew Lamb
Adviser for Vocational Education: Mrs Margaret
    Matthews, Finstall Centre, Stoke Road,
    Bromsgrove, Worcester. Tel: 01527 570566.
    Fax: 01527 570763
Telephone: 01905 765477
Facsimile: 01905 765527

Hereward SATRO
GPtec
Unit 1, Blenheim Court
Peppercorn Close
Peterborough PE1 2DU
Director: Mrs Liz Wade
SATRO Coordinator: Mike Palmer
Telephone: 01733 890808
Facsimile: 01733 890809 and marked for the
    attention of Hereward SATRO

Hertfordshire SATRO
The Institution of Electrical Engineers
Schools Education & Liaison
Michael Faraday House
Six Hills Way
Stevenage, Hertfordshire
SG1 2AY
Director: Mrs Sue Allenby
Accreditation: Sue Allenby
Young Engineers: Peter Young
CREST: John Nightingale
BP/SATRO Fellow: Mike Allen
Young Engineers (8-13): Anne Abbot
Rotary/SATRO Re-Use Scheme: Barbara
    Redway
National Science Week: Bill Blackburn
Telephone: 01438 767308
Facsimile: 01438 767309

The Curriculum
Science & Technology Regional Organisations

Humberside SATRO
Newlands House
Newlands Science Park
Inglemire Lane
Hull
HU6 7TQ
Director: Dr Wendy Richardson
Telephone: 01482 856622
Facsimile: 01482 806972

Kent SATRO
Kent Education Business Partnership
60 Churchill Square
Kings Hill
West Malling
Kent
ME19 6DU
Director: Mr Gareth Marshall, CITB Project
   Coordinator
Telephone: 01732 220111
Facsimile: 01732 220222

Lancashire SATRO
SATRO National Coordinator
c/o Cheshire SATRO
Director: David Merrell

Leicestershire SATRO
Leicestershire EBP Ltd
7 de Montfort Mews
off de Montfort Street
Leicester
LE1 7FW
SATRO Project Coordinator: Mr Derek Akers
SET Project Manager: Mr Garth Lee
Telephone: 0116 254 0033
Facsimile: 0116 254 1724

London - North SATRO
c/o The Engineering Council
Essex House
12/13 Essex Street
London
WC2R 3EG
Director: Mr Bernie Holloway
Telephone: 0171-240 7891 ext 3005
Facsimile: 0171-379 5586

London - NorthEast & Essex (NELEX)
   SATRO
NELEX
University of East London
Longbridge Road
Dagenham
Essex
RM8 2AS
Director: Mr Arthur Catterall
Telephone: 0181-597 0513/0181-590 7722 ext
   2238
Facsimile: 0181-590 7799 and marked for the
   attention of NELEX

London - West SATRO
Brunel Education Liaison Centre
Brunel University
Uxbridge
Middlesex
UB8 3PH
Director: Mr Malcolm Mander
Telephone: 01895 274000
Facsimile: 01895 232806 and marked for the
   attention of M Mander/Eileen Wright,
   Education Liaison Centre

Merseyside SATRO
MSTEC
Middlesex University
Trent Park
Bramley Road
London
N14 4XS
Director: Mr Terry Russell
Telephone: 0181-362 5690
Facsimile: 0181-441 4672 and marked for the
   attention of Middlesex Science and
   Technology Education Centre

Mid-Anglia SATRO
Cambridge Regional College
Arbury Centre
110a Arbury Road
Cambridge
CB4 2JF
Director: Mr Alan Rowe
Telephone: 01223 460317
Facsimile: 01223 315989

The Curriculum
Science & Technology Regional Organisations

Norfolk SATRO
County Technology Centre
Turner Road
Norwich
NR2 4DF
SATRO Activities Link: Ms Jenny Jealous
Telephone: 01603 620337, mobile 0850 567271
Facsimile: 01603 760448

North Yorkshire SATRO
North Yorkshire Business Education
    Partnership
5 Pioneer Business Park
Amy Johnson Way
York
YO3 4TN
Director: Mrs Diane Christon
SATRO Associates: Ms Sue McGinnis tel
    01653 668530; Mr Tom Smith tel 01904
    769396
Telephone: 01904 693632
Facsimile: 01904 693070

Northamptonshire SATRO
Spencer Centre
Lewis Road
Northampton
NN5 7BG
Director: Mr Phil Garnham
Telephone: 01604 232843/756134
Facsimile: 01604 604937
*Further information: Centre for training,
    consultancy and resource purchase in the
    fields of science, technology, maths and
    engineering.*

Northern Ireland SATRO
NISTRO
University of Ulster at Jordanstown
Shore Road
Newtownabbey
County Antrim
BT37 0QB
Director: Mr Brian Campbell
Deputy Director: Ms Fionnuala O'Gorman
Telephone: 01232 366682
Facsimile: 01232 852747 and marked for the
    attention of B Campbell, NISTRO

Northern SATRO
University of Northumbria at Newcastle
Kielder House
Coach Lane Campus
Newcastle upon Tyne
NE7 7XA
Director: Joseph Hornsby
Telephone: 0191-227 4178
Facsimile: 0191-227 4419

Salford SATRO
Salford Education Centre
London Street
Salford
M6 6QT
Director: Dr David Ward
Co-Directors: Mr Brian Sharples & Mr Paul
    Craig
Telephone: 0161-743 4262
Facsimile: 0161-745 7269

SATRO - Cumbria
Catherine Street
Whitehaven
Cumbria
CA28 7QX
Director: Mr Roger Day
Telephone: 01946 692163
Facsimile: 01946 67053 and marked for the
    attention of Cumbria SATRO

Scotland - North SATRO
University of Aberdeen
Marischal College
Broad Street
Aberdeen
AB9 1AS
Director: Dr Lesley Glasser
Administrative Assistant & TechFest
    Coordinator: Mrs Doreen Skinner
Telephone: 01224 273161
Facsimile: 01224 273160
*Further information: Activities include: Opening
    Windows in Engineering, Young Investigators
    and Primary INSET.*

The Curriculum

Science & Technology Regional Organisations

South Wales SATRO
Design & Technology Centre
Southey Street
Cardiff
CF2 1AP
Director: Mr Selwyn Gale
Telephone: 01222 483347
Facsimile: 01222 492852

South Yorkshire & North Derbyshire SATRO
Sheffield Education Department
Sheffield Education Business Partnership
Leopold Street
Sheffield
S1 1RJ
Director: Eur Ing John H Carter
EBP Manager: Mrs Deidre Eastburn
Telephone: 01742 727544
Facsimile: 01742 786641

Southern SATRO
Southern Science & Technology Forum
The University of Southampton
Southampton
SO17 1BJ
Director: Mr Paul Barnes
Telephone: 01703 553404
Facsimile: 01703 672714

St Helens SATRO
Community Education Department
The Rivington Centre
Rivington Road
St Helens
Merseyside WA10 4ND
Director: Mr Dave Roscoe
Co-Director: Anne Witt, tel 01744 455379
Telephone: 01744 453479
Facsimile: 01744 455350

Staffordshire SATRO
Staffordshire Design & Technology Education
  Programme
Kingston Centre
Harrowby Street
Stafford
ST16 3TU
Director: Mr John Hindhaugh
Telephone: 01785 277974
Facsimile: 01785 56193
EMail: qlsstepscc@bbcnc.org.uk

Strathclyde SATRO
University of Strathclyde
Graham Hills Building
50 Richmond Street
Glasgow
G1 1XP
Director: Dr R H Nuttall
Telephone: 0141-552 4400 ext 3743
Facsimile: 0141-552 0775 and marked for the
  attention of SSTF - Graham Hills Building ext
  3105

Sunderland SATRO
Broadway Education Centre
Springwell Road
Sunderland
SR4 8NW
Director: Mr Bill Smiles
TIC Coordinator: Mr Phil Marley
Telephone: 0191-511 2067
Facsimile: 0191-511 0006
Mailbox: YNX043

Surrey SATRO
Surrey Technology Centre
Occam Road
Surrey Research Park
Guildford
GU2 5YG
Director: Mr David Chesters
Telephone: 01483 295754
Facsimile: 01483 300433
*Further information: Centre for Young
  Engineers, Primary Science, Nuffield Bursary
  Scheme, CREST awards, and Problem-
  Solving Challenge.*

Sussex SATRO
East Sussex Education Business Partnership
Careers Office
16 Buckhurst Road
Bexhill-on-Sea
Sussex
TN40 1QF
Director: Mrs Gill Hamilton
Telephone: 01424 217660
Facsimile: 01424 843633

SATROs

The Curriculum
Science & Technology Regional Organisations

Trafford/Manchester SATRO
Trafford Education Business Partnership
Trafford Park Business Centre
Lloyd House, 392 Third Avenue
Trafford Park
Manchester
M17 1JE
Director: Mr David Roberts
Telephone: 0161-848 4305
Facsimile: 0161-848 4307

Trafford/Manchester SATRO
Manchester Compact Partnership
Greehays Business Park
Pencroft Way
Manchester
M15 6JJ
Director: Mr Alan Bell
Telephone: 0161-226 7491
Facsimile: 0161-226 8397

Warwickshire SATRO
Warwickshire Education Business Partnership
Educational Development Service
Manor Hall, Sandy Lane
Leamington Spa
Warwickshire
CV32 6RD
Director: Mr Brian Richardson
Telephone: 01926 413777
Facsimile: 01926 413773

West Yorkshire SATRO
School of Education
The University of Huddersfield
Hollybank Road
Lindley, Huddersfield
HD3 3BP
Director: Mrs Ann Gibson
Telephone: 01484 422288 ext 8267
Facsimile: 01484 514784

Wirral SATRO
Professional Development Centre
Acre Lane
Bromborough
Wirral
L62 7BZ
Director: Mr Tim Sibthorp
Telephone: 0151-334 0783
Facsimile: 0151-343 1608

STUDENTS

Students

Welfare

Association for Student Counselling
Learning Support, College of St Mark and St
  John
Derriford Road
Plymouth
Devon
PL6 8BH
Contact: David Acres, Chair, Press & Publicity
  Sub-Committee
Telephone: 01752 761133
Facsimile: 01752 761133

Association of Jewish Sixth-Formers
128 East Lane
Wembley
Middlesex
HA0 3NL
Contact: Olivia Marks, National Fieldworker
Telephone: 0181-904 4357
Facsimile: 0181-904 4323
*AJ6 aims to prepare Jewish fifth- and sixth-
  formers for life after school, particularly life on
  campus. A range of social and educational
  events are organised for the membership,
  open to all Jewish fifth- and sixth-formers
  regardless of affiliation.*

Brook Advisory Centre
153 East Street
London
SE17 2SD
Telephone: 0171-708 1234
Facsimile: 0171-833 8182
*The prevention and mitigation of the suffering
  caused by unwanted pregnancy by educating
  young persons in matters of sex and
  contraception and developing among them a
  sense of responsibility in regard to sexual
  behaviour.*

Catholic Children's Society (Westminster)
73 St Charles Square
London
W10 6EJ
Contact: Jim Richards, Director
Telephone: 0181-969 5305
Facsimile: 0181-960 1464
Helping children and families, irrespective of
*race or creed, living in Hertfordshire, Essex
  and London boroughs north of the Thames,
  the Society works with the homeless and
  travellers and advises on adoption,
  playgroups and family centres via counselling
  in school.*

EPOCH: End Physical Punishment of Children
77 Holloway Road
London
N7 8JZ
Telephone: 0171-700 0627
Facsimile: 0171-700 1105
*A non-membership body seeking to end the
  legal legitimisation of physical punishment of
  children by parents and other carers, and to
  find alternatives.*

National Association of Citizens' Advice Bureaux
115-123 Pentonville Road
London
N1 9LZ
Contact: Press and Publicity
Telephone: 0171-833 2181
Facsimile: 0171-833 4371
*Seeks to ensure that individuals do not suffer
  through lack of knowledge of their rights and
  responsibilities, or of the services available to
  them, or through an inability to express their
  needs effectively.*

National Union of Students of the United Kingdom
461 Holloway Road
London
N7 6LJ
Contact: Cindy Rowley, Manager of Research
Telephone: 0171-272 8900
Facsimile: 0171-263 5713
*NUS exists to represent the needs of its
  member student unions and their students
  nationally. It provides training, research, legal
  assistance, advice and information for its
  members.*

WELFARE

Students

Welfare

Salvation Army Territorial Headquarters
P.O. Box 249
101 Queen Victoria Street
London
EC4P 4EP
Contact: Director for Schools and Colleges
Telephone: 0171-236 5222
Facsimile: 0171-236 6272
An integral part of the universal Christian Church, its message is based on the Bible and its motivation is the love of God as revealed in Jesus Christ. Its mission is to proclaim His Gospel and engage in a programme of practical concern for the needs of humanity regardless of race, creed, colour, age or gender.

Scottish Child Law Centre
Lion Chambers
170 Hope Street
Glasgow
G2 2TU
Contact: Rosemary Gallagher, Solicitor
Telephone: 0141-333 9305
Facsimile: 0141-353 3861
Seeks to promote the knowledge of, and use of, Scots law for the benefit of children and young people in Scotland. The Centre also has an interest in all law as it affects the rights of children and young people.

Student Loans Company Ltd
100 Bothwell Street
Glasgow
G2 7JD
Telephone: 0141-306 2000
Facsimile: 0141-306 2005
Student Loans, which were introduced in 1990, are part of the financial support package available to students. Loans are governed by regulations which are revised by the government from time to time.

The Prince's Trust
8 Bedford Row
London
WC1R 4BA
Telephone: 0171-430 0524/0800 842 842
Aims to enable disadvantaged young people to achieve positive things for themselves or their community. 'Disadvantaged' means the young people are either homeless, unemployed, disabled or have just had it tougher than most.

WELFARE

Students

Youth organisations

Air Training Corps
HQ University & Air Cadets
RAF Cranwell
Sleaford
Lincolnshire
NG34 8HB
Contact: Public Relations Officer
Telephone: 01400 261201
Facsimile: 01400 261201
Seeks to promote and encourage a practical interest in aviation and the RAF by providing training which will be useful in both service and civilian life. Open to anyone aged 13-22 years.

Army Cadet Force Association
E Block, Duke of York's Headquarters
London
SW3 4RR
Telephone: 0171-730 9733
Participants must be between 13 and 18 years old.

Association for Jewish Youth
128 East Lane
Wembley
Middlesex
HA0 3NL
Telephone: 0181-908 4747
Facsimile: 0181-904 4323
Minicom: 0181-904 4393
Email: ajy@ort.org
A national voluntary Jewish youth organisation providing a range of services to affiliated clubs, centres, movements and projects.

Boys' Brigade (Incorporated)
Felden Lodge
Felden
Hemel Hempstead
Hertfordshire
HP3 0BL
Contact: Sydney Jones, Brigade Secretary
Telephone: 01442 231681
Facsimile: 01442 235391
A uniformed youth organisation for boys and girls aged 6-18 years. Each company is connected to a Christian church but membership is open to those of any faith or no faith.

British Association of Settlements and Social Action Centres
13 Stockwell Road
London
SW9 9AU
Contact: Julian Altshul, Information Assistant
Telephone: 0171-733 7428
Facsimile: 0171-737 0988
A national network of multi-purpose community centres. Working with the 60 member centres, the BASSAC aims to tackle the effects of poverty and discrimination in inner city areas. The centres provide a range of services in their local communities.

British Schools Exploring Society
Royal Geographical Society
1 Kensington Gore
London
SW7 2AR
Contact: Executive Director
Telephone: 0171-584 0710
Facsimile: 0171-581 7995
A registered charity which runs expeditions for young people aged 16-20 to trackless wilderness areas where they carry out adventure survival and scientific fieldwork as an integral aid to their self-development and growing-up process.

British Youth Council
57 Chalton Street
London
NW1 1HU
Telephone: 0171-387 7559
Facsimile: 0171-383 3545
Representing young people aged 16-25 to government and decision-makers, BYC provides an opportunity for the collective voice of youth to be heard on matters which concern them. It is run by young people from all walks of life.

Students

Youth organisations

Campaigners
Campaigner House
St Marks Close
Colney Heath
St Albans
Hertfordshire
AL4 0NQ
Telephone: 01727 824065
Facsimile: 01727 825049
The aim of the organisation is, through local Campaigner Groups, to bring young people to personal Christian faith and train them in Christian discipleship and lifestyle.

Church Lads' and Church Girls' Brigade
2 Barnsley Road
Wath-upon-Dearne
Rotherham
South Yorkshire
S63 6PY
Contact: J S Cresswell, General Secretary
Telephone: 01709 876535
Facsimile: 01709 878089
An Anglican uniformed youth organisation for those aged 5-21. Seeks to help young people grow as balanced citizens in society, offering them fun and friendship within a Christian setting.

Combined Cadet Force Association
E Block, Duke of York's Headquarters
London
SW3 4RR
Contact: Brig R G MacGregor-Oakford, Secretary
Telephone: 0171-730 9733
Facsimile: 0171-730 8264

Crusaders
2 Romeland Hill
St Albans
AL3 4ET
Contact: Gill Martin
Telephone: 01727 855422
Facsimile: 01727 848518
Seeks to provide resources and back-up for Christians who want to share the Christian gospel with young people aged 4-18 through weekly youth groups.

Duke of Edinburgh's Award, The
Gulliver House
Madeira Walk
Windsor
Berkshire
SL4 1EU
Telephone: 01753 810753
Facsimile: 01753 810666
The Duke of Edinburgh's Award is a programme of leisure-time activities for young people aged between 14 and 25, giving opportunities for personal achievement, social and community involvement, adventure and the discovery of new interests.

GFS Platform for Young Women
126 Queen's Gate
London
SW7 5LQ
Contact: Hazel Crompton, General Secretary
Telephone: 0171-589 9628
Facsimile: 0171-225 1458
The GFS seeks to enable girls and women to develop their potential personally, socially and spiritually.

Girls' Venture Corps Air Cadets
Redhill Aerodrome
Kings Mill Lane
South Nutfield, Redhill
Surrey
RH1 5JY
Telephone: 01737 823345
A voluntary, uniformed youth organisation for girls aged 11-18 providing activities which help to give a wider outlook and a greater sense of purpose. Activities include work in the community and air experience flights.

Kids' Clubs Network
Bellerive House
3 Muirfield Crescent
London E14 9SZ
Contact: Debi Jones, Information Services Manager
Telephone: 0171-512 2100
Facsimile: 0171-512 1020
Promotes and supports the provision of high-quality out-of-school clubs offering play for 5-12-year-olds, before and after school and during the holidays.

Students

Youth organisations

NABC - Clubs for Young People
396 Kennington Lane
London
SE11 5QY
Telephone: 0171-793 0787
Facsimile: 0171-820 9815
*Offers young people (11-25) the knowledge,
understanding and help they need, which will
utilise to the full their potential as they
prepare for life in society and their
responsibilities as adults.*

**National Council of Young Men's Christian
Associations**
640 Forest Road
London
E17 3DZ
Telephone: 0181-520 5599
Facsimile: 0181-509 3190
*The YMCA is a Christian charity committed to
helping young people, particularly at times of
need, regardless of gender, race, ability or
faith.*

National Federation of Gateway Clubs
117 Golden Lane
London
EC1Y 0RT
Contact: Robert Hunter, National Officer
Telephone: 0171-454 0454
Facsimile: 0171-608 3254
*Seeks to assist those with learning difficulties to
integrate themselves into the community by
providing leisure opportunities.*

Scout Association
Baden-Powell House
Queen's Gate
London
SW7 5JS
Telephone: 0171-584 7030
Facsimile: 0171-590 5103
*Seeks to promote the development of young
people in achieving their full physical,
intellectual, social and spiritual potentials as
individuals, as responsible citizens and as
members of their local, national and
international communities. Beaver Scouts 6-8
years. Cub Scouts 8-10 1/2 years. Scouts
10 1/2-15 1/2 years. Venture Scouts 15 1/2-20
years.*

Scripture Union in Schools
130 City Road
London
EC1V 2NJ
Contact: Emlyn Williams
Telephone: 0171-782 0013
Facsimile: 0171-782 0014
*Fosters voluntary Christian groups in schools in
England and Wales, and runs residential
activities.*

Scripture Union (Scotland)
9 Canal Street
Glasgow G4 0AB
Contact: Kenny McKie, Regional Activities
Director (Schools)
Telephone: 0141-332 1162
Facsimile: 0141-332 5925
*Provides holiday camps and residential activities,
outreach youth work and missions, and works
in schools and the community with the aim of
encouraging systematic Bible reading and the
promotion of Christian resources.*

Sea Cadet Corps
202 Lambeth Road
London SE1 7JF
Telephone: 0171-928 8978
Facsimile: 0171-401 2537
*A uniformed, voluntary, independent national
youth organisation for boys and girls aged
12-18, with junior sections for 10-12 year
olds. It has a nautical emphasis drawing upon
the British seafaring tradition and the high
standards of the Royal Navy.*

Toc H
1 Forest Close
Wendover
Aylesbury
Buckinghamshire
NP22 6BT
Contact: John A Biggerstaff, Methods
Administration Officer
Telephone: 01296 623911
Facsimile: 01296 696137
*Runs short-term residential projects in Britain,
Belgium and Germany lasting from a
weekend to 3 weeks. Projects include
working with people and children in need,
conservation work and study sessions.*

Students

Youth organisations

Urdd Gobaith Cymru
Swyddfa'r Urdd
Aberystwyth
Dyfed
SY23 1EN
Contact: J Eric Williams, Director
Telephone: 01970 623744
Facsimile: 01970 626120
Seeks to ensure that its members are given the opportunity to develop into mature individuals through the medium of Welsh, and to enable them to play an important part in the community by learning personal and social skills.

Young Explorers' Trust
at The Royal Geographical Society
1 Kensington Gore
London
SW7 2AR
Telephone: 01623 861027
Facsimile: 01623 861027
Seeks to encourage young people (aged 14-20) to take part in expeditions. YET offers an advice service and operates an approval/grant aid scheme for youth expeditions. It does not organise expeditions itself.

Young Women's Christian Association
Clarendon House
52 Cornmarket Street
Oxford
OX1 3EJ
Contact: Youth and Community Department
Telephone: 01865 726110
Facsimile: 01865 204805
Part of a worldwide Christian movement open to all (men and women), working for the full participation of women and young people in society.

Youth Clubs Scotland
19 Bonnington Grove
Edinburgh
EH6 4BL
Contact: Steven Greig, Project Coordinator
Telephone: 0131-554 2561
Facsimile: 0131-555 2553
Provides a national focus for good youth work in conjunction with the regional associations by, with and for young people.

Youth Clubs UK
11 St Bride Street
London
EC4A 4AS
Contact: John Bateman, Chief Executive
Telephone: 0171-353 2366
Facsimile: 0171-353 2369
Exists to support and develop high-quality voluntary work and educational opportunities for all young people.

YOUTH ORGANISATIONS

Students

Sports and interests

HOBBIES AND INTERESTS

Association of Football Badge Collectors
18 Hinton Street
Fairfield
Liverpool
L6 3AR
Contact: Keith Wilkinson, Chairman
Telephone: 0151-260 0554
Promotion of the hobby of collecting official enamel football club lapel badges, and encouraging clubs to issue quality badges.

Backpackers Club
P.O. Box 381
Reading
RG4 5YY
Contact: Dr Eric R Gurney, Director
Telephone: 01491 680684
Supports and promotes backpacking, for walkers, cyclists, canoeists and lightweight cross-country skiers.

British Association of Symphonic Bands and Wind Ensembles
6 Colehurst Croft
Monkspath
Solihull
West Midlands
B90 4XQ
Contact: Kevin Cooke, National Secretary
Telephone: 0121-744 0087
Facsimile: 0121-744 0087
Promotes interest in wind bands and wind ensembles to all ages and abilities throughout the country.

British Astrological and Psychic Society
124 Trefoil Crescent
Broadfield
Crawley
Sussex
RH11 9EZ
The Society exists to bring together those actively working in or interested in learning about Astrology, Palmistry, Tarot, Numerology, Psychic Perception and Healing. Membership is open to anyone.

British Chess Federation
9a Grand Parade
St Leonards-on-Sea
Sussex
TN39 4DY
Telephone: 01424 442500
Facsimile: 01424 435439
The governing body for chess in England, the BCF is responsible for fostering chess played in clubs, schools and competitions held throughout the country.

British Correspondence Chess Society
Barbican YMCA
2 Fann Street
London
EC2Y 8BR
Contact: Alon Risdon
Telephone: 0370 430 706 (mobile)
Promotes correspondence chess of good playing standard and according to the highest standards of courtesy.

British Driving Society
27 Dugard Place
Barford
Warwick
CV35 8DX
Contact: Mrs C Dale-Leech, Commissioner for Juniors
Telephone: 01926 624420
Facsimile: 01926 624633
To encourage and assist those interested in the driving of horses and ponies.

British Elastic Rope Sports Association
33A Canal Street
Oxford
OX2 6BQ
Contact: David Boston, Chairman
Telephone: 01865 311179
Facsimile: 01865 311189
Regulates and promotes the sport of bungee jumping in Great Britain. Those between 14 and 18 years require parental consent to participate.

Students

Sports and interests

British Falconers' Club
Home Farm
Hints
Tamworth
Staffordshire
B78 3DW
Contact: John R Fairclough Esq, Director
Telephone: 01534 481737
Facsimile: 01534 481737
*Promotion of the sport of falconry, the welfare
and survival of hawks in the wild, and the
upholding of the highest standards of welfare,
housing and feeding of hawks.*

British Federation of Brass Bands
4 Albury Road
Studley
Warwickshire
B80 7LW
*All activities to further the interests of brass
bands, and publishes the Directory of British
Brass Bands.*

British Field Sports Society
59 Kennington Road
London
SE1 7PZ
Contact: Juliet Bryan-Brown, Public Relations
Telephone: 0171-928 4742
Facsimile: 0171-620 1401
To promote and protect all field sports.

British Horse Society
Boreland Riding Centre
Fearnan
Aberfeldy
Perthshire
PH15 2PG
Telephone: 01887 830606
Facsimile: 01887 830606
*Promotes horse riding through regional
organisations and centres.*

British Lawn Mower Racing Association
Hunts Cottage
Wisborough Green
Billingshurst
Sussex
RH14 0HN
Telephone: 01403 700220
Facsimile: 01403 700037
*Organises lawn mower races between May and
October for anyone over 14 years.*

British Microlight Aircraft Association
Bullring
Deddington
Banbury
Oxfordshire
OX15 0TT
Contact: Jim Bell, Chief Executive
Telephone: 01869 338888
Facsimile: 01869 337116
*Promotes the sport of microlight flying.
Minimum age for solo flying is 17 years.*

British Numismatic Society
Hunterian Museum
Glasgow University
Glasgow
G12 8QQ
Contact: Dr J D Bateson, Hon Secretary
Telephone: 0141-330 4289
Facsimile: 0141-307 8059
*Encourages the study of British coinage in all its
forms. Junior members welcome.*

British Philatelic Bureau
20 Brandon Street
Edinburgh
EH3 5TT
*A department of the British Post Office which
supplies information, stamps and first day
covers to collectors and dealers.*

British Show Pony Society
124 Green End Road
Sawtry
Huntingdon
Cambridgeshire
PE17 5XA
Contact: Mrs P J Hall, Secretary
Telephone: 01487 831376
Facsimile: 01487 832779
*Protects and improves the showing of children's
riding ponies, for those aged under 25.*

Students

Sports and interests

British Trust for Ornithology
The Nunnery
Thetford
Norfolk
IP24 2PU
Contact: Dr Jeremy Greenwood, Director
Telephone: 01842 750050
Facsimile: 01842 750030

Central Council of Church Bell Ringers
50 Cramhurst Lane
Witley
Godalming
Surrey
GU8 5QZ
Contact: Mr C H Rogers, Hon Secretary
Telephone: 01428 682790
Promoting and fostering the ringing of bells for Christian worship and other occasions. Minimum age for participation is usually 9 years.

Crossword Club
Coombe Farm
Awbridge
Romsey
Hampshire
SO51 0HN
Contact: Brian Head, Editor
Telephone: 01794 524346
Facsimile: 01794 524346
Promotes the true art of the crossword through discussion and setting and solving challenging puzzles in their monthly publication. Advice is not available to non-members.

English Tiddlywinks Association
123 Clare Court
Judd Street
London
WC1H 9QR
Contact: Dr Patrick Barrie
Telephone: 0171-278 0476
Promotion of the game of tiddlywinks throughout the UK and organisation of national tournaments.

Federation of Scottish Skateboarders
16 Northwood Park
Livingstone
Edinburgh
EH54 8BD
Telephone: 01506 415308
Manages the affairs of all aspects of skateboarding, promotes competitions and seeks financial sponsorship. The Federation advises on the design, location and operation of facilities for skateboarding, rollerblading and freestyle bicycling.

Great Britain Postcard Club
34 Harper House
St James Crescent
London
SW9 7LW
Contact: Mrs D Brennan
Telephone: 0171-733 0720

Handbell Ringers of Great Britain
9 Dale Road
Grantham
Lincolnshire
NG31 8EF
Contact: Vaughan P Evans, Hon Secretary
Telephone: 01476 591986
Facsimile: 01476 591986
A registered charity which aims to encourage Handbell Tune Ringing in all its forms. Offers educational opportunities, help and advice, music, text and interest-free loans.

Historical Model Railway Society
'The Lawns'
9 Park Place
Worksop
Nottinghamshire
S80 1HL
Telephone: 01909 477566
Dedicated to the study, recording, publishing and dissemination of information on the railways of Britain and the construction, operating and public display of accurate models of those railways. Membership open to those over 17 years.

Students

Sports and interests

Long-Distance Walkers' Association
10 Temple Park Close
Leeds
West Yorkshire
LS15 0JJ
Contact: Brian Smith, Hon Secretary
Telephone: 0113 264 2205
To further the interests of people who enjoy long-distance walking.

Model Railway Club
4 Calshot Street
London
N1 9DA
Contact: The Secretary
Telephone: 0171-833 1840
Facsimile: 0171-833 1840
Promotes model railways as a hobby, building model railways and putting on exhibitions. Membership open to those aged 12 years and over.

Motorcycle Action Group
P.O. Box 750
Kings Norton
Birmingham
B30 3BA
Telephone: 0121-459 5860
Facsimile: 0121-628 1992
Promotes and protects all positive aspects of motorcycling in the UK and Europe, encourages greater road safety, and aims to improve other road users' awareness of motorcycles by positive promotion.

National Fancy Rat Society
4 Salisbury Road
London
W13 9TX
Contact: Mr Greg Baker, Hon Secretary
The promotion of the fancy rat as companion animals and pets, and ensuring continuing propagation of named varieties.

National Scooter Riders Association
P.O. Box 32
Mansfield
Nottinghamshire
NG19 0AZ
Contact: Jeff Smith, President
Telephone: 01623 651658
Facsimile: 01623 651658
Promotes social events and rallies for scooter enthusiasts nationwide and abroad.

Pony Club
British Equestrian Centre
Stoneleigh
Kenilworth
Warwickshire
CV8 2LR
Contact: Mr P R Lord, Development Officer
Telephone: 01203 696697
Facsimile: 01203 696836
Encourages young people to ride and learn to enjoy all kinds of connected sport, provides instruction in riding and horsemanship, instilling the proper care of animals, and promotes the ideals of sportsmanship, citizenship and loyalty. Open to those under 21 years.

Puppet Centre, The
Battersea Art Centre
Lavender Hill
London
SW11 5TN
Contact: Allyson Kirk, General Administrator
Telephone: 0171-228 5335
Facsimile: 0171-978 5207
Aims to promote and further the arts of puppetry and animation in all their forms. Services the needs of anyone interested in professional, amateur and educational puppetry.

Radio Society of Great Britain
Lambda House
Cranborne Road
Potters Bar
Hertfordshire
EN6 3JE
Contact: Mrs Marcia Brimson, Marketing and PR Manager
Telephone: 01707 59015
Facsimile: 01707 645105
The national society supporting radio amateurs in the UK. Radio amateurs are licensed by the DTI and issued with an individual call sign once qualified. A Novice Licence is available to encourage young people into the electronics field. A hobby which can lead to an interesting career.

HOBBIES & INTERESTS

Students

Sports and interests

Rehearsal Orchestra
c/o London College of Music
Thames Valley University, St Mary's Road
London
W5 5RF
Contact: Miss Jean Shannon, Administrator
Telephone: 0181-231 2643
The Orchestra, founded in 1957, provides an opportunity to rehearse under professional conditions with professional leaders and conductors. Soloists may rehearse with the Orchestra. Courses are held at weekends in London and elsewhere, with a week-long residential course in Edinburgh during the Festival.

Royal Photographic Society of Great Britain, The
The Octagon
Milsom Street
Bath
BA1 1DN
Telephone: 01225 462841
Facsimile: 01225 448688
An educational charity which promotes the development of scientific and fine art photography to both amateurs and professionals.

Scottish Ornithologists' Club
21 Regent Terrace
Edinburgh
EH7 5BT
Contact: Sylvia Laing, Secretary
Telephone: 0131-556 6042
Promotes ornithology in Scotland and assists with various surveys.

Society of Model Shipwrights, The
5 Lodge Crescent
Orpington
Kent
BR6 0QE
Contact: Peter Rogers, Hon Secretary
Telephone: 01689 827213
Promotes and preserves the traditional skills of ship modelling to a museum standard. Members, who range from beginners to experts, have interests covering all historical periods and both static and working models.

Society of Roadcraft
41 South Road
Hailsham
Sussex
BN27 3JE
Contact: Bruce Gillett, Chairman
Telephone: 01323 847466
Raises the standards of road usage by making the study of all aspects of the subject into a hobby in which all trainees both teach and learn to ever-rising standards.

Society of Scribes and Illuminators
The Art Workers' Guild
6 Queen Square
London
WC1N 3AR
Contact: Mrs Clare Turvey, Secretary
The aims of the Society are to perpetuate a tradition of craftsmanship in the production of manuscript books and documents, and to encourage the practice and influence of calligraphy and fine lettering.

St John Ambulance
1 Grosvenor Crescent
London
SW1X 7EF
Contact: Caroline Whitehead, Schools Development Officer
Telephone: 0171-235 5231
Facsimile: 0171-235 0796
Promotes the Three Cross Award scheme for schools, and aims to train every school child through the scheme at school (8 years and up), and to train teachers in first aid techniques.

United Kingdom Harp Association
Pooks Hill
Woodland Way
Kingswood
Surrey
KT20 6NX
Telephone: 01737 832740
An association for harpists, harp makers and repairers and harp enthusiasts.

Students

Sports and interests

Welsh Amateur Music Federation
Federasiwn Cerddoriaeth Amatur Cymru
9 Museum Place
Cardiff
CF1 3NX
Contact: Keith Griffin, Director
Telephone: 01222 394711
Facsimile: 01222 221447
Support for amateur music-making throughout Wales.

Welsh Chess Union
57 Treharne Street
Cwmparc
Rhondda
Mid Glamorgan
CF42 6LH
Contact: Kevin Staveley, Executive Director
Telephone: 01443 772750
Facilitates and develops the playing of chess in Wales. Enquiries are welcome from schools and pupils of all school ages wishing to know their nearest club.

Youth and Music
28 Charing Cross Road
London
WC2H 0DB
Telephone: 0171-379 6722
Facsimile: 0171-497 0345
Aims to increase young people's access to the arts. The main project is Stage Pass, a membership scheme which provides discounted tickets and an informative monthly arts magazine. School and individual subscriptions are available.

Students

Sports and interests

THE SPORTS COUNCIL

WHAT IS THE SPORTS COUNCIL?

The Sports Council is an independent body, established in 1972 by Royal Charter, which plays a strong strategic role in the development of sport and physical recreation.

The Council's headquarters is located in London with a network of ten regional offices and six National Sports Centres, England-wide.

It is currently undergoing a process of reorganisation in order to establish both a UK Sports Commission and an English Sports Council in place of the current GB Sports Council.

The UK Sports Council will

◆ oversee those areas where there is a need for a UK-wide policy – for example, on doping control, sports science, sports medicine and coaching – and identify areas of unnecessary overlap and duplication

◆ represent the UK on the international scene and coordinate policy for bringing major international sporting events to the UK

The Sports Council for England will

◆ concentrate its resources on an increased programme of support to the governing bodies to help 'grass roots' sport (with particular emphasis on young people) and to develop services in support of sporting excellence

◆ take responsibility for the distribution of National Lottery funds for sport in England

◆ provide a range of services in support of these three key programmes

This reorganisation is scheduled to take place by April 1996 with the aim of providing a strong framework to take sport forward into the 21st century.

Increasingly the Sports Council's emphasis is on work with young people. For more precise details on the work initiatives, products and services currently available it is advisable to telephone your nearest Sports Council office in the first instance. The developing strategic plan for the new bodies will affect the range of opportunities available resulting in some changes to traditional practice.

The Sports Council
16 Upper Woburn Place
London WC1H 0QP
Telephone: 0171-388 1277
Facsimile: 0171-383 5740

East Midland Region
(Derbyshire, Nottinghamshire, Lincolnshire, Leicestershire and Northamptonshire)
Grove House
Bridgford Road
West Bridgford
Nottinghamshire NG2 6AP
Telephone: 0115 982 1887
Facsimile: 0115 945 5236

Eastern Region
(Norfolk, Cambridgeshire, Suffolk, Bedfordshire, Hertfordshire and Essex)
Crescent House
19 The Crescent
Bedford
MK40 2QP
Telephone: 01234 345222
Facsimile: 01234 359046

Students

Sports and interests

Greater London Region
(Greater London)
P.O. Box 480
Crystal Palace National Sports Centre
Ledrington Road
London SE19 2BQ
Telephone: 0181-778 8600
Facsimile: 0181-676 9812

North West Region
(Lancashire, Cheshire, Greater Manchester and
  Merseyside)
Astley House
Quay Street
Manchester M3 4AE
Telephone: 0161-834 0338
Facsimile: 0161-835 3678

Northern Region
(Northumberland, Cumbria, Durham, Cleveland
  and Tyne and Wear)
Aykley Heads
Durham
DH1 5UU
Telephone: 0191-384 9595
Facsimile: 0191-384 5807

Scottish Sports Council
Caledonia House
South Gyle
Edinburgh EH12 9DQ
Contact: Information Assistant
Telephone: 0131-317 7200
Facsimile: 0131-317 7202
*The national agency, funded by the Scottish
  Office, to lead the development of sport and
  physical recreation in Scotland. With limited
  human resources, replies to written enquiries
  are normally restricted to one or more of their
  publications: What is Your Sport? leaflets,
  Where to Play? leaflets, and reading lists
  prepared.*

South East Region
(Surrey, Kent, East and West Sussex)
P.O. Box 480
Crystal Palace National Sports Centre
Ledrington Road
London SE19 2BQ
Telephone: 0181-778 8600
Facsimile: 0181-676 9812

South Western Region
(Avon, Cornwall, Devon, Dorset, Somerset,
  Wiltshire and Gloucestershire)
Ashlands House
Ashlands
Crewkerne
Somerset
Telephone: 01460 73491
Facsimile: 01460 77263

Southern Region
(Hampshire, Isle of Wight, Berkshire,
  Buckinghamshire and Oxfordshire)
51A Church Street
Caversham
Reading
Berkshire
RG4 8AX
Telephone: 01734 483311
Facsimile: 01734 475935

The Sports Council for Northern Ireland
House of Sport
Upper Malone Road
Belfast BT9 5LA
Telephone: 01232 381222

West Midlands Region
(West Midlands Metropolitan Authorities,
  Hereford & Worcester, Shropshire,
  Staffordshire and Warwickshire)
Metropolitan House
1 Hagley Road, Five Ways
Edgbaston
Birmingham B16 8TT
Telephone: 0121-456 3444
Facsimile: 0121-456 1583

Yorkshire and Humberside Region
(W Yorkshire, S Yorkshire, N Yorkshire and
  Humberside)
Coronet House
Queen Street
Leeds LS1 4PW
Telephone: 0113 243 6443
Facsimile: 0113 242 2189

SPORTS

Students

Sports and interests

SPORTING BODIES

British Association of Sport and Exercise Sciences, The
114 Cardigan Road
Headingley
Leeds
LS6 3BJ
Contact: The General Secretary
Telephone: 0113 230 7558
Facsimile: 0113 275 5019
The professional body for all those with an interest in science, sport and exercise, BASES aims to develop and spread knowledge about the application of science to sport and exercise.

British Olympic Association
1 Wandsworth Plain
London
SW18 1EH
Telephone: 0181-871 2677
Facsimile: 0181-871 9104
Disseminates the ideals of the Olympic Games in Great Britain and organises Britain's representation at the games.

Commonwealth Games Federation
10 Melton Street
London
NW1 2EB
Contact: Mr David Dixon, Hon Secretary
Telephone: 0171-383 5596
Facsimile: 0171-383 5506
The promotion of the Commonwealth Games every four years and the development of sport throughout the Commonwealth.

Northern Ireland Commonwealth Games Council
22 Mountcoole Park
Cave Hill
Belfast BT14 8JR
Contact: R J McColgan MBE, Gen Secretary
Telephone: 01232 716558
Facsimile: 01232 716558
Seeks to ensure that Northern Ireland is represented by the best available team at the Commonwealth Games, wherever they are held.

SPORTING CENTRES

Crystal Palace National Sports Centre
P.O. Box 676
Upper Norwood
London
SE19 2BL
Contact: Karen Murphy, Sports Coordinator
Telephone: 0181-778 0131
Facsimile: 0181-676 8754

Holme Pierrepont National Water Sports Centre
Adbolton Lane
Holme Pierrepont
Nottinghamshire
NG12 2LU
Contact: Mr John Morris, Events Manager, Sports Council
Telephone: 0115 982 1212
Facsimile: 0115 981 1359

SPORTS ASSOCIATIONS FOR THE DISABLED

British Deaf Sports Council
7a Bridge Street
Otley
West Yorkshire
LS21 1BQ
Contact: Roland Haythornthwaite, Chief Executive
Telephone: 01943 850214
Facsimile: 01943 850828
Promotes, develops and controls a wide range of sporting activities for deaf people in the UK. They are particularly concerned with providing opportunities of choice for young people.

SPORTS

Students

Sports and interests

British Disabled Water Ski Association
The Tony Edge National Centre
Heron Lake, Hythe End
Wraysbury, Staines
Middlesex
TW19 6HW
Telephone: 01784 483664
Facsimile: 01784 482747
Teaches people with disability to water ski.

British Motor Sports Association for the Disabled
P.O. Box 120
Aldershot
Hampshire
GU11 3TF
Contact: Tony Reynolds, Chairman
Telephone: 01252 319070
Facsimile: 01252 319070
Advice on how the disabled with an interest in motorsport can get started.

British Paralympic Association
Delta Point
35 Wellesley Road
Croydon
CR9 2YZ
Contact: Jane Swan, Assistant General Secretary
Telephone: 0181-666 4556
Facsimile: 0181-666 4617
The BPA is the central fundraising organisation for British teams competing in paralympic and other international events sanctioned by the International Paralympic Committee. The future aim is for greater integration between able-bodied athletes and athletes with a disability.

British Sports Association for the Disabled
13-27 Brunswick Place
London
N1 6DX
Contact: Gordon Neale, Marketing Manager
Telephone: 0171-490 4919
Facsimile: 0171-490 4914
Committed to encouraging children with a disability to participate in and enjoy sport of all kinds, and to developing opportunities at a local, regional and national level.

British Wheelchair Sport Foundation
Guttman Sports Centre
Harvey Road
Stoke Mandeville
Buckinghamshire
HP21 9PP
Telephone: 01296 84848
Facsimile: 01296 24171
The governing body of wheelchair sport for men, women and children paralysed by injury to the spinal cord and other related disabilities.

Riding for the Disabled Association
National Agricultural Centre
Avenue R, Stoneleigh Park
Kenilworth
Warwickshire
CV8 2LY
Telephone: 01203 696510
Facsimile: 01203 696532
Provides disabled people with the opportunity to ride and drive, helping their general health and well-being.

AIKIDO

see Martial Arts

AMERICAN FOOTBALL

British American Football Association Senior League
22a Market Place
Boston
Lincolnshire
PE21 6EH
Contact: Mr D S Quincey, League Commissioner
Telephone: 01205 363522
Facsimile: 01205 358139
Administers the sport of British American football (amateur) in the UK.

SPORTS

Students

Sports and interests

British Youth American Football Association (Flag League)
65 The Hayes
Summer Hayes
Willenhall
West Midlands
WV12 4RV
Contact: Mr Nick Russell, Development Officer
Telephone: 01902 631535
Facsimile: 0121-585 5912
Introduces 10-19-year-olds (boys and girls) to American football, a game which requires skills other than just athletic.

World League of American Football
Mellier House
26a Albermarle Street
London
W1X 3FA
Contact: Stephen Davies
Telephone: 0171-629 1300
Facsimile: 0171-629 4003
Seeks to introduce the excitement of American football as a participation sport into the school and youth sports programmes.

ANGLING

Anglers Conservation Association
23 Castlegate
Grantham
Lincolnshire
NG31 6SW
Telephone: 01476 61008
Facsimile: 01476 60900
Provides education about pollution problems within rivers.

Angling Foundation, The
Federation House
National Agricultural Centre
Stoneleigh Park
Warwickshire
CV8 2RF
Telephone: 01203 414999
Facsimile: 01203 414990
To protect and promote the welfare of the sport of angling, with special reference to the environment.

National Federation of Anglers
Halliday House
Eggington Junction
Hilton
Derbyshire
DE65 6GU
Contact: K E Watkins, Chief Administration Officer
Telephone: 01283 734735
Facsimile: 01332 734799
The governing body of coarse angling.

National Federation of Sea Anglers
51A Queen Street
Newton Abbott
Devon
TQ12 2QJ
Contact: Mr David Rowe, NFSA Development Officer
Telephone: 01626 331330
Facsimile: 01626 331330
The governing body for the sport of sea angling in England. The members (over 32,000) are contained within 550 affiliated clubs.

Scottish Federation of Sea Anglers
Caledonia House
South Gyle
Edinburgh EH12 9DQ
Telephone: 0131-317 7192
Promotes the sport of sea angling by holding junior and youth sections in open competitions, and by holding an annual 3-day coaching course and boat championship.

ARCHERY

National Field Archery Society
67 Seaburn Road
Toton
Beeston
Nottinghamshire
NG9 6HN
Contact: Hon Secretary
Telephone: 0115 972 4615
Exists to foster and promote field archery as a sport in which archers shoot at inanimate objects set in natural undulating terrain with trees and shrubbery and few or no clear-laned targets.

SPORTS

ASSOCIATION FOOTBALL

see Football

ATHLETICS

Amateur Athletics Association of England
225A Bristol Road
Edgbaston
Birmingham
B5 7UB
Telephone: 0121-440 5000
Facsimile: 0121-440 0555
The governing body for athletics in England.

Athletics Association of Wales
Morfa Stadium
Landore
Swansea
SA1 7DF
Telephone: 01792 456237
Facsimile: 01792 474916
Promotes and develops athletics for all ages in Wales.

British Athletic Federation
225A Bristol Road
Edgbaston
Birmingham
B5 7UB
Contact: Bill Adcocks, Information Officer
Telephone: 0121-440 5000
Facsimile: 0121-440 0555
Governing body for athletics in the UK, promoting the sport through award schemes for schools and coaching courses.

Fell Runners Association
15 New Park View
Farsley
Pudsey, Leeds
LS28 5TZ
Contact: Mike Rose, General Secretary
Telephone: 0113 255 6603
Advice can be provided for anyone interested in fell running, including the nearest club catering for junior (age 11-18) fell running.

Hammer Circle, The - The Association of British Hammer Throwers
38 Leeds Road
Mirfield
Leeds
WF14 0DA
Contact: M J Morley, Hon Secretary
Telephone: 01484 422133 ext 782210 (business), 01924 493340 (home)
Seeks to advance and promote hammer throwing in the UK.

Road Runners Club
21 Station Road
Digswell
Welwyn
Hertfordshire
AL6 0DU
Contact: J C Legge, Chairman of Council
Telephone: 01438 716508
Facsimile: 01438 840277
The promotion of road running.

Scottish Athletics Federation
Caledonia House
Redheughs Rigg, South Gyle
Edinburgh
EH12 9DQ
Contact: Mr G Ross, SAF Development Officer
Telephone: 0131-317 7320
Facsimile: 0131-317 7321
Provides opportunities for children of primary and secondary school age to participate in athletics and to achieve their desired level of performance.

BADMINTON

Badminton Association of England
National Badminton Centre
Bradwell Road, Loughton Lodge
Milton Keynes
MK8 9LA
Telephone: 01908 568822
Facsimile: 01908 566922
The governing body for the game of badminton in England. Their aim is to introduce badminton into all schools, and they advocate short badminton for primary schools.

SPORTS

Students

Sports and interests

Badminton Union of Ireland
The House of Sport
Upper Malone Road
Belfast
BT9 5LA
Contact: Mrs A E Kinkead, Hon Secretary
Telephone: 01232 381222
Facsimile: 01232 682757
*Promotes, develops and supports the sport of
badminton at school and club level
throughout Ireland.*

Scottish Badminton Union
40 Bogmoor Place
Glasgow
G51 4TQ
Contact: Anne Smillie, Chief Executive
Telephone: 0141-445 1218
Facsimile: 0141-425 1218
*Acts as the governing body for the sport of
badminton in Scotland, and seeks to promote
and encourage the development of the game.*

Welsh Badminton Union
Undeb Badminton Cymru
3rd Floor, 3 Westgate Street
Cardiff
CF1 1DD
Contact: Andrew Burke, Administration Officer
Telephone: 01222 222082
Facsimile: 01222 343961

BASEBALL

British Baseball Federation
66 Belvedere Road
Hessle
North Humberside
HU13 9JJ
Contact: Kevin Macadam, Executive Director
Telephone: 01482 643551
Facsimile: 01482 640224
*Seeks to promote the game of baseball in the
UK, with particular emphasis on schools.*

BASKETBALL

Basketball Association of Wales
Connies House
Rhymney River Bridge Road
Cardiff
CF3 7ZY
Telephone: 01222 454395
Governing body for basketball in Wales.

British and Irish Basketball Federation
Carnegie National Sports Development Centre
Beckett Park
Leeds
LS6 3QS
Telephone: 0113 283 2600 ext 3574
Facsimile: 0113 283 3170
*Administers the regional associations and has
no direct contact with schools.*

English Basket Ball Association
48 Bradford Road
Stanningley
Pudsey
West Yorkshire
LS28 6DF
Contact: Helen Kendall, Young Persons
Development Officer
Telephone: 0113 236 1166
Facsimile: 0113 236 1022
The promotion of basketball in England.

English Mini-Basketball Association
P.O. Box 22
Royston
Hertfordshire
SG8 7BD
Contact: Ken Charles, General Secretary
Telephone: 01223 207213
Facsimile: 01223 207213
*Develops the game of mini-basketball for
children of 10 years and under in schools,
clubs and at local authority and private sports
centres.*

SPORTS

Students

Sports and interests

Great Britain Wheelchair Basketball Association
The Woodlands
Brook End
Keysoe
Bedfordshire MK44 2HR
Contact: Gordon Perry, National Development
    Officer
Telephone: 01234 708741
Facsimile: 01234 708741
Promotion of wheelchair basketball for children
    and adults throughout Great Britain. A mobile
    'Roadshow' vehicle is available to visit
    schools, and has everything needed to
    demonstrate and play the game.

Scottish Basketball Association
Caledonia House
South Gyle
Edinburgh EH12 9DQ
Contact: The Secretary
Telephone: 0131-317 7260
Facsimile: 0131-317 7489
Seeks to develop, promote and control the sport
    of basketball in Scotland, including that
    played in Scottish primary and secondary
    schools.

BATON TWIRLING

National Baton Twirling Association
24 Cargate Terrace
Aldershot
Hampshire GU11 3EL
Contact: Tony Lloyd, Secretary
Telephone: 01252 311053
Promotion of the sport of baton twirling,
    provision of competition and a sales service
    to members for equipment.

BICYCLE POLO

Bicycle Polo Association of Great Britain
5 Archer Road
South Norwood
London
SE25 4JN
Contact: Garry Beckett, General Secretary
Telephone: 0181-656 9724

BILLIARDS AND SNOOKER

World Ladies Billiards and Snooker Association
3 Felsted Avenue
Wisbech
Cambridgeshire
PE13 3SL
Telephone: 01945 589589
Facsimile: 01945 589589
Seeks to promote billiards and snooker for girls
    at school and youth club level.

World Professional Billiards and Snooker Association
27 Oakfield Road
Clifton
Bristol
BS8 2AT
Contact: Malcolm L Hulley, Company Secretary
Telephone: 0117 974 4491
Facsimile: 0117 974 4931
Promotes the games of snooker and billiards to
    all, but especially to young people through
    coaching and participation.

BOBSLEIGH

British Bobsleigh Association Ltd
Chestnuts
85 High Street
Codford, Warminster
Wiltshire
BA12 0ND
Contact: Henrietta Alderman, General Secretary
Telephone: 01985 850064
Facsimile: 01985 850064
Aims to achieve a medal at the next Olympics
    and to develop the sport of bobsleigh for men
    and women at all levels in the UK. Open to
    those over 18.

BOULES

see Pétanque

SPORTS

Students

Sports and interests

BOWLS

British Crown Green Bowling Association
14 Leighton Avenue
Maghull
Merseyside
L31 0AH
Contact: Mr R Holt, Secretary/Treasurer
Telephone: 0151-526 8367
Promotes the game of crown green bowls.

British Isles Bowling Council
28 Woodford Park
Lurgan
Craigavon
Co Armagh
BT66 7HA
Contact: W A Gracey, Hon Secretary
Telephone: 01762 322036
Facsimile: 01762 322036
Promotes the game of bowls among young people by providing coaching and organising junior international matches.

English Bowling Association
Lyndhurst Road
Worthing
Sussex
BN11 2AZ
Telephone: 01903 820222
Facsimile: 01903 820444
Promotes, fosters and safeguards the game of outdoor level green bowls for males in England.

English Bowling Federation
62 Frampton Place
Boston
Lincolnshire
PE21 8EL
Contact: John Webb, Secretary/Hon Treasurer
Telephone: 01205 366201
Promotes, fosters and safeguards the flat green game of bowls, and formulates and adopts rules and laws of the game.

English Bowls Council
18 Margaret Paston Avenue
Norwich
NR3 2LT

Contact: Ray Springfield MBE, Secretary/ Treasurer
Telephone: 01603 427551
Places some importance on the promotion of the game in schools, providing support in the form of coaching.

English Indoor Bowling Association
David Cornwell House
Bowling Green, Leicester Road
Melton Mowbray
Leicestershire
LE13 0DA
Contact: Mr David Brown, National Secretary
Telephone: 01664 481900
Promotes, fosters and safeguards the level green game of indoor bowls for men. Local clubs may have age restrictions, the national competitions are open to those over 14.

English Short Mat Bowling Association
21 Croft Road
Benfleet
Essex
SS7 5RQ
Telephone: 01268 792950
Facsimile: 01268 792950
Seeks to promote the sport to young people, and administers national under-18 championships.

English Women's Bowling Association
2 Case Gardens
Seaton
Devon
EX12 2AP
Telephone: 01297 21317
Facsimile: 01297 21317
Promotes and fosters the level green game of bowls in England.

English Women's Indoor Bowling Association
3 Duncan Close
Moulton Park
Northampton
NN3 6WL
Contact: M E Ruff, Secretary
Telephone: 01604 494163
Promotes and organises women's indoor bowling.

Students

Sports and interests

Scottish Bowling Association
50 Wellington Street
Glasgow
G2 6EF
Contact: William S Forbes, Secretary
Telephone: 0141-221 8999
Facsimile: 0141-221 8999
*Fosters the sport of lawn bowls in Scotland. A
minimum age of 16 years is required for entry
in competitive events.*

Scottish Indoor Bowling Association
41 Montfode Court
Ardrossan
Strathclyde KA22 7NJ
Telephone: 01294 468372
*The promotion and fostering of indoor bowls in
Scotland.*

**Scottish Women's Indoor Bowling
Association**
39/7 Murrayburn Park
Edinburgh EH14 2PQ
Contact: Mrs Muriel Old, Hon Secretary
Telephone: 0131-453 2305
*The Association has a minimum age of 16 for
membership. However, most Indoor Clubs
have junior sections where the minimum age
is generally in the region of 10 years.*

Welsh Bowling Association
48 Pochin Crescent
Tredegar
Gwent
NP2 4JS
Contact: Alan H Williams, Hon Secretary
Telephone: 01495 253836
Facsimile: 01495 723836
*Fosters and promotes the level green game of
bowls for male bowlers of all ages in Wales.*

Welsh Indoor Bowls Association
16 Hendre Avenue
Ogmore Vale
Bridgend
Mid Glamorgan
CF32 7HD
Contact: Brian Davies, Hon Secretary
Telephone: 01656 841361
*Promotes the game of indoor bowls for all
people throughout Wales.*

BOXING

**Amateur Boxing Association of England Ltd,
The**
Crystal Palace National Sports Centre
London
SE19 2BB
Contact: Mr C Brown, Secretary
Telephone: 0181-778 0251
Facsimile: 0181-778 9324
*Promotes the sport and practice of amateur
boxing in England. Restricted to those aged
over 11.*

Association of Women Boxers
1 Fayland Avenue
Streatham
London
SW16
Contact: Pauline Dickson, General Secretary
Telephone: 0181-769 0645
*Aims to provide a platform for legitimate
sporting opportunities for women in the
sphere of boxing. Young people are
encouraged to come forward and learn the
skills and keep fit, although no competitive
opportunities are available for those under 18
years old. A programme for juniors is under
development.*

British Amateur Boxing Association
96 High Street
Lochee
Dundee
DD2 3AY
Telephone: 01382 508261
Facsimile: 01382 509425
*Scheme to introduce school-age boys to boxing
through the 'Kid Gloves' scheme, aimed at
10-15.*

British Boxing Board of Control
Jack Petersen House
52A Borough High Street
London SE1 1XW
Telephone: 0171-403 5879
Facsimile: 0171-378 6670
*Licenses, regulates and controls professional
boxing in Great Britain and Northern Ireland,
and represents British interests in
international boxing.*

SPORTS

Students

Sports and interests

Scottish Amateur Boxing Association
96 High Street
Lochee
Dundee
DD2 3AY
Contact: Frank Hendry, President: Executive
Director
Telephone: 01382 611412/508261
Facsimile: 01382 509425
Schoolboys (12-18 years) are catered for at three levels: non-contact, domestic and international. National and international championships entered.

Welsh Amateur Boxing Association
8 Erw Wen
Rhiwbina
Cardiff
CF4 6JW
Contact: Schools Section
Telephone: 01222 623566
Promotes and controls amateur boxing in Wales. Open to boxers of school age up to 15 years.

CANOEING

British Canoe Union
John Dudderidge House
Adbolton Lane
West Bridgford, Nottingham
NG2 5AS
Telephone: 0115 982 1100
Facsimile: 0115 982 1797
Promotes the sport of canoeing in the UK.

Scottish Canoe Association
Caledonia House
South Gyle
Edinburgh
EH12 9DQ
Telephone: 0131-317 7314
Facsimile: 0131-317 7319
The national governing body for canoeing in Scotland.

CAVING

National Caving Association
27 Old Gloucester Street
London
WC1N 3XX
Contact: Mr Frank S Baguley, Hon Secretary
Acts as the governing body of the sport of caving in the UK. It promotes cave conservation and correct caving techniques, including safety and equipment. It produces and distributes information leaflets.

CRICKET

Cricket Council
Lord's Cricket Ground
London
NW8 8QZ
Telephone: 0171-286 4405
Facsimile: 0171-289 5619

Marylebone Cricket Club
Lord's Cricket Ground
London
NW8 8QZ
Telephone: 0171-289 1611
Facsimile: 0171-289 5619

National Cricket Association
Lord's Cricket Ground
London NW8 8QZ
Contact: David Clarke, Marketing Executive
Telephone: 0171-286 4405
Facsimile: 0171-289 5619
Seeks to increase the opportunities for young people at school to experience cricket.

Scottish Cricket Union
Caledonia House
South Gyle
Edinburgh EH12 9DQ
Contact: Iain G Kennedy, Team Sport Scotland
Coordinator
Telephone: 0131-317 7247

Students

Sports and interests

Facsimile: 0131-317 7103
Provides opportunities for young people of school age to play cricket and develop their talents to the full.

Test and County Cricket Board
Lord's Cricket Ground
London
NW8 8QZ
Telephone: 0171-286 4405
Facsimile: 0171-289 9100

Women's Cricket Association
Warwickshire County Cricket Ground
Edgbaston Road
Birmingham
B5 7QX
Contact: Ms Maria Grant, Executive Director
Telephone: 0121-440 0520
Facsimile: 0121-446 6344
Seeks to encourage participation of girls and young women in the game of cricket at school, and provide opportunities for representation at county and country level.

CROQUET

Scottish Croquet Association
13 Park Place
Dunfermline
KY12 7QL
Telephone: 01383 722368
Is able to provide general information and coaching on croquet in Scotland.

The Croquet Association
c/o The Hurlingham Club
Ranelagh Gardens
London
SW6 3PR
Telephone: 0171-736 3148
Facsimile: 0171-736 3148
Seeks to encourage youngsters and teachers to take up the game and join their local croquet club.

CURLING

English Curling Association
Little Wethers
Sandy Lane
Northwood
Middlesex
HA6 3HA
Contact: Eric G Hinds, National Secretary
Telephone: 01895 256541 (business), 01923 825004 (home)
Facsimile: 01895 273481
Seeks to forward the cause of curling by fostering the game where possible. Because of the weight of the curling stones, the game is only usually suitable for those aged about 12 or 13.

Royal Caledonian Curling Club
Cairnie House
Avenue K, Ingliston Showground
Newbridge
Midlothian
EH28 2NB
Contact: W J Duthie Thompson, Secretary
Telephone: 0131-333 3003
Facsimile: 0131-333 3323
The governing body for the sport of curling in Scotland.

Welsh Curling Association
27 Holm Lane
Oxton
Birkenhead
Merseyside L43 2HN
Contact: Miss Ann Meikle, Secretary
Telephone: 0151-608 3691
Promotes the sport of curling in Wales.

SPORTS

Students

Sports and interests

CYCLING

Bicycle Association of GB Ltd
Starley House
Eaton Road
Coventry
CV1 2FH
Contact: David Collins, Public Relations
  Consultant
Telephone: 01203 553838
Facsimile: 01203 228366
Provides information on cycling.

British Cycle Speedway Council
57 Rectory Lane
Poringland
Norwich
NR14 7SW
Contact: The Administrator
Telephone: 01508 493880
Facsimile: 01508 493880
*Seeks to further the sport of cycle speedway by
  organising competitions, and co-ordinating
  leagues.*

British Cycling Federation
National Cycling Centre
Stuart Street
Manchester
M11 4DQ
Telephone: 0161-230 2301
Facsimile: 0161-231 0592

British Cyclo-Cross Association
14 Deneside Road
Darlington
Co Durham
DL3 9HZ
Contact: Brian Furness, General Secretary
Telephone: 01325 482052
Facsimile: 01325 482052
*Governing body for the sport in England and
  Wales with over 250 promotions a year. All
  promotions include races for under-12s (free
  entry) and under-16s, with no membership
  requirement for those under 16.*

British Mountain Biking
National Cycling Centre
Stuart Street
Manchester
M11 4DQ
Telephone: 0161-230 2301
Facsimile: 0161-231 0591
*Provides a comprehensive source of
  information relating to everything connected
  with mountain biking as a sport and
  recreation.*

English Schools Cycling Association
21 Bedhampton Road
North End
Portsmouth
Hampshire
PO2 7JX
Contact: Mrs Susan Knight, General Secretary
Telephone: 01705 642226
Facsimile: 01705 660187

Road Time Trials Council
77 Arlington Drive
Pennington
Leigh
Lancashire
WN7 3QP
Contact: Phil Heaton, National Secretary
Telephone: 01942 603976
Facsimile: 01942 262326
*Controls unpaced cycling time trials held on the
  public roads of England and Wales.*

Scottish Cyclists' Union
The Velodrome, Meadowbank Stadium
London Road
Edinburgh EH7 6AD
Telephone: 0131-652 0187
Facsimile: 0131-661 0474
*The development of the sport of cycling in
  Scotland.*

DANCE

see Movement and Dance

DRIVING

see Equestrian or Motor Sports

Students

Sports and interests

ETON FIVES

see Fives

EQUESTRIAN

British Equestrian Federation
British Equestrian Centre
Stoneleigh
Kenilworth
Warwickshire
CV8 2LR
Contact: Col J D Smith-Bingham, Director
General
Telephone: 01203 696697
Facsimile: 01203 696484
Helps in the furtherance of equestrian sport.

British Horse Society
British Equestrian Centre
Stoneleigh Park
Kenilworth
Warwickshire
CV8 2LR
Contact: Alison Taylor, Information Officer
Telephone: 01203 696697
Facsimile: 01203 692351
The prime objective is the well-being of horse and rider. It aims to improve standards of riding establishments, safety and training, horse care and welfare, and preserve our riding routes.

British Show Jumping Association
British Equestrian Centre
Stoneleigh Park, National Agricultural Centre
Kenilworth
Warwickshire
CV8 2LR
Contact: Mr A N K Shipton, Administration
Manager
Telephone: 01203 696516
Facsimile: 01203 696685
Improving and maintaining standards of show jumping, while encouraging members of all standards and at all levels to enjoy fair competition over safe and attractive courses.

British Show Jumping Association (Scottish Branch)
'Glenauld'
Hamilton Road
Strathaven
ML10 6SX
Contact: Mrs Janice Mair, Administrator
Telephone: 01357 22853
Facsimile: 01357 20022

Ponies UK Ltd
Chesham House
56 Green End Road
Sawtry, Peterborough
Cambridgeshire
PE17 5UY
Contact: John G Gadsby, Executive Officer
Telephone: 01487 830118
Facsimile: 01487 832086

Riding for the Disabled Association
National Agricultural Centre
Avenue R, Stoneleigh Park
Kenilworth
Warwickshire
CV8 2LY
Telephone: 01203 696510
Facsimile: 01203 696532
Provides disabled people with the opportunity to ride and drive, helping their general health and well-being.

Trekking and Riding Society of Scotland
Boreland
Fearnan
Aberfeldy
Perthshire
PH15 2PG
Contact: Liz Menzies, Secretary
Telephone: 01887 830274
Facsimile: 01887 830606
Member societies provide an introduction to the care of horses and ponies and offer riding for both the novice and experienced rider.

SPORTS

231

Students

Sports and interests

FENCING

Amateur Fencing Association
1 Barons Gate
33-35 Rothschild Road
London
W4 5HT
Telephone: 0181-742 3032
Facsimile: 0181-742 3033
The governing body for fencing in the UK.

Scottish Fencing
The Cockburn Centre
40 Bogmoor Place
Glasgow
G51 4TQ
Contact: Colin Grahamslaw, Administrator
Telephone: 0141-445 1602
Facsimile: 0141-445 1602
Seeks to aid the development and organisation of fencing in Scotland.

FIVES

Eton Fives Association
The Welches
Bentley
Farnham
Surrey
GU10 5HZ
Contact: Mr M P Powell
Telephone: 01420 22107
Promotes and maintains a general interest in the game of Eton Fives.

FLYING

British Model Flying Association
31 St Andrews Road
Leicester
LE2 8RE
Telephone: 0116 244 0028
Facsimile: 0116 244 0645
Promotes model flying to youngsters as a Design and Technology subject designed to fit in with the National Curriculum.

Royal Aero Club of the United Kingdom
Kimberley House
47 Vaughan Way
Leicester
LE1 4SG
Telephone: 0116 253 1051
Promotes sporting aviation for young persons.

Scottish Aeromodellers Association
2 Forth Avenue
Kirkcaldy
KY2 5PN
Contact: Mr Alan Gibson, Secretary
Telephone: 01592 592265
Facsimile: 01592 592265
Seeks to encourage the younger generation into the sport of aeromodelling and to promote competition at local and international level.

FOOTBALL

Football Association Ltd
9 Wyllyotts Place
Potters Bar
Hertfordshire
EN6 2JD
Telephone: 01707 651840
Facsimile: 01707 644190
The promotion, control, administration and organisation of association football in England.

Football Association of Wales Ltd
3 Westgate Street
Cardiff
CF1 1DD
Contact: D G Collins, Secretary
Telephone: 01222 372325
Facsimile: 01222 343961
Administration of association football in Wales at all levels.

Students

Sports and interests

Scottish Football Association
6 Park Gardens
Glasgow
G3 7YF
Contact: J Farry, Chief Executive
Telephone: 0141-332 6372
Facsimile: 0141-332 7559
Committed to promote and develop football at all levels, particularly in the formative years. A comprehensive development programme is now in operation.

Scottish Football League
188 West Regent Street
Glasgow
G2 4RY
Telephone: 0141-248 3844
Facsimile: 0141-221 7450
Provides league championship and league cup competitions for, and promotes and guards the interests of, the clubs comprising the league.

Scottish Women's Football Association
5 Park Gardens
Glasgow
G3 7YE
Telephone: 0141-353 1162
Facsimile: 0141-353 1823
Develops and promotes girls' and women's football throughout Scotland.

FRISBEE

British Ultimate Federation
74 Old High Street
Headington
Oxford
OX3 9HW
Telephone: 01865 69789
Facsimile: 01865 843952
Organises and promotes the sport of ultimate frisbee, a unisex 7-a-side team sport. Membership open to anyone over 9 years.

GAMES, HIGHLAND & BORDER

Scottish Games Association
24 Florence Place
Perth
PH1 5BH
Contact: Andrew Rettie, Secretary
Telephone: 01738 627782
Facsimile: 01738 639622
Seeks to encourage and foster the highest standards of ethics and performances in open athletic and traditional Highland games activities, and lays down and enforces rules and regulations covering them.

GLIDING

British Gliding Association
Kimberley House
47 Vaughan Way
Leicester LE1 4SE
Telephone: 0116 253 1051
Facsimile: 0116 251 5939
The governing body of the sport, the BGA promotes gliding and can supply an information pack (free) and a list of all the clubs in the country. Solo flying only possible after age 16.

Scottish Gliding Union Ltd
Portmoak Airfield
Scotlandwell
Tayside KY13 7JJ
Telephone: 01592 840543
Aims to inculcate a love of flying, an appreciation of teamwork and initiative for solo work. Open to those aged 14 and over.

GOLF

English Golf Union
1-3 Upper King Street
Leicester LE1 6XF
Telephone: 0116 255 3042
Facsimile: 0116 247 1322
Promotes, administers and encourages amateur golf in England.

SPORTS

Students

Sports and interests

English Ladies' Golf Association
Edgbaston Golf Club
Church Road
Edgbaston, Birmingham
B15 3TB
Contact: Mrs M Carr, Secretary
Telephone: 0121-456 2088
Facsimile: 0121-454 5542
Promotes golf for girls through schools and county junior organisers.

English Schools Golf Association
20 Dykenook Close
Whickham
Newcastle upon Tyne
NE16 5TD
Contact: Mr R Snell, Hon Secretary
Telephone: 0191-488 3538
Seeks to regulate and control schools golf in England and to give boys and girls an equal opportunity to participate in organised events. Open to both maintained and independent schools.

Golf Club – Great Britain, The
3 Sage Yard
Off Douglas Road
Surbiton
Surrey
KT6 7TS
Telephone: 0181-390 3113
Facsimile: 0181-399 9371
Encourages all golfers and would-be golfers to join the organisation so that they can obtain a handicap and play competitive golf.

Golf Foundation
Foundation House
Hanbury Manor
Ware
Hertfordshire
SG12 0UH
Telephone: 01920 484044
Facsimile: 01920 484055
Supports and promotes the playing of golf among young people, through coaching schemes (in school and out) and tournaments. Help can be provided for children and young people with special needs or handicaps.

Ladies' Golf Union
The Scores
St Andrews
Fife
KY16 9AT
Telephone: 01334 475811
Facsimile: 01334 472818
The governing body for women's golf in the UK and Commonwealth.

Scottish Golf Union
181a Whitehouse Road
Edinburgh
EH4 6BY
Contact: Ian Hume, Secretary
Telephone: 0131-339 7546
Facsimile: 0131-339 1169
The governing body for amateur golf in Scotland.

GYMNASTICS

British Amateur Gymnastics Association
Lilleshall National Sports Centre
Ford Hall
Lilleshall, Newport
Shropshire
TF10 9NB
Contact: Martin Reddin, National Development Officer
Telephone: 01952 677137
Facsimile: 01952 820326
Helps teachers fulfil National Curriculum requirements for gymnastics through teachers' awards and LEA courses.

Welsh Amateur Gymnastic Association
WAGA Office, Thornbury House
Thornbury Close
Rhiwbina, Cardiff
CF4 1UT
Contact: Mrs S John, General Secretary
Telephone: 01222 522012
Facsimile: 01222 529543
The encouragement, promotion and control of the sport and practice of gymnastics for the benefit of amateurs in Wales.

Students

Sports and interests

HANDBALL

British Handball Association
40 Newchurch Road
Rawtenstall
Rossendale
Lancashire
BB4 7QX
Contact: B J Rowland, Chairman/Chief
   Executive
Telephone: 01706 229354
Facsimile: 01706 229354
*The governing body for handball in the UK,
BHA administers Coach Education and a
'Play Handball' campaign designed to
introduce young people to the sport.*

Handbalito Association of Great Britain
P.O. Box 2284
Chingford
London
E4 9UP
Contact: Mr Aldridge, Director
Telephone: 0181-559 4490
Facsimile: 0181-529 9448
*Seeks to establish a new concept of mini-
handball by providing a teaching and
coaching aid, a stepping stone towards the
'real game'.*

HANG GLIDING

**Airborne Hang Gliding and Paragliding
   Centre**
Hey End Farm
Luddendenfoot
Halifax
West Yorkshire
HX2 6JN
Telephone: 01422 834989
Facsimile: 01422 836442
*Tuition in hang gliding and paragliding offered
for those over 14 years.*

**British Hang Gliding and Paragliding
   Association**
The Old School Room
Loughborough Road
Leicester
LE4 5PJ
Telephone: 0116 261 1322
Facsimile: 0116 261 1323
*Develops, promotes and regulates the sport of
hang gliding and paragliding.*

**Scottish Hang Gliding and Paragliding
   Federation**
42a Cumberland Street
Edinburgh
EH3 6RG
Contact: Mr Steve Senior
Telephone: 0131-557 2128
A sport suitable for people aged 16 and above.

HOCKEY

All England Women's Hockey Association
51 High Street
Shrewsbury
SY1 1ST
Telephone: 01743 233572
Facsimile: 01743 233583
*As the governing body of women's hockey in
England, it seeks to promote amateur hockey
for women and girls.*

British Skater Hockey Association
Grammont
Chiddingly Road
Horam
Heathfield
Sussex TN21 0JH
Contact: Stella van der Geyten, General
   Secretary
Telephone: 01435 812359
Facsimile: 01435 812359
*Promotes the fast physical sport of skater
hockey (was known as street hockey) which
is played by teams in all age groups (10-14,
14-18, 18+) throughout the country. Skater
hockey is similar to ice hockey but played
with a ball and on roller skates.*

235

Students

Sports and interests

England Mixed Hockey Association
Unicorn House
3 Plough Yard
London
EC2A 3LP
Contact: Simon Austin, Hon Secretary
Telephone: 0171-377 9750
Facsimile: 0171-247 3381
*Promotes the game of mixed hockey to those
over the age of 15.*

Hockey Association
Norfolk House
102 Saxon Gate West
Milton Keynes
Buckinghamshire
MK9 2EP
Telephone: 01908 241100
Facsimile: 01908 241106
*As the governing body for male hockey in
England, it seeks to promote the game by
running courses for coaches and young
players. Also has a resource bank that can
be used by schools.*

Scottish Hockey Union
48 Pleasance
Edinburgh
EH8 9TJ
Contact: Brent Deans, Director of Hockey
Telephone: 0131-650 8170
Facsimile: 0131-650 8169
Seeks to develop hockey in Scotland.

Welsh Hockey Association
1 White Hart Lane
Caerleon
Gwent
NP6 1AB
Contact: John G Williams, Secretary
Telephone: 01633 420326
Facsimile: 01222 221757
*Seeks to promote the game of hockey in Wales
by encouraging every school in Wales to play
hockey and supporting them with officers
from the Association.*

Welsh Women's Hockey Association
Welsh Hockey Office, Deeside Leisure Centre
Chester Road West
Queensferry

Clwyd
CH5 1SA
Contact: Miss M A Ellis MBE, President
Telephone: 01244 811825
Facsimile: 01244 822662
*Development of all aspects of women's hockey
in Wales at all ages and levels of play.*

ICE HOCKEY

British Ice Hockey Association
2nd Floor, 517 Christchurch Road
Bournemouth
Dorset
BH1 4AG
Telephone: 01202 303946
Facsimile: 01202 398005

JOUSTING

Jousting Federation of Great Britain
British Jousting Centre
Tapeley Park
Instow, Bideford
Devon
EX39 4NT
Contact: Max Diamond, President
Telephone: 01271 861200
Jousting and medieval period.

JUDO

British Judo Association Ltd
7A Rutland Street
Leicester LE1 1RB
Telephone: 0116 255 9669
Facsimile: 0116 255 9660
The governing body for the sport of judo.

Scottish Judo Federation
Caledonia House
South Gyle
Edinburgh EH12 9DQ
Contact: Kirsteen Hogg, Administration Officer
Telephone: 0131-317 7270
Facsimile: 0131-317 7050
*Promotes, fosters and develops the sport of
judo in Scotland.*

SPORTS

Students

Sports and interests

KARATE

see Martial Arts

KENDO

see Martial Arts

KORFBALL

British Korfball Association
P.O. Box 179
Maidstone
Kent
ME14 1LU
Telephone: 01622 813115
Facsimile: 01622 813115
Co-ordinates, develops and promotes the sport of korfball in Great Britain.

LACROSSE

All England Women's Lacrosse Association
4 Western Court
Bromley Street
Digbeth, Birmingham
B9 4AN
Contact: Anita Chesses, Administrator
Telephone: 0121-773 4422
Facsimile: 0121-753 0042

English Lacrosse Union, The
70 High Road
Rayleigh
Essex
SS6 7AD
Contact: Ron Bales, Hon Secretary
Telephone: 01268 770758
Facsimile: 01268 771372
Promotion and control of the game of men's lacrosse in England.

LAND YACHTING

see Sand and Land Yachting

LAWN TENNIS

British Women's Tennis Association
33 Princes Avenue
London
W3 8LX
Telephone: 0181-993 3397
Facsimile: 0181-993 6889
The promotion of women's tennis generally by providing tournaments and events for all age groups. Short tennis tournaments for school-age groups.

Tennis and Rackets Association
c/o The Queen's Club
Palliser Road
West Kensington
London
W14 9EQ
Contact: The Chief Executive
Telephone: 0171-386 3448
Facsimile: 0171-385 7424
Encourages young players.

Welsh Lawn Tennis Association
Plymouth Chambers
3 Westgate Street
Cardiff
CF1 1DD
Telephone: 01222 371838
Facsimile: 01222 343961
Assists schools, both primary and secondary, in the teaching of tennis in the school environment. Both tennis and short tennis is covered and most of the courses are directed at the various Key Stages.

MARTIAL ARTS

British Aikido Board
6 Halkingcroft
Langley
Slough
SL3 7AT
Contact: Mrs Shirley Timms, General Secretary
Telephone: 01753 819086

SPORTS

Students

Sports and interests

British Council of Chinese Martial Arts
46 Oaston Road
Nuneaton
Warwickshire
CV11 6JZ
Contact: Bob Wetherall, Secretary
Telephone: 01203 329461
Seeks to advance the case for the benefits of Chinese martial arts in schools and among LEAs.

British Ju-Jitsu Association
5 Avenue Parade
Accrington
Lancashire
BB5 6PN
Telephone: 01254 237216
Facsimile: 01254 396806
Places importance on the integration of young people in all aspects of club life, including officiating, coaching and administration.

British Karate Federation
Ein O'r Diwedd
Tramroadside
Treharris
Mid Glamorgan
CF46 5EF
Contact: Mr D Lund-Regan, Hon Secretary
Telephone: 01443 411944
Facsimile: 01443 411944
Promotes the sport of karate in the UK.

British Kendo Association
Security House, Littleton Business Park
Cocksparrow Lane
Huntington
Staffordshire
WS12 4TS
Contact: D Ratbould, Secretary
Telephone: 01543 466334
Facsimile: 01543 505882
Seeks to foster sport, independence, respect and discipline.

English Karate Governing Body
58 Bloomfield Drive
Bath
BA2 2BG
Contact: Mr B J Porch, General Administrator
Telephone: 01225 834008

Facsimile: 01225 834008
Seeks to introduce young people to the disciplines of mind and body taught in karate.

Scottish Ju-Jitsu Association
3 Dens Street
Dundee
DD4 6BU
Telephone: 01382 458262
Facsimile: 01382 458262
Promotes and encourages the education of all through participation in ju-jitsu; controls, regulates and organises the sport in Scotland; acts as an advisory body on the sport, and provides members with services. Membership is open to anyone over 6 years.

United Kingdom Tang Soo Do Federation
P.O. Box 184
Watford
Hertfordshire WD1 3LS
Telephone: 01582 402248
Facsimile: 01582 4002248

MODERN PENTATHLON

Modern Pentathlon Association of Great Britain, The
Pentathlon House
Baughurst Road
Baughurst, Tadley
Hampshire RG26 5JF
Telephone: 01734 817181
Facsimile: 01734 816618
Promotes multi-sport in schools through the National Schools Biathlon Championship, also through the Triathlon, Tetrathlon and Pentathlon.

MOTOR CYCLING

Amateur Motor Cycle Association
28 Mill Park
Hawks Green Lane
Cannock
Staffordshire WS11 2XT
Contact: D T Green, Chief Executive
Telephone: 01543 466282
Facsimile: 01543 466283

Students

Sports and interests

Auto-Cycle Union Ltd
ACU House
Wood Street
Rugby
Warwickshire
CV21 2YX
Telephone: 01788 540519
Facsimile: 01788 573585
The governing body of British motor cycle sport, whose aims are to provide participants with an enjoyable, safe and competitive day's sport. Youth events are for those aged 6-17.

Motor Cycling Club Ltd, The
Haven Bank
21 Madresfield Road
Malvern
Worcestershire
WR14 2AS
Contact: Geoffrey Margetts, Secretary and Treasurer
Telephone: 01684 565761
The club organises five principal events in the year, all of which require the driver to hold a driving licence.

National Scooter Sport Association
P.O. Box 32
Mansfield
Nottinghamshire
NG19 0AZ
Contact: Jeff Smith, Chairman
Telephone: 01623 651658
Facsimile: 01623 651658
Promotes road racing and off-road events for scooters. Road races open to those over 16 years.

Scottish Auto-Cycle Union
Block 2, Unit 6
Whiteside Industrial Estate
Bathgate
EH48 2RX
Contact: Mr Adam M Brownlie, Secretary
Telephone: 01506 630262
Facsimile: 01506 634972
Promotes and licenses motor cycle sport in Scotland, open to those aged over 6 years.

MOTOR SPORTS

AWDC - All Wheel Drive Club
P.O. Box 6
Fleet
Hampshire
GU13 9YY
Organises events for 4-wheel-drive vehicles of any sort and publishes a bi-monthly magazine.

British Motor Sports Association for the Disabled
P.O. Box 120
Aldershot
Hampshire
GU11 3TF
Contact: Tony Reynolds, Chairman
Telephone: 01252 319070
Facsimile: 01252 319070
Advice on how the disabled with an interest in motor sport can get started.

RAC Motor Sports Association Ltd
Motor Sports House
Riverside Park
Colnbrook, Slough
SL3 0HG
Contact: Derek Tye, Corporate Executive
Telephone: 01753 681736
Facsimile: 01753 682938
Promotes motor sport throughout the UK.

MOUNTAINEERING

Alpine Club
55-56 Charlotte Road
London
EC2A 3QT
Contact: Sheila Harrison, Assistant Secretary
Telephone: 0171-613 0755
A mountaineering club catering specifically for those who climb in the Alps and the greater ranges of the world. Library of over 40,000 items open to non-members by appointment. Minimum age for membership is 18.

SPORTS

Students

Sports and interests

British Mountaineering Council
177-179 Burton Road
West Didsbury
Manchester
M20 2BB
Telephone: 0161-445 4747
Facsimile: 0161-445 4500
National representative body for climbers, hill
walkers and mountaineers.

Mountain Bothies Association
26 Ryecroft Avenue
Deeping St James
Peterborough
PE6 8NT
Contact: Ted Butcher, Information Officer
Telephone: 01778 345062
A charity founded in 1965 to maintain simple
unlocked shelters in remote country for the
use and benefit of all who love wild and
lonely places.

Mountain Rescue Committee of Scotland
12 Hazel Avenue
Dundee
DD2 1QD
Contact: Alfred Ingram, Secretary
Telephone: 01382 68193
Provides advice and education in safe practice
on open and mountain environments, and
assists with statistics for projects on study
work.

MOVEMENT AND DANCE

Imperial Society of Teachers of Dancing
Euston Hall
Birkenhead Street
London
WC1H 8BE
Telephone: 0171-837 9967
Facsimile: 0171-833 5981
Seeks to educate the public in the art of dance
in all its forms, and to promote knowledge of
dance.

International Dance Teachers Association
International House
76 Bennett Road
Brighton
Sussex
BN2 5JL
Telephone: 01273 685652
Facsimile: 01273 674388
Promotes the art of dancing in all its forms,
creates and maintains dance syllabuses for
structured examinations, and arranges
programmes and courses for those wishing to
become a professional dancer.

NETBALL

All England Netball Association Ltd
9 Paynes Park
Hitchin
Hertfordshire
SG5 1EH
Contact: Sheelagh Redpath, Senior
Administrator
Telephone: 01462 442344
Facsimile: 01462 442343
Fosters the growth and quality of netball within
and beyond the school environment, thereby
creating the necessary bridge to continue into
the adult game.

Scottish Netball Association
Kelvin Hall Sports Complex
Argyle Street
Glasgow
G3 8AA
Contact: Liz Wilson, Administrator
Telephone: 0141-334 3650
Increases participation, enjoyment and the
profile of netball for all.

Welsh Netball Association
82 Cathedral Road
Cardiff
CF1 9LN
Telephone: 01222 237048
Facsimile: 01222 226430
Governing body for the sport of netball in
Wales, providing courses for teachers in
umpiring and coaching skills.

SPORTS

Students

Sports and interests

ORIENTEERING

British Orienteering Federation
Riversdale
Dale Road North
Darley Dale, Matlock
Derbyshire
DE4 2HX
Telephone: 01629 734042
Facsimile: 01629 733769
The governing body for the sport of
orienteering. Publishes books linking
orienteering with the National Curriculum.

Scottish Orienteering Association
Riversdale
Slitrig Crescent
Hawick
Roxburghshire
TD9 0EN
Contact: Mrs Lindsey Knox, Secretary
Telephone: 01450 377383
Seeks to promote and administer the sport of
orienteering in Scotland, and can provide
details of coaching awards for all levels
(including teachers) and also details of
regional schools orienteering groups.

PARACHUTING

British Parachute Association
5 Wharf Way
Glen Parva
Leicester
LE2 9TF
Contact: David Oddy, Office Manager
Telephone: 0116 278 5271
Facsimile: 0116 247 7662
The governing body for all sport parachuting in
the UK, and is responsible for the safe
conduct of all parachuting activities at its 32
affiliated clubs and centres. Minimum age 16
years.

Scottish Sport Parachute Association
c/o Skydive Strathallan
Strathallan Airfield
Auchterarder
PH3 1LA
Contact: Scotty Milne, Chief Instructor
Telephone: 01374 686161
There is a minimum age of 16 with parental
consent for participants.

PARAGLIDING

Scottish Paragliding and Hang Gliding
Federation
2 Inchmurrin Drive
Cathkin
Glasgow
G73 5RT
Contact: Peter Shields
Telephone: 0141-634 6688
Facsimile: 0141-631 3556
Promotes the sport of hang gliding and
paragliding in Scotland, and promotes
training and competitions for both.

PETANQUE

British Pétanque Association
18 Ensign Business Centre
Westwood Park
Coventry
CV4 8JA
Telephone: 01203 421408
Facsimile: 01203 422269
Promotes the playing of pétanque (the French
game of boules) at all levels for people of all
ages and abilities.

Scottish Pétanque Association
1 Arbroath Crescent
Causewayhead
Stirling
Central FK9 5SQ
Contact: Bob Boyle, Secretary
Telephone: 01786 470619
Promotes the game of pétanque in Scotland
including increasing public awareness, and
organises, co-ordinates and controls the
sport.

SPORTS

Students

Sports and interests

POLO

Hurlingham Polo Association
Winterlake
Kirtlington
Oxford
OX5 3HG
Contact: Mr J W M Crisp
Telephone: 01869 350044
Facsimile: 01869 350625
The governing body of polo, the Association runs scholarship schemes for 12- to 18-year-olds, mostly taught through the Pony Club.

RACKETBALL

British Racketball Association
50 Tredegar Road
Wilmington
Dartford
Kent
DA2 7AZ
Contact: I D W Wright, Hon Secretary
Telephone: 01322 272200
Facsimile: 01322 289295
Promotes racketball.

RACQUETBALL

Great Britain Racquetball Federation
145 Beccles Drive
Barking
Essex
IG11 9HZ
Contact: Wendy Hackett, General Secretary
Telephone: 0181-924 0842
Seeks to promote the game of racquetball for everyone to participate regardless of age, gender, race and disability.

RIDING & DRIVING

see Equestrian

ROLLER HOCKEY

National Roller Hockey Association of England Ltd
82 Greenfield Road
Farnham
Surrey
GU9 8TQ
Contact: Mrs G Whattingham, Publicity & Promotions Executive
Telephone: 01252 723635
Facsimile: 01252 723635
Promotes and develops roller hockey from grass roots to performance of excellence.

ROUNDERS

National Rounders Association
3 Denehurst Avenue
Nottingham
NG8 5DA
Contact: Brian Mackinney, Administrative Secretary
Telephone: 0115 978 5514
Promotes and encourages the development of the game of rounders in every way. Award scheme available.

ROWING

Amateur Rowing Association Ltd
6 Lower Mall
London
W6 9DJ
Telephone: 0181-748 3632
Facsimile: 0181-741 4658
To protect and advance the interests of amateur rowing.

Women's Rowing Commission
30 Denton Grove
Walton-on-Thames
Surrey KT12 3HE
Telephone: 01932 240459
Promotes women's senior and junior rowing throughout the country. The Commission's aims are to help interested parties meet and to assist with the establishment of new organisations.

SPORTS

Students

Sports and interests

RUGBY LEAGUE

British Amateur Rugby League Association
4 New North Parade
Huddersfield
HD1 5JP
Contact: Maurice F Oldroyd, Chief Executive
Telephone: 01484 544131
Facsimile: 01484 519985
The governing body of amateur rugby league football in Great Britain.

English Schools Rugby League
6 Brook House
Warrington Lane
Wigan
Lancashire
WN1 3RP
Telephone: 01942 239588
Promotes the game of rugby league football in schools by organising matches at all levels.

RUGBY UNION

Rugby Football Union
Twickenham
Middlesex
TW1 1DZ
Telephone: 0181-892 8161
Facsimile: 0181-892 9816
The promotion, encouragement and extension of rugby union football.

Rugby Football Union for Women
33 Rice Mews
St Thomas
Exeter
Devon
EX2 9AY
Telephone: 01635 298906
Actively encourages the participation of young women in all forms of rugby. A Youth Development Officer is available for advice.

Scottish Rugby Union Inc
7-9 Roseburn Street
Edinburgh
EH12 5PJ
Contact: James W Telfer, Director of Rugby
Telephone: 0131-346 5000

The promotion and development of school rugby by means of their staged development programme.

Welsh Rugby Union
P.O. Box 22
Westgate Street
Cardiff CF1 1JL
Contact: Mr Edward H Jones, Secretary
Telephone: 01222 390111
Facsimile: 01222 378472
Promotes, encourages, fosters and develops the game of rugby union football in Wales.

SAILING

Cruising Association
1 Northey Street
Limehouse Basin
London E14 8BT
Contact: Mrs Lorna Hammett, General
    Secretary
Telephone: 0171-537 2828
Facsimile: 0171-537 2266
Provides a crewing and skipper service for all age groups.

International Sail Training Association
5 Mumby Road
Gosport
Hampshire PO12 1AA
Telephone: 01705 586367
Facsimile: 01705 584661
Organises the Cutty Sark Tall Ships races and promotes the challenge of sail training in an international environment for 15-25-year-old male and female trainees through the medium of tall ships racing.

Royal Yachting Association
RYA House
Romsey Road
Eastleigh
Hampshire SO50 9YA
Contact: Mark Howell, Public Relations Officer
Telephone: 01703 627400
Facsimile: 01703 629924
Promotes and encourages participation in sailing, windsurfing and motor boating in the UK.

SPORTS

Royal Yachting Association, Scotland
Caledonia House
South Gyle
Edinburgh
EH12 9DQ
Telephone: 0131-317 7388
Facsimile: 0131-317 8566
The governing body of sport for sailing,
windsurfing and powerboating.

United Kingdom Sailing Centre
West Cowes
Isle of Wight PO31 7PQ
Contact: Donna Lett, Bookings Manager
Telephone: 01983 294941
Facsimile: 01983 295938
A registered charity whose main aim is to
introduce youngsters to the great outdoors
via a watersports medium in the largest
residential watersports centre in Europe.
Minimum age 8 years.

SAND AND LAND YACHTING

British Land Speedsail Association
155 Waldegrave Road
Teddington
Middlesex TW11 8LU
Contact: Martyn Coates
Telephone: 0181-287 2998
Promotes land speed sailing (windsurfing on
wheels). National Speedsailing school phone:
01736 762950.

SHINTY

Camanachd Association
Algarve
Badabrie, Banavie
Fort William
Highland
PH33 7LX
Contact: Alastair MacIntyre,
Secretary/Treasurer
Telephone: 01397 772772
Facsimile: 01397 772255
Seeks to foster and develop the Scottish
national game of shinty.

SHOOTING

British Association for Shooting and
Conservation
Marford Mill (HQ)
Rossett
Wrexham
Clwyd
LL12 0HL
Contact: Education and Training Department
Telephone: 01244 570881
Facsimile: 01244 571678
Seeks to educate through courses for 'Young
Shots' aged 8+, courses for mixed age
groups, a proficiency award scheme, a
teachers' resource pack, the provision of
speakers for schools and organisations, and
leaflets. Phone (Scotland) 01350 723226.

British Sporting Rifle Club
c/o National Rifle Association
Bisley Camp
Brookwood, Weybridge
Surrey
GU24 0PB
Contact: The Hon Secretary
Telephone: 01483 797777
Facsimile: 01483 797285
The encouragement of moving target shooting
and the provision of range facilities for this
and static shooting with sporting rifles.
Minimum age 14 years.

Clay Pigeon Shooting Association
107 Epping New Road
Buckhurst Hill
Essex
IG9 5TQ
Contact: Schools Liaison Officer
Telephone: 0181-505 6221
Facsimile: 0181-506 0739
Seeks to promote clay pigeon shooting as a
recreational activity available to all young
people throughout the UK either on an
informal or competitive basis.

SPORTS

Students

Sports and interests

National Pistol Association
21 Letchworth Gate Centre
Protea Way, Pixmore Avenue
Letchworth
Hertfordshire
SG6 1JT
Contact: Mr I McConchie, General Secretary
Telephone: 01462 679887
Facsimile: 01462 481183
Promotes the sport of target shooting for handguns in the UK. Organises shoot meetings and lobbies for the good of the sport. Provides advice and a helpline service.

National Rifle Association
Bisley Camp
Brookwood
Woking
Surrey
GU24 0PB
Telephone: 01483 797777
Facsimile: 01483 797285
The provision of a shooting centre of excellence for competitors from all over the world.

National Small-Bore Rifle Association
Lord Roberts House
Bisley Camp
Brookwood, Woking
Surrey
GU24 0NP
Telephone: 01486 76969
Facsimile: 01486 76392
Promotes the sport of small-bore, airgun and match crossbow shooting in the UK.

Scottish Air Rifle and Pistol Association
45 Glenartney Court
Glenrothes
KY7 6YF
Contact: Eric B Wallace, Hon Secretary
Telephone: 01592 743929
The governing body for field target shooting in Scotland. Promotes all forms of safe air weapon shooting at inanimate objects.

Scottish Pistol Association
Sandhole
Furnace
Inveraray
Argyll
PA32 8XU
Contact: T & M A M McCarthy, Joint Secretaries
Telephone: 01499 500640
Facsimile: 01499 500640
Promotion and encouragement of all types of target pistol shooting in Scotland.

Scottish Rifle Association
1 Mortonhall Park Terrace
Edinburgh
EH17 8SU
Contact: Colin R Aitken, Hon Secretary
Telephone: 0131-664 9674
Seeks to promote and develop fullbore target rifle shooting whenever and wherever possible.

Scottish Target Shooting Federation
1 Tipperlinn Road
Edinburgh
EH10 5ET
Contact: J H Mason, Shooting Development Officer
Telephone: 0131-452 8200
Seeks to encourage an interest in target shooting through coaching courses, liaison with local clubs and advertising.

Shooters' Rights Association
P.O. Box 3
Cardigan
Dyfed
SA43 1BN
Contact: Richard Law, Secretary
Telephone: 01239 698607
Facsimile: 01239 698614
The Association is a membership organisation for people whose activities are or may become subject to the Firearms Acts 1968-94. Membership includes both legal costs and public liability insurance, newsletters and advice.

SPORTS

Students

Sports and interests

SKATING

British Federation of Roller Skating
Lilleshall National Sports Centre
Newport
Shropshire TF10 9AT
Contact: Mrs M Brooks, Chairman
Telephone: 01952 825253
Facsimile: 01952 825228
Runs a 'Basic Skills' course for young people wishing to try roller skating.

National Ice Skating Association of UK Ltd
15-27 Gee Street
London EC1V 3RE
Contact: Celia Godsall, Chief Executive Officer
Telephone: 0171-253 3824
Facsimile: 0171-490 2589
Promotes, encourages and furthers the growth of ice skating as a sport and leisure activity. Coach; Dance; Figure; Precision; Speed.

SKIING

English Ski Council
Area Library Building
Queensway Mall, The Cornbow
Halesowen
West Midlands
B63 4AJ
Telephone: 0121-501 2314
Facsimile: 0121-585 6448
The governing body of the sport in England. Membership is open to schools, colleges and youth organisations. Various award schemes are administered, competitions organised and teaching and coaching qualifications administered.

Scottish National Ski Council
Caledonia House
South Gyle
Edinburgh
EH12 9DQ
Telephone: 0131-317 7280
Facsimile: 0131-339 8602
The national governing body representing and regulating the sport of skiing in Scotland. Both individuals and clubs may become members.

Ski Club of Great Britain
118 Eaton Square
London
SW1W 9AF
Contact: David Hearns, Information Services Manager
Telephone: 0171-245 1033
Facsimile: 0171-245 1258
Offers a wide-ranging number of services to members to enable them to get more from their skiing.

SNOOKER

see Billiards and Snooker

SOCCER

see Football

SOFTBALL

British Softball Federation
P.O. Box 210
Redhill
Surrey
RH1 1FN
Contact: Ms Maria Anderson, Gen Secretary
Telephone: 01737 765303
Seeks to foster, develop, promote and regulate the playing of all forms of softball in the UK. Coaching can be offered at primary schools in T-Ball, and youth/adult softball for higher-level schools.

SPEEDWAY

Speedway Riders Association
334 Kidmore Road
Caversham
Reading
Berkshire
RG4 7NG
Contact: Paul King, Secretary
Telephone: 01734 478475
Facsimile: 01734 468475
The SRA represents the riders' interests in all matters in much the same way as a union would in industry.

SPORTS

Students

Sports and interests

SQUASH

Scottish Squash
Caledonia House
South Gyle
Edinburgh
EH12 9DQ
Contact: Norman Brydon, Chief Executive
Telephone: 0131-317 7343
Facsimile: 0131-317 7734
*Seeks to promote the game of squash in
schools and to introduce young people to the
game through mini-squash.*

Squash Rackets Association Ltd
33-34 Warple Way
London
W3 0RQ
Contact: Matthew McFahn, National
Development Coordinator
Telephone: 0181-746 1616
Facsimile: 0181-746 0580
*Seeks to provide youngsters with the
opportunity to try squash. This is being
tackled through the Youth Sport Trusts -
National Sports Programme. The SRA Junior
Skills Awards Scheme is very suitable for use
in schools.*

STOOLBALL

National Stoolball Association
3 Bramber Way
Burgess Hill
Sussex
RH15 8JU
Contact: Mrs Delia Saunders, Hon
Chairman/Secretary
Telephone: 01444 241644
*Seeks to promote the game of stoolball as
much as possible.*

SUB-AQUA

British Sub-Aqua Club
Telford's Quay
Ellesmere Port
South Wirral
L65 4FY
Telephone: 0151-357 1951
Facsimile: 0151-357 1250

Scottish Sub-Aqua Club
Cockburn Centre
40 Bogmoor Place
Glasgow
G51 4TQ
Contact: Gus Furrie, Development Officer
Telephone: 0141-425 1021
Facsimile: 0141-425 1021
*Teaches the skills of scuba diving through a
structured training schedule, developing
leadership and instructional qualities in young
people and making them respect their aquatic
surroundings.*

SURF LIFE-SAVING

Surf Life-Saving Association of Great Britain
Verney House
4th Floor, 115 Sidwell Street
Exeter
Devon
EX4 6RY
Contact: Mrs E D Little, National Secretary
Telephone: 01392 54364
Facsimile: 01392 496563
*Promotes public safety in the enjoyment of
beach and off-shore sports and recreation
and furthers the competitive sport of surf life-
saving. Suitable for anyone over 7 years.*

SPORTS

Students

Sports and interests

SURFING

British Surfing Association
Champion Yard
Penzance
Cornwall
TR18 2TA
Contact: Colin Wilson,
    Administrator/Development Officer
Telephone: 01736 60250
Facsimile: 01736 331077
*Represents surfers and the sport of surfing in
    Britain and abroad, and develops the sport
    for all in all areas.*

Scottish Surfing Federation
20 Strichen Road
Fraserburgh
Grampian
AB43 5QZ
Contact: Chris Noble, Secretary
Telephone: 01346 513736
*Seeks to bring together all Scottish surfers of
    whatever age, to enable them to practise and
    participate in the sport with an emphasis on
    safety and healthy competition.*

SWIMMING

Amateur Swimming Association
Harold Fern House
Derby Square
Lougborough
Leicestershire
LE11 0AL
Contact: Amanda Richards, Customer Services
Telephone: 01509 230431
Facsimile: 01509 610720
*Administers and organises swimming, diving,
    water polo, synchronised swimming and open
    water swimming, from parent & baby to
    Olympic level.*

British Long Distance Swimming
Association
16 Elmwood Road
Barnton
Northwich
Cheshire
CW8 4NB

Contact: M Ferguson, Hon General Secretary
Telephone: 01606 75298
Facsimile: 01900 68829
*Promotes and encourages the sport of long-
    distance swimming, particularly in open water
    (minimum age 12 years). A one-hour-duration
    pool swimming scheme also operates for
    under 10 years and up.*

Royal Life Saving Society UK
Mountbatten House
Studley
Warwickshire
B80 7NN
Telephone: for enquiries about training or
    membership 01527 853943
*The RLSS UK is the premier drowning
    prevention agency in the UK, teaching life-
    saving and training lifeguards.*

Scottish Amateur Swimming Association
Holmhills Farm
Greenlee Road
Cambuslang, Glasgow
G72 8DT
Contact: Mrs Elaine Mackenzie, Administration
    Manager
Telephone: 0141-641 8818
Facsimile: 0141-641 4443
*Seeks to ensure that all school-age pupils are
    given the opportunity to learn to swim, helps
    school-age pupils fulfil their potential, and
    ensures that schools and clubs are
    interactive.*

Swimming for People with Disabilities
National Coordinating Committee
3 Knoll Crescent
Northwood
Middlesex
HA6 1HH
Contact: J E Hughes, Hon Secretary
Telephone: 01923 827142
*Promotes swimming for people with any
    physical disability. Membership is open to
    any organisation whose constitution indicates
    its interest in this work.*

SPORTS

Students

Sports and interests

TABLE TENNIS

English Schools Table Tennis Association
36 Froom Street
Chorley
Lancashire
PR6 0AM
Contact: Geoff Gardiner, General Secretary
Telephone: 01257 264873
Promotes and encourages the playing of table tennis in schools by organising courses for teachers and players and arranging schools' competitions.

English Table Tennis Association
Queensbury House
Havelock Road
Hastings
Sussex TN34 1HF
Contact: D C Gray, National Development Manager
Telephone: 01424 722525
Facsimile: 01424 422103
Governing body for the sport in England, providing help for teachers in the form of advice and information, local clubs and contacts, the Dunlop Skills Awards, the Woolwich Junior Leagues, help from local coaches and national schemes.

Table Tennis Association of Wales
31 Maes-y-Celyn
Griffithstown
Pontypool
Gwent NP4 5DG
Contact: Stephen Gibbs, General Secretary
Telephone: 01495 756112
Facsimile: 01495 763025
Seeks to promote table tennis at all levels throughout Wales.

TCHOUKBALL

British Tchoukball Association
50 Mallard Way
Great Cornard
Sudbury
Suffolk
CO10 0YQ
Telephone: 01787 374434

Suitable for primary schoolchildren upwards, a game which allows for the development of a high level of agility, speed and skill with the ball.

TENNIS

see Lawn Tennis

TENPIN BOWLING

British Tenpin Bowling Association
114 Balfour Road
Ilford
Essex
IG1 4JD
Contact: Rob Andrews, Assistant Secretary
Telephone: 0181-478 1745
Facsimile: 0181-514 3665
Promotes and encourages active participation in the sport of tenpin bowling at all levels, trains and educates all abilities, and promotes youth bowling.

TRIATHLON

British Triathlon Association
BTA Ltd
P.O. Box 26
Ashby-de-la-Zouch
Leicestershire
LE65 2ZR
Telephone: 01530 414234
Facsimile: 01530 560279
Seeks to increase participation in triathlon in schools and among school-age children.

Scottish Triathlon Association
Aberfeldy Recreation Centre
Crieff Road
Aberfeldy
PH15 2DU
Contact: D Thompson, Development Officer
Telephone: 01887 890922

SPORTS

Students

Sports and interests

TUG-OF-WAR

Scottish Tug-of-War Association
2 Davaar Avenue
Craigens
Cumnock
KA18 3BB
Contact: Mrs Fiona Shankland
Telephone: 01290 420493
Facsimile: 01290 420493
Willing to help any school in Scotland interested in establishing the sport.

UNDERWATER SWIMMING

see Sub-Aqua

VOLLEYBALL

English Volleyball Association
27 South Road
West Bridgford
Nottingham
NG2 7AG
Contact: George Bulman, National Director
Telephone: 0115 981 6324
Facsimile: 0115 945 5429
The EVA wants volleyball to be a major participant sport in England. It seeks to have volleyball included on the curriculum in every school in England, with mini-volleyball taught in primary schools.

Scottish Volleyball Association
48 The Pleasance
Edinburgh
EH8 9TJ
Contact: Executive Officer
Telephone: 0131-556 4633
Facsimile: 0131-557 4314
Seeks to promote, develop and control volleyball in Scotland by organising courses and exams for teachers and coaches, organising competitions and building a library of information.

Welsh Volleyball Association
70 Swakeleys Road
Ickenham
Uxbridge
Middlesex
UB10 8BD
Contact: Bryan Goodman
Telephone: 01895 673369 (evenings)
Governing body for the sport of volleyball in Wales. Arranges coaching courses and encourages schools to play the game.

WALKING

Race Walking Association
Hufflers
Shenfield
Brentwood
Essex
CM15 0SF
Contact: Peter Cassidy, Hon General Secretary
Telephone: 01277 220687
Seeks to encourage race walking among the young by liaising with schools and clubs, promoting competitions, establishing area young athletics squads, organising 10-race Grand Prix series, and taking leading young walkers abroad each summer for a taste of 'international' competition.

WATER SKIING

British Disabled Water Ski Association
The Tony Edge National Centre
Heron Lake, Hythe End
Wraysbury, Staines
Middlesex
TW19 6HW
Telephone: 01784 483664
Facsimile: 01784 482747
Teaches people with disability to water ski.

British Water Ski Federation
390 City Road
London
EC1V 2QA
Telephone: 0171-833 2855
Facsimile: 0171-837 5879

Students

Sports and interests

Scottish Water Ski Association
Scottish National Water Ski Centre
Townhill Country Park
Dunfermline
KY12 0HT
Telephone: 01382 620123
Facsimile: 01382 620122
Seeks to give young people the opportunity to try the sport of waterskiing and promote its inclusion on the list of school sports in areas where facilities exist.

WEIGHT LIFTING

British Amateur Weight Lifters Association
3 Iffley Turn
Oxford
OX4 4DU
Contact: W Holland OBE, General Secretary
Telephone: 01865 778319
Facsimile: 01865 778319
Promotes weight lifting and weight training, and organises the Strongest Schoolchild competition.

WINDSURFING

RYA Windsurfing
RYA House
Romsey Road
Eastleigh
Hampshire
SO50 9YA
Contact: Alan Hillman, RYA Windsurfing Manager
Telephone: 01703 629962
Facsimile: 01703 629924
The national governing body for the sport.

Scottish Windsurfing Association
c/o The Royal Yachting Association Scotland
Caledonia House, South Gyle
Edinburgh
EH12 9DQ
Contact: John Jameson, National Sailing Coach
Telephone: 0131-317 7217
Facsimile: 0131-317 8566
The governing body of the sport of windsurfing in Scotland.

United Kingdom Boardsailing Association
P.O. Box 36
Sarisbury Green
Southampton
SO31 7SB
Contact: Louise Roberts
Telephone: 01489 579642
Facsimile: 01489 889088
Organisation of regional and national windsurfing racing events. Under-15s are particularly encouraged to participate and they have their own fleet.

WRESTLING

British Amateur Wrestling Association
41 Great Clowes Street
Salford
Manchester M7 1RQ
Contact: Robin Tomlinson, National Development Officer
Telephone: 0161-832 9209
Facsimile: 0161-833 1120
Fosters the development of all styles of wrestling recognised by the International Wrestling Federation (FILA). Wrestling in schools is supported by the BAWA's development project 'Wrestling at the Grassroots' and is designed to meet the requirements of PE in the National Curriculum.

British Sombo Federation
Clarke's Sports Studio
Vicarage Road
Milton Regis, Sittingbourne
Kent ME10 2BL
Contact: Martin Clarke, Chairman
Telephone: 01795 470659
Facsimile: 01795 421644
A jacket wrestling sport from Russia, which helps to teach fitness, responsibility and a respect for others.

English Olympic Wrestling Association
41 Great Clowes Street
Salford
M7 1RQ
Telephone: 0161-832 9209
Facsimile: 0161-833 1120

SPORTS

Students

Sports and interests

Scottish Amateur Wrestling Association
Kelvin Hall Sports Centre
Argyle Street
Glasgow
G3 8AW
Telephone: 0141-334 3843
Raises awareness of wrestling in Scotland by running demonstrations and short courses in local schools

YACHTING

see Sailing

YOGA

British Wheel of Yoga
1 Hamilton Place
Boston Road
Sleaford
Lincolnshire
NG34 7ES
Contact: Karin Rice, Secretary
Telephone: 01529 306851
Facsimile: 01529 306851
Encourages and helps all persons to a greater knowledge and understanding of all aspects of yoga and its practice by a provision of study, education and training.

Students

Seeking help

Aberlour Child Care Trust
36 Park Terrace
Stirling
FK8 2JR
Contact: Mr Wm Grieve, Director
Telephone: 01786 450335
Facsimile: 01786 473238
*The Trust provides a wide range of services for
children and young people in Scotland whose
development or well-being is threatened by
disadvantage or deprivation. It is not a grant-
making trust.*

Action for Sick Children
Argyle House
29-31 Euston Road
London
NW1 2SD
Contact: Mrs Penny King, Library
Telephone: 0171-833 2041
Facsimile: 0171-837 2110
*A charity which aims to improve health services
for sick children and to increase public
understanding of their particular needs, with
advice for parents and publications for
parents and professionals.*

Association for the Prevention of Addiction
67-69 Cowcross Street
London
EC1V 6BP
Telephone: 0171-251 5860
Facsimile: 0171-251 5890
*Seeks to reduce the harm caused by drugs and
alcohol. Provides community-based services
for drug users and their families.*

Centrepoint
Leaving Home Project
Bewlay House, 2 Swallow Place
London W1R 7AA
Contact: Gillian Gholan, Schools Development
Worker
Telephone: 0171-629 2229
Facsimile: 0171-409 2027
*Centrepoint aims to ensure that no young
person is at risk because they do not have a
place to stay. The Leaving Home Project
aims to ensure that young people develop
skills and access information on leaving
home.*

Childline
2nd Floor, Royal Mail Building
50 Studd Street
London
N1 0QW
Contact: Information Officer
Telephone: 0171-239 1000 office. Helpline:
0800 1111
Facsimile: 0171-239 1001
*A free 24-hour national telephone helpline for
children and young people in trouble or
danger.*

Children's Society, The
Edward Rudolf House
Margery Street
London WC1X 0JL
Telephone: 0171-837 4299
Facsimile: 0171-837 0211
*Provides safe houses for runaways under 17;
runs independent living projects for teenagers
leaving care, family centres and home-finding
projects for children with special needs; and
provides housing for young people with
disabilities, and advocacy for those in trouble
with the law.*

Fairbridge
Central Office
1 Westminster Bridge Road
London SE1 7PL
Telephone: 0171-928 1704
Facsimile: 0171-928 6016
*A national charity providing a programme of
training and long-term support to young
people deemed to be at risk, especially those
excluded or at risk of exclusion from school.*

Gifted Children's Information Centre
Hampton Grange
21 Hampton Lane
Solihull
West Midlands B91 2QJ
Telephone: 0121-705 4547
*Supplies books, guides, teaching packs and
equipment for gifted children, dyslexic
children and left-handed children. Can
arrange psychological assessments and offer
legal advice and guidance for children with
special educational needs.*

Students

Seeking help

National Society for the Prevention of Cruelty to Children
42 Curtain Road
London
EC2A 3NH
Telephone: 0171-825 2500
Facsimile: 0171-825 2525
The NSPCC exists to prevent children suffering from all forms of child abuse and to protect children at risk from such harm.

RELEASE - Drugs in Schools
388 Old Street
London
EC1V 9LT
Contact: Sally Taylorson, Drugs in Schools Advisor
Telephone: 0345 36 66 66
Facsimile: 0171-729 2599
Provides information, advice and support to anyone concerned about a drug incident at school. Also offers advice on managing drug incidents and drug policy.

Terrence Higgins Trust, The
52-54 Grays Inn Road
London
WC1X 8JU
Contact: Nick Partridge
Telephone: 0171-242 1010 (helpline)
Facsimile: 0171-242 0121
A registered charity to inform, advise and help on AIDS and HIV infection.

Students

Seeking help

Advisory Committee for the Education of Romany and Other Travellers
Nott House
Bestow
Harlow
Essex
CM20 3HE
Telephone: 01279 418666
Works for equal access to education, health and other community services for gypsies and travellers, and campaigns for safe and secure accommodation and good community relations by eliminating discrimination.

Commission for Racial Equality
Elliott House
10-12 Allington Street
London
SW1E 5EH
Telephone: 0171-828 7022
Set up and funded by government, the CRE's duties are to work towards the elimination of racial discrimination.

Gypsy Council for Education, Culture, Welfare and Civil Rights
8 Hall Road
Aveley
Romford
Essex
RM15 4HD
Telephone: 01708 868986
Supports gypsies and travellers by campaigning for their civil rights, respecting their culture and demanding a good education for their children.

Institute of Race Relations
2-6 Leeke Street
London
WC1X 9HS
Contact: Jenny Bourne, Secretary
Telephone: 0171-837 0041
Facsimile: 0171-278 0623
Collects and exchanges information on racism and race relations throughout the world. Publishes materials for young people.

Minority Rights Group
379 Brixton Road
London
SW9 7DE
Contact: Rachel Warner, Head of Education
Telephone: 0171-978 9498
Facsimile: 0171-738 6265
Provides educational materials about and for minorities, with particular reference to young refugees in the UK.

National Association of Teachers of Travellers
The Graiseley Centre
Pool Street
Wolverhampton
West Midlands
WV2 4NE
Telephone: 01902 714646
Facsimile: 01902 714202
Works to promote and improve the education of travellers.

MINORITY GROUPS

255

Students

Seeking help

Anaphylaxis Campaign
8 Wey Close
Ash
Aldershot
Hampshire
GU12 6LY
Contact: David Reading, Chairman
*Offers support and guidance to those at risk
    from potentially fatal food allergies, and their
    carers.*

**Association for Children with Heart
    Disorders**
Killieard House
Killiecrankie
Pitlochry
Perthshire
PH16 5LN
Contact: Sandra Parkins, Scottish Secretary
Telephone: 01796 473204
*Provides support and understanding in
    everyday care and welfare to parents and
    families of children with heart disorders.*

**Association for Spina Bifida and
    Hydrocephalus**
42 Park Road
Peterborough
Cambridgeshire
PE1 2UQ
Contact: Peter Walker, Education Adviser
Telephone: 01733 555988
Facsimile: 01733 555985
*Offers advice and help for children at school
    and young people going on to FE. Helps to
    anticipate possible educational problems and
    is prepared to visit schools. Various
    publications are also available.*

**Association to Aid the Sexual and Personal
    Relationships of People with a Disability**
286 Camden Road
London
N7 0BJ
Contact: Mr Morgan Williams, Director
Telephone: 0171-607 8851

Body Positive
51b Philbeach Gardens
London
SW5 1EB

Telephone: 0171-835 1045
Facsimile: 0171-373 5327
*Self-help organisation providing support, advice
    and information to people affected by HIV
    and AIDS.*

Bridges
Greytree Lodge
Second Avenue
Ross-on-Wye
Herefordshire
HR9 7HT
Telephone: 01594 834120
Facsimile: 01989 563533
*Committed to working in partnership with
    people with learning disabilities, their carers
    and professionals to promote and maintain
    valued lifestyles, rights and choices.*

British Deaf Association
38 Victoria Place
Carlisle
Cumbria
CA1 1HV
Telephone: 01228 48844
Facsimile: 01228 41420
*Seeks to further the cultural and educational
    advancement of deaf people by organising
    appropriate courses and visits both at home
    and abroad.*

British Epilepsy Association
Anstey House
40 Hanover Square
Leeds
LS3 1BE
Telephone: 0800 309030
Facsimile: 0113 242 8804
*Provides practical support, information and
    advice to anyone with an interest in epilepsy,
    and campaigns for the rights of people with
    epilepsy.*

British Institute of Learning Difficulties
Wolverhampton Road
Kidderminster
Worcestershire DY10 3PP
Telephone: 01562 850251
Facsimile: 01562 851970
*Seeks to improve the quality of life for people
    with learning disabilities.*

HANDICAPS

Students

Seeking help

British Migraine Association
178a High Road
Byfleet
Surrey
KT14 7ED
Telephone: 01932 352468
Supports and promotes research into the cause and treatment of migraine, and provides encouragement and information to sufferers.

Centre for Accessible Environments
Nutmeg House
60 Gainsford Street
London
SE1 2NY
Telephone: 0171-357 8182
Facsimile: 0171-357 8183
The Centre is committed to the provision of built environments which are accessible for all people, including older and disabled people. It is an information and training resource and can answer queries by letter or phone.

Centre for Micro-Assisted Communication
Charlton Park School
Charlton Park Road
London
SE7 8HX
Contact: Myra Tingle, Director
Telephone: 0181-316 7589
Facsimile: 0181-317 3843
Provides an advisory and assessment service for students whose physical disability is hindering their access to social or written communication. Funding is normally via the LEA or FE college.

Cheyne Centre for Children with Cerebral Palsy
61 Cheyne Walk
London
SW3 5LX
Telephone: 0181-846 6488
Provides an assessment, education, treatment and resource service for children with cerebral palsy aged 18 months to 8 years. Also provides outpatient treatment for children aged 0-19 years.

Child Growth Foundation
2 Mayfield Avenue
Chiswick
London
W4 1PW
Telephone: 0181-995 0257
Facsimile: 0181-995 9075
Parent/patient support for children and adults with growth disorders.

Cystic Fibrosis Research Trust
5 Blyth Road
Bromley
Kent
BR1 3RS
Telephone: 0181-464 7211
Facsimile: 0181-313 0472
Seeks to raise funds to finance research and improve the care and treatment of people with CF, to establish groups for those affected and their families, and to educate and raise public awareness about CF.

David Lewis Centre
Mill Lane
Warford
Alderley Edge
Cheshire
SK9 7UD
Contact: Mrs Sally Harte, School Principal
Telephone: 01565 872613
Facsimile: 01565 872829
The Centre provides residential assessment, treatment and rehabilitation of people, including schoolchildren, suffering from epilepsy. It aims to maximise each student's potential by enabling them to achieve as much independence as possible and to enjoy a life which is both stimulating and rewarding.

Down's Syndrome Association
153-155 Mitcham Road
London
SW17 9PG
Telephone: 0181-682 4001
Facsimile: 0181-682 4012
Provides information and support for people with Down's Syndrome, their families and professionals who work with them.

HANDICAPS

Students

Seeking help

Epilepsy Association of Scotland
National Headquarters
48 Govan Road
Glasgow
G51 1JL
Telephone: 0141-427 4911
Facsimile: 0141-427 7414
*Provides information, support, advice and
counselling for people with epilepsy, their
families, carers and the professionals who
work with these groups.*

Hyperactive Children's Support Group
71 Whyke Lane
Chichester
Sussex
PO19 2LD
Contact: Mrs Sally Bunday, Director & National
Coordinator
Telephone: 01903 725182
*Advises and supports parents and professionals
of hyperactive/ADHD/allergic children by
suggesting dietary therapies and behaviour
modification ideas, with information on other
therapies that could prove beneficial.*

I CAN
Barbican City Gate
1-3 Dufferin Street
London
EC1Y 8NA
Contact: Information Coordinator
Telephone: 0171-374 4422
Facsimile: 0171-374 2762
*I CAN is a children's charity specialising in the
education of children with speech and
language disorders and asthma and eczema.*

JOLT (The Journey of a Lifetime Trust)
High Brow
Harrow Park
Harrow-on-the-Hill
Middlesex
HA1 3JE
Contact: Dorothy Dalton, Chairman of Trustees
Telephone: 0181-869 1214
Facsimile: 0181-869 1214
*JOLT exists to take physically, medically and
socially disadvantaged teenagers on
challenging month-long journeys of a lifetime.*

**Michael Palin Centre for Stammering
    Children, The**
Finsbury Health Centre
Pine Street
London
EC1R 0JH
Telephone: 0171-837 0031
*Provides a consultation service for stammering
children aged 2-18 years. Children are
referred by their GP or local therapist.*

National Asthma Campaign
Providence House
Providence Place
London
N1 0NT
Contact: Joanna Taylor
Telephone: 0171-226 2260
Facsimile: 0171-704 0740
*Provides information and support for those with
asthma, their carers and health professionals.
Helpline 0345 010203 9am-9pm Mon-Fri.*

National Autistic Society
276 Willesden Lane
London
NW2 5RB
Telephone: 0181-451 1114
Facsimile: 0181-451 5865
*Seeks to offer families and carers information,
advice and support, and develops a range of
educational and support services for people
with autism.*

National Deaf Children's Society
15 Dufferin Street
London
EC1Y 9PD
Telephone: 0171-250 0123
Facsimile: 0171-251 5020
*An organisation of families, parents and
professionals providing support, information
and advice to families with deaf children. Also
produces publications.*

Students

Seeking help

National Eczema Society
163 Eversholt Street
London
NW1 1BU
Telephone: 0171-388 4097
Facsimile: 0171-388 5882
*Provides practical advice and information about
eczema and its management. Publications
are available including a booklet about
eczema in schools.*

National Library for the Blind
Cromwell Road
Bredbury
Stockport
SK6 2SG
Telephone: 0161-494 0217
Facsimile: 0161-406 6728
*A registered charity providing literature in
embossed and large types for the blind and
partially sighted.*

National Society for Epilepsy
Chalfont Centre for Epilepsy
Chalfont St Peter
Gerrards Cross
Buckinghamshire
SL9 0RJ
Contact: Information and Education Department
Telephone: 01494 873991
Facsimile: 01494 871927
*Provides information resources and a helpline,
and runs conferences about the condition.*

Partially-Sighted Society
P.O. Box 322
Doncaster
DN1 2XA
Telephone: 01302 323132
*Helps the visually impaired make the best use
of their remaining sight.*

**PHAB (Physically Disabled and Able-
Bodied)**
12-14 London Road
Croydon
Surrey
CR0 2TA
Contact: Peter Gooch, Chief Executive

Telephone: 0181-667 9443
Facsimile: 0181-681 1399
*Exists to integrate people with and without
physical disabilities.*

Rathbone C.I.
Head Office, 1st Floor
The Excalibur Building
77 Whitworth Street
Manchester
M1 6QZ
Contact: Information Officers
Telephone: 0161-236 5358
Facsimile: 0161-236 4539
*Aims to ensure that those people in the UK who
have special education and training needs
realise their full potential and participate fully
in the social and economic life of the
community. Rathbone C.I. runs employment
and training schemes, residential schemes
for young adults, and a national information
line which deals with enquiries related to
learning difficulties.*

Restricted Growth Association
P.O. Box 18
Rugeley
Staffordshire
WS15 2GH
Telephone: 01889 576571
*Aims to help reduce the distress and
disadvantages of persons of restricted growth
by providing support for them and their
families.*

Royal National Institute for the Blind (RNIB)
224 Great Portland Street
London
W1N 6AA
Contact: RNIB Education Information Service
Telephone: 0171-388 1266
Facsimile: 0171-383 4921
*Aims to enable children and young people to
achieve all they are capable of, whether in
the classroom, in sports, in creative pursuits
or in everyday life. Support is also provided
for families with a visually impaired child.*

HANDICAPS

Students

Seeking help

Scoliosis Association (UK), The
2 Ivebury Court
323-327 Latimer Road
London
W10 6RA
Telephone: 0181-964 5343
Facsimile: 0181-964 5343
SAUK supports people with scoliosis (sideways curving and twisting of the spine) and seeks to spread knowledge about scoliosis, alerting the public and those in contact with children and young people to the need for early detection.

Scottish Association for the Deaf
Moray House Institute of Education
Holyrood Road
Edinburgh
EH8 8AQ
Telephone: 0131-557 0591
Facsimile: 0131-557 6922
Acts as a clearing house for information relating to deaf people and the hearing impaired, and educates hearing people concerning deafness and its implications.

Scottish Society for Autistic Children
Hilton House
Alloa Business Park, Whins Road
Alloa
FK10 3SA
Telephone: 01259 720044
Facsimile: 01259 720051
Provides care, support and education for people with autism in Scotland.

Shaftesbury Society, The
16 Kingston Road
London
SW19 1JZ
Contact: Allan Giles, Education Officer (Schools)
Telephone: 0181-542 5550
Facsimile: 0181-545 0605
A registered charity which exists to enable people in great need to achieve security, self-worth and significance, and through this to show Christian care in action.

Spinal Injuries Association
Newpoint House
76 St James's Lane
London
N10 3DF
Contact: Information Officer
Telephone: 0181-444 2121
Facsimile: 0181-444 3761
The national organisation for spinal cord-injured people and their families. Provides information on the effects of paralysis and a wide range of services.

STEPS
15 Statham Close
Lymn
Cheshire
WA13 9NN
Telephone: 01925 757525
A charity which gives support, contact, help, advice and information to children with lower limb abnormalities (club foot, congenital dislocated hip, lower limb deficiency) through a national helpline, publications and local contact.

The Children's Trust
Tadworth Court
Tadworth
Surrey
KT20 5RU
Contact: Sarah Watts, Communications Manager
Telephone: 01737 357171
Facsimile: 01737 373848
A charity providing care, treatment and education to children with profound disabilities, and support for their families.

UK Rett Syndrome Association
29 Carlton Road
London
N11 3EX
Contact: Christine Freeman, Administrator
Telephone: 0181-361 5161
Facsimile: 0181-361 5161
Offers practical help, friendship and support to Rett Syndrome sufferers, their families and carers.

HANDICAPS

TEACHERS

Teachers
Initial teacher training establishments

Aberystwyth University of Wales
Department of Education
Old College, King Street
Aberystwyth
Dyfed
SY23 2AX
Contact: Mrs Barbara Bevan, Administrator
Telephone: 01970 622104/5
Facsimile: 01970 622258

Anglia Polytechnic University
East Road
Cambridge
CB1 1PT
Telephone: 01223 363271
Facsimile: 01223 352973

Bishop Grosseteste College
Lincoln
LN1 3DY
Contact: Karen Boot, College Registry
Telephone: 01522 527347
Facsimile: 01522 530243

Bolton Institute of Higher Education
School of Education and Health Studies
Chadwick Street
Bolton
BL2 1JW
Telephone: 01204 28851
Facsimile: 01204 399074

Bradford and Ilkley Community College
Great Horton Road
Bradford
West Yorkshire
BD7 1AY
Contact: Information Desk
Telephone: 01274 753004
Facsimile: 01274 741060

Brunel University
The School of Education
Twickenham Campus
St Margaret's Road
Twickenham
Middlesex
TW1 1PT
Telephone: 0181-891 4618
Facsimile: 0181-744 2960

Canterbury Christ Church College
North Holmes Road
Canterbury
Kent
CT1 1QU
Contact: Mrs M A Alfrey, Head Teacher
  Education
Telephone: 01227 767700

Cardiff Institute of Higher Education
Cyncoed
Cardiff
CF2 6XT
Telephone: 01222 551111
Facsimile: 01222 506589

**Cheltenham & Gloucester College of Higher
  Education**
The Park
Cheltenham
Gloucestershire
GL50 2QF
Contact: Gill Thatcher, Schools Liaison Officer
Telephone: 01242 532825
Facsimile: 01242 256759

Chester College
Cheyney Road
Chester
CH1 4BJ
Contact: The Registry
Telephone: 01244 375444
Facsimile: 01244 373379

Coleg Normal
Bangor
Gwynedd
LL57 2PX
Telephone: 01248 370171
Facsimile: 01248 370461

De Mountfort University
37 Lansdowne Road
Bedford
MK40 2BZ
Telephone: 01234 351966
Facsimile: 01234 350833

INITIAL TEACHER TRAINING

Teachers

Initial teacher training establishments

Edge Hill College of Higher Education
St Helen's Road
Ormskirk
Lancashire
L39 4QP
Contact: Mr Terry Kershaw, Head of
Admissions
Telephone: 01695 575171
Facsimile: 01695 579997

Faculty of Education, Jordanhill Campus
University of Strathclyde
76 Southbrae Drive
Glasgow
G13 1PP
Contact: Registry Education
Telephone: 0141-950 3000
Facsimile: 0141-950 3268

Goldsmith's College, University of London
New Cross
London
SE14 6NW
Contact: The Registry
Telephone: 0171-919 7171
Facsimile: 0171-919 7517

Gwent College of Higher Education
P.O. Box 101
Newport
Gwent
NP6 1YH
Contact: Admissions Office
Telephone: 01633 430088
Facsimile: 01633 432006

Homerton College
Hills Road
Cambridge
CB2 2PH
Contact: The Registry
Telephone: 01223 411141

Hull University
School of Education
Cottingham Road
Hull
HU6 7RX
Contact: Mr I D Marriott, Secretary to Education
Telephone: 01482 465987
Facsimile: 01482 465406

King Alfred's College, Winchester
Sparkford Road
Winchester
Hampshire
SO22 4NR
Telephone: 01962 841515
Facsimile: 01962 842280

Lancaster University
Department of Teaching and Educational
Studies
Ambleside
Cumbria
LA22 9BB
Contact: Cliff Skelding, Head of Department
Telephone: 015394 30218
Facsimile: 015394 30305

Leeds Metropolitan University
Faculty of Cultural and Education Studies (TES)
Beckett Park
Leeds
LS6 3QS
Contact: P Clarke, Programme Administrative
Officer
Telephone: 0113 283 7410

Liverpool Institute of Higher Education
P.O. Box 6
Stand Park Road
Liverpool
L16 9KD
Contact: Dr John Hill, Deputy Registrar
(Admissions)
Telephone: 0151-737 3000
Facsimile: 0151-737 3100

Liverpool John Moores University
School of Education and Community Studies
I M Marsh Campus, Barkhill Road
Liverpool
L17 6BD
Telephone: 0151-231 5240
Facsimile: 0151-729 0136

Loughborough University of Technology
Department of Education
Loughborough
Leicestershire LE11 3TU
Telephone: 01509 222780
Facsimile: 01509 231948

Teachers

Initial teacher training establishments

LSU College of Higher Education
The Avenue
Southampton SO17 1BG
Contact: The Registry
Telephone: 01703 228761 mainline
Facsimile: 01703 230944

Manchester Metropolitan University
Didsbury School of Education
799 Wilmslow Road
Didsbury
Manchester M20 2RR
Telephone: 0161-247 2020
Facsimile: 0161-247 6392

Middlesex University
Trent Park
Bramley Road
Oakwood
London N14 4XS
Contact: School of Education
Telephone: 0181-362 5000
Facsimile: 0181-441 4672

Moray House Institute of Education
Heriot-Watt University
Cramond Campus, Cramond Road North
Edinburgh
EH4 6JD
Contact: Dr David Jenkins, Registrar
Telephone: 0131-312 6001
Facsimile: 0131-312 6355

Newman College
Genners Lane
Bartley Green
Birmingham
B32 3NT
Contact: Miss C M Wilkinson, Admissions
  Registrar
Telephone: 0121-476 1181
Facsimile: 0121-476 1196

North East Wales Institute, Wrexham
Mold Road
Wrexham
Clwyd
LL11 2AW
Contact: Keith Mitchell, Admissions Officer
Telephone: 01978 290666
Facsimile: 01978 290008

Northern College of Education
Aberdeen Campus
Hilton Place
Aberdeen
AB9 1FA
Telephone: 01224 283500
Facsimile: 01224 487046

Nottingham Trent University
Faculty of Education
Clifton Hall
Clifton
Nottingham
NG11 8NJ
Contact: Dean of Education
Telephone: 0115 9418418 ext 6711
Facsimile: 0115 948 6747

Open University
School of Education
Walton Hall
Milton Keynes
MK7 6AA
Telephone: 01908 653765
Facsimile: 01908 654111

Oxford Brookes University
School of Education
Wheatley
Oxford
OX33 1HX
Contact: The Administrator
Telephone: 01865 485930
Facsimile: 01865 485838

Roehampton Institute
Roehampton Lane
London
SW15 5PU
Telephone: 0181-392 3000

St Andrew's College
Duntocher Road
Bearsden
Glasgow
G61 4QA
Contact: Miss P Devine, Student Services
  Officer
Telephone: 0141-943 1424
Facsimile: 0141-943 0106

Teachers

Initial teacher training establishments

St Mary's University College
Strawberry Hill
Twickenham
Middlesex
TW1 4SX
Telephone: 0181-892 0051
Facsimile: 0181-744 2080

Sheffield Hallam University
School of Education, Southbourne
36 Collegiate Crescent
Sheffield
S10 2BP
Telephone: 0114 253 2306
Facsimile: 0114 253 2333

South Bank University
103 Borough Road
London
SE1 1AA
Telephone: 0171-928 8989
Facsimile: 0171-815 8155

Trinity and All Saints
Brownberrie Lane
Horsforth
Leeds
LS18 5HD
Contact: Mr D Baldasera, Schools Liaison
Telephone: 0113 283 7100
Facsimile: 0113 283 7200

University College of Ripon and York St John
York Campus
Lord Mayor's Walk
York
YO3 7EX
Contact: The Registrar
Telephone: 01904 656771
Facsimile: 01904 612512

University College of St Martin
Bowerham Road
Lancaster
LA1 3JD
Contact: General Office
Telephone: 01524 63446
Facsimile: 01524 68943

University College, Scarborough
Filey Road
Scarborough
North Yorkshire
YO11 3AZ
Contact: Dr E J Payne-Ahmadi, Head of
   External Relations Recruitment
Telephone: 01723 632392
Facsimile: 01723 370815

University of Bath
School of Education
Claverton Down
Bath
Avon
BA2 7AY
Contact: Mrs C Smith, PGCE Course Secretary
Telephone: 01225 826341
Facsimile: 01225 462508

University of Birmingham School of Education
Edgbaston
Birmingham
B15 2TT
Telephone: 0121-414 4860
Facsimile: 0121-414 4865

University of Brighton
Mithras House
Lewes Road
Brighton
Sussex
BN2 4AT
Contact: Academic Registrar
Telephone: 01273 600900
Facsimile: 01273 642825

University of Bristol School of Education
Helen Wodehouse Building
35 Berkeley Square
Bristol
Avon
BS8 1JA
Telephone: 0117 928 9000
Facsimile: 0117 929 9110

Teachers

Initial teacher training establishments

University of Central England in Birmingham
Faculty of Education
Westbourne Road
Edgbaston
Birmingham
B15 3TN
Telephone: 0121-331 6100
Facsimile: 0121-331 6147

University of Durham
School of Education
Leazes Road
Durham
DH1 1TA
Telephone: 0191-374 2000
Facsimile: 0191-374 3506

University of East Anglia, Norwich
School of Education and Professional
  Development
Norwich
NR4 7TJ
Telephone: 01603 56161
Facsimile: 01603 593446

University of Exeter School of Education
Heavitree Road
Exeter
Devon
EX1 2LU
Contact: Initial Professional Studies Office
Telephone: 01392 264837
Facsimile: 01392 264736

**University of Greenwich School of
  Education**
Avery Hill Campus
Bexley Road
Eltham
London
SE9 2PQ
Contact: Head of School
Telephone: 0181-331 8444
Facsimile: 0181-331 9504

University of Hertfordshire
P.O. Box 109
College Lane
Hatfield
Hertfordshire AL10 9AB
Contact: Geoff Ward, Higher Education Liaison
Telephone: 01707 284458
Facsimile: 01707 284738

University of Huddersfield
Hollybank Road
Lindley
Huddersfield HD3 3BP
Contact: Helen Shaw, Admissions Officer
Telephone: 01484 478232
Facsimile: 01484 514784

University of Leeds
School of Education
Hilary Place
Leeds
LS2 9JT
Contact: Rosemarie J Temple, Schools Liaison
  Officer
Telephone: 0113 233 4525
Facsimile: 0113 233 4541

University of Leicester
School of Education
21 University Road
Leicester
LE1 7RF
Telephone: 0116 252 3688
Facsimile: 0116 252 3653

University of London, Institute of Education
20 Bedford Way
London
WC1H 0AL
Contact: Mr David Warren
Telephone: 0171-612 6012
Facsimile: 0171-612 6089

**University of London, King's College
  London**
School of Education
Cornwall House
Waterloo Road
London
SE1 8WA
Telephone: 0171-836 5454

Teachers

Initial teacher training establishments

University of Manchester
School of Education
Manchester
M13 9PL
Contact: Mr G R Wedlock, Senior
 Administrative Assistant
Telephone: 0161-275 3682
Facsimile: 0161-275 3519

University of Newcastle upon Tyne
Department of Education
St Thomas Street
Newcastle upon Tyne
NE1 7RU
Telephone: 0191-222 6568
Facsimile: 0191-222 8170

University of Nottingham
School of Education
University Park
Nottingham
NG7 2RD
Contact: Mrs D E Herrod, PGCE Admissions
 Secretary
Telephone: 0115 951 4487
Facsimile: 0115 951 4516

University of Paisley
Craigie Campus in Ayr
Faculty of Education
Beech Grove
Ayr
KA8 0SR
Contact: Prof Gordon M Wilson
Telephone: 01292 260321
Facsimile: 01292 611705

University of Plymouth
Faculty of Arts and Education, Rolle School of
 Education
Douglas Avenue
Exmouth
EX8 2AT
Telephone: 01395 255324
Facsimile: 01395 255303

University of Reading, The
Faculty of Education and Community Studies
Bulmershe Court
Earley, Reading
Berkshire
RG6 1HY
Telephone: 01734 318810
Facsimile: 01734 352080

University of Southampton
School of Education
Southampton
SO9 5NH
Telephone: 01703 592413
Facsimile: 01703 592745

University of the West of England, Bristol
Coldharbour Lane
Frenchay
Bristol
BS16 1QY
Contact: Head of Admissions
Telephone: 0117 965 6261
Facsimile: 0117 976 3804

University of Wales Swansea
Department of Education
Hendrefoelan
Swansea
SA2 7NB
Contact: Alwena Morgan, Administrator
Telephone: 01792 281183
Facsimile: 01792 290219

INITIAL TEACHER TRAINING

267

Teachers

In-service training

**Centre for Educational Development,
   Appraisal and Research**
University of Warwick
Coventry
CV4 7AL
Contact: Mrs Su Powell
Telephone: 01203 523806
Facsimile: 01203 524472

**Centre for Research and Education on
   Gender**
Institute of Education
University of London
20 Bedford Way
London
WC1H 0AL
Telephone: 0171-612 6313
Facsimile: 0171-612 6330

College of Preceptors
Coppice Row
Theydon Bois
Epping
Essex
CM16 7DN
Contact: Tim Wheatley, Chief Executive Officer
   & Academic Registrar
Telephone: 01992 812727
Facsimile: 01992 814690

Teacher Placement Service
UBI, Sun Alliance House
New Inn Hall Street
Oxford
OX1 2QE
Contact: Mrs Jan Hussey, Senior Information
   Officer
Telephone: 01865 722585
Facsimile: 01865 790014

Teachers

Teacher representation and support

ACITT
Brondale Cottage
Spring Gardens
Narberth
SA67 7BN
Telephone: 0181-698 3713
The national association for teachers and co-ordinators of Information Technology.

All Saints Educational Trust
St Katharine Cree Church
86 Leadenhall Street
London
EC3A 3DH
Contact: Mr A W Bush, Secretary
Telephone: 0171-283 4485
The advancement of higher or further education by granting awards to enable beneficiaries to become qualified or better qualified as teachers.

Association for Language Learning
150 Railway Terrace
Rugby
Warwickshire
CV21 3HN
Contact: Christine Wilding, Secretary General
Telephone: 01788 546443
Facsimile: 01788 544149
Support for Language teachers and lecturers through journals, newsletters and INSET for specific languages.

Association for Science Education
College Lane
Hatfield
Hertfordshire
AL10 9AA
Telephone: 01707 267411
Facsimile: 01707 266532
Seeks to help teachers teach Science.

Association for Teaching Psychology
c/o The British Psychological Society
St Andrew's House, 48 Princess Road East
Leicester
LE1 7TR
Contact: Ms S Hirschler, Hon Secretary
Telephone: 0116 254 568

Supports teachers of Psychology at pre-degree level by producing and supplying resources suitable for teaching at this level and organising conferences to update and help teachers.

Association of Teachers and Lecturers
7 Northumberland Street
London
WC2N 5DA
Contact: Peter Smith, General Secretary
Telephone: 0171-930 6441
Facsimile: 0171-930 1359
Represents the interests of teachers.

Association of Tutors Incorporated
63 King Edward Road
Northampton
NN1 5LY
Contact: Dr D J Cornelius, Secretary
Telephone: 01604 24171
Facsimile: 01604 24718
Professional association for those involved in independent private tuition.

British Association for Counselling
1 Regent Place
Rugby
Warwickshire
CV21 2PJ
Contact: Isobel Palmer, Information & Publications Manager
Telephone: 01788 578328
Facsimile: 01788 562189
Professional association for counsellors.

British Association for the Study and Prevention of Child Abuse and Neglect
10 Priory Street
York
YO1 1EZ
Telephone: 01904 613605
Facsimile: 01904 642239
A multi-disciplinary association for professionals working in the field of child protection, providing a forum for the exchange of views, opinions, issues, research and experience.

TEACHER SUPPORT

269

Teachers

Teacher representation and support

British Association of Teachers of Dancing
23 Marywood Square
Glasgow
G41 2BP
Contact: Mrs Katrina Allan, General Secretary
Telephone: 0141-423 4029
Facsimile: 0141-423 0677
The professional dance teachers' association offering comprehensive syllabuses in 17 different branches of dance.

British Association of Teachers of the Deaf
41 The Orchard
Leven
Beverley
North Humberside
HU17 5QA
Contact: Mrs Ann Underwood, Hon Secretary
Telephone: 01964 544243
Facsimile: 01964 544243
Represents the interests of teachers of the deaf.

British Dietetic Association
7th Floor, Elizabeth House
22 Suffolk Street
Birmingham
B1 1LS
Telephone: 0121-643 5483
The professional association for qualified dietitians in the UK.

British Educational Research Association
c/o SCRE
15 St John Street
Edinburgh
EH8 8JR
Telephone: 0131-557 2944
Facsimile: 0131-556 9454
Supports its membership with conferences, a journal ('The British Educational Research Journal'), newsletters, workshops and groups formed to tackle current issues.

British Psychological Society
St Andrews House
48 Princess Road East
Leicester
LE1 7DR
Contact: Dr Colin V Newman, Executive Secretary
Telephone: 0116 254 9568
Facsimile: 0116 247 0787
A professional body for qualified psychologists, dedicated to promoting the advancement of a knowledge of psychology and the efficiency and usefulness of its members by setting a high standard of professional education and knowledge.

Christian Education Movement
Royal Buildings
Victoria Street
Derby
DE1 1GW
Telephone: 01332 296655
Facsimile: 01332 343253
Works throughout the UK to support the work of teachers of RE by publishing teacher materials, and offering a subscription service, INSET, and advisory services through its professional staff.

Church Schoolmasters' and Schoolmistresses' Benevolent Institution
Glen Arun
9 Athelstan Way
Horsham
Sussex
RH13 6HA
Telephone: 01403 253881
Helping retired teachers who are in severe difficulties and running a nursing home for 21 residential and 10 nursing care residents.

Design and Technology Association
16 Wellesbourne House
Walton Road
Wellesbourne
Warwickshire
CV23 9JB
Telephone: 01789 470007
Facsimile: 01789 841955
Represents everyone involved in Design & Technology education in the National Curriculum, seeks to promote and disseminate good practice, organises a wide range of events, and publishes journals and reports which are free to members.

Teachers

Teacher representation and support

Economics and Business Education Association
1a Keymer Road
Hassocks
Sussex BN6 8AD
Contact: Richard Young, Director of Education and Marketing
Telephone: 01273 846033
Facsimile: 01273 844646
Represents the interests of teachers and lecturers of Economics, Business Studies and related subjects in schools and colleges throughout the UK.

Headmasters' Conference
1 Russell House
Bepton Road
Midhurst
Sussex
GU29 9NB
Contact: Mr R N P Griffiths, Membership Secretary
Telephone: 01730 815635
Facsimile: 01730 815225
Seeks to promote the exchange of good ideas and practice, to participate in debate on national educational issues, and to look after the professional interests of members and their schools.

Incorporated Society of Musicians
10 Stratford Place
London
W1N 9AE
Contact: Neil Hoyle, Chief Executive
Telephone: 0171-629 4413
Facsimile: 0171-408 1538
Protects the interests of those who work with music.

Institute of Linguists
24a Highbury Grove
London
N5 2DQ
Telephone: 0171-359 7445
Facsimile: 0171-354 0202
Aims to serve all professional linguists by promoting the learning and use of Modern Languages, improve the status of professional linguists and establish and maintain high standards of work.

Institute of Swimming Teachers and Coaches
63 Forest Road
Loughborough
Leicestershire
LE11 3NW
Contact: B W Relf, Secretary
Telephone: 01509 264357/218827
Facsimile: 01509 219349
Provides support for swimming teachers with ASA and RLSS Teaching qualifications.

Library Association, The
7 Ridgemount Street
London
WC1E 7AE
Contact: Mary Knowles, Professional Adviser, Youth & Schools Libraries
Telephone: 0171-636 7543
Facsimile: 0171-436 7218
The professional body for those who work in libraries and information services, with a duty to promote high-quality library services. Some guidelines on school libraries have been produced by the Association.`

National Association for Environmental Education
University of Wolverhampton
Walsall Campus
Gorway, Walsall
WS1 3BD
Contact: Brian Milton, General Secretary
Telephone: 01922 31200
A teacher organisation promoting environmental education in schools. Produces the termly journal 'Environmental Education'.

National Association for Pastoral Care in Education
Department of Education
University of Warwick
Coventry
CV4 7AL
Telephone: 01203 523810
Facsimile: 01203 524110
Supports those professionals involved in pastoral care in education.

TEACHER SUPPORT

Teachers

Teacher representation and support

National Association for Special Educational Needs
York House
Exhall Grange, Wheelwright Lane
Coventry
CV7 9HP
Telephone: 01203 362414
Facsimile: 01203 362414
Promotes the development of children and young people with special educational needs and supports those who work with them by publishing two journals, a termly magazine and supporting practical publications.

National Association for the Teaching of English
50 Broadfield Road
Broadfield Business Centre
Sheffield
S8 0XJ
Contact: Anne Barnes, General Secretary
Telephone: 0114 255 4419
Facsimile: 0114 255 5296
Supports the teaching of English at all age levels by organising conferences, INSET, branch activities and by publishing books written by teachers for teachers.

National Association of Advisory Officers for Special Education
32a Pleasant Valley
Saffron Walden
Essex
CB11 4AP
Contact: Christopher Dyer, Hon Secretary
Telephone: 01799 521257
Facsimile: 01799 521257
The Association provides a means for those professionally concerned with the quality of education for pupils with special educational needs to keep in touch, receive support and feel that they have a representative voice through the Council.

National Association of Head Teachers
1 Heath Square
Boltro Road
Haywards Heath
Sussex
RH16 1BL
Contact: David M Hart, General Secretary

Telephone: 01444 458133
Facsimile: 01444 416326
Represents the interests of headteachers and deputy heads.

National Association of Hospital Play Staff
c/o Mrs M P Patterson
40 High Street
Landbeach, Cambridge
CB4 4DT
Supports those hospital staff responsible for play facilities in hospitals.

National Association of Schoolmasters/Union of Women Teachers
Hillscourt Education Centre
Rednal
Birmingham
B45 8RS
Contact: General Secretary
Telephone: 0121-453 6150
Facsimile: 0121-453 7224
Represents the interests of teachers.

National Association of Schoolmasters/Union of Women Teachers (Scotland)
34 West George Street
Glasgow
G2 1DA
Contact: Jim O'Neill, Regional Official
Telephone: 0141-332 2688
Facsimile: 0141-332 0608
Represents the interests of teachers.

National Association of Teachers of Home Economics and Technology
Hamilton House
Mabledon Place
London
WC1H 9BJ
Contact: Geoffrey Thompson, Association Secretary
Telephone: 0171-387 1441
Facsimile: 0171-383 7230
Supports all teachers of Food, Textiles Technology and Home Economics with specialist materials, publications and professional, legal and insurance services.

Teachers

Teacher representation and support

National Association of the Teachers of Wales
Prif Swyddfa, UCAC
Pen Roc, Rhodfa'r Mor
Aberystwyth
Dyfed
SY23 2AZ
Contact: G Wyn James, General Secretary
Telephone: 01970 615577
Facsimile: 01970 626765
Promotes the Welsh language and culture, protects and improves the working conditions of teachers, safeguards teachers' welfare, provides legal and professional advice and maintains funds to provide financial assistance.

National Primary Centre
Westminster College
Oxford
OX2 9AT
Contact: Information Officer
Telephone: 01865 245242
Facsimile: 01865 251847
Support for primary teachers through shared information and partnerships, and a network of centres throughout Britain. It publishes books based on teacher research in schools, has a newsletter and issues two regular journals.

National Society for Education in Art and Design
The Gatehouse
Corsham Court
Corsham
Wiltshire
SN13 0BZ
Telephone: 01249 714825
Facsimile: 01249 716138
A trade union and professional association for teachers and lecturers of Art and Design. It publishes the Journal of Art and Design Education and protects the interests of those engaged in Art and Design education in the UK.

Professional Association of Teachers
2 St James' Court
Friar Gate
Derby
DE1 1BT
Telephone: 01332 372337
Facsimile: 01332 290310
A body representing the interests of teachers.

Professional Association of Teachers in Wales
Cymdeithas Broffesiynol Athrawon
Bodnant
Borth
Dyfed
SY24 5NL
Contact: Richard Wynn Cowell, Secretary for Wales
Telephone: 01970 871401
Facsimile: 01970 871401
Represents the interests of teachers in Wales.

Professional Classes Aid Council
10 St Christopher's Place
London
W1M 6HY
Contact: The Secretary
Telephone: 0171-935 0641
A charity which can assist individuals of professional background. Help with school fees only considered in short term or at a crisis.

Professional Council for Religious Education
Royal Buildings
Victoria Street
Derby
DE1 1GW
Contact: Mr Lat Blaylock, Executive Officer
Telephone: 01332 296655
Facsimile: 01332 343253
Supports and represents classroom RE teachers by publishing periodicals, organising conferences and courses, offering consultancy services and giving RE a national voice.

Teachers

Teacher representation and support

School Library Association
Liden Library
Barrington Close
Liden, Swindon
Wiltshire
SN3 6HF
Contact: Valerie Fea, Executive Secretary
Telephone: 01793 617838
An independent organisation for everyone
interested in the development of school
libraries, primary and secondary. Provides an
information/advisory service and publishes
guidelines, booklists and a quarterly journal.
Also offers training courses.

Scottish Library Association
Motherwell Business Centre
Coursington Road
Motherwell
Lanarkshire
ML1 1PW
Contact: Robert Craig, Director
Telephone: 01698 252526
Facsimile: 01698 252057
Professional organisation for Scotland's 2500
librarians, which supports and promotes the
role of library and information specialists.

Scottish Secondary Teachers' Association
15 Dundas Street
Edinburgh
EH3 6QG
Contact: Alan M Lamont, General Secretary
Telephone: 0131-556 0605
Facsimile: 0131-556 1419
Represents the interests of Scottish secondary
teachers.

Secondary Heads Association, Northern
Ireland
Cambridge House Boys' Grammar School
Cambridge Avenue
Ballymena
Co Antrim
BT42 2EN
Contact: Mr W J Wallace, President
Telephone: 01266 43151
Facsimile: 01266 651239
Represents the interests of headteachers.

Society of Assistants Teaching in
Preparatory Schools Ltd
Cherry Trees
Stebbing
Great Dunmow
Essex
CM6 3ST
Contact: Mrs P Harrison, Administrator
Telephone: 01371 856369
Facsimile: 01371 856369
Professional support for staff in independent
schools.

Society of Schoolmasters
Dolton's Farm
Woburn
London
MK17 9HX
Contact: D J Skipper, Chairman
Will make a small grant to schoolmasters of
more than 10 years' standing or their
dependants when they are in need and all
normal sources of help have failed.

Society of Teachers of Speech and Drama
73 Berry Hill Road
Mansfield
Nottinghamshire
NG18 4RU
Contact: Mrs Ann Jones, Secretary
Telephone: 01623 27636
Facsimile: 01623 27636
Seeks to protect the professional interests of
qualified specialist teachers of Speech and
Drama, encourages good standards of
teaching and promotes the study and
knowledge of Speech and Dramatic Art in
every form by providing courses, publications
and advice.

Teachers

Teaching, learning and child behaviour

Anna Freud Centre for the Psychoanalytic Study and Treatment of Children
12-14 & 21 Maresfield Gardens
London
NW3 5SH
Telephone: 0171-794 2313
Facsimile: 0171-794 6506
Schools can refer children to the Centre for assessment or treatment. The Centre regularly runs workshops and study days which may be of interest to teachers.

British Association for Early Childhood Education, The
111 City View House
463 Bethnal Green Road
London
E2 9QY
Contact: Mrs Barbara Boon, Senior Administrative Officer
Telephone: 0171-739 7594
Facsimile: 0171-739 7594
BAECE promotes the right of children to education of the highest quality. It provides a network of support and advice for everyone concerned with the education and care of young children.

British Educational Research Association
c/o SCRE
15 St John Street
Edinburgh
EH8 8JR
Telephone: 0131-557 2944
Facsimile: 0131-556 9454
Supports its membership with conferences, a journal ('The British Educational Research Journal'), newsletters, workshops and groups formed to tackle current issues.

Centre for Community & Social Paediatric Research
University of Warwick
Coventry
CV4 7AL
Contact: Prof Nick Spencer
Telephone: 01203 523167
Facsimile: 01203 521145

Centre for the Study of Comprehensive Schools
Queen's Building, University of Leicester
Barrack Road
Northampton
NN2 6AF
Contact: Liza Griffiths, Information Officer
Telephone: 01604 24969/36326
Facsimile: 01604 29735
Main activities: promoting the values and good practice evident in comprehensive secondary education; encouraging effective partnership with a network of schools, LEAs, government, industry, FE and HE and TECs/EBPs; supporting the development needs of schools and teachers, and recognising education as a life-long activity for all.

Enuresis Resource and Information Centre
65 St Michael's Hill
Bristol
Avon BS2 8DZ
Contact: Lizzie Chambers, Information Officer
Telephone: 0117 926 4920
Facsimile: 0117 925 1640
Provides leaflets and posters which can be sent to schools.

Institute for the Study and Treatment of Delinquency
King's College London
Strand
London WC2R 2LS
Contact: Julia Braggins, Director
Telephone: 0171-873 2822
Facsimile: 0171-873 2823

Learning Through Action Centre
Cumberland Road
Reading RG1 3JY
Contact: Annette Cotterill, Director
Telephone: 01734 665556
Facsimile: 01734 665556
Offers: half-day and full-day interactive primary and secondary projects on behavioural themes and a wide range of curriculum subjects delivered by highly skilled, specialist teacher/advisers; INSET training on behaviour and bullying; photocopiable resource packs; and full-time certificate and diploma courses.

Teachers

Teaching, learning and child behaviour

National Association for Gifted Children
Park Campus
Boughton Green Road
Northampton
NN2 7AL
Telephone: 01604 792300
Facsimile: 01604 720636
*Assists teachers to identify gifted children,
giving them strategies on coping with them.
Also provides advice on whole-school
policies towards the gifted. INSET is available
from an Education Consultants team.*

National Children's Bureau
8 Wakley Street
London
EC1V 7QE
Telephone: 0171-843 6000
Facsimile: 0171-278 9512
*A membership organisation promoting the
interests of children and young people and
seeking to improve their status in a diverse
and multi-racial society. Enquiries (not
appropriate for students) should be
accompanied by a large SAE.*

National Play Information Centre
359-361 Euston Road
London
NW1 3AL
Telephone: 0171-383 5455
Facsimile: 0171-387 3152
*Acts as information resource on all aspects of
children's play, and provides booklists,
information sheets and details of commercial
suppliers. A number of publications may be
purchased direct from the Centre.*

Scottish Council for Research in Education
15 St John Street
Edinburgh
EH8 8JR
Contact: Information Services
Telephone: 0131-557 2944
Facsimile: 0131-556 9454
*Conducts research on various aspects of
education covering all sectors.*

276

Teachers

Physical and learning handicaps

AFASIC (Association for All Speech Impaired Children)
347 Central Markets
Smithfield
London
EC1A 9NH
Contact: Mrs Norma Corkish, Chief Executive
Telephone: 0171-236 3632/6487
Facsimile: 0171-236 8115
Represents children and young people with speech and language impairments. Provides information, advice and support for parents and professionals, and produces publications and information leaflets.

Anaphylaxis Campaign
8 Wey Close
Ash
Aldershot
Hampshire
GU12 6LY
Contact: David Reading, Chairman
Offers support and guidance to those at risk from potentially fatal food allergies, and their carers.

Association for Spina Bifida and Hydrocephalus
42 Park Road
Peterborough
Cambridgeshire
PE1 2UQ
Contact: Peter Walker, Education Adviser
Telephone: 01733 555988
Facsimile: 01733 555985
Offers advice and help for children at school and young people going on to FE. Helps to anticipate possible educational problems and is prepared to visit schools. Various publications are also available.

Association to Aid the Sexual and Personal Relationships of People with a Disability
286 Camden Road
London
N7 0BJ
Contact: Mr Morgan Williams, Director
Telephone: 0171-607 8851

Body Positive
51b Philbeach Gardens
London
SW5 1EB
Telephone: 0171-835 1045
Facsimile: 0171-373 5327
Self-help organisation providing support, advice and information to people affected by HIV and AIDS.

Boys' and Girls' Welfare Society
Central Offices
Schools Hill
Cheadle
Cheshire
SK8 1JE
Contact: David Seddon, Director of Educational Services
Telephone: 0161-428 5256
Facsimile: 0161-491 5056
Provides education in two special schools for young people with disabilities, learning difficulties and autistic behaviours.

Bridges
Greytree Lodge
Second Avenue
Ross-on-Wye
Herefordshire
HR9 7HT
Telephone: 01594 834120
Facsimile: 01989 563533
Committed to working in partnership with people with learning disabilities, their carers and professionals to promote and maintain valued lifestyles, rights and choices.

British Deaf Association
38 Victoria Place
Carlisle
Cumbria
CA1 1HV
Telephone: 01228 48844
Facsimile: 01228 41420
Seeks to further the cultural and educational advancement of deaf people by organising appropriate courses and visits both at home and abroad.

LEARNING CONSTRAINTS

Teachers

Physical and learning handicaps

British Epilepsy Association
Anstey House
40 Hanover Square
Leeds
LS3 1BE
Telephone: 0800 309030
Facsimile: 0113 242 8804
*Provides practical support, information and
advice to anyone with an interest in epilepsy,
and campaigns for the rights of people with
epilepsy.*

British Institute of Learning Difficulties
Wolverhampton Road
Kidderminster
Worcestershire
DY10 3PP
Telephone: 01562 850251
Facsimile: 01562 851970
*Seeks to improve the quality of life for people
with learning disabilities.*

British Migraine Association
178a High Road
Byfleet
Surrey
KT14 7ED
Telephone: 01932 352468
*Supports and promotes research into the cause
and treatment of migraine, and provides
encouragement and information to sufferers.*

Centre for Accessible Environments
Nutmeg House
60 Gainsford Street
London
SE1 2NY
Telephone: 0171-357 8182
Facsimile: 0171-357 8183
*The Centre is committed to the provision of built
environments which are accessible for all
people, including older and disabled people.
It is an information and training resource and
can answer queries by letter or phone.*

Centre for Left-Handed Studies
P.O. Box 52
South DO
Manchester
M20 8PJ
Contact: Miss Diane Paul, Principal

Telephone: 0161-445 0159
Facsimile: 0161-445 0159
*Assists those researching left-handedness,
organises lectures and workshops and
publishes books on the subject. Dextral
Books (same address) can supply books on
the subject and school equipment for left-
handers.*

Centre for Micro-Assisted Communication
Charlton Park School
Charlton Park Road
London
SE7 8HX
Contact: Myra Tingle, Director
Telephone: 0181-316 7589
Facsimile: 0181-317 3843
*Provides an advisory and assessment service
for students whose physical disability is
hindering their access to social or written
communication. Funding is normally via the
LEA or FE college.*

Child Growth Foundation
2 Mayfield Avenue
Chiswick
London
W4 1PW
Telephone: 0181-995 0257
Facsimile: 0181-995 9075
*Parent/patient support for children and adults
with growth disorders.*

College of Speech and Language Therapists
7 Bath Place
Rivington Street
London
EC2A 3DR
Contact: Mrs P Evans, Professional Director
Telephone: 0171-613 3855
Facsimile: 0171-613 3854
*Speech and language therapists offer
assessment, treatment, advice and
counselling to people of all ages with a
communication disorder and related eating
and swallowing problems.*

LEARNING CONSTRAINTS

Teachers

Physical and learning handicaps

Cystic Fibrosis Research Trust
5 Blyth Road
Bromley
Kent
BR1 3RS
Telephone: 0181-464 7211
Facsimile: 0181-313 0472
Seeks to raise funds to finance research and improve the care and treatment of people with CF, to establish groups for those affected and their families, and to educate and raise public awareness about CF.

David Lewis Centre
Mill Lane
Warford
Alderley Edge
Cheshire
SK9 7UD
Contact: Mrs Sally Harte, School Principal
Telephone: 01565 872613
Facsimile: 01565 872829
The Centre provides residential assessment, treatment and rehabilitation of people, including schoolchildren, suffering from epilepsy. It aims to maximise each student's potential by enabling them to achieve as much independence as possible and to enjoy a life which is both stimulating and rewarding.

Down's Syndrome Association
153-155 Mitcham Road
London
SW17 9PG
Telephone: 0181-682 4001
Facsimile: 0181-682 4012
Provides information and support for people with Down's Syndrome, their families and professionals who work with them.

Epilepsy Association of Scotland
National Headquarters
48 Govan Road
Glasgow
G51 1JL
Telephone: 0141-427 4911
Facsimile: 0141-427 7414
Provides information, support, advice and counselling for people with epilepsy, their families, carers and the professionals who work with these groups.

Gifted Children's Information Centre
Hampton Grange
21 Hampton Lane
Solihull
West Midlands
B91 2QJ
Telephone: 0121-705 4547
Supplies books, guides, teaching packs and equipment for gifted children, dyslexic children and left-handed children. Can arrange psychological assessments and offer legal advice and guidance for children with special educational needs.

HAPA
Fulham Palace
Bishop's Avenue
London
SW6 6EA
Contact: Mary Januarius, Information Officer
Telephone: 0171-731 1435
Facsimile: 0171-731 4426
A national charity whose purpose is to develop play opportunities for children with disabilities and special needs. Provides year-round play service for disabled children at five adventure playgrounds in London.

Hyperactive Children's Support Group
71 Whyke Lane
Chichester
Sussex
PO19 2LD
Contact: Mrs Sally Bunday, Director & National Coordinator
Telephone: 01903 725182
Advises and supports parents and professionals of hyperactive/ADHD/allergic children by suggesting dietary therapies and behaviour modification ideas, with information on other therapies that could prove beneficial.

LEARNING CONSTRAINTS

279

Teachers

Physical and learning handicaps

JOLT (The Journey of a Lifetime Trust)
High Brow
Harrow Park
Harrow-on-the-Hill
Middlesex
HA1 3JE
Contact: Dorothy Dalton, Chairman of Trustees
Telephone: 0181-869 1214
Facsimile: 0181-869 1214
JOLT exists to take physically, medically and
socially disadvantaged teenagers on
challenging month-long journeys of a lifetime.

Michael Palin Centre for Stammering
Children, The
Finsbury Health Centre
Pine Street
London
EC1R 0JH
Telephone: 0171-837 0031
Provides a consultation service for stammering
children aged 2-18 years. Children are
referred by their GP or local therapist.

MIND (National Association for Mental
Health)
Granta House
15-17 Broadway
London
E15 4BQ
Telephone: 0171-519 2122
Facsimile: 0181-522 1725
The leading mental health charity in England
and Wales, MIND works for a better life for
people diagnosed, labelled or treated as
mentally ill, and campaigns for their right to
lead an active and valued life in the
community.

National Association for Gifted Children
Park Campus
Boughton Green Road
Northampton
NN2 7AL
Telephone: 01604 792300
Facsimile: 01604 720636
Assists teachers to identify gifted children,
giving them strategies on coping with them.
Also provides advice on whole-school
policies towards the gifted. INSET is available
from an Education Consultants team.

National Association for Special Educational
Needs
York House
Exhall Grange
Wheelwright Lane
Coventry
CV7 9HP
Telephone: 01203 362414
Facsimile: 01203 362414
Promotes the development of children and
young people with special educational needs
and supports those who work with them by
publishing two journals, a termly magazine
and supporting practical publications.

National Asthma Campaign
Providence House
Providence Place
London
N1 0NT
Contact: Joanna Taylor
Telephone: 0171-226 2260
Facsimile: 0171-704 0740
Provides information and support for those with
asthma, their carers and health professionals.
Helpline 0345 010203 9am-9pm Mon-Fri.

National Deaf Children's Society
15 Dufferin Street
London
EC1Y 9PD
Telephone: 0171-250 0123
Facsimile: 0171-251 5020
An organisation of families, parents and
professionals providing support, information
and advice to families with deaf children. Also
produces publications.

National Eczema Society
163 Eversholt Street
London
NW1 1BU
Telephone: 0171-388 4097
Facsimile: 0171-388 5882
Provides practical advice and information about
eczema and its management. Publications
are available including a booklet about
eczema in schools.

LEARNING CONSTRAINTS

280

Teachers

Physical and learning handicaps

**National Federation of the Blind of the
 United Kingdom**
Unity House
Smyth Street, Westgate
Wakefield
West Yorkshire
WF1 1ER
Telephone: 01924 291313
Facsimile: 01924 200244
*Through its membership of blind and partially
 sighted people, the Federation seeks to
 convey to the authorities the real needs of the
 blind and partially sighted.*

National Left-Handers Association
57 Brewer Street
London
W1R 3FB
Telephone: 0181-770 3722
Facsimile: 0181-715 1220
*Provides guidance, support and equipment for
 left-handers. The Left-Handers Club can
 support schools with a Group Membership
 which includes newsletters, workshops and
 product discounts. A Teachers' Guide is also
 available.*

National Library for the Blind
Cromwell Road
Bredbury
Stockport
SK6 2SG
Telephone: 0161-494 0217
Facsimile: 0161-406 6728
*A registered charity providing literature in
 embossed and large types for the blind and
 partially sighted.*

National Society for Epilepsy
Chalfont Centre for Epilepsy
Chalfont St Peter
Gerrards Cross
Buckinghamshire
SL9 0RJ
Contact: Information and Education Department
Telephone: 01494 873991
Facsimile: 01494 871927
*Provides information resources and a helpline,
 and runs conferences about the condition.*

Partially-Sighted Society
P.O. Box 322
Doncaster
DN1 2XA
Telephone: 01302 323132
*Helps the visually impaired make the best use
 of their remaining sight.*

**PHAB (Physically Disabled and Able-
 Bodied)**
12-14 London Road
Croydon
Surrey
CR0 2TA
Contact: Peter Gooch, Chief Executive
Telephone: 0181-667 9443
Facsimile: 0181-681 1399
*Exists to integrate people with and without
 physical disabilities.*

Raised Dot Computing
408 S Baldwin Street
Madison
WI 53703
USA
Telephone: 001 608 257 9595
Facsimile: 001 608 257 4143
*Braille production hardware and software,
 suitable for use by any age.*

Rathbone C.I.
Head Office, 1st Floor, The Excalibur Building
77 Whitworth Street
Manchester
M1 6QZ
Contact: Information Officers
Telephone: 0161-236 5358
Facsimile: 0161-236 4539
*Aims to ensure that those people in the UK who
 have special education and training needs
 realise their full potential and participate fully
 in the social and economic life of the
 community. Rathbone C.I. runs employment
 and training schemes, residential schemes
 for young adults, and a national information
 line which deals with enquiries related to
 learning difficulties.*

Teachers

Physical and learning handicaps

Reach Resource Centre
National Library for the Handicapped Child
Wellington House
Wellington Road
Wokingham
Berkshire
RG11 2AG
Contact: Desmond L Spiers, Librarian &
    Information Officer
Telephone: 01734 891101
Facsimile: 01734 790989
Provides a resource and information centre for
    those working with children whose disability,
    illness or learning problem affects their
    reading, language or communication. The
    collection, which includes books, tapes,
    videos, software and microelectronic
    equipment, is for reference only.

Research Trust for Metabolic Diseases in
    Children
Golden Gates Lodge
Weston Road
Crewe
Cheshire
CW1 1XN
Contact: Mrs Lesley Greene, Director of
    Support Services
Telephone: 01270 250221
Facsimile: 01270 250244
Seeks to support families of children suffering
    from metabolic diseases by making grants for
    medical treatment and care, and by putting
    parents into contact with each other for their
    mutual support.

Royal Association for Disability and
    Rehabilitation, The
12 City Forum
250 City Road
London
EC1V 8AF
Telephone: 0171-250 3222
Facsimile: 0171-250 0212
Works with and for disabled people.

Royal London Society for the Blind
    (Incorporated)
Dorton House School
Seal
Sevenoaks
Kent
TN15 0ED
Contact: Mrs Pauline Davies, Head of
    Information Support Services
Telephone: 01732 761477
Facsimile: 01732 763363
Seeks to promote excellence in education for
    blind and partially sighted children aged 3-16
    years, improving independence and
    confidence within a challenging curriculum.

Royal National Institute for the Blind (RNIB)
224 Great Portland Street
London W1N 6AA
Contact: RNIB Education Information Service
Telephone: 0171-388 1266
Facsimile: 0171-383 4921
Aims to enable children and young people to
    achieve all they are capable of, whether in
    the classroom, in sports, in creative pursuits
    or in everyday life. Support is also provided
    for families with a visually impaired child.

Scoliosis Association (UK), The
2 Ivebury Court
323-327 Latimer Road
London
W10 6RA
Telephone: 0181-964 5343
Facsimile: 0181-964 5343
SAUK supports people with scoliosis (sideways
    curving and twisting of the spine) and seeks
    to spread knowledge about scoliosis, alerting
    the public and those in contact with children
    and young people to the need for early
    detection.

Scope
12 Park Crescent
London W1N 4EQ
A charity in England and Wales only offering
    assistance for the welfare and treatment and
    education of people with cerebral palsy
    (spasticity) and support to parents and
    carers. Anyone requiring information should
    write to their regional office, as follows:

Teachers
Physical and learning handicaps

Scope (East Region)
The Anderson Centre
Ermine Business Park, Spitfire Close
Huntingdon
Cambridgeshire
PE18 6YB
*Enquiries must be accompanied by an A4
stamped addressed envelope. Areas covered
by this office: Bedfordshire,
Buckinghamshire, Cambridgeshire, Essex,
Lincolnshire, Norfolk, Northamptonshire and
Suffolk.*

Scope (London & South-East Region)
Shackleton Square
Priestly Way
Crawley
Sussex
RH10 2GZ
*Enquiries must be accompanied by an A4
stamped addressed envelope. Areas covered
by this office: Berkshire, Greater London,
Hampshire, Isle of Wight, Kent, Surrey and
Sussex.*

Scope (Midlands Region)
Shapland House
Clews Road
Oakenshaw, Redditch
Worcestershire
B98 7ST
*Enquiries must be accompanied by an A4
stamped addressed envelope. Areas covered
by this office: Derbyshire, Hereford &
Worcester, Leicestershire, Nottinghamshire,
Oxfordshire, Shropshire, Staffordshire,
Warwickshire and West Midlands.*

Scope (North Region)
8 Brindley Way
41 Business Park North
Wakefield
WF2 0XJ
*Enquiries must be accompanied by an A4
stamped addressed envelope. Areas covered
by this office: Cheshire, Cleveland, Cumbria,
Co Durham, Greater Manchester,
Lancashire, the Isle of Man, Merseyside,
Northumberland, Tyne & Wear and
Yorkshire.*

Scope (Wales Region)
3 Links Court
Links Business Park
St Mellons, Cardiff
CF3 0SP
*Enquiries must be accompanied by an A4
stamped addressed envelope. Areas covered
by this office: Clwyd, Dyfed, Glamorgan,
Gwent, Gwynedd, Powys.*

Scope (West Region)
Pamwell House
160 Pennywell Road
Easton, Bristol
BS5 0TX
*Enquiries must be accompanied by an A4
stamped addressed envelope. Areas covered
by this office: Avon, Cornwall, Devon, Dorset,
Gloucestershire, Somerset, Wiltshire.*

Scottish Association for the Deaf
Moray House Institute of Education
Holyrood Road
Edinburgh
EH8 8AQ
Telephone: 0131-557 0591
Facsimile: 0131-557 6922
*Acts as a clearing house for information relating
to deaf people and the hearing impaired, and
educates hearing people concerning
deafness and its implications.*

Scottish Council for Spastics
Etas Centre
11 Ellersly Road
Edinburgh
EH12 6HY
Contact: Sheila Williams, Senior Advice Worker
Telephone: 0131-313 5510
Facsimile: 0131-346 7864
*Exists to enable the needs of people with
cerebral palsy (and those with a disability
resulting in similar needs) to be met, by
providing accommodation, advice, education,
employment, social services and therapy.*

LEARNING CONSTRAINTS

Teachers

Physical and learning handicaps

Scottish Sensory Centre
Moray House Institute of Education
Holyrood Road
Edinburgh
EH8 8AQ
Telephone: 0131-558 6501
Facsimile: 0131-558 6502
Seeks to promote and disseminate effective
practices and innovation in the education of
children and young people with a range of
sensory impairments. Services available:
courses, conferences, research, outreach
service, advice and resource library.

Scottish Society for Autistic Children
Hilton House
Alloa Business Park, Whins Road
Alloa
FK10 3SA
Telephone: 01259 720044
Facsimile: 01259 720051
Provides care, support and education for people
with autism in Scotland.

Shaftesbury Society, The
16 Kingston Road
London
SW19 1JZ
Contact: Allan Giles, Education Officer
(Schools)
Telephone: 0181-542 5550
Facsimile: 0181-545 0605
A registered charity which exists to enable
people in great need to achieve security, self-
worth and significance, and through this to
show Christian care in action.

Society for Mucopolysaccharide Diseases
55 Hill Avenue
Amersham
Buckinghamshire
HP6 5BX
Contact: Christine Lavery, Director
Telephone: 01494 434156
Facsimile: 01494 434252
Supports families of children with
mucopolysaccharide diseases through the
publication of specific disease booklets,
annual conferences, specialist clinics and
holidays.

Society for the Autistically Handicapped
199 Blandford Avenue
Kettering
Northamptonshire
NN16 9AT
Contact: Keith Lovett, Director
Telephone: 01536 523274
Facsimile: 01536 523274
Seeks to improve services in care and
education for those with autism thus helping
to achieve a better quality of life for them and
their carers, by organising and running
regular training seminars and hands-on
workshops for the professionals who work
with them.

STEPS
15 Statham Close
Lymn
Cheshire
WA13 9NN
Telephone: 01925 757525
A charity which gives support, contact, help,
advice and information to children with lower
limb abnormalities (club foot, congenital
dislocated hip, lower limb deficiency) through
a national helpline, publications and local
contact.

Turner Syndrome Society
2 Mayfield Avenue
London
W4 1PW
Telephone: 0181-995 0257
Facsimile: 0181-995 9075
Comes under the umbrella of the Child Growth
Foundation, which provides support for
parents and funds research for running
educational programmes.

UK Rett Syndrome Association
29 Carlton Road
London
N11 3EX
Contact: Christine Freeman, Administrator
Telephone: 0181-361 5161
Facsimile: 0181-361 5161
Offers practical help, friendship and support to
Rett Syndrome sufferers, their families and
carers.

PARENTS

Parents

Care of children

Action for Sick Children
Argyle House
29-31 Euston Road
London
NW1 2SD
Contact: Mrs Penny King, Library
Telephone: 0171-833 2041
Facsimile: 0171-837 2110
A charity which aims to improve health services for sick children and to increase public understanding of their particular needs, with advice for parents and publications for parents and professionals.

Association for the Prevention of Addiction
67-69 Cowcross Street
London
EC1V 6BP
Telephone: 0171-251 5860
Facsimile: 0171-251 5890
Seeks to reduce the harm caused by drugs and alcohol. Provides community-based services for drug users and their families.

National Association for Maternal and Child Welfare Ltd
First Floor
40-42 Osnaburgh Street
London
NW1 3ND
Telephone: 0171-383 4117
Facsimile: 0171-383 4541
Seeks to contribute towards the education of young people for responsible parenthood and family life by providing relevant and up-to-date courses on child care and child development.

National Association of Toy and Leisure Libraries/Play Matters
68 Churchway
London
NW1 1LT
Telephone: 0171-387 9592
Facsimile: 0171-383 2714
Supports parents and children by the provision of practical resources and effective models of adult-child interaction. All enquiries from teachers or students relating to their studies must be accompanied by a £5 donation.

National Child Care Campaign/Day Care Trust
4 Wild Court
London
WC2B 4AU
Contact: Carol Sherriff, Director
Telephone: 0171-405 5617
Facsimile: 0171-831 6632
Promotes high-quality, affordable, accessible child care facilities based on equal opportunities principles. Day Care Trust provides information and advice to parents, employers and all those interested in child care provision.

National Childminding Association
8 Masons Hill
Bromley
Kent
BR2 9EY
Contact: Communications Officer
Telephone: 0181-464 6164
Facsimile: 0181-290 6834
Only enquiries made by teaching staff (or parents) are responded to.

National Portage Association
127 Monks Dale
Yeovil
Somerset
BA21 3JE
Telephone: 01935 71641
Facsimile: 01935 71641
Portage is a home teaching scheme for pre-school children with special needs.

One Parent Families Scotland
13 Gayfield Square
Edinburgh
EH1 3NX
Contact: Ian Maxwell, Information Officer
Telephone: 0131-556 3899/4563
Facsimile: 0131-557 9650
Enables lone parents to achieve their full potential as individuals and parents by promoting public recognition of achievements and needs, and by providing information, encouragement and support.

Parents

Care of children

Scottish Pre-School Play Association
14 Elliot Place
Glasgow
G3 8EP
Telephone: 0141-221 4148
Facsimile: 0141-221 6043
*An education charity committed to the
development of quality care and education in
pre-school groups which respect the rights,
responsibilities and needs of all children and
their parents.*

Parents

Education and school

Advisory Centre for Education
1b Aberdeen Studios
22-24 Highbury Grove
London
N5 2EA
Telephone: 0171-354 8321 (advice line)
Facsimile: 0171-354 9069
ACE works for an open and accountable state education service that supports all children. It provides information, advice and support to parents and others by letter and phone.

Boys' and Girls' Welfare Society
Central Offices
Schools Hill
Cheadle
Cheshire
SK8 1JE
Contact: David Seddon, Director of Educational Services
Telephone: 0161-428 5256
Facsimile: 0161-491 5056
Provides education in two special schools for young people with disabilities, learning difficulties and autistic behaviours.

British Association for Early Childhood Education, The
111 City View House
463 Bethnal Green Road
London
E2 9QY
Contact: Mrs Barbara Boon, Senior Administrative Officer
Telephone: 0171-739 7594
Facsimile: 0171-739 7594
BAECE promotes the right of children to education of the highest quality. It provides a network of support and advice for everyone concerned with the education and care of young children.

Church Schools Company Ltd
Church Schools House
Titchmarsh
Kettering
Northamptonshire
NN14 3DA
Telephone: 01832 735105
Facsimile: 01832 734760
Founded as an educational charity in 1882 with the principal objective of creating schools that would offer pupils a good academic education based on Christian principles, with particular reference to the Church of England.

Gabbitas Educational Consultants
Broughton House
6-8 Sackville Street
Piccadilly
London
W1X 2BR
Telephone: 0171-734 0161
Facsimile: 0171-437 1764
Offers parents and students individual, independent guidance on education at all levels, from age 5 upwards. For schools in the UK and overseas a full range of staff recruitment and consultancy services are available.

Home and School Council
40 Sunningdale Mount
Sheffield
S11 9HA
Contact: Mrs B Bullivant, Hon Secretary
Telephone: 0114 236 4181
Facsimile: 0114 236 4181
The Council exists to publish reasonably priced booklets for parents, governors and teachers on aspects of home-school contact, and how parents can help their children. It also links the main parents' and teachers' associations.

Independent Schools Information Service
56 Buckingham Gate
London
SW1E 6AG
Telephone: 0171-630 8793
Facsimile: 0171-630 5103
Answers parents' questions about independent schools and helps them with educational problems, and ensures that the general public have an accurate image of independent schools.

Parents

Handicaps

AFASIC (Association for All Speech Impaired Children)
347 Central Markets
Smithfield
London
EC1A 9NH
Contact: Mrs Norma Corkish, Chief Executive
Telephone: 0171-236 3632/6487
Facsimile: 0171-236 8115
Represents children and young people with speech and language impairments. Provides information, advice and support for parents and professionals, and produces publications and information leaflets.

Anaphylaxis Campaign
8 Wey Close
Ash
Aldershot
Hampshire
GU12 6LY
Contact: David Reading
Offers support and guidance to those at risk from potentially fatal food allergies, and their carers.

Association for Children with Heart Disorders
Killieard House
Killiecrankie
Pitlochry
Perthshire
PH16 5LN
Contact: Sandra Parkins, Scottish Secretary
Telephone: 01796 473204
Provides support and understanding in everyday care and welfare to parents and families of children with heart disorders.

Association of Children with Hand or Arm Deficiency
12 Wilson Way
Earls Barton
Northamptonshire
NN6 0NZ
Contact: Mrs Sue Stokes, National Coordinator
Telephone: 01604 811041
Facsimile: 01604 811041
Provides contact and support for families with children having any form of hand or arm deficiency.

Bridges
Greytree Lodge
Second Avenue
Ross-on-Wye
Herefordshire
HR9 7HT
Telephone: 01594 834120
Facsimile: 01989 563533
Committed to working in partnership with people with learning disabilities, their carers and professionals to promote and maintain valued lifestyles, rights and choices.

British Deaf Association
38 Victoria Place
Carlisle
Cumbria
CA1 1HV
Telephone: 01228 48844
Facsimile: 01228 41420
Seeks to further the cultural and educational advancement of deaf people by organising appropriate courses and visits both at home and abroad.

British Epilepsy Association
Anstey House
40 Hanover Square
Leeds
LS3 1BE
Telephone: 0800 309030
Facsimile: 0113 242 8804
Provides practical support, information and advice to anyone with an interest in epilepsy, and campaigns for the rights of people with epilepsy.

British Institute for Brain Injured Children
Knowle Hall
Bridgwater
Somerset
TA7 8PJ
Contact: The Administrator
Telephone: 01278 684060
Facsimile: 01278 685573
BIBIC provides a positive answer for parents who want to give their child every opportunity to develop his full potential. Parents are shown how to provide their own treatment at home, with additional support as necessary.

Parents

Handicaps

British Migraine Association
178a High Road
Byfleet
Surrey
KT14 7ED
Telephone: 01932 352468
Supports and promotes research into the cause and treatment of migraine, and provides encouragement and information to sufferers.

Centre for Accessible Environments
Nutmeg House
60 Gainsford Street
London
SE1 2NY
Telephone: 0171-357 8182
Facsimile: 0171-357 8183
The Centre is committed to the provision of built environments which are accessible for all people, including older and disabled people. It is an information and training resource and can answer queries by letter or phone.

Cheyne Centre for Children with Cerebral Palsy
61 Cheyne Walk
London
SW3 5LX
Telephone: 0181-846 6488
Provides an assessment, education, treatment and resource service for children with cerebral palsy aged 18 months to 8 years. Also provides outpatient treatment for children aged 0-19 years.

Child Growth Foundation
2 Mayfield Avenue
Chiswick
London
W4 1PW
Telephone: 0181-995 0257
Facsimile: 0181-995 9075
Parent/patient support for children and adults with growth disorders.

Cystic Fibrosis Research Trust
5 Blyth Road
Bromley
Kent BR1 3RS
Telephone: 0181-464 7211
Facsimile: 0181-313 0472
Seeks to raise funds to finance research and improve the care and treatment of people with CF, to establish groups for those affected and their families, and to educate and raise public awareness about CF.

Down's Syndrome Association
153-155 Mitcham Road
London
SW17 9PG
Telephone: 0181-682 4001
Facsimile: 0181-682 4012
Provides information and support for people with Down's Syndrome, their families and professionals who work with them.

Enuresis Resource and Information Centre
65 St Michael's Hill
Bristol
Avon
BS2 8DZ
Contact: Lizzie Chambers, Information Officer
Telephone: 0117 926 4920
Facsimile: 0117 925 1640
Provides leaflets and posters which can be sent to schools.

Epilepsy Association of Scotland
National Headquarters
48 Govan Road
Glasgow
G51 1JL
Telephone: 0141-427 4911
Facsimile: 0141-427 7414
Provides information, support, advice and counselling for people with epilepsy, their families, carers and the professionals who work with these groups.

HAPA
Fulham Palace
Bishop's Avenue
London SW6 6EA
Contact: Mary Januarius, Information Officer
Telephone: 0171-731 1435
Facsimile: 0171-731 4426
A national charity whose purpose is to develop play opportunities for children with disabilities and special needs. Provides year-round play service for disabled children at five adventure playgrounds in London.

Parents

Handicaps

Hyperactive Children's Support Group
71 Whyke Lane
Chichester
Sussex
PO19 2LD
Contact: Mrs Sally Bunday, Director & National
  Coordinator
Telephone: 01903 725182
*Advises and supports parents and professionals
  of hyperactive/ADHD/allergic children by
  suggesting dietary therapies and behaviour
  modification ideas, with information on other
  therapies that could prove beneficial.*

I CAN
Barbican City Gate
1-3 Dufferin Street
London
EC1Y 8NA
Contact: Information Coordinator
Telephone: 0171-374 4422
Facsimile: 0171-374 2762
*I CAN is a children's charity specialising in the
  education of children with speech and
  language disorders and asthma and eczema.*

IN TOUCH Trust
10 Norman Road
Sale
Cheshire
M33 3DF
Contact: Ann Worthington
Telephone: 0161-905 2440
*Supports parents of children with special needs,
  specialising in assisting those caring for
  children affected by rare and complex
  conditions.*

JOLT (The Journey of a Lifetime Trust)
High Brow
Harrow Park
Harrow-on-the-Hill
Middlesex
HA1 3JE
Contact: Dorothy Dalton, Chairman of Trustees
Telephone: 0181-869 1214
Facsimile: 0181-869 1214
*JOLT exists to take physically, medically and
  socially disadvantaged teenagers on
  challenging month-long journeys of a lifetime.*

LOOK
Queen Alexander College
49 Court Oak Road
Birmingham
B17 9TG
Contact: Louise Williams, Office Manager
Telephone: 0121-428 5038
Facsimile: 0121-428 5048
*A national organisation providing practical help,
  support and advice to families with children
  who are visually impaired.*

**Michael Palin Centre for Stammering
  Children, The**
Finsbury Health Centre
Pine Street
London
EC1R 0JH
Telephone: 0171-837 0031
*Provides a consultation service for stammering
  children aged 2-18 years. Children are
  referred by their GP or local therapist.*

**MIND (National Association for Mental
  Health)**
Granta House
15-17 Broadway
London
E15 4BQ
Telephone: 0171-519 2122
Facsimile: 0181-522 1725
*The leading mental health charity in England
  and Wales, MIND works for a better life for
  people diagnosed, labelled or treated as
  mentally ill, and campaigns for their right to
  lead an active and valued life in the
  community.*

National Asthma Campaign
Providence House
Providence Place
London
N1 0NT
Contact: Joanna Taylor
Telephone: 0171-226 2260
Facsimile: 0171-704 0740
*Provides information and support for those with
  asthma, their carers and health professionals.
  Helpline 0345 010203 9am-9pm Mon-Fri.*

HANDICAPS

Parents

Handicaps

National Autistic Society
276 Willesden Lane
London
NW2 5RB
Telephone: 0181-451 1114
Facsimile: 0181-451 5865
*Seeks to offer families and carers information,
advice and support, and develops a range of
educational and support services for people
with autism.*

National Deaf Children's Society
15 Dufferin Street
London
EC1Y 9PD
Telephone: 0171-250 0123
Facsimile: 0171-251 5020
*An organisation of families, parents and
professionals providing support, information
and advice to families with deaf children. Also
produces publications.*

National Eczema Society
163 Eversholt Street
London
NW1 1BU
Telephone: 0171-388 4097
Facsimile: 0171-388 5882
*Provides practical advice and information about
eczema and its management. Publications
are available including a booklet about
eczema in schools.*

National Library for the Blind
Cromwell Road
Bredbury
Stockport
SK6 2SG
Telephone: 0161-494 0217
Facsimile: 0161-406 6728
*A registered charity providing literature in
embossed and large types for the blind and
partially sighted.*

National Society for Epilepsy
Chalfont Centre for Epilepsy
Chalfont St Peter
Gerrards Cross
Buckinghamshire
SL9 0RJ
Contact: Information and Education Department
Telephone: 01494 873991
Facsimile: 01494 871927
*Provides information resources and a helpline,
and runs conferences about the condition.*

Partially-Sighted Society
P.O. Box 322
Doncaster
DN1 2XA
Telephone: 01302 323132
*Helps the visually impaired make the best use
of their remaining sight.*

**PHAB (Physically Disabled and Able-
Bodied)**
12-14 London Road
Croydon
Surrey
CR0 2TA
Contact: Peter Gooch, Chief Executive
Telephone: 0181-667 9443
Facsimile: 0181-681 1399
*Exists to integrate people with and without
physical disabilities.*

Rathbone C.I.
1st Floor, The Excalibur Building
77 Whitworth Street
Manchester
M1 6QZ
Telephone: 0161-236 5358
Facsimile: 0161-236 4539
*The Society, a registered charity, exists to help
people with learning difficulties achieve their
full potential and participate fully in the
community. It offers practical help and
support to parents and professionals who
care for them.*

HANDICAPS

Parents

Handicaps

Research Trust for Metabolic Diseases in Children
Golden Gates Lodge
Weston Road
Crewe
Cheshire
CW1 1XN
Contact: Mrs Lesley Greene, Director of Support Services
Telephone: 01270 250221
Facsimile: 01270 250244
Seeks to support families of children suffering from metabolic diseases by making grants for medical treatment and care, and by putting parents into contact with each other for their mutual support.

Restricted Growth Association
P.O. Box 18
Rugeley
Staffordshire
WS15 2GH
Telephone: 01889 576571
Aims to help reduce the distress and disadvantages of persons of restricted growth by providing support for them and their families.

Royal London Society for the Blind (Incorporated)
Dorton House School
Seal
Sevenoaks
Kent
TN15 0ED
Contact: Mrs Pauline Davies, Head of Information Support Services
Telephone: 01732 761477
Facsimile: 01732 763363
Seeks to promote excellence in education for blind and partially sighted children aged 3-16 years, improving independence and confidence within a challenging curriculum.

Royal National Institute for the Blind (RNIB)
224 Great Portland Street
London
W1N 6AA
Contact: RNIB Education Information Service
Telephone: 0171-388 1266
Facsimile: 0171-383 4921
Aims to enable children and young people to achieve all they are capable of, whether in the classroom, in sports, in creative pursuits or in everyday life. Support is also provided for families with a visually impaired child.

Royal Society for Mentally Handicapped Children & Adults
MENCAP National Centre
123 Golden Lane
London
EC1Y 0RT
Telephone: 0171-454 0454
Facsimile: 0171-608 3245
Provides support and help for parents and carers of people with learning disabilities by providing residential services, training and employment services and leisure facilities.

Scoliosis Association (UK), The
2 Ivebury Court
323-327 Latimer Road
London
W10 6RA
Telephone: 0181-964 5343
Facsimile: 0181-964 5343
SAUK supports people with scoliosis (sideways curving and twisting of the spine) and seeks to spread knowledge about scoliosis, alerting the public and those in contact with children and young people to the need for early detection.

Scope
12 Park Crescent
London
W1N 4EQ
A charity in England and Wales only offering assistance for the welfare and treatment and education of people with cerebral palsy (spasticity) and support to parents and carers. Anyone requiring information should write to their regional office, as follows:

Parents

Handicaps

Scope (East Region)
The Anderson Centre
Ermine Business Park, Spitfire Close
Huntingdon
Cambridgeshire
PE18 6YB
*Enquiries must be accompanied by an A4
stamped addressed envelope. Areas covered
by this office: Bedfordshire,
Buckinghamshire, Cambridgeshire, Essex,
Lincolnshire, Norfolk, Northamptonshire and
Suffolk.*

Scope (London & South-East Region)
Shackleton square
Priestly Way
Crawley
Sussex
RH10 2GZ
*Enquiries must be accompanied by an A4
stamped addressed envelope. Areas covered
by this office: Berkshire, Greater London,
Hampshire, Isle of Wight, Kent, Surrey and
Sussex.*

Scope (Midlands Region)
Shapland House
Clews Road
Oakenshaw, Redditch
Worcestershire
B98 7ST
*Enquiries must be accompanied by an A4
stamped addressed envelope. Areas covered
by this office: Derbyshire, Hereford &
Worcester, Leicestershire, Nottinghamshire,
Oxfordshire, Shropshire, Staffordshire,
Warwickshire and West Midlands.*

Scope (North Region)
8 Brindley Way
41 Business Park North
Wakefield
WF2 0XJ
*Enquiries must be accompanied by an A4
stamped addressed envelope. Areas covered
by this office: Cheshire, Cleveland, Cumbria,
Co Durham, Greater Manchester,
Lancashire, the Isle of Man, Merseyside,
Northumberland, Tyne & Wear and
Yorkshire.*

Scope (Wales Region)
3 Links Court
Links Business Park
St Mellons, Cardiff
CF3 0SP
*Enquiries must be accompanied by an A4
stamped addressed envelope. Areas covered
by this office: Clwyd, Dyfed, Glamorgan,
Gwent, Gwynedd, Powys.*

Scope (West Region)
Pamwell House
160 Pennywell Road
Easton, Bristol
BS5 0TX
*Enquiries must be accompanied by an A4
stamped addressed envelope. Areas covered
by this office: Avon, Cornwall, Devon, Dorset,
Gloucestershire, Somerset, Wiltshire.*

Scottish Association for the Deaf
Moray House Institute of Education
Holyrood Road
Edinburgh
EH8 8AQ
Telephone: 0131-557 0591
Facsimile: 0131-557 6922
*Acts as a clearing house for information relating
to deaf people and the hearing impaired, and
educates hearing people concerning
deafness and its implications.*

Scottish Council for Spastics
Etas Centre
11 Ellersly Road
Edinburgh
EH12 6HY
Contact: Sheila Williams, Senior Advice Worker
Telephone: 0131-313 5510
Facsimile: 0131-346 7864
*Exists to enable the needs of people with
cerebral palsy (and those with a disability
resulting in similar needs) to be met, by
providing accommodation, advice, education,
employment, social services and therapy.*

Scottish Society for Autistic Children
Hilton House
Alloa Business Park, Whins Road
Alloa FK10 3SA
Telephone: 01259 720044
Facsimile: 01259 720051
Provides care, support and education for people with autism in Scotland.

Shaftesbury Society, The
16 Kingston Road
London
SW19 1JZ
Contact: Allan Giles, Education Officer (Schools)
Telephone: 0181-542 5550
Facsimile: 0181-545 0605
A registered charity which exists to enable people in great need to achieve security, self-worth and significance, and through this to show Christian care in action.

Society for Mucopolysaccharide Diseases
55 Hill Avenue
Amersham
Buckinghamshire
HP6 5BX
Contact: Christine Lavery, Director
Telephone: 01494 434156
Facsimile: 01494 434252
Supports families of children with mucopolysaccharide diseases through the publication of specific disease booklets, annual conferences, specialist clinics and holidays.

Society for the Autistically Handicapped
199 Blandford Avenue
Kettering
Northamptonshire
NN16 9AT
Contact: Keith Lovett, Director
Telephone: 01536 523274
Facsimile: 01536 523274
Seeks to improve services in care and education for those with autism thus helping to achieve a better quality of life for them and their carers, by organising and running regular training seminars and hands-on workshops for the professionals who work with them.

Spinal Injuries Association
Newpoint House
76 St James's Lane .
London
N10 3DF
Contact: Information Officer
Telephone: 0181-444 2121
Facsimile: 0181-444 3761
The national organisation for spinal cord-injured people and their families. Provides information on the effects of paralysis and a wide range of services.

STEPS
15 Statham Close
Lymn
Cheshire
WA13 9NN
Telephone: 01925 757525
A charity which gives support, contact, help, advice and information to children with lower limb abnormalities (club foot, congenital dislocated hip, lower limb deficiency) through a national helpline, publications and local contact.

The Children's Trust
Tadworth Court
Tadworth
Surrey
KT20 5RU
Contact: Sarah Watts, Communications Manager
Telephone: 01737 357171
Facsimile: 01737 373848
A charity providing care, treatment and education to children with profound disabilities, and support for their families.

Tracheo-Oesophageal Fistula Society
St George's Centre
91 Victoria Road
Netherfield
Nottinghamshire
NG4 2NN
Telephone: 0115 940 0694
Provides mutual support to parents of children born with oesophageal atresia (gap in the oesophagus), tracheo-oesophageal fistula and conditions associated with swallowing.

HANDICAPS

Turner Syndrome Society
2 Mayfield Avenue
London
W4 1PW
Telephone: 0181-995 0257
Facsimile: 0181-995 9075
*Comes under the umbrella of the Child Growth
Foundation, which provides support for
parents and funds research for running
educational programmes.*

UK Rett Syndrome Association
29 Carlton Road
London
N11 3EX
Contact: Christine Freeman, Administrator
Telephone: 0181-361 5161
Facsimile: 0181-361 5161
*Offers practical help, friendship and support to
Rett Syndrome sufferers, their families and
carers.*

Parents

Coping with the worst

Association of Parents of Vaccine Damaged Children
2 Church Street
Shipston-on-Stour
Warwickshire
CV36 4AP
Contact: Rosemary Fox, Hon Secretary
Seeks to secure compensation for children injured by routine immunisation programmes. A request for information must be accompanied by an SAE.

Compassionate Friends, The
53 North Street
Bristol
Avon
BS3 1EN
Contact: Pastoral Administrator
Telephone: 0117 953 9639 (helpline)
Facsimile: 0117 966 5202
A nationwide self-help organisation of bereaved parents offering friendship, understanding and support to other bereaved parents after the death of a son or daughter from any cause.

David Lewis Centre
Mill Lane
Warford
Alderley Edge
Cheshire
SK9 7UD
Contact: Mrs Sally Harte, School Principal
Telephone: 01565 872613
Facsimile: 01565 872829
The Centre provides residential assessment, treatment and rehabilitation of people, including schoolchildren, suffering from epilepsy. It aims to maximise each student's potential by enabling them to achieve as much independence as possible and to enjoy a life which is both stimulating and rewarding.

Parentline
Endway House
The Endway
Benfleet
Essex
SS7 2AN
Telephone: 01702 559900 (helpline)
Facsimile: 01702 554911

Seeks to promote, safeguard, protect and preserve good health, both mental and physical, of parents and children, and to prevent physical, emotional and sexual abuse of children and young people. The helpline is there for parents under stress.

Parents Against Injustice (PAIN)
3 Riverside Business Park
Stansted
Essex
CM24 8PL
Contact: Sue Amphlett, Director
Telephone: 01279 64717
Facsimile: 01279 812612
Specialises in providing advice and support to those who state they have been mistakenly involved in investigations of alleged child abuse.

Re-Unite: National Council for Abducted Children
P.O. Box 4
London
WC1X 8XY
Contact: Samantha Edwards, Administrator
Telephone: 0171-404 8356
Advice, support and information for parents and families whose children have been abducted or who fear abduction. Advice is also given to professionals whose work involves any aspect of child abduction. Helpline 0171-404 8356.

Roadpeace
P.O. Box 2579
London
NW10 3PW
Contact: Brigitte Chakdhry, National Secretary
Telephone: 0181-964 1021
Facsimile: 0181-964 1021
Provides emotional and practical support to road traffic victims and to bereaved families and friends, and aims to raise awareness of the dangers on the road and encourage their reduction.

Parents

Coping with the worst

**SAMM - Support After Murder &
  Manslaughter**
Cranmer House
39 Brixton Road
London
SW9 6DZ
Contact: Jane Cooper, Coordinator
Telephone: 0171-735 3838
Facsimile: 0171-735 3900
*Offers understanding and support to families
  and friends who have been bereaved as a
  result of murder and manslaughter.*

Index of establishments

Index of establishments

Index of establishments

Index of establishments

Index of establishments

Index of establishments

Index of establishments

Index of establishments

Index of establishments

Index of establishments

Index of establishments

Index of establishments

Index of establishments

Index of establishments

Index of establishments

Index of establishments

Index of establishments

Index of establishments

Index of establishments

Index of establishments

Index of establishments

Index of establishments

Subject index

Subject index

Subject index

Subject index

Subject index

Subject index

Subject index

Subject index

GOLDMINE

Finding free and low-cost resources for teaching

1995–1996

Compiled by David Brown

"It can be highly recommended because the choice of subjects, the organisation of the entries, and an index make a mass of information very easily accessible. Having used this directory to acquire resources for a couple of ad hoc topic areas, I can confidently state that it works - with ease and practicability. In the saving of teachers' time, let alone in access to materials, it really is a goldmine. I would advise any school to acquire this book. The title of the book is wholly accurate and the outlay is modest compared with the returns." **School Librarian**

David Brown has been teaching in primary, middle and secondary schools for 23 years. It was through David's need to find resources within a limited school budget that he began to uncover a wealth of low-cost, good quality material which was just what he was looking for.

Goldmine places these resources into topic areas, describes them and tells you where you can get them from. Since the first edition in 1985, **Goldmine** has developed into the country's leading directory of free and sponsored teaching resources, providing the wherewithal to obtain over 6000 resources from some 235 suppliers.

Budget-conscious schools will find it saves its purchase price many times over, and parents and teachers are safe in the knowledge that all the items described in here ar personally recommended by a teacher, the compiler himself.

1995   329 pages   1 85742 137 X   £15.00

Price subject to change without notification

arena